T0399487

The End of Compassion

This book brings together the most recent and the most comprehensive collection of articles on a population at risk: the children of immigrants in the United States, especially those children whose parents came to the country without legal authorization.

The end of compassion and the shift to temporary migration to source the labour needs of the American economy have brought in their wake a series of consequences, some of which were predictable and others unexpected. The chapters fully document the nature and implications of the enforcement initiatives implemented by the American government in recent years and their interaction with state policies and local contexts of reception. This collection provides an exhaustive testimony of the severe conditions faced by unauthorized migrant families and their children today and their repercussions in both countries of origin and those where they currently live.

The End of Compassion will be of interest to researchers and academics studying migration in the United States and ethnic and racial studies, and to advanced students of sociology, public policy, law and political science. This book was originally published as a special issue of the journal *Ethnic and Racial Studies*.

Alejandro Portes is Professor of Sociology (Emeritus) at Princeton University, USA, and Professor of Law and Sociology at the University of Miami, USA.

Patricia Fernández-Kelly is Professor of Sociology and Director of the Centre for Migration and Development, Princeton University, USA.

Ethnic and Racial Studies

Series editors:
Martin Bulmer, *University of Surrey, UK*,
and John Solomos, *University of Warwick, UK*

The journal *Ethnic and Racial Studies* was founded in 1978 by John Stone to provide an international forum for high quality research on race, ethnicity, nationalism and ethnic conflict. At the time the study of race and ethnicity was still a relatively marginal sub-field of sociology, anthropology and political science. In the intervening period the journal has provided a space for the discussion of core theoretical issues, key developments and trends, and for the dissemination of the latest empirical research.

It is now the leading journal in its field and has helped to shape the development of scholarly research agendas. *Ethnic and Racial Studies* attracts submissions from scholars in a diverse range of countries and fields of scholarship, and crosses disciplinary boundaries. It is now available in both printed and electronic form. Since 2015 it has published 15 issues per year, three of which are dedicated to *Ethnic and Racial Studies Review* offering expert guidance to the latest research through the publication of book reviews, symposia and discussion pieces, including reviews of work in languages other than English.

The *Ethnic and Racial Studies* book series contains a wide range of the journal's special issues. These special issues are an important contribution to the work of the journal, where leading social science academics bring together articles on specific themes and issues that are linked to the broad intellectual concerns of *Ethnic and Racial Studies*. The series editors work closely with the guest editors of the special issues to ensure that they meet the highest quality standards possible. Through publishing these special issues as a series of books, we hope to allow a wider audience of both scholars and students from across the social science disciplines to engage with the work of *Ethnic and Racial Studies*.

Most recent titles in the series include:

The End of Compassion
Children of Immigrants in the Age of Deportation

Edited by
Alejandro Portes and Patricia Fernández-Kelly

Routledge
Taylor & Francis Group

LONDON AND NEW YORK

ETHNIC
◄ AND ►
RACIAL
STUDIES

First published 2021
by Routledge
2 Park Square, Milton Park, Abingdon, Oxon OX14 4RN

and by Routledge
52 Vanderbilt Avenue, New York, NY 10017

Routledge is an imprint of the Taylor & Francis Group, an informa business

British Library Cataloguing in Publication Data
A catalogue record for this book is available from the British Library

ISBN 13: 978-0-367-47265-8

Typeset in MyriadPro
by Newgen Publishing UK

Publisher's Note
The publisher accepts responsibility for any inconsistencies that may have arisen during the conversion of this book from journal articles to book chapters, namely the inclusion of journal terminology.

Disclaimer
Every effort has been made to contact copyright holders for their permission to reprint material in this book. The publishers would be grateful to hear from any copyright holder who is not here acknowledged and will undertake to rectify any errors or omissions in future editions of this book.

Contents

Citation Information

The chapters in this book were originally published in *Ethnic and Racial Studies*, volume 43, issue 1 (January 2020). When citing this material, please use the original page numbering for each article, as follows:

Chapter 11

Chapter 12

For any permission-related enquiries please visit:
www.tandfonline.com/page/help/permissions

Notes on Contributors

Carl L. Bankston III, Department of Sociology, Tulane University, New Orleans, USA.

Kristina Brant, Department of Sociology, Harvard University, Cambridge, USA.

M. Priscilla Brietzke, Department of Health Behavior, University of North Carolina, Chapel Hill, USA.

Meghan Conley, Department of Sociology, University of Tennessee, Knoxville, USA.

Richard Durán, Gevirtz Graduate School of Education, University of California, Santa Barbara, USA.

Cynthia Feliciano, Department of Sociology, Washington University, St. Louis, USA.

Patricia Fernández-Kelly, Department of Sociology, Princeton University, Princeton, USA.

Patricia Gándara, Graduate School of Education and Information Studies, University of California, Los Angeles, USA.

Roberto G. Gonzales, Graduate School of Education, Harvard University, Cambridge, USA.

David Griffith, Department of Coastal Studies, East Carolina University, Greenville, USA.

Rubén Hernández-León, Department of Sociology, University of California, Los Angeles, USA.

Sarah M. Lakhani, Immigrant Legal Resource Center, San Francisco, USA.

Helen B. Marrow, Department of Sociology, Tufts University, Medford, USA.

Douglas S. Massey, Office of Population Research, Princeton University, Princeton, USA.

Krista M. Perreira, Department of Social Medicine, University of North Carolina, Chapel Hill, USA.

Alejandro Portes, Department of Sociology, Princeton University, Princeton, USA; Department of Sociology and School of Law, University of Miami, Coral Gables, USA.

Stephanie Potochnick, Truman School of Public Affairs, University of Missouri, Columbia, USA.

Benjamin Roth, College of Social Work, University of South Carolina, Columbia, USA.

Rubén G. Rumbaut, Department of Sociology, University of California, Irvine, USA.

Jon Shefner, Department of Sociology, University of Tennessee, Knoxville, USA.

Min Zhou, Department of Sociology, University of California, Los Angeles, USA.

Víctor Zúñiga, Department of Political Sciences, Tecnologico de Monterrey, Monterrey, Mexico.

Preface

The set of papers included in this Special Issue were presented originally at a conference in the American Academy of Arts and Sciences in Cambridge, Mass. in April 2017. The editors are indebted to the then President of the Academy, Jonathan Fanton, and to its staff for steady support for this initial conference. Its title was *"Children of Immigrants in New Places of Destination"*.

A year and a half later, in October 2018, a second conference took place at Princeton University where revised and updated versions of the original papers were presented and discussed. The conference was sponsored by the Princeton Institute of International and Regional Studies (PIIRS) under its Migration Lab Initiative sponsored by the Andrew W. Mellon Foundation. The editors are also deeply indebted to Sandra Newman, director of the PIIRS Lab, for her unwavering and enthusiastic support of this project.

The editors of *Ethnic and Racial Studies* also contributed significantly to its success by signaling their interest in publishing revised versions of the conference papers as a Special Issue of this journal. This interest encouraged authors both to participate in the October event and to revise their papers for publication subsequently.

Given the turn of events of Federal immigration policy in the United States, we deemed appropriate to title this Issue, *"Children of Immigrants in the Age of Deportation."* The following articles fully document the nature and implications of the enforcement initiatives implemented by the American government in recent years and their interaction with state policies and local contexts of reception. It is our hope that this collection will provide an exhaustive testimony of the severe conditions faced by unauthorized migrant families and their children at today and their repercussions in both countries of origin and that where they currently live.

Alejandro Portes and Patricia Fernandez-Kelly
Guest Editors
Princeton, August 2019.

Bifurcated immigration and the end of compassion

Alejandro Portes

ABSTRACT
Impressions to the contrary, the United States continue to be a country of immigration. I review recent statistics showing the size of the present migrant flow and its progressive bifurcation between a high human capital flow coming primarily from Asia and a manual labour flow originating mainly in Latin America. There are parallel splits between permanent migration and temporary labour flows, the latter becoming increasingly the preferred form of sourcing labour needs at both ends of the labour market. Combined the shift from permanent to temporary labour contract migration, the persecution of the unauthorized, and the closure of the country's doors to asylum seekers have ushered a new era in American immigration policy marked by the end of compassion and the consequent loss of the country's unique moral stature in the world. I sketch the evolution of international labour migration since the onset of the world capitalist system ushering the present situation in the United States.

Despite appearances, the United States continues to be quite receptive to new immigration. In 2017, the last complete year of record as of this writing, more than one million persons (1,127,167) were admitted for legal permanent residence in the country. As enshrined in immigration law, the two primary channels for legal permanent entry are family re-unification and occupational qualifications. Family re-unification, responding primarily to petitions by U.S. citizens, is the primary driver of the process. In 2017, immediate relatives of U.S. citizens (spouses, children, parents) accounted for almost half to the total legal flow (516,508). To this must be added another 232,238 brought in as more distant relatives of citizens or immediate relatives of non-citizen residents. Figures for 2018, incomplete as of this writing, indicate similar trends.[1]

In total, family connections accounted for about three-fourths of the legal permanent inflow during the last decade. Built into the system, there are other quaint features like "lottery visas", originally designed primarily to encourage migration from European countries. In 2017, 51,592 new immigrants took advantage of this channel. The sizable inflow of migrants, reflected but not limited to legal permanent entry, is responsible for the sustained growth of the foreign-born population of the nation that, in 2017, reached 44.5 million or 14 per cent of the total. If to this number are added the children of immigrants, we have accounted for more than one-fourth of the total population of the country. Without doubt, the United State continues to be a nation of immigrants.

To these trends must be added others that are a source of greater concern. Foremost among them is the bifurcation of the foreign-born population, both geographically and educationally. Overwhelmingly, new immigrants come from less developed countries situated either in Latin America or Asia. For many years, Mexico has been the most important contributor to U.S.-bound immigration and this role continues today. In 2017, 170,581 Mexicans received legal permanent residence, about 25 per cent of the total. Mexico was followed, however, by Cuba (65,028), and three Asian countries: China (71,565); India (60,394) and the Philippines (49,147). As we shall see presently, the legal permanent flow is only part of the story because to it must be added sizable contingents of temporary legal migrants and those in unauthorized status.

Geographical bifurcation is superimposed on that based on human capital. Overwhelmingly, Mexican and Central American immigrants are manual workers with low average education and skills, while those coming from China, India, Korea, and the Philippines tend to arrive with above-average educational credentials. The educational split is not due to low average human capital in Mexico and Central American nations, but to a key geographical fact, namely the Pacific Ocean. Indian and Chinese peasants would also love to gain access to the United States and other countries in the rich world but the huge oceanic barrier effectively keeps them from doing so.

Be it as it may, the educational gap between Asian and Latin American nationalities is quite large. According to the last census, 44.5 per cent foreign-born Chinese, 51.1 per cent Koreans, 70.0 per cent of the Taiwanese, and 75 per cent of Indians were college graduates. By comparison only 8.4 per cent of Hondurans, 6.7 per cent of Salvadorians and just 5.3 per cent of Mexicans had the same level of education. The high number and high educational achievement of many Asian groups are the determining factors accounting for the non-existent gap in average levels of education between the U.S. native-born and all the foreign-born populations. By the time of the last census, exactly the same proportion of both groups, 28 per cent, had college degrees. In 2015, average years of education for both groups, aged 25 and older, were almost at par: 13.4 years among natives and 12.6 years among immigrants who entered during the last five years. Among younger workers, aged 25–34, average educational attainment was the same.

Differences in human capital and, subsequently, socio-economic status among first generation immigrants go on to decisively affect the achievement patterns in the second generation (Portes and Rumbaut 2014, Ch.4). Such differences are then essentialized in stereotypes about the below-average "Hispanic" ability and the superior achievement of Asian youths. The cultural myths grounded on obvious educational differences in the parental immigrant generation have been eloquently analyzed and exposed by Jennifer Lee and Min Zhou (Lee and Zhou 2015).

An emerging, and equally important form of bifurcation exists between permanent and temporary immigrants. Since the end of the Bracero Program in 1964, the country subscribed to the idea of immigration as permanent settlement, at least among those coming legally. Accordingly, the federal government sought to suppress unauthorized border crossing, while simultaneously expanding avenues for legal migration. Starting in 1990, things started to change with passage of legislation authorizing temporary entry visas for foreigners of high ability. This was the basis for a new H1-B visa programme that authorizes legal residence in the United States for three years for professional immigrants in high demand. The visa can be extended for another three years.

By 2010, 99 per cent of H1-B visa holders had attained a Bachelor's degree or higher. Forty-two percent were working in computer-related fields and an additional twelve percent in engineering, surveying, and architecture. Geographically, countries of origin of H1-B workers compound the regional disparities observed previously because they come overwhelmingly from Asia. India has pride of place with approximately half of all H1-B visa holders coming from that country. It is followed by China (10 per cent in 2009), Canada (4.1 per cent), and the Philippines (7.3 per cent) (Portes and Celaya 2013). The significance of the H1-B programme is that it opens a path for legal entry of high human capital flows that it is not conditional on permanent residence in the country. This conditional character of the visa, tied to a single employer, at least initially, increases the precarious legal status of the worker. A complaining or otherwise troublesome H1-B Indian engineer may not get his visa renewed and must go back home.

Unsurprisingly, the H1-B programme has been widely popular with high-tech information, electronics, and engineering companies in the United States which have repeatedly lobbied for its expansion. This popularity is well reflected in the present size of the flow. In 2017, 531,280 H1-B workers and their families were authorized for legal residence in the United States.

The figure is larger than the number of visas granted for family reunification of U.S. citizens and more than twelve times the number of professionals with advanced degrees admitted for permanent residence (39,331). Again, India was the dominant presence in the temporary professional inflow, accounting for about half of the total H1-B visas granted in 2017 (276,178).

More recently, another temporary labour channel has been greatly expanded – the H-2 programme for manual labour. In the wake of the Great Recession of 2008–10, the clandestine flow of Mexican workers going north dried up, being discouraged by both greater repression at the border and the shrinkage of job opportunities in the U.S. (Massey and Pren 2012; Portes and Rumbaut 2014, Ch. 1). As a consequence, crops started rotting in the fields in states like Arizona and Alabama which had been at the forefront of the anti-immigrant campaign. Alarmed by the situation, farmers' and ranchers' urged their lobbyists in Washington to prevail upon the government to do something. The federal government responded by discreetly expanding the H-2A temporary programme for agricultural labourers. H-2A visas are granted for one year and linked to a single employer. The number of such visas tripled between 2006 and 2010 from 46,000to 139,000 workers. By 2017, the programme had expanded to 412,800; of these 393,849 came from Mexico. In addition, 124,300 non-agricultural manual workers were admitted with H2-b and H2-r visas in the same year.

What these figures mean is that, tacitly but effectively, the United States has started sourcing its labour needs, at both ends of the skills spectrum, on the bases of temporary contracts. Like H1-B professionals, H2 manual workers are tied to a single employer and, in their case, without a path to permanent residence. While this is convenient from the standpoint of firms that hire these workers, it confines them to a condition of permanent insecurity and vulnerability. In 2017, 1,068,430 H1-B, H2-A, H2-B workers and their families were admitted. This is about the same as the total for legal permanent immigration in the same year, including family reunifications.

The other side of the coin is what has happened to the estimated twelve million (in 2012) unauthorized workers and their families who were already in the country prior to the resurrected H-2 programme (Robertson 2019). They came in the years prior to the Great Recession responding to labour demand north of the border. In the absence of a regular legal programme to do so, they crossed the border clandestinely. In subsequent years, they stayed in the United States because of the dangers and costs of repeating that journey. Instead, they sought to consolidate and improve their economic situation in American soil, while seeking facilities for their children to enter the school system (Massey forthcoming).

While exceptions exist, this has proven to be a population of law-abiding, hard-working individuals and families seeking to carve their share of the

American dream. The response by the federal government has not been to try to normalize their situation, given the fact that most have committed no crime other than crossing the border clandestinely and that they did so because there was no other alternative. Instead the federal government through its agency, Immigration and Customs Enforcement (ICE), has engaged in a campaign of mass deportations that, over the last decade, saw over 8.1 million migrants removed or returned to their countries of origin. Mexico alone received over three million deportees during the last five years. While such removals are justified by government authorities as a response to the crimes committed by unauthorized immigrants, the fact is that the vast majority of the deportees committed no crimes or were guilty only of misdemeanors (Hernandez-Leon and Zuñiga forthcoming; Massey, Durand, and Malone 2003).

Be it as it may, in 2017 the U.S. government apprehended 265,747 Mexicans, while admitting 332,445 for temporary agricultural labour and another 90,301 for unskilled non-rural labour. In effect, the federal government has set up a revolving door at the border where the same kind of migrant deported by one of its agencies (ICE), is received and granted a work visa by another (USCIS). How much easier, less costly, and less painful would it have been to regularize the situation of individuals and families already in the country. As is well-known, the campaign of mass deportation has caused untold suffering – tearing families and communities apart, "orphaning" children prematurely, or compelling them to accompany deported parents to a country they don't know and whose language they don't speak. Articles in this issue document in detail the plight of these new Americans cut off from any possible avenue to legalize their status.

Hundreds of thousands now find themselves in that situation in order to satisfy the ire of nativists and anti-immigration activists. Along with the replacement of legal permanent residents by temporary precarious workers, the deportation campaign reflects a shift from an immigration policy governed by relative tolerance and concern for human rights to one where the selfish interests of employers at both ends of the labour market and the narrow views of militant nationalists rule the day. It is *the end of compassion* as we have known it in the past and, along with it, the end of the claim to a unique American moral standing in the world.

A parallel story pertains to refugees. Compared with the effort led by Germany to resettle hundreds of thousands of Syrian and other Middle Eastern refugees in Western Europe, the 85,000 refugees admitted by the United States in 2016 look paltry. Of these, only 12,587 came from Syria. The total number is actually much smaller than the number of refugees admitted in 1980 under President Carter (207,116) or even under the first Bush Administration in 1990 (122,066) (Portes and Rumbaut 2014, Ch. 1).

No effort has been made to help Western European countries cope with the refugee crisis. Instead, the new Trump Administration is seeking ways to bar new refugee entries from Middle Eastern countries and other regions under the theory that they represent a threat to national security. In 2018, approximately 20,000 refugees were admitted in the U.S., the number represents a 68 per cent drop just from the prior year (Homeland Security 2018).

So far, no Middle Eastern refugee in the U.S. has been convicted of committing or seeking to commit a terrorist act. No such acts or attempts have been reported in the very few areas of Muslim immigrants' concentration in the United States, such as Dearborn or Detroit. But the politics of fear and intransigent nativism have pretty much done away with the rationality and relative openness guiding America's approach toward its newcomers in the past. The famous words of Emma Lazarus's poem inscribed at the base of the Statue of Liberty might as well be taken down.[2]

Explaining the changes

There is no question that immigration policy in all advanced nations has been governed primarily by domestic economic and political interests. But along with them, a measure of humanitarianism and concern for the most downtrodden populations on earth has grown in recent years spearheaded by, among others, the UN High Commission for Refugees (UNCHR). The category of "refugee" and the increasing admission of people under this label reflect this growing concern. The label did not exist, for example, at the start of the XXth century where the U.S. was granting access to millions of Russian Jews, in effect the political refugees of the time. (Portes and Rumbaut 2014, Ch. 1; Zolberg 2006)

Immigration has been a constant in the development of capitalism, although it has taken the most varied forms. To make the story short, attracting settlers to the empty lands of new colonies was a high priority for the monarchies of all major European powers since the discovery of the Americas in 1492. This was as true for the pioneering Iberian powers, Spain and Portugal, as for their fast-rising competitors in the Netherlands, England, and France (Thomas 1973; Zolberg 2006). In a context where land was abundant and essentially free but suitable people to till it absent, the colonial powers' goal was to entice enough migrants from the home countries to come and settle the new territories. These settler migrations created the grounds for emerging colonial societies in the Americas, Oceania, and Africa (Lebergott 1964; Thomas 1973).

Agricultural production for subsistence was short-lived, however, giving way to production for the market. Mines were also opened and production organized for the same purpose. The problem then became how to secure enough hands that the European settlers themselves were unable or unwilling to provide. Enslaving the indigenous population proved a short-term remedy, as they were promptly decimated by the colonists' imported European diseases or escaped into inaccessible areas of country, only known to them (Thompson 1939; Portes and Walton 1981). Migration of indentured servants imported from Europe and elsewhere, was tried next, but it suffered from the fatal flaw of lack of motivation among the newcomers. They had little incentive to work for others and, instead every incentive to work for themselves, just as the original settlers were doing. Hence, they escaped at the first chance (Thomas 1973).

As sociologist Edgar Thompson (1939, 1975) noted, the solution was to find a source of labour so alien to their new environment in plantations or mines that they would have no way to escape. African slaves were that solution and the organized trans-Atlantic migration of these early victims of capitalism became the normative form of labour migration for several centuries (Arrighi 1994; Calvo 1944). Slavery and others coerced labour flows only receded in the XIX Century, victims of their own cruelty and of the very development of the global capitalist economy.

The rising industrial economy of the XIX Century did not recruit slaves, but formally free labour that was paid a wage. This is the moment in which, according to Marx, capitalism ceased to be a mode of *exchange*, to become an actual mode of *production* (Dobb 1946; Marx 1962). In the pioneer industrializers, primarily Britain, the requisite labour force for the rising industrial economy was sourced internally – from a peasantry forced from the land by the Enclosure movement and other related political measures. Former colonies of the Americas had no such recourse and, when their own era of industrialization arrived, they had to go abroad in search of needed workers. Slavery was out of the question and thus it was substituted by deliberate recruitment. Paid recruiters were dispatched by American industrialists to remote confines of Southern Italy and the Austro-Hungarian empire to apprise peasants of the "better meals and higher wages" to be had in factory and casual work in the Northeast and Midwest (Lebergott 1964; Thomas 1973; Zolberg 2006).

A similar method was used by Southwestern ranchers and growers to recruit peasant labour from the recently defeated Mexican republic (Samora 1971). The flows triggered by deliberate labour recruitment gave rise to massive out-migrations from southeastern Europe to North America and, to a lesser extent, to Argentina and Brazil, and from Mexico to the American West. The arrival of these recruited migrants and their subsequent incorporation in the receiving societies led, eventually, to the "canonical" story of migrant assimilation, featuring a working-class first generation that toiled hard at menial industrial jobs in order to pave the way for a second generation who moved ahead to better positions made possible by its command of the language and access to education. The happy story was completed by a third and fourth generations who joined *en masse* the native middle-class "mainstream". (Alba and Nee 2003; Gordon 1964).

This assimilation story was fashioned with little regard for another development taking place right next to it. Unlike early settlers, slaves, and the first waves of recruited migration, the new labourers coming by the thousands from Southern, Eastern Europe, and Mexico were increasingly confronted with a native population made up of the descendants of earlier migrants. These natives regarded themselves as having a proprietary claim on the land and came to increasingly resent the new arrivals as taking away, by force of numbers, what was rightfully "theirs". While an open frontier still existed, the natives still had the option of going west, settling still unoccupied land and becoming self-employed proprietors (Lebergott 1964; Rosenblum 1973). But when the frontier closed, they had to face the competition of new arrivals head on, giving rise to increasing unrest and political confrontations.

The increasing dislike of the native working class for immigrant workers was helped along by two other developments, both characteristic of the late XIX and XX centuries. First, employers perfected the practice of bringing in foreign labour to counter mobilizations and strikes by native workers. Immigrants could be counted on to work "hard and scared", in the process undermining the efforts of locals for a better life. Commonly, natives blamed migrants for their plight, while absolving employers who were the real cause of their situation (Bonacich 1976; Portes and Walton 1981, Ch. 2).

Second, immigrants increasingly started coming *on their own*, rather than being recruited by industrialists and growers. These "spontaneous" flows were the consequence of the social networks connecting earlier recruited labourers to those left behind and through which information about the better living conditions in places of destination and the best means to get there flowed (Massey 1987; Portes and Rumbaut 2014, Ch. 1). The emergence of spontaneous migration brought to an end the successive stages of labour flows accompanying the development of the world economy, as portrayed in Figure 1. Thereafter, the initiative for such movements would devolve from employers to the migrants themselves, making these movements less predictable and less controlled (Bustamante 1973; Massey, Durand, and Malone 2003). Simultaneously, tensions rose between the native population, especially its working-class component, and immigrants who became frequent targets of citizens' ire fuelled by professional agitators. That situation lasts to our day (Bonacich 1976; Massey and Pren 2012).

The intransigence of nativists who, it must be remembered, were themselves descendants of earlier migrants was crystallized in a number of political measures that sought, in various ways, to prevent the arrival of newcomers, deport those without documents, and compel the ones who remained to assimilate to American ways and language as quickly as possible. Major

Immigration and the World Capitalist Economy

<u>Type</u>	<u>Origin</u>[1]	<u>Centuries</u>[2]
-Settler migrations	European Powers: Spain, Portugal, Great Britain, France, Netherlands	XVI – XVIII
-Coerced labor migration (slavery)	Africa	XVII – XIX
-Indentured labor migration	British Isles, ⟶ China and India ⟶	XVI – XVII XIX
-Recruited labor migrations	Southern Europe, ⟶ Mexico, China	XIX—XX
-Self-motivated (spontaneous)migrations	Southeastern Europe ⟶ Latin America, Asia, ⟶ Africa	XIX – XX XX – XXI

1. Main sending countries or regions.
2. Main periods where each type of migration was predominant.

Figure 1. Immigration and the world capitalist economy.

examples of these policy measures range from the Chinese Exclusion Act and the 1925 National Origins Act to the series of "propositions" passed by states as varied as California, Arizona, and Alabama to get rid of unauthorized migrants in the recent past (Marrow forthcoming; Massey forthcoming; Zolberg 2006).

However, the forces governing contemporary immigration are not limited to the reactions by nativists. On the other side of the spectrum, there is a need for foreign labour that, if always changing, is perennial. In the American post-industrial economy, the labour market has evolved into the now familiar "hourglass" where demand concentrates at the top for positions requiring advanced education and training and at the bottom for menial, hard, and poorly-paid work. This hourglass labour market is also in need of foreign workers because the domestic education system does not produce software engineers, programmers, computer scientists, and mathematicians in sufficient numbers, and because bottom-tier jobs – crop picking, dishwashing, cleaning, bedpan emptying, etc. ... are disdained by citizens, often the same ones attacking the migrants who do accept these positions (Hernandez-Leon and Zuñiga forthcoming; Portes and Rumbaut 2014, Chs. 1, 9) (Figure 2).

Hence, the stage is set for the confrontation between capital and its needs and a native population increasingly distraught by the very process of industrial re-structuring and downsizing that has given rise to the "hourglass". If we conceive of these two collective actors as players in a game, the situation may be ideally portrayed as in Figure 3. For the native working-class, the best situation is represented by cell A, where employers would refrain from hiring foreign labour. This cannot happen, however, because of the objective need for such labour, at both ends of the labour market, as seen previously. For employers, on the other hand, the ideal outcome is cell C where they would have a free hand to hire as many foreign workers as they please.

That situation is not to happen either because of the discontent and subsequent political mobilization of a native population threatened by a rising foreign presence. The "game" thus converges in cell D which corresponds fairly well to the present situation in the United States. This convergence

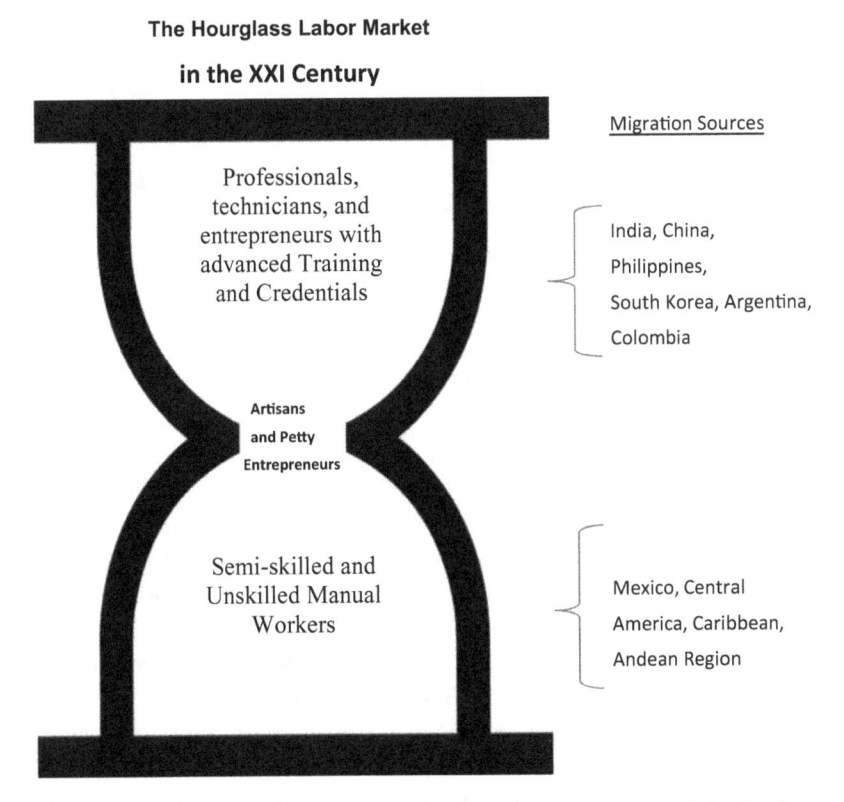

Figure 2. The hourglass labour market mid-XX, XXI centuries. Source: Alejandro Portes and Ruben G. Rumbaut, *Immigrant America: A Portrait, IV Edition*. Berkeley, CA: University of California Press. Figure 2.

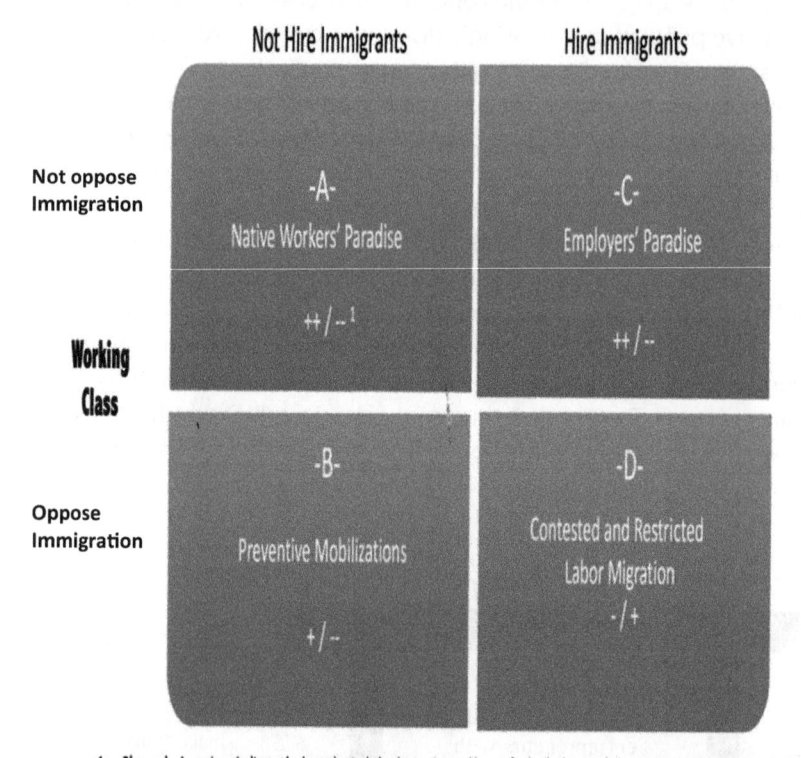

Figure 3. Outcomes of labour/capital interests in labour immigration employers. Source: Alejandro Portes, "Tensions that Make a Difference: Institutions, and the Immigrant Drive", Sociological Forum 27, #3 (September 2012): 563–578.

has held up for some time, but the conflict concerning foreign labour and immigration in general has risen to new heights, propelled by increasing native discontent with industrial downsizing and consequent job losses and the parallel rising visibility of foreigners in many regions of the country. The situation is reflected in the consolidation of the Tea Party at the extreme right of Republicanism and, more recently, by the unexpected election of Donald Trump to the presidency (Griffith forthcoming).

Up to the recent past, growers, ranchers, construction companies and other employers of manual labour were quite accustomed to hire unauthorized immigrants, knowing that the penalties for doing so were non-existent or minimal and that the supply of these workers was almost inexhaustible. But the political mobilization of the native population, especially its working-class component, has had a series of practical consequences including a much reinforced Border Patrol and, in particular, the rapid growth of Immigration and Custom Enforcement (ICE), a branch of the Department of Homeland Security tasked with identifying and summarily deporting unauthorized migrants (Gandara forthcoming; Office of Immigration Statistics 2018b).

As seen previously, ICE has succeeded in this mission, deporting millions in the few years of its existence. A direct consequence of that success has been to render problematic the hiring of unauthorized workers for industries previously accustomed to that practice. ICE raids can disrupt, at any time, normal production activities and the continued presence of unauthorized workers cannot be taken for granted, as they could be here today and deported to their home countries tomorrow (Hernandez-Leon and Zuñiga forthcoming). The contested relationship portrayed in Figure 3 had thus taken a decided turn for the worse, at least for a segment of the employer class.

The solution to this situation has been to revive the old *Bracero* Program for temporary agricultural labour, a ploy implemented quietly but efficiently by the Obama Administration. The programme was promptly extended to non-agricultural manual workers to meet the labour needs of the construction and personal services industries (Office of Information Statistics 2018; Portes and Rumbaut 2014, Ch. 1). Relative to unauthorized immigrants, H-2A and H-2B workers possess three crucial advantages. First, they cannot be summarily deported, and, hence, normal production routines in firms hiring them are not disrupted. Second, nativists have a much harder time attacking these immigrants since they have a legal right to be in the country. Third, labour discipline can be easily enforced since H-2 workers are consigned to a single employer and their permanence in the United States or a possible extension of their visa depend on the goodwill of that employer (Griffith forthcoming; Massey and Pren 2012).

A final advantage of the H-2 programme is to bring the sourcing of manual labour for the bottom tier of the labour market in line with the programmes sourcing its top tier. The result of this policy change is clearly portrayed in the figures reviewed previously. Legal, temporary labour migration has rapidly become *the* dominant component of the American immigration system, relegating stable permanent immigration to a secondary role. The obvious benefit of a well-run temporary migration programme is that the host society can gain from the labour of foreigners without having to absorb the costs of their permanent settlement or subsequent challenge of educating their children. The nation can thus remain culturally and linguistically homogenous, without the supposed threat posed by large contingents of foreign workers.

The less obvious disadvantage of such a policy is that it takes away the demographic contribution made by settled immigrants to a declining and aging native population. Perhaps more importantly, it deprives society of

the vibrancy and energy brought about by cultural diversity and of the potential for social change and innovation inherent in it. Such a country would have
many "bowling leagues" joined by old-timers; but few inventors, innovators,
and competitive teams in sports requiring both youth and energy (Portes
and Vickstrom 2011; Putnam 2007).

In this policy context, what has happened to the category "refugee"
becomes understandable. Refugees are either economically unnecessary or
redundant. There is no "practical" reason for their admission, since it is
mainly motivated by value imperatives. Growing nativist pressure trumps
these considerations, as humanitarian concerns give way to "taking care of
our own first" (Brimelow 1997). Blocking or drastically reducing refugee arrivals corresponds perfectly well to this orientation. Since satisfying demands
for ending all immigration is impossible, given powerful economic interests
supporting its continuation, such demands can be at least partially met by
attacking the most vulnerable category of migrants.

Conclusion

The end of compassion and the shift to temporary migration to source the
labour needs of the American economy have brought in their wake a series
of consequences, some of which were predictable and others unexpected.
Most poignant is the plight of youths brought at an early age by their
parents to the United States and who have been educated in American institutions. As Gonzales (2016) has put it, these youths "live in limbo" having no
clear path to legalize their situation and finally join a society that they see as
their own (See also Gonzales forthcoming). A second tragic consequence is
what awaits those children of immigrants who have actually been repatriated
to a country that they do not know and whose language they do not speak.
Consequences for themselves and for the communities to which they return
are vividly portrayed in the articles by Gandara and by Hernandez-Leon and
Zuñiga, in this issue.

The recent "caravans" of asylum seekers from Central America add a still
new dimension to the present situation. As Massey (this issue) notes, these
are not job seekers but desperate escapees from violent conditions in their
ungoverned countries. The fact that they have not been immediately
deported, despite President Trump's denunciations against them and the
deployment of troops to the border, is a credit to the resilience of American
institutions. The law stipulates that asylum claimers must be given the opportunity to explain their situation before a judge and the entire American legal
system supports this right. Most of these claims, however, will be denied and
many unsuccessful claimants will then join the unauthorized masses at the
bottom of society. They will go to increase the population targeted by ICE
for continuing its mass deportation campaign for years to come.

We live in tragic times rendered still more unsettling by the nativist chorus supporting the politics of no compassion. The situation will not change in the foreseeable future and is likely to have additional grim consequences for the existing population of unauthorized migrants and their children, the American communities where they currently hide, and the cities and towns in the sending countries having to cope with their enforced return. These issue is dedicated to document these realities and their aftermath.

Notes

1. The data cited here and in the following pages is drawn from the *2016 and 2017 Yearbooks of Immigration Statistics,* Office of Immigration Statistics, Department of Homeland Security 2018a. In the first three-quarters of 2018, according to data from the same source permanent admissions declined slightly (3 per cent). Immediate relatives of U.S. citizens again represented close to half of the permanent flow, 43 per cent.
2. Give me your tired, your poor, your huddled masses yearning to be free, the wretched refuse of your teeming shore … I lift my lamp beside the golden door.

Acknowledgement

I acknowledge with thanks the comments of David Abraham and Patricia Fernandez-Kelly to an earlier version of this paper. Responsibility for the contents is exclusively mine.

Disclosure statement

No potential conflict of interest was reported by the author.

References

Alba, Richard, and Victor Nee. 2003. *Remaking the American Mainstream: Assimilation and Contemporary Immigration.* Cambridge, MA: Harvard University Press.
Arrighi, Giovanni. 1994. *The Long Twentieth Century: Money, Power and the Origins of Our Time.* London: Verso Books.
Bonacich, Edna. 1976. "Advanced Capitalism and Black/White Relations in the United States: A Split Labor Market Interpretation." *American Sociological Review* 41 (2): 34–51.
Brimelow, Peter. 1997. *Alien Nation: Common Sense about American Immigration Disaster.* New York: Harper.
Bustamante, Jorge. 1973. "The Historical Context of Undocumented Mexican Migration to the United States." *Aztlan* 5 (3): 257–281.
Calvo, Lino Novas. 1944. *El Negrero: Vida Novelada de Pedro Blanco.* Buenos Aires: Espasa Calpe.
Dobb, Maurice. 1946. *Studies in the Development of Capitalism.* London: Routledge and Kegan Paul.

Gandara, Patricia. Forthcoming. "The Students We Share: Falling through the Cracks on Both Sides of the U.S.-Mexican Border." *Ethnic and Racial Studies* 43 (1).

Gonzalez, Roberto. 2016. *Lives in limbo: Undocumented and Coming of Age in America.* Berkeley, CA: University of California Press.

Gonzalez, Roberto. 2020. "The DACAmented in the Age of Deportation: Navigating Spaces of Belonging and Vulnerability." *Ethnic and Racial Studies* 43 (1).

Gordon, Milton, M. 1964. *Assimilation in American Life: The Role of Race, Religion, and National Origins.* New York: Oxford University Press.

Griffith, David. Forthcoming. "The Value of Reproduction: Multiple Livelihoods, Cultural Labor, and Immigrants in Iowa and North Carolina." *Ethnic and Racial Studies* 43 (1).

Hernandez-Leon, Ruben, and Victor Zuñiga. Forthcoming. "An Imperfect Realignment: the Movement of Children of Immigrants and their Families from the United States to Mexico." *Ethnic and Racial Studies* 43 (1).

Homeland Security. 2018. "Legal Immigration and Adjustment of Status. Fiscal Year 2018". Third Quarter Report. *Office of Immigration Statistics.*

Lebergott, Stanley. 1964. *Manpower in Economic Growth: The American Record Since 1800.* New York: Academic Press.

Lee, Jennifer, and Min Zhou, 2015. *The Asian American Achievement Paradox.* New York: Russell Sage Foundation.

Marrow, Helen. Forthcoming. "Hope Turned Sour: Second-Generation Incorporation and Mobility in U.S. New Immigrant Destinations." *Ethnic and Racial Studies* 43 (1).

Marx, Karl. 1962. *Capital,* Vol II. New York: International Publishers.

Massey, Douglas. S. 1987. "Understanding Mexican Migration to the United States." *American Journal of Sociology* 92 (6): 1372–1403.

Massey, Douglas S. Forthcoming. "Creating the Exclusionist Society: From the War on Poverty to the War on Immigrants." *Ethnic and Racial Studies* 43 (1).

Massey, Douglas, Jorge Durand, and Nolan J. Malone. 2003. *Beyond Smoke and Mirrors: Mexican Immigration in an Era of Economic Integration.* New York: Russell Sage Foundation.

Massey, Douglas, and Karen Pren. 2012. "Unintended Consequences of U.S. Immigration Policy." *Population and Development Review* 38 (March): 1–29.

Office of Immigration Statistics. 2018a. *Annual Report, 2017.* Washington, DC: Department of Homeland Security.

Office of Immigration Statistics. 2018b. *Yearbook of Immigration Statistics.* 2017. Washington, DC: Department of Homeland Security.

Portes, Alejandro, and Adrienne Celaya. 2013. "Modernization for Emigration: Determinants and Consequences of the Brain Drain." *Daedalus* 142 (3): 170–184.

Portes, Alejandro, and Ruben Rumbaut. 2014. *Immigrant America.* 4th ed. Berkeley, CA: University of California Press.

Portes, Alejandro, and Erik Vickstrom. 2011. "Diversity, Social Capital, and Cohesion." *Annual Review of Sociology* 37: 461–479.

Portes, Alejandro, and John Walton. 1981. *Labor Class and the International System.* New York: Academic Press.

Putnam, Robert. 2007. "E Pluribus Urum: Diversity and Community in the Twenty-First Century." *Scandinavian Political Studies* 30: 137–174.

Robertson, Lori. 2019. "Illegal Immigration Statistics." *The Wire.* www.factcheck.org, Jan.9.

Rosenblum, Gerals. 1973. *Immigrant Workers: Their Impact on American Radicalism.* New York: Basic Books.

Samora, Julian. 1971. *Los Mojados: The Wetback Story.* Notre Dame, Indiana: Notre Dame University Press.

Thomas, Brinley. 1973. *Migration and Economic Growth: A Study of Great Britain and the Atlantic Economy.* Cambridge: Cambridge University Press.

Thompson, Edgar, T. 1939. "The Plantation: The Physical Basis for Traditional Race Relations." In *Race Relations and Race Problems,* edited by E. T. Thompson, 180–218. Durham, NC: Duke University Press.

Thompson, Edgar, T. 1975. *The Plantation Societies, Race Relations, and the South: the Regimentation of Populations: Selected Papers of Edgar T. Thompson.* Durham, NC: Duke University Press.

Zolberg, Aristide. 2006. *A Nation by Design: Immigration Policy in the Fashioning of America.* Cambridge, MA: Harvard University Press.

Creating the exclusionist society: from the War on Poverty to the war on immigrants

ABSTRACT
A series of policy decisions beginning in 1965 produced an exclusionist climate in the United States. Lyndon Johnson sought to eliminate prejudice from the nation's immigration system but inadvertently curtailed opportunities for legal entry from Mexico that created a large undocumented population. In waging the Cold War, Ronald Reagan launched an intervention in Central America that displaced many more thousands who also became undocumented residents. The Wars on Crime and Drugs of Presidents Nixon and Reagan created a prison industrial complex that imprisoned blacks and Hispanics. George Bush's War on Terror unleashed a rising tide of deportations swept Latino migrants into the immigrant detention system. Finally, President Trump transformed a humanitarian problem affecting Central American families and children into a manufactured immigration crisis for the nation as a whole. The result is among the most repressive and exclusionist context of immigrant reception in American history.

Politicians in the United States display a remarkable fondness for martial metaphors. When they seek to address a social problem, they don't just promise vigorous efforts to solve it; they declare all-out war on it. Thus Lyndon Johnson famously declared a War on Poverty, Richard Nixon a War on Crime, and Ronald Reagan a War on Drugs while all three simultaneously prosecuted a Cold War (Hinton 2016); and beginning with George W. Bush, of course, U.S. Presidents began to wage a never-ending War on Terror (Mayer 2008). The resulting symbolic (and all too often real) "warfare" did little to mitigate the problems of poverty, crime, drug abuse, and terrorism. More often than naught, these self-declared wars served to assuage the partisan grievances of favoured constituencies so politicians could achieve domestic political goals that bore only the most tenuous connections to the purported problems being addressed.

Decades of symbolic and at times more concrete warfare may not have solved the nation's problems, but they did have profound consequences for certain vulnerable segments of the U.S. population. The succession of America's politically-inspired "wars" brought the repressive power of the state down upon poor women, minority men, and immigrants, especially migrants from Latin America. In this article I document the forces of exclusion and repression that have successively been unleashed in the name of the nation's putative wars and describe how they have accumulated to create an unprecedentedly harsh context of reception for first and second generation Latino immigrants in the United States today.

The War on Poverty

Lyndon Johnson's War on Poverty sought to combat the racial and class foundations of disadvantage on two fronts, simultaneously pursuing an aggressive civil rights agenda while also creating federal programmes to transfer power and resources to those left behind in America's otherwise affluent society. The War on Poverty was officially declared in 1964 with the passage of two pieces of legislation: the Civil Rights Act and the Economic Opportunity Act. These landmark acts were followed in 1965 by the passage of the Voting Rights Act and amendments to the Social Security Act that created the Medicare and Medicaid Programs (Quadagno 1994). In that same year, Congress also passed amendments in an effort to eliminate prejudice from the Immigration and Nationality Act.

At the time, these amendments were not seen as a significant shift in immigration policy so much as a long overdue civil rights reform. Just as Johnson sought to deracialize the social welfare system that had been constructed in the 1930s to exclude blacks and Hispanics (see Katznelson 2005), he sought also to deracialize an immigration system that earlier had been fashioned to exclude presumed racial inferiors from the United States (Zolberg 2006).

Thus the 1965 Hart-Cellar act repealed national origin quotas that for decades had discriminated against Southern and Eastern Europeans while also lifting long-standing bans on the entry of immigrants from Africa, the Middle East, and Asia. In addition, at midnight on January 1, 1965 Congress let a binational labour accord with Mexico known as the Bracero Agreement expire, having come to see it as an exploitative system on a par with southern sharecropping.

The new immigration system legislation sought to admit only legal permanent residents selected impartially on the basis of family ties to U.S. residents and U.S. labour needs. Total immigration was capped at 290,000 visas annually, with 170,000 reserved for immigrants from the Eastern Hemisphere and 120,000 allocated to persons from the Western Hemisphere (i.e. the Americas). Beginning in 1968, visas allocated to the Eastern Hemisphere were capped at 20,000 per country, and starting in 1976 these country caps were applied to nations in the Western Hemisphere as well.

These reforms were enacted with the noblest of intentions: to end racism in immigrant admissions and curtail the exploitation of Mexican farmworkers. However, lawmakers paid little attention to what would happen to existing migratory flows when the new limits took effect. Prior to 1965, there was no statutory quota regulating the number of Mexicans who could enter the United States as legal immigrants. At the same time, Mexicans also enjoyed access to an expansive supply of temporary work visas under the Bracero Program. In 1957, legal entries from Mexico totalled 485,000 persons, with 49,000 entering on permanent resident visas and 436,000 arriving on temporary work visas. However, by 1977 after the end of the Bracero Program and the imposition of country quotas, the legal inflow of Mexicans to the United States stood at just 47,000 persons (a figure that exceeded the annual 20,000-visa quota because immediate relatives of U.S. citizens are exempt from the law's numerical limits).

The conditions of binational labour supply and demand had not changed, however, and over the 22 years of the Bracero Program millions of Mexicans had established strong ties to employers and job markets in the United States. As a result, migratory inflows from Mexico did not stop after 1965; they simply reestablished themselves under undocumented auspices, as demonstrated in Figure 1. Whereas total legal entries from Mexico were quite large before the new restrictions, averaging around 346,000 per year from 1955 to 1965, they dropped to an average of just 57,000 per year from 1965 to 1979. After 1965, legal entries were steadily replaced by undocumented entries, here proxied by the number of border apprehensions per 1,000 Border Patrol officers (creating a serviceable index that adjusts total apprehensions for temporal variations in the enforcement effort). As can be seen, this index rose from 37,000 in 1965–464,000 in 1977 after which the increase ended and the level fluctuated around an average value of 407,000 through 1985.

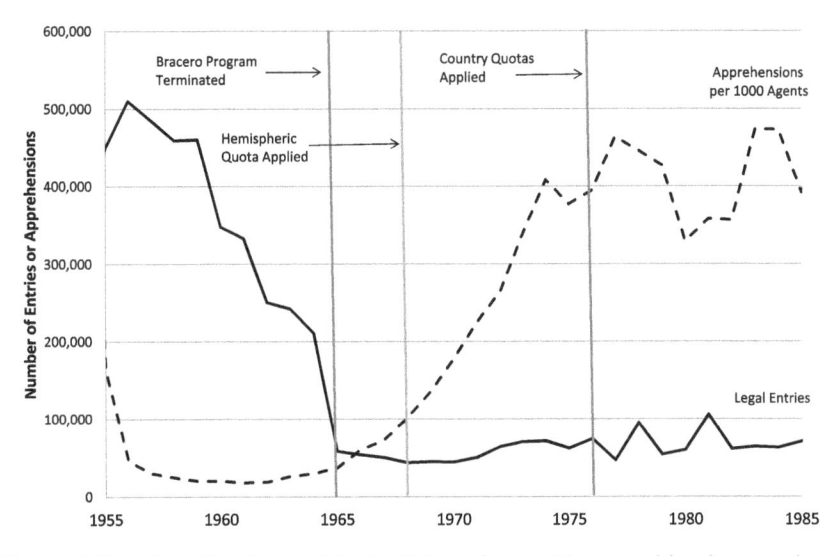

Figure 1. Total legal Mexican entries for U.S. work or residence and border apprehensions per 1,000 agents 1955–1985. Source: Mexican Migration Project (2018).

In one sense little had changed in the Mexico-U.S. migration system. Migrants still followed the same routes northward from the same communities in Mexico, crossing the border at much the same places, and generally going on to the same jobs in the same destination areas. In another sense, however, everything had changed because now the entries were "illegal" and so by definition the migrants could be portrayed as "criminals" and "lawbreakers" (Chavez 2001). After 1965, migration from south of the border was increasingly framed as a profound threat to the United States, portrayed in the media either as a *rising tide* of "illegal aliens" that would "flood" American society to "drown" its culture, or as an *alien invasion* of migrants who would "overrun" border defenses to "conquer" and "occupy" the nation (Santa Ana 2002; Massey and Pren 2012a).

Year after year, each annual increase in the number of border apprehensions was trumpeted by immigration officials, politicians, and pundits as proof of the ongoing alien invasion, steadily solidifying a new "Latino threat narrative" in public discourse (Chavez 2013). The propagation of this narrative pushed popular opinion in an ever more conservative direction, leading to rising demands for more restrictive immigration and border policies, which then produced more apprehensions, which justified even more enforcement actions. The ultimate result was a self-perpetuating cycle of rising enforcement, apprehensions, more enforcement, and still more apprehensions (Massey and Pren 2012b).This militarization of the Mexico-U.S. border occurred despite the fact that the underlying volume of undocumented migration had stopped rising around 1977 (Massey, Durand, and Pren 2014).

The escalation of border enforcement began slowly after the passage of the 1986 Immigration Reform and Control Act, accelerated with the passage of the Immigration Act of 1990, and rose again with the launching of Operations Blockade in El Paso in 1993 and Operation Gatekeeper in San Diego in 1994. Border enforcement accelerated further with the passage of the Illegal Immigration Reform and Immigrant Responsibility Act of 1996 and climbed exponentially after the passage of the 2001 USA PATRIOT Act.

The effect of these measures in militarizing the border is shown in Figure 2, which plots trends in the number of Border Patrol agents, the size of the Border Patrol's budget (in $2016), and the number of linewatch hours spent patrolling the border. Each series is expressed relative to its value in 1986, thereby putting the trend lines on a common scale. The resulting graphs reveal little change in the level of border enforcement effort prior to 1986 followed by a steady trend upward over the next quarter century. By around 2010 the real value of the Border Patrol budget had increased by a factor of nearly 12 (the solid line), the number of officers had risen nearly six times (the dotted line), and linewatch hours (total person-hours spent patrolling the border) had grown over five times (the dashed line).

Research shows that the militarization of the border had little effect on the likelihood of apprehension along the border, even less effect on the odds of ultimately achieving an unauthorized entry, and no effect whatsoever on the likelihood that Mexicans would decide to head northward with intent of becoming undocumented migrants (Massey, Durand, and Pren 2014, 2016). Nonetheless border apprehension *did* have other powerful effects on the

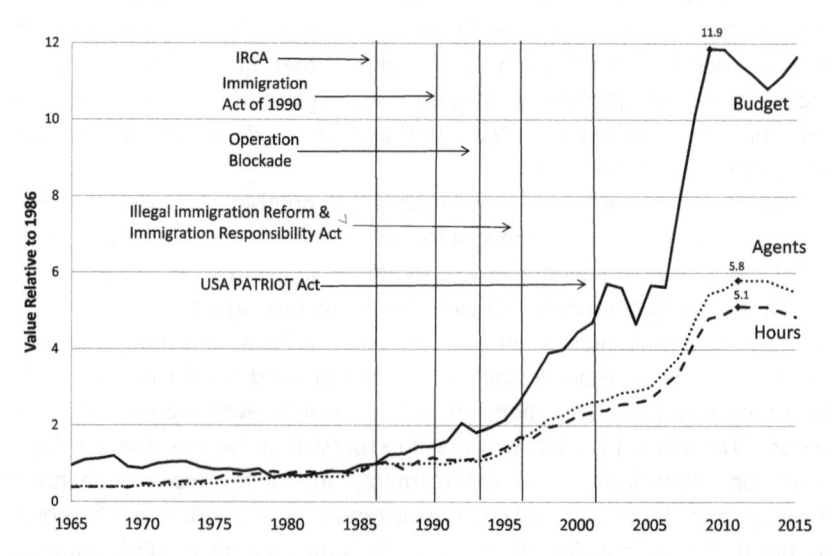

Figure 2. Border Patrol agents, real budget, and linewatch hours 1965–2015 (1986=1.0). Source: Mexican Migration Project (2018).

behaviour of undocumented migrants. It diverted them away from traditional crossing points in the San Diego and El Paso sectors and channeled them instead through the Sonoran Desert into Arizona as well as toward more remote locations in the Rio Grande Valley (Massey, Durand, and Malone 2002; Massey, Durand, and Pren 2016). These shifts geographic were accompanied by a sharp increase in the financial costs and physical risks of unauthorized border crossing. Since 1985 at least 8,644 migrants have died along the Mexico-U.S. border and the average cost of an unauthorized entry has risen from around $825 in constant 2016 dollars before 1986 to over $5,000 today (Massey 2018).

Given that the costs and risks undocumented border crossing had increased dramatically but the odds of gaining entry to the United States remained unchanged, migrants did the logical thing. They minimized border crossing—not by remaining Mexico but by staying longer in the United States once they had run the gauntlet at the border. As border militarization increased in intensity and spread geographically, the likelihood that an undocumented migrant would return to Mexico fell at an accelerating pace during the 1990s and 2000s (Massey, Durand, and Pren 2015, 2016). With the volume of in-migration holding steady but the level of return migration to Mexico falling, the net inflow of unauthorized migrants increased and the rate of undocumented population growth accelerated (Massey and Pren 2012b; Massey, Durand, and Pren 2014). From 1988 to 2008, the population of undocumented Mexicans grew from 1.1 million to 7 million (Wasem 2011). At the latter date, around 7 per cent of all persons born in Mexico were living without authorization in the United States.

The Cold War

In 1979, a leftist guerilla faction known as the Sandinistas toppled Nicaragua's longtime dictator Anastasio Somoza to establish a left-wing regime friendly with the Soviet Union and Cuba. At the same time, leftist insurgents were challenging repressive right-wing governments in Guatemala and El Salvador backed by the United States. In 1981, Ronald Reagan ascended to the Presidency with a promise to confront the Soviet Union's "evil empire" politically and militarily on all fronts. Upon assuming office, he immediately scaled up political and military support for the region's right-wing governments while turning a blind eye to the death squads they supported and the murders they committed. Reagan then went on secretly to finance and arm a clandestine army known as the Contras with bases in Honduras whose goal was to drive the Sandinistas from power.

As a result of Reagan's political and military intervention, waves of civil violence swept across frontline nations of El Salvador, Guatemala, Honduras, and Nicaragua and crippled their economies. From 1978 to 1989, average GDP in these four nations dropped by 27 per cent in real terms and did not climb back to its 1978 level until 2011 (Massey 2018). Although open warfare gradually died out in the early 1990s, levels of violence never returned to pre-intervention levels. In 1995 when reliable statistics first become available, the homicide rate in the four frontline nations averaged 53.9 per 100,000 compared to a value of just 11.9 per 100,000 in the neighbouring non-frontline nations of Belize, Costa Rica, and Panama. Although the murder rate in frontline nations fell to 35.6 in 1999, thereafter it rose to peak at 51.6 in 2019; and as of 2016 the murder rate in the frontline nations remained very high at 43.5, compared to 19.7 elsewhere in Central America (Massey 2018).

The combination of economic decline and civil violence displaced tens of thousands of people from their homes, many of whom headed northward to the United States looking for refuge. Although Nicaraguans were welcomed as refugees fleeing communist tyranny under the Sandinistas, those fleeing El Salvador, Guatemala, and Honduras were labelled economic migrants rather than political refugees and denied asylum in the United States (Lundquist and Massey 2005). Whereas the 1997 Nicaraguan Adjustment and Central American Relief Act authorized undocumented Nicaraguans to apply for legal permanent residence if they had been in the U.S. since December 1, 1995 and forgave any legal infractions related to their unauthorized entry, Salvadorans and Guatemalans were allowed only to apply for a *temporary* suspension of deportation or cancelation of removal, not legal permanent residence; and Honduran migrants received no benefits under the legislation (Massey, Durand, and Pren 2014).

The result was predictable: a surge of undocumented Guatemalans, Hondurans, and Salvadorans joined their Mexican counterparts north of the border. According to estimates developed by Massey, Durand, and Pren (2014) undocumented migration to the United States from Central America prior to the downfall of the Somoza regime was rare, but afterward the likelihood of taking an undocumented trip steadily rose and by 1989 was seven times the likelihood observed in 1977 before the Sandinista takeover. In the end, the combination of America's Cold War intervention in the region and its restrictive stance towards Salvadoran, Guatemalan, and Honduran refugees increased the number of unauthorized Central Americans from around 100,000 in 1980 to around 2 million today.

Although the signing of the Central American Peace Accords in 1987 and the Sandinista's loss of political power in 1990 reduced the likelihood of leaving for the U.S. without documents, departure probabilities never returned to the *status quo ante*. Salvadorans, Guatemalans, and Hondurans who faced endemic violence and economic stagnation in the region were by then socially connected to many thousands of compatriots living without authorization in the United States, whose presence gave them access to an important source of social capital they could draw upon to escape to the United States (Massey, Durand, and Pren 2014).

The effect of Reagan's intervention on out-migration from the region is not only apparent in the likelihood of undocumented migration but is also seen in official statistics on legal immigration. As shown in Figure 3, prior to 1979 few legal immigrants entered the United States from the frontline nations of El Salvador, Guatemala, Honduras, and Nicaragua. However, beginning with a total of 10,545 legal immigrants in 1979 the number rose steadily to reach 25,381 in 1988 before skyrocketing to 136,602 in 1990. Although the number fell to 27,861 in 1995 by 2001 it had risen back up to 71,350. As with undocumented migration, after the end of the Contra War the trend in legal immigration did not return to the *status quo ante* because of the social capital that had by then accumulated through connections to the large population of legal immigrants living in the United States. Whereas legal immigration from frontline countries averaged 7,834 per year from 1970 to 1979, from 1995 to 2016 it averaged 48,100 and at the latter date the number of legal entrants stood at 53,239. The effect of the U.S. intervention is underscored by the lack of a similar trend in out-migration from Belize, Costa Rica, and Panama. In those nations, the level of migration remained flat throughout the period.

Figure 4 shows what happened to the size of the undocumented population as a result of the United States' militarization of the border and its military and political intervention in Central America. In the case of Mexico, the number of undocumented migrants grew from around 114,000 in 1965–2.2

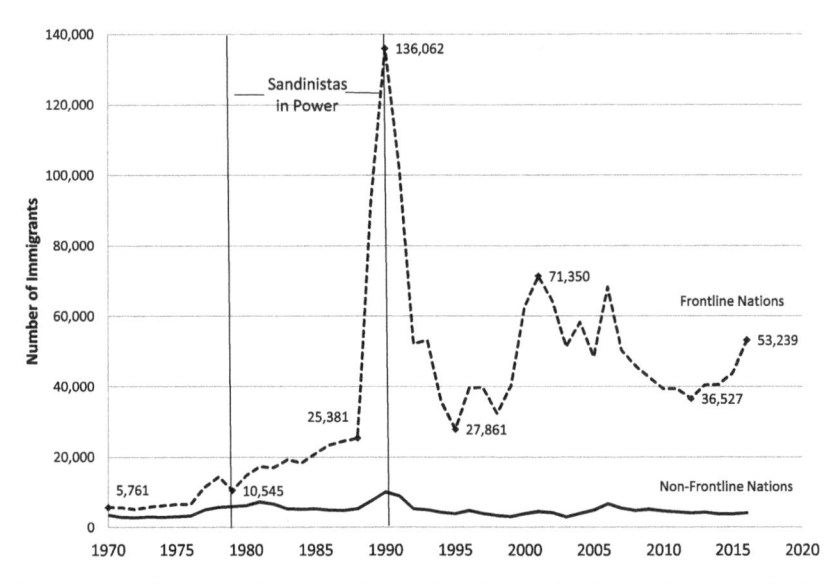

Figure 3. Legal immigration from Central America to the United States 1970–2016. Source: U.S. Office of Immigration Statistics (2018).

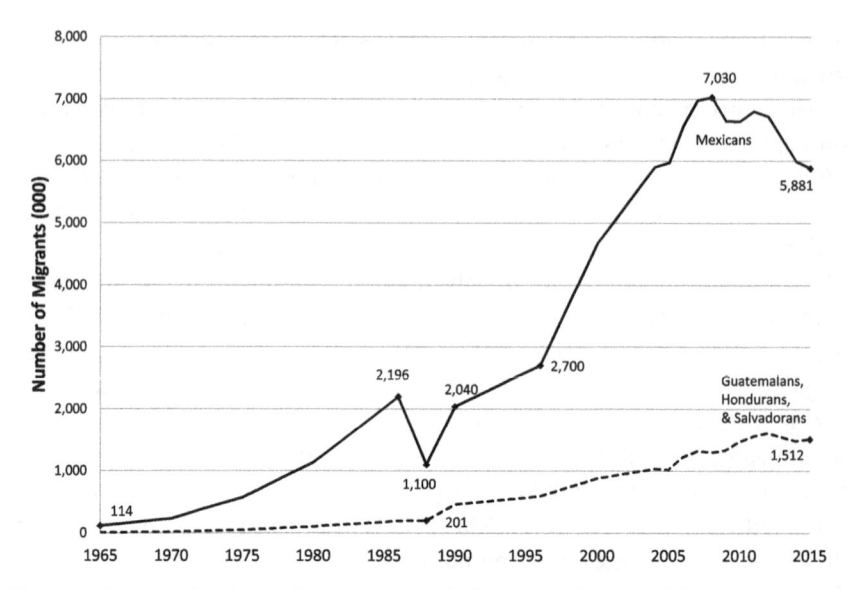

Figure 4. Estimated number of undocumented migrants in the United States 1965–2015. Sources: Wasem 2011 and Cohen, Passel, and Gonzalez-Barrera 2017.

million in 1986 when IRCA's legalization cut the number down to reach 1.1 million in 1988. By 1990, however, it had once again crossed the two million mark and reached 2.7 million in 1996. At this point, growth accelerated as declining rates of return migration served to increase the size of the net inflow. The Mexican undocumented population ultimately reached a maximum of a little over seven million persons in 2008 before declining to around 5.9 million in 2015.

In contrast, the undocumented population of Central Americans rose very slowly through the 1970s and 1980s, reaching a total of just 201,000 in 1990. Thereafter, the rate of growth accelerated and continued even after the undocumented Mexican population began to decline, reaching 1.5 million persons in 2015. Since 2008, the *total* number of Central Americans living in the United States has steadily risen and by 2015 reached around three million persons, about half documented and half undocumented (Cohn, Passel, and Gonzalez-Barrera 2017).

The War on Terror

The U.S. intervention in Central America during the 1980s was the last major battle of the Cold War. However, no sooner had the communist threat disappeared with the Soviet Union's collapse in 1991 than a new threat appeared, heralded by the 1993 bombing of the World Trade Center in New York. This terrorist attack was followed in 1995 by the bombing of the Murrah federal building in Oklahoma City, the 1998 bombing of the U.S. Embassies in Kenya and Tanzania, the 2000 bombing of the USS Cole in Yemen, and finally by the airborne attacks on targets in New York City and Washington, DC on September 11, 2001. In response, President George W. Bush declared a War on Terror, telling the nation that "our war on terror begins with Al Qaeda, but it does not end there. It will not end until every terrorist group of global reach has been found, stopped and defeated" (Bush 2001).

In reality, the first salvo in the war on terror had been fired much earlier, with the passage of the Anti-terrorism and Effective Death Penalty Act in 1996. Its provisions were then augmented by enforcement provisions contained in the 2001 USA PATRIOT Act. The former law, in concert with the 1996 Illegal Immigration Reform and Immigrant Responsibility Act, increased deportations dramatically by criminalizing acts and behaviours that theretofore had been treated as civil violations or misdemeanors, a process now known as "crimmigration" (García Hernández 2015). It also expanded the range of offenses meriting punishment by deportation and gave the federal government expanded powers for detention and removal while deputizing state and local authorities to assist in immigration enforcement. The PATRIOT Act, in turn, authorized enhanced surveillance procedures and expanded the police powers of federal authorities (Golash-Boza 2015).

The end result of these legislative changes was a massive expansion of deportations from the United States. Ironically the new deportation regime had its most powerful effect on immigrants from Latin America, not on migrants from nations that actually launched the terrorist attacks of 2001 and earlier. Paradoxically, although the hijackers on September 11 came from Saudi Arabia, the United Arab Emirates, Egypt, and Lebanon, the United States chose to demonstrate its resolve in combatting Al Qaeda by deporting its Latinos. The scale of the deportation effort is indicated by Figure 5, which plots the trend in total deportations from 1965 to 2016. From 1965 to 1995 the annual number of deportations rose slowly, going from 10,572–50,924 over the course of 30 years. Over the next six years removals from the United States jumped by some 138,000 to reach 189,026 in 2001. After a brief decline in 2002, the number shot upward to peak at 434,015 in 2013 before dropping back to 340,156 at the end of the Obama administration.

The brunt of this massive deportation effort fell not Arab terrorists, but instead swept up ordinary Latino migrants with no conceivable connection to Islamic terrorism. Between 1996 and 2016, some 5.8 million persons were deported from the United States, with 94 per cent originating in just ten nations, nine of which were Latin American (with the tenth being Jamaica). Mexico led the way with around 4.2 million removals, followed by Guatemala with 431,212, Honduras with 372,960, and El Salvador with 267,599. These four nations by themselves comprised 80 per cent of all deportations over the

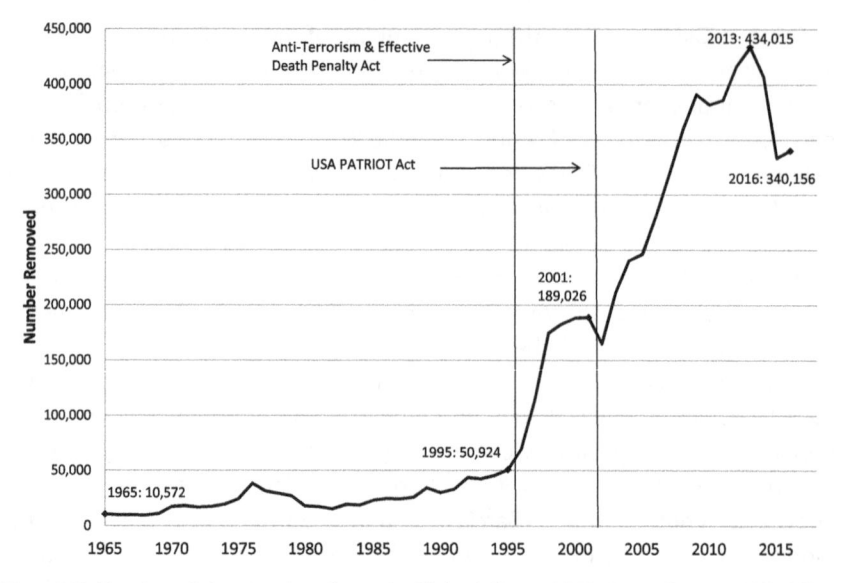

Figure 5. Number of deportations from the United States 1965–2016. Source: U.S. Office of Immigration Statistics (2018).

period. Of all those forcibly removed from the United States after 1996, just 6,995 were from nations associated with the 9–11 attackers, constituting 0.1 per cent of all removals after 1996.

The Wars on crime and drugs

Although the Cold War gave way to the War on Terror after 1991, throughout the period under study the United States was also busy pursuing its twin wars on crime and drugs. Lyndon Johnson's effort to create a "Great Society" coincided with a precipitous rise in crime and a wave of urban riots, provoking a white backlash that gave Richard Nixon the political capital he needed to begin dismantling Johnson's War on Poverty (Perlstein 2008) and to replace it with a racialized War on Crime (Alexander 2010). Although Nixon's hardline efforts at policing faltered during the Watergate scandal, the anti-crime juggernaut returned under Ronald Reagan who in 1986 amplified the War on Crime with a new War on Drugs, labelling drug trafficking as a threat to national security and authorizing the military to cooperate with civilian authorities in anti-drug enforcement along the border and elsewhere (Andreas 2000).

Over the course of the 1980s and into the 1990s, U.S. incarceration rates increased to unprecedented of levels, creating a racialized carceral state that not only imprisoned record numbers of African Americans but also a disproportionate number of Latinos (Alexander 2010). At present nearly a third of all federal prisoners are Hispanic, almost double their share of the U.S. population (U.S. Bureau of Prisons 2018). Although the incarceration boom was initially driven by the imposition of ever-harsher punishments for drug-related crimes and violent offenses, over the last decade the fastest growing portion of the nation's prison industrial complex has been the immigrant detention system.

Consistent with the portrayal of "illegal" migrants as criminals, lawbreakers, and a threat to public safety, infractions of immigration law that formerly were treated as civil offenses in the 1970s and 1980s were criminalized and prosecuted as felonies during the 1990s and 2000s (Meissner et al. 2013; Ewing, Martínez, and Rumbaut 2015; García Hernández 2015). As already noted, the 1996 Illegal immigration Reform and Immigration Responsibility Act expanded the number of acts punishable by deportation and streamlined removal proceedings (Juárez, Gómez-Aguiñaga, and Bettez 2018). At the same time, profits increasingly came to incentivize the arrest and detention of immigrants, with around two thirds of all spaces in the immigrant detention system now being owned and managed by private corporations such as the Geo Group and CoreCivic (Luan 2018). In 2009 lobbyists for the private prison industry successfully prevailed upon Congress to set a quota of 34,000 detention beds to be filled each day (Gilman and Romero 2018).

As a result of these shifts in policy and practice, the immigration detention system grew rapidly. Figure 6 shows the average daily number of persons in the U.S. immigrant detention system from 1979 through the first 11 months of

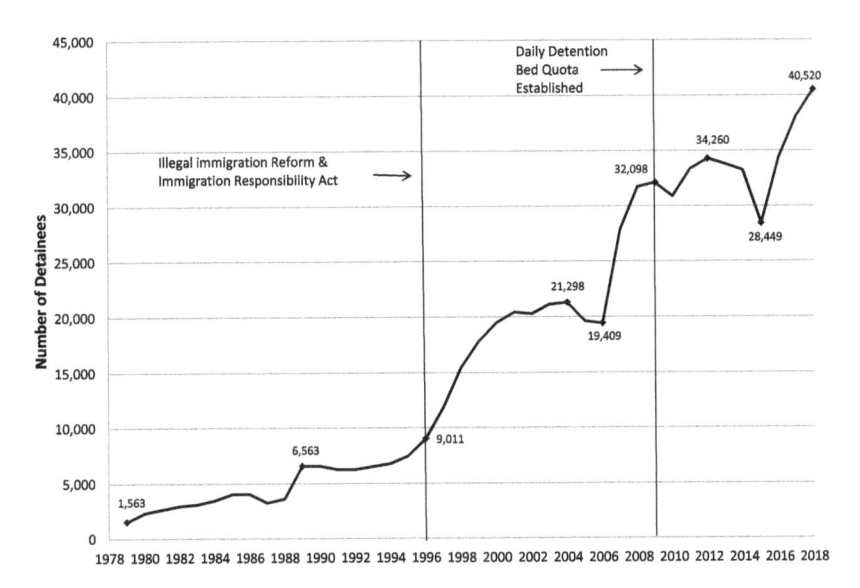

Figure 6. Average daily population in the U.S. immigrant detention system 1979–2018. Source: Reyes (2018).

2018. As indicated by the graph, in 1979 the detention system was very small, holding only 1,563 persons on an average day. This average rose slowly until 1989 when it suddenly jumped to 6,563 and then rose further to reach 9,011 in 1996. At this point the curve bends sharply upwards to plateau briefly at 21,298 in 2004. It then dips slightly to 19,309 in 2006 but in the following year the daily number of detentions shoots almost straight upward to reach a local maximum 32,098 in 2009. It was at this point that Congress enacted the daily 34,000 bed quota, which was achieved in 2012 when the average daily detainee population hit 34,260 persons. Although the average number of detainees dropped to 28,449 in 2015, by 2018 the average had soared to a record 40,520 under the aegis of President Donald Trump.

The War on immigrants

Unlike the Wars on Poverty, Crime, Drugs, and Terror, and the Cold War, the War on Immigrants remains undeclared by any prominent political leader or government official, though Donald Trump perhaps came close when announcing his candidacy for President of the United States. In his speech, he told Americans that "when Mexico sends its people, they're not sending their best ... They're sending people that have lots of problems, and they're bringing those problems with them. They're bringing drugs. They're bringing crime. They're rapists." He then went on to assure his audience that to fix that problem he would "build a great, great wall on our southern border ... [and] have Mexico pay for that wall." Although he may not explicitly have declared a War on Immigrants, reporters and the media have accurately labelled his immigration policies as such (see Collinson 2018; Gessen 2018; Suarez 2018).

As described earlier, the War on Immigrants emerged out of the various other declared "wars," symbolic and real, that U.S. political leaders have launched since the 1960s (Massey 2007). Today's large undocumented population grew out of Lyndon Johnson's War on Poverty and Ronald Reagan's Cold War actions in Central America. Johnson sought to eliminate racism from the U.S. immigration system, but in the process curtailed opportunities for legal entry from Mexico, giving rise to an unauthorized circular inflow that was later converted into a settled population by an unprecedented militarization of the border. In his prosecution of the Cold War, Reagan funded a rebel army and murderous paramilitary units to check the spread of communism in Central America, unleashing waves of violence that wrecked the economy and sent waves of people fleeing northward. Unfortunately most were escaping nations led by right-wing governments allied with the United States and therefore could not be admitted as refugees or asylum seekers for ideological reasons. The ultimate result was the growth of a large population of undocumented migrants living north of the border, one composed overwhelmingly of Mexicans and Central Americans.

The War on Poverty ended in the early 1970s when Nixon replaced it with his War on Crime and Reagan later piled on with a War on Drugs. Together these "wars" led to a regime of mass incarceration that swept young black and Latino men into the nation's prisons. When Bush declared the War on Terror in the aftermath of 9–11, deportations rose to record levels and the immigrant detention system emerged as the fastest growing component of the prison industrial complex. Although the War on Terror was launched to combat Islamic terrorism, the vast majority of those caught up in the deportation machine are from Mexico and Central America. The War on Terror also brought about increases in border enforcement despite a sharply declining inflow of undocumented migrants. Trump's adoption of a "zero-tolerance" policy of vigorously prosecuting all those who appear at the southern border without authorization, irrespective of their claims for asylum refuge, has further expanded the immigrant detention system to record levels.

The scale of exclusion and repression is indicated by a simple comparison of data points in 1988 and today. In 1988, the number of undocumented migrants was estimated at around 1.9 million persons, but after two decades of border militarization the number peaked at nearly 12 million in 2008 and today it fluctuates at around 11 million persons, with the number of Mexicans slowly declining and the number of Central Americans slowly rising. This population is now subject to intense policing both internally and along the border. From 1988 to 2018 the Border Patrol's budget increased from $411 million to $3.6 billion in real terms and the number of officers rose from 3,700 to more than 19,000 to become the largest arms-bearing agency in the U.S. except for the military itself. Over the same period the internal enforcement budget went from $1.6 billion to $6.2 billion in real terms, and deportations rose from 26,000–340,000 while average daily detentions grew from 3,600 to nearly 41,000 (Massey 2018).

Ironically, today's massive anti-immigrant effort occurs at a time when undocumented migration from Mexico has effectively ceased, though Mexicans continue to play an important role in the U.S. economy (Blau and Mackie 2017). At this writing, the net volume of undocumented Mexican entries has been negative for twelve years, with very few people arriving and many more departing (often through deportation). In 2017 the number of apprehensions along the Mexico-U.S. border reached a 46 year low, dropping from a peak of 1.6 million in 2000 to just 304,000 in 2017. Over the same period the share of Mexicans among those apprehended dropped from 98 to 42 per cent. Although the net inflow from El Salvador, Guatemala, and Honduras remains positive, the numbers are modest and those arriving at the border are increasingly not workers but children and families.

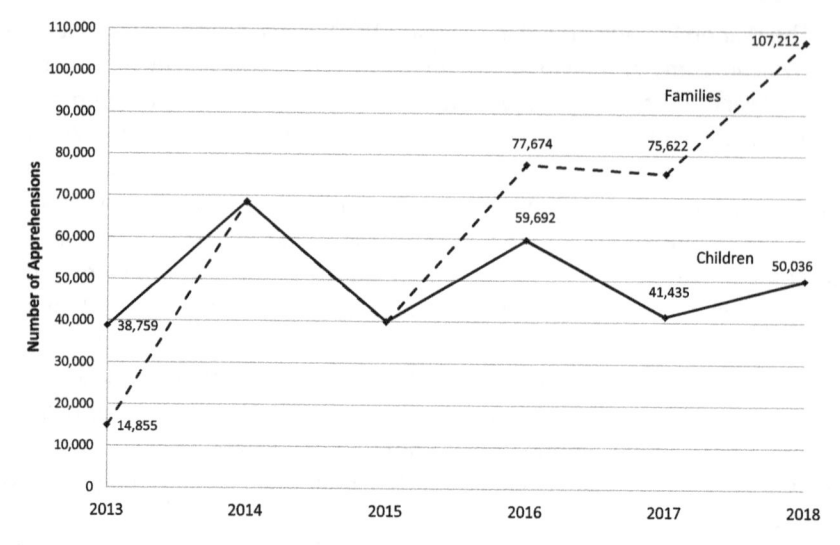

Figure 7. Apprehensions of children and families at the Mexico-U.S. Border 2013–2018. Source: U.S. Customs and Border Enforcement (2018).

The new reality at the border is indicated by trends in the number of people apprehended as members of family units or as unaccompanied minors. Although the available data only go back five years, Figure 7 reveals that from 2013 to 2018 the number of persons apprehended as part of a family unit rose from around 15,000–107,000 persons. Over the same period, the number of unaccompanied minors apprehended fluctuated between 40,000 and 70,000 and stood at around 50,000 in 2018. As a share of total apprehensions, the percentage of unaccompanied minors rose from 9 to 13 per cent over the same period and the number apprehended in families grew from 4 to 27 per cent.

Unlike single undocumented migrants travelling alone, those arriving at the border in family groups or as children are overwhelming from Central America rather than Mexico. As shown in Figure 8, in 2018 only 20 per cent of the unaccompanied minors apprehended at the border came from Mexico, whereas 45 per cent come from Guatemala, 22 per cent from Honduras, and 10 per cent from El Salvador. Likewise, among those apprehended while travelling with other family members, 47 per cent were from Guatemala, 37 per cent were from Honduras, and 13 per cent came from El Salvador, with just 2 per cent originating in Mexico. Thus the current situation at the border is not an immigration crisis, but a humanitarian crisis, one that ultimately derives from the America's military and political intervention in the region. A very large inflow of Mexican workers seeking jobs in the United States has been replaced by a much smaller inflow of families and children seeking not jobs but refuge.

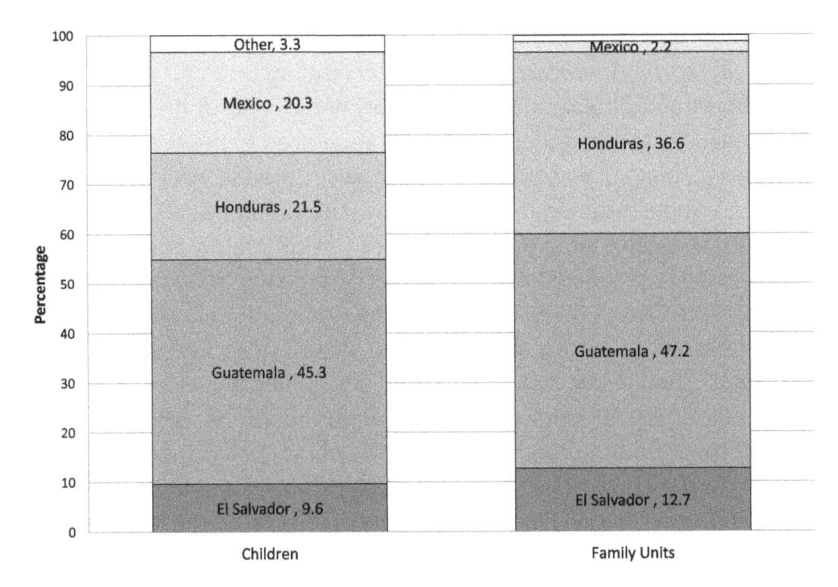

Figure 8. Origins of families and children apprehended at the Mexico-U.S. border in 2018. Source: U.S. Customs and Border Enforcement (2018).

Conclusion

What used to be a very large annual flow of undocumented Mexican male workers before 2000 has now become a much smaller flow of Central American women and children seeking to escape horrendous social and economic conditions growing out of the armed U.S. intervention in the region as part of the Cold War. During the 1970s and 1980s the United States took in and successfully integrated a much larger inflow of refugees from Indochina. Between 1975 and 1985 some 761,000 refugees entered the United States from Cambodia, Laos, and Vietnam, seeking to escape the chaos that engulfed the region in the aftermath of the U.S. withdrawal from Vietnam (Gordon 1987). Currently we face a much smaller number of Central Americans arriving at our southern border seeking refuge from collateral damage linked to another U.S. intervention to stop the spread of communism.

The current exodus stems from economic stagnation and endemic violence that has come to characterize the region since 1980. As noted earlier, income in the frontline nations of Central America declined in real terms after the U.S. intervention and did not return to the *status quo ante* for three decades, dramatically increasing the income gap relative to other countries in the region. From 1977 to 2017 the size of the gap in GDP per capita between frontline and non-frontline Central American nations rose in real terms from $1,027 to $6,420. In a very real way, the permanent economic stagnation of the region is a direct result of the damage to infrastructure and markets caused by America's Cold War intervention.

Although political violence in the region diminished in the 1990s, it was soon supplanted by gang-related violence also linked to the U.S. intervention. The infamous Mara Salvatrucha gang formed in the Pico-Union neighbourhood of Los Angeles during the mid-1980s, incorporating young undocumented Salvadoran males who, unlike their Mexican counterparts, had no access to established institutions and networks connected to employment and assistance (Menjivar 2000). Lacking a clear pathway to advance in the United States, these young men turned to street gangs for mutual support and were subsequently swept into the U.S. criminal justice system and deported (Wolf 2012). Although criminal deportations into frontline nations remained small through the early 1990s, they accelerated rapidly thereafter and as of 2017 a cumulative total of 161,000 criminals had been repatriated, jump-starting gang activity in the region and exacerbating the exodus of refugees northward (Massey 2018).

Rather than meeting these new arrivals at the border with humanitarian aid and asylum, the Trump administration instead is funnelling them into the maw of an expanding gulag of detention centres (see Dow 2005). Since 1996, the United States has only admitted 28,500 refugees and asylum seekers from El Salvador, Guatemala, and Honduras instead of the hundreds of thousands of Indochinese taken in earlier. The grudging acceptance of Central American and their harsh treatment in the detention system prevails despite the fact that circa 1980 the demographic potential for out-migration from Cambodia, Laos, and Vietnam was much greater (with a combined population 64 million) than in El Salvador, Guatemala, and Honduras today (with a total population 32 million).

In policy terms, it would not be very difficult to address the current humanitarian crisis at the border by enacting the same policies and procedures used earlier to incorporate a much larger number of arrivals from Indochina. However, one distinctive barrier to the smooth integration of Central Americans today is the fact that half of their potential sponsors living in the United States are unauthorized; but this problem also could be solved if Congress were to create a pathway to legal status for the nation's 11 million undocumented residents. The legalization of presently undocumented Central Americans would create a firm platform for the social support and integration of newly arrived refugees and asylum seekers. Such a policy, however, would require Americans to recognize their ultimate responsibility for the current exodus from El Salvador, Guatemala, and Honduras, just as they accepted responsibility for the exodus from Cambodia, Laos, and Vietnam two generations ago. Unfortunately the current surge of nativism and xenophobia in the United States, which is both cultivated and accommodated by political leaders in the Republican Party, renders that scenario rather unlikely, at least for the time being.

Disclosure statement

No potential conflict of interest was reported by the author.

Funding

This work was supported by Eunice Kennedy Shriver National Institute of Child Health and Human Development: [Grant Number R01 HD35643,5P2CHD047879].

References

Alexander, Michelle. 2010. *The New Jim Crow: Mass Incarceration in the Age of Colorblindness*. New York: The New Press.

Andreas, Peter. 2000. *Border Games: Policing the U.S.-Mexico Divide*. Ithaca, NY: Cornell University Press.

Blau, Francine, and Christopher Mackie. 2017. *The Economic and Fiscal Consequences of Immigration*. Washington, DC: National Academies Press.

Bush, George W. 2001. "Text: President Bush Addresses the Nation." *Washington Post*, September 20. http://www.washingtonpost.com/wp-srv/nation/specials/attacked/transcripts/bushaddress_092001.html.

Chavez, Leo. 2001. *Covering Immigration: Popular Images and the Politics of the Nation*. Berkeley: University of California Press.

Chavez, Leo. 2013. *The Latino Threat: Constructing Immigrants, Citizens, and the Nation*. Stanford, CA: Stanford University Press.

Cohen, D'Vera, Jeffrey S. Passel, and Ana Gonzalez-Barrera. 2017. *Rise in U.S. Immigrants From El Salvador, Guatemala, and Honduras Outpaces Growth From Elsewhere*. Washington, DC: Pew Research Center. Accessed 17 December 2018. http://www.pewhispanic.org/wp-content/uploads/sites/5/2017/12/Pew-Research-Center_Central_American-migration-to-U.S._12.7.17.pdf.

Cohn, D'Vera, Jeffrey S. Passel, and Ana Gonzalez-Barrera. 2017. *Rise in Immigrants From El Salvador, Guatemala, and Honduras Outpaces Growth From Elsewhere*. Washington, DC: Pew Research Center.

Collinson, Stephen. 2018. "US Reckons with Trump's War on Immigration." *CNN*, June 14. https://www.cnn.com/2018/06/14/politics/donald-trump-immigration-jeff-sessions/index.html.

Dow, Mark. 2005. *American Gulag: Inside U.S. Immigration Prisons*. Berkeley: University of California Press.

Ewing, Walter A., Daniel E. Martínez, and Rubén G. Rumbaut. 2015. *The Criminalization of Immigration in the United States*. Washington, DC: American Immigration Council.

García Hernández, César Cuauhtémoc. 2015. *Crimmigration Law*. Chicago: American Bar Association.

Gessen, Masha. 2018. "Trump's New War on Immigrants." *The New Yorker*, April 10.

Gilman, Denise, and Luis A. Romero. 2018. "Immigration Detention, Inc." *Journal of Migration and Human Security*, 1–16. doi:10.1177/2311502418765414.

Golash-Boza, Tanya M. 2015. *Deported: Immigrant Policing, Disposable Labor and Global Capitalism*. New York: NYU Press.

Gordon, Linda. 1987. "Southeast Asian Refugee Migration to the United States." In *Pacific Bridges: The New Immigration From Asia and the Pacific Islands*, edited by James T. Fawcett, 153–173. New York: Center for Migration Studies.

Hinton, Elizabeth. 2016. *From the War on Poverty to the War on Crime: The Making of Mass Incarceration*. Cambridge, MA: Harvard University Press.

Juárez, Melina, Bárbara Gómez-Aguiñaga, and Sonia P. Bettez. 2018. "Twenty Years After IIRIRA: The Rise of Immigrant Detention and its Effects on Latinx Communities Across the Nation." *Journal of Migration and Human Security* 6 (1): 74–96.

Katznelson, Ira. 2005. *When Affirmative Action Was White: An Untold History of Racial Inequality in Twentieth-Century America*. New York: W.W. Norton.

Luan, Livia. 2018. *Profiting from Enforcement: The Role of Private Prisons in U.S. Immigration Detention*. Migration Policy Institute, May 2. https://www.migrationpolicy.org/ article/profiting-enforcement-role-private-prisons-us-immigration-detention.

Lundquist, Jennifer H., and Douglas S. Massey. 2005. "Politics or Economics? International Migration During the Nicaraguan Contra War." *Journal of Latin American Studies* 37: 29–53.

Massey, Douglas S. 2007. *Categorically Unequal: The American Stratification System*. New York: Russell Sage Foundation.

Massey, Douglas S. 2018. "Doubling Down on a Bad Bet: U.S. Immigration Policy Before and after Trump." Paper presented at the Conference "A 21st Century Immigration Policy for the West," sponsored by the Lefrak Forum and the Department of Political Science, Michigan State University, October 11–13.

Massey, Douglas S., Jorge Durand, and Nolan J. Malone. 2002. *Beyond Smoke and Mirrors: Mexican Immigration in an Age of Economic Integration*. New York: Russell Sage Foundation.

Massey, Douglas S., Jorge Durand, and Karen A. Pren. 2014. "Explaining Undocumented Migration." *International Migration Review* 48 (4): 1028–1061.

Massey, Douglas S., Jorge Durand, and Karen A. Pren. 2015. "Border Enforcement and Return Migration by Documented and Undocumented Mexicans." *Journal of Ethnic and Migration Studies* 41 (7): 1015–1040.

Massey, Douglas S., Jorge Durand, and Karen A. Pren. 2016. "Why Border Enforcement Backfired." *American Journal of Sociology* 121 (5): 1557–1600.

Massey, Douglas S., and Karen A. Pren. 2012a. "Origins of the New Latino Underclass." *Race and Social Problems* 4 (1): 5–17.

Massey, Douglas S., and Karen A. Pren. 2012b. "Unintended Consequences of U.S. Immigration Policy: Explaining the Post-1965 Surge From Latin America." *Population and Development Review* 38 (1): 1–29.

Mayer, Jane. 2008. *The Dark Side: The Inside Story of How the War on Terror Turned Into a War on American Ideals*. New York: Doubleday.

Meissner, Doris, Donald M. Kerwin, Musaffar Chisti, and Claire Bergeron. 2013. *Immigration Enforcement in the United States: The Rise of a Formidable Machinery*. Washington, DC: Migration Policy Institute.

Menjivar, Cecilia. 2000. Fragmented Ties: Salvadoran Immigrant Networks in America. Berkeley: University of California Press.

Mexican Migration Project. 2018. *Supplementary Data File: NATLYEAR*. Princeton, NJ: Office of Population Research, Princeton University. Accessed 17 December 2018. https://mmp.opr.princeton.edu/databases/supplementaldata-en.aspx.

Perlstein, Rick. 2008. *Nixonland: The Rise of a President and the Fracturing of America*. New York: Scribner.

Quadagno, Jill. 1994. *The Color of Welfare: How Racism Undermined the War on Poverty*. New York: Oxford University Press.

Reyes, J. Rachel. 2018. Immigration Detention: Recent Trends and Scholarship. New York: Center for Migration Studies. Accessed 17 December 2018. http://cmsny.org/publications/virtualbrief-detention/.

Santa Ana, Otto. 2002. *Brown Tide Rising: Metaphors of Latinos in Contemporary American Public Discourse*. Austin: University of Texas Press.

Suarez, Cyndi. 2018. "The War on Immigrants (of Color): Who's Really Crossing the Line?" *Nonprofit Quarterly*, June 20. https://nonprofitquarterly.org/2018/06/20/war-on-immigrants-of-color-crossing-the-line/.

U.S. Bureau of Prisons. 2018. *Inmate Statistics: Inmate Ethnicity*. Washington, DC: U.S. Bureau of Prisons, August 25, 2018. https://www.bop.gov/about/statistics/statistics_inmate_ ethnicity.jsp.

U.S. Customs and Border Enforcement. 2018. *Stats and Summaries*. Washington, DC: U.S. Department of Homeland Security. Access 17 December 2018. https://www.cbp.gov/newsroom/media-resources/stats.

U.S. Office of Immigration Statistics. 2018. *Yearbook of Immigration Statistics*. Washington, DC: U.S. Department of Homeland Security. Accessed 17 December 2018. https://www.dhs.gov/immigration-statistics/yearbook.

Wasem, Ruth E. 2011. *Unauthorized Aliens Residing in the United States: Estimates Since 1986*. Washington, DC: Congressional Research Service.

Wolf, Sonja. 2012. "Mara Salvatrucha: The Most Dangerous Street Gang in the Americas?" *Latin American Politics and Society* 54 (1): 65–99.

Zolberg, Aristide R. 2006. *A Nation by Design: Immigration Policy in the Fashioning of America*. Cambridge, MA: Harvard University Press.

The students we share: falling through the cracks on both sides of the US-Mexico border

Patricia Gándara

ABSTRACT
This article describes the significant and increasing challenges faced by children of Mexican immigrants on both sides of the border. US schools that serve these students overwhelmingly in low-resource, segregated settings are under attack by ICE, disrupting their education. Meanwhile, more than half a million US born, as well as many Mexican born but US educated (generation 1.5) students, are attempting to integrate into Mexican schools that lack training in teaching and supporting them. In the face of data that show a plummeting birth rate in the US and a high demand for bilingual, multi-cultural workers in both Mexico and the U.S, the enormous asset represented by the students we share is being squandered.

This paper argues that millions of children are caught in the crucible of migration in which neither Mexico nor the United States takes their educational needs sufficiently into account and risks consigning them to a permanent underclass in both countries. This includes more than a million students who have experienced some part of their young lives in both the US and Mexico, often going to school in both systems. More than 500,000 Mexico-born children under 18 live in the United States (Childtrends 2018) and another 600,000 U.S. born and raised citizen children are now in Mexican schools as a result of their families returning to Mexico from the U.S. (Jacobo and Jensen 2018, 1). Still more students born in Mexico but educated in the U.S. (generation 1.5), though not officially counted, are returnees in Mexican classrooms. All of these students are considered "the students we share".

This, however, does not account for the students who accompany their families to Mexico only to end their schooling prematurely because of the challenges they face in trying to enrol, or the immediate need to help support the family. That number is potentially large but not known. Additionally, there are nearly 7 million students who are the U.S. born children of Mexican immigrants (Childtrends 2018), but whose educational experience is partially shaped by their parents' lack of experience with the U.S. schooling system, and still many thousands of others whose parents have come to the U.S. while they remain behind in Mexico, creating binational families. These too are sometimes referred to as the "students we share", (Jensen and Gándara forthcoming) as these young people often lead uniquely binational lives.

In the Mexican state of Baja California alone there are 53,000 U.S. citizen students in the Mexican schools (López 2018) for whom both countries have a stake in their future. These students are potentially enormous assets to both nations. But often these binational students are traumatized, mis-educated, and fall through the cracks of both educational systems.

Immigration status of the students we share

Individuals of Mexican origin are far and away the largest segment of the Hispanic/Latino group, representing 63.5% of the group. An estimated 17 million children are of Mexican origin in 2020. Thirty-eight percent or about 7 million of these children are the children of Mexican immigrants (Childtrends 2018). While approximately 90% are either U.S. citizens by birth or legal residents (Annie E Casey Foundation 2017; Zong, Batalova, and Hallock 2018), it is important to note that children who are born abroad as well as those born in the U.S. to immigrant parents are often grouped together as first and second generation "immigrants". As a group, Mexican origin students often struggle in U.S. schools (Gándara and Contreras 2009).

Educational outcomes for the students we share in the U.S.

Given that federal education data are collected for Hispanic or Latino students, but not by Mexican origin or by immigration status, we are limited in our ability to report achievement for Mexican origin students alone. However, we know that approximately two-thirds of Hispanic students are of Mexican origin (Childtrends 2018). Therefore, in order to provide an estimate of Mexican students' educational trajectories in contemporary United States of America, I present data for Hispanic/Latino students with the caveat that Mexican origin students are among the most socio-economically disadvantaged of the Latino/Hispanic group (Hernandez, Denton, and McCartney 2009) and SES is very closely correlated with academic achievement (Carnavale et al. 2019). Thus, if anything, these data likely over-estimate Mexican origin students' academic achievement.

On the 2017 National Assessment of Educational Progress (NAEP), known as "The Nation's Report Card", only 26% of Latino 4th graders tested proficient in math, compared to 51% of white students and 67% of Asians. At 8th grade just 20% of Latinos achieved proficiency in math compared to 44% of white students and 64% of Asians (NCES 2017a). (Score gaps for English Language Arts are very similar.) Thus, as Latino students head towards high school, their preparation is very different from their white or Asian peers, which is then reflected in substantially different high school graduation rates. In 2016, the 4-year high school graduation rate for Asian students was 91%, for white students and 88%, for Latino students, 79%, although this represents a major leap from only about 68% a decade prior (NCES 2017b). Perhaps the most telling statistic about opportunity in America, however, is the enormous gap in college completion, which has become increasingly critical for entering the middle class. Among Asians 25 years and older, 55.9% hold a bachelor's degree or higher, as do 37.3% of whites. For Latinos, the figure is 16.4% (NCES 2017c). This enormous gap in college completion rates makes it impossible for Latinos, and especially Latino immigrants, to compete effectively in the U.S. economy and is strong evidence of the marginalization of Latino, and especially Mexican-origin students in American society.

The schooling context for Latino students in the U.S.

Whether born in the U.S. or abroad, Latino students do not fare well as a group in U.S. schools, with the exception of those who gain a strong education in their home country before immigrating to the U.S. For these students a good foundation in the home language is a major asset, as developing concepts in one's strongest language "is half the battle" (Bialystok and Hakuta 1994, 101). But most of their teachers cannot communicate with them or their families, nor do they understand the students' backgrounds, cultures or even their prior schooling experiences. In most of the Southwest, the students in public schools are now majority or near majority Latino, and overwhelmingly Mexican origin. For decades these students have been encountering schools and teachers that are not adequately prepared to educate them (López 2017). Surveys of teachers in California – a state in which Latino students are the majority and 84% of English learners speak Spanish – note that inability to communicate with students and their parents is a primary concern of teachers with English Learners (ELs) in their classrooms (Gándara, Maxwell-Jolly, and Driscoll 2005, 5; Santibañez and Gándara 2017). A study by Hopkins (2013) conducted in California, Arizona and Texas with about 600 teachers of immigrant students –both bilingual and English only – found that teachers who spoke only English were much more likely than bilingual teachers to expect parents to reach out to them, rather than the reverse. Thus, there was very limited communication between the two. This lack of connection between schools, students and their parents is an important element in low academic achievement for many Latino children of immigrants, as the parents do not know how to support their children's school work and the schools have little knowledge of the circumstances or challenges faced by these families.

For the 7 million students who are children of Mexican immigrants, language is typically a major challenge upon entering school. If they cannot communicate with their teachers and feel isolated and estranged from the other students, they are likely to under-perform. Although bilingual programmes have been shown to be superior to English only programmes with respect to long term outcomes in English (Umansky and Reardon 2014; Valentino and Reardon 2015; Steele et al. 2017), relatively few EL students are provided with this option. The exact number of students in bilingual programmes is not known as these data are not collected nationally and local definitions of programme types are inconsistent and unreliable. Sometimes programmes that serve "bilingual students" are labelled bilingual even though no bilingual instruction is actually offered. The last time the federal government commissioned a study of educational services for English learners was nearly two decades ago and researchers found that 48% of students had no primary language support at all, much less a bilingual programme (Zehler et al. 2003). California, with nearly one-third of all English learners in the country prohibited bilingual instruction in most cases until very recently, as does Arizona.

Perhaps even more important than academic outcomes are the socio-emotional challenges students face when they are stripped of their home language in the school. Portes and Hao (2002) found that students whose bilingualism is supported had more cohesive family relations and fewer behaviour problems in school than students without this linguistic advantage, and Rumbaut (2014) found that immigrant students educated bilingually are less likely to drop out of school than those who lose or do not develop their home language. He argues that this is likely the result of closer family relations and thus greater adherence to parental authority. Cummins (1996) has argued, based on decades of research and theory development, that language is inextricably bound up with culture and because immigrant cultures are not held in very high regard in many places in the U.S., the denial of a student's language can also undermine the student's self-esteem and disempower the student in the academic setting. But language is not the only, nor possibly even the most important challenge that immigrant students experience in U.S. schools.

Latinos are also now the most segregated major subgroup in most parts of the nation (Frankenberg et al. 2019). Moreover, one analysis conducted in California found that immigrant students (85% of whom are Latino and overwhelmingly of Mexican origin) were more likely than any other sub-group to be assigned to the lowest performing schools in the state (Gándara 2016, 370). One well-known characteristic of these struggling schools is that teacher turn-over is double that of schools that serve middle-income students (Goldring, Taie, and Riddles 2014) and many students report never having had a single consistent teacher in some core subjects like math or science, only a series of substitutes throughout the year.

It would be wrong, however, to place all the blame for dismal educational outcomes on the schools. Nationally, 54% of Latino children live at or near poverty, more than double the percentage of white children, and 10% live in deep poverty (below1/2 the federal poverty level) (Childtrends 2019); 30% of Mexican immigrant families routinely experience food insecurity (Potochnick, Chen, and Perreira 2017, 1047), which under even stable circum-stances puts them at risk for poor health. However, in the study by Potochnick, Chen and Perreira, the researchers found that local immigration enforcement reduced families' use of social services, increasing the rate of food insecurity by another 10%. Forty percent (40%) of adult undocumented immigrants also have no health insurance, which means that an accident or chronic illness can reduce parents' ability to work, increasing children's risk of food insecurity. Twenty-three percent (23%) of undocumented children have no health insur-ance themselves (Kaiser Family Foundation 2017) . However, even where undocumented families may have some access to health care for their U.S. born children, undocumented parents are often reluctant to interact with public institutions for fear of being reported. As a result, immigrant children – most of whom are U.S. citizens– may go without corrective lenses to help them see properly and they generally suffer from chronic health problems that can keep them out of school (Berliner 2006).

Extremely deleterious educational and social conditions paired with segre-gated schools in poor neighbourhoods conspire to place educational success out of reach of many Latino and immigrant students. Yet, even these con-ditions may be less important than the immigration enforcement policies of the current federal administration with respect to children's wellbeing.

The context of immigration enforcement

President Donald Trump made immigration enforcement a centrepiece of his campaign for the presidency. He promised to build a wall across the whole southern border and to get Mexico to pay for it. He also referred to immigrants from Mexico as rapists, drug dealers and criminals. He has stirred up an enor-mous amount of fear and resentment among some sectors of the public with the idea that criminal immigrants were taking their jobs and threatening their security (Newsday, November 9, 2016). Once in office he lost no time cracking down on immigrants in random and unannounced raids in places that had not previously been considered targets, as in the case of Mr. Avelica, a more than twenty-year resident of Los Angeles who was apprehended as he left his U.S.-born daughter at school in July of 2017. The story went viral and caused panic in immigrant communities across the nation (Castillo 2017).

While deportations were high, and sometimes even higher, during the Obama administration, in the last years of that administration they were mostly confined to felons and to individuals interdicted at the border. "Felons not families" became the policy (The Economist 2017). Under Trump, all immigrants are targets, including those who have lived in the U.S. for decades without incident and those raising U.S. born children (The Economist 2017). As a result, stories abound of children terrified to go to school for fear that their parents will no longer be there when they return home and children afraid to sleep at night, waiting for the knock on the door from ICE. Even students in mixed status families, where one or more members of the household lack documentation, are also at risk, even though most family members are legal immigrants.

Civil rights project study of impact of immigration enforcement on schools

Between October of 2017 and January of 2018, the Civil Rights Project at the University of California at Los Angeles conducted a survey of school personnel in approximately 750 schools in 24 districts– urban, suburban, and rural–in 12 states. All four U.S. Census regions were surveyed. More than 5,000 educators (teachers, principals, counsellors and other certificated school staff) responded initially, and of these, approximately 3500 noted that they had observed an impact of heightened immigration enforcement on their students. It is important to note as well that 83% of the educators responding were working in Title I schools – designated by the federal government as serving high percentages of students meeting the criteria for free and reduced price lunch– that were already challenged beyond their limits. In order to keep the survey short and increase the probability that educators would respond, we kept it to nine substantive questions plus five questions about the place they worked and their role there. We also offered an open-ended question allowing respondents to write about their experience. Almost everyone chose to write something and the comments below are illustrative of the kinds of responses we received. (For more in depth description of the study see Gándara and Ee 2018; Ee and Gándara 2019).

Across all schools in this study, 76% of educators responded that they had observed behavioural or emotional problems among immigrant youth and 26% reported that these problems were "extensive". For example, one educator from the Northeast wrote:

> Several students have arrived at school crying, withdrawn and refusing to eat lunch because they have witnessed deportation of a family member. Some students show anxiety symptoms … All of this impacts their ability to focus and complete work, which further affects them academically.

Likewise, more than 80% of respondents reported that their immigrant students had talked about fearing ICE[1], and almost 40% said that this was extensive. One counsellor in the South noted:

> The kids are scared and sometimes they hide for days when there are immigration raids in the area. Some of the students have no food or place to live because the parents do not have a job and they go day by day.

The counsellor's comment points up an issue that is not widely reported but that we heard repeatedly: immigration enforcement is creating both housing and food insecurity for students, in addition to psychological trauma. Even very young children are suffering on many levels. One first grade girl was reported to have asked her teacher: "How will we eat?" It is hard to imagine that under these conditions children would be able to apply themselves in school.

Not surprisingly, two-thirds of respondents reported that, as a consequence of the enforcement regime, their immigrant students were experiencing a decline in academic performance, and many educators commented that even their most outstanding, college bound students were giving up on school because their futures were now so uncertain. As a principal in Tennessee noted:

> They are not thinking about college, or the test next week, or what is being taught in the classroom today. They are thinking about their family and whether they will still be a family; whether their family will remain intact.

Although most of these students are U.S. citizens, deportation of a parent can mean they too will be leaving the country, or that they will no longer have the resources to continue their education and may need to leave school to help support the family as the primary breadwinner or caregiver has been deported. Deciding to stay or go is a wrenching decision for these young people – to follow a parent to a country they do not know, giving up their dream of an education, or carrying the guilt of staying behind while other family members leave to an uncertain future. Of course, there is also the challenge of figuring out a way – and place – to live if one decides to remain.

But it is not just the students whose families are targets of these enforcement practices that are affected. Nearly two –thirds (62%) of educators reported that the other students in the classroom or school were also affected. As one teacher shared about the impact of losing one student from her classroom:

> This [a student picked up by ICE] understandably had an immense impact on the rest of my students, as well, as his empty seat in the classroom confirmed the reality of their fears every day.

Students are anxious for their friends and classmates even when they are not directly affected, and the loss of students from the classroom creates a pall over the whole class (Minikwu 2017). The image of empty desks where classmates and friends had sat haunts the other students, as frequently no one knows what has happened to them.

Teachers, too, are deeply affected by the impact on their students. One teacher told us that a parent had come to her pleading that she take her children because she was so worried about who would care for them if they detained and deported her. Teachers also reported having to interrupt lessons to deal with students crying or acting out in class. But perhaps the greatest impact on the schools is the declining sense of trust and community in the schools. Some teachers reported they didn't know whom they could trust among their colleagues with information about a student's immigration status. Revealing information about a student's family situation to the wrong person could result in severe consequences for that family. In addition to the concerns about trust in the school, teachers also have to worry about how they are perceived by parents with varying perspectives on immigration. An Arizona teacher lamented that "[the students] want to know about what's going on but anytime it is discussed in class I get an upset parent phone call". It was clear from educators' responses that many feel pressured from all sides and unsure where to turn for support.

The children of immigrants in the U.S. are an especially vulnerable group, especially if they are Latinos. While most are U.S. citizens, an estimated 5.9 million (American Immigration Council 2018) have at least one unauthorized family member, which puts them at risk for sudden deportation or family loss of livelihood.

Not all the undocumented are Latinos, but Latinos are the targets of ICE. Although Asians are the fastest growing undocumented group, ICE tends to leave them alone (Shan 2018, 9).

The migrant experience

The decision for a family to leave their home and migrate is often fraught with fear, anxiety, and a deep sense of loss (Suárez-Orozco and Suárez-Orozco 1995). Most who arrive at the U.S. border are also desperately poor and traumatized by the journey. Only the most dire of circumstances would prompt most families to leave all behind to take a chance in another country where they are considered illegal and unwelcome. Falicov (2002) describes the response to migration as grief or mourning, not unlike losing a loved one.

For children this can be especially stressful if the family migrates in stages with one parent going and one staying behind or if children are separated from their parents at the border (as has occurred under Trump administration policies in 2018). These separations can have damaging life-long psychological and physical health consequences, including alterations in brain development (SRCD 2018).

Even U.S. citizen children are affected by family separations resulting from immigration enforcement, increasing the risk for these children's mental health, including anxiety, depression, behaviour problems, and symptoms of post-traumatic stress disorder (Zayas et al. 2015; Rojas-Flores, Hwang-Koo, and Judy London 2017). Of course, some migrants come to the US to find a better life in their youth and form a family after having lived in the U.S. for a number of years, and some are brought as children and build their lives in the U.S. as the only home they have ever really known. But what they all have in common is constant fear and anxiety about their status in this country and a sense that they may have no future here.

Those brought as children form the group that the Deferred Action for Childhood Arrivals (DACA) programme was created to help. Not infrequently they do not even know they are undocumented until the need to produce a birth certificate in order to apply for a college loan or driver's license reveals the fact (Gonzalez 2011). DACA was created in 2012 by the Obama administration and at its height enrolled approximately 900,000 young people, 20% of whom were high school students, another 18% college students, 9,000 teachers, and most of the rest in the workforce in other areas including medicine and the clergy (Wong 2017). However, in September of 2017 President Trump announced the end of the DACA programme as of March 2018. The courts have since stayed its elimination, but currently about 680,000 DACA recipients are holding their breath to see what their future will be. These young people, too, experience enormous stress not being able to plan for their futures.

In sum, immigrant students suffer from a host of disadvantages that affect their overall health, make normal development challenging and create high levels of stress. When they are additionally faced with the possibility of being separated from their families, the level of stress can be so distracting that it is impossible to concentrate in school, jeopardizing their futures.

En el Otro Lado/On the other side

Hundreds of thousands of the students we share are experiencing another form of trauma on the Mexican side of the border (and increasingly in Central America as well). These students, often with weak academic Spanish (having been educated in English only classrooms in the United States), are attempting to continue their educations, but with schools and teachers that have little understanding of their educational history, experiences, or expectations and are very unlikely to be able to communicate with them in English as it estimated that no more than 5% of Mexican teachers speak English (Gándara 2016). If teachers notice them at all, since they tend to look like the other students, it is often to see them as intellectually inferior or lazy because they are unable to keep up with lessons presented in Spanish, a language most have not been taught to read or write in. Hamann, Zuñiga, and Sánchez Garcia (2008) found that when asked about immigrant students in their classroom, many teachers would deny having any. But when researchers then asked students to raise their hands if they had immigrated to Mexico, several hands would go up.

This invisibility ensures that no special accommodations will be made for them. But even if teachers knew of their backgrounds, there is virtually no chance they would be treated any differently. In a study that included teachers from five Mexican states, Sánchez Garcia and Hamann (2017) found that many teachers didn't believe there needed to be any accommodation for these students. They located the students' problems outside of the school. Mexican teachers spend almost all of their time in front of the class; nearly twice that of US teachers according to OECD rankings, and they are paid only to provide direct instruction, not improve their skills or consult with parents or others on behalf of their students (OECD 2014). The school day in Mexico is also shorter than the U.S. at first through sixth grade, resulting in many fewer hours of instruction, and this is especially true in rural schools where most migrants relocate (Jacobo and Jensen 2018).

With respect to academic achievement, Mexico does not test all students annually in a way that would allow for monitoring students' learning over time. However, Mexico does participate in international OECD (Organization for Economic Cooperation and Development) assessments. U.S. students do not fare particularly well on these international assessments, but Mexican students perform even worse. One quarter (25.8%) of students in U.S. schools scored below the basic level (Level 2) on the PISA mathematics exam in 2012, but more than half of students in Mexico scored at this low level (54.5%) (OECD 2014). This is attributed, at least in part, to the very uneven preparation of teachers, especially in rural schools. The national teacher examination instituted with Mexico's major 2013 education reform was boycotted by teachers in the lowest performing areas of the country and ultimately abandoned under the new administration that took power in December of 2018. Teachers, especially in the upper grades, are also challenged – and sometimes resentful– by the idea that they need to be teaching immigrant students basic Spanish reading, writing, and academic forms at a grade level in which Mexican students have long mastered the material.

Turning to the Mexican education system, the failure of U.S. and Mexican education systems to communicate with each other often derails students' aspirations when they are denied credit for courses they have taken and passed in the other country or are placed in lower grades with younger students "to catch up", which is a fairly common practice in Mexico (Zuñiga and Vivas-Romero 2014). One study found that U.S. migrant students in Mexico were three times as likely to be held back as native students Hamann, Zuñiga, and Sánchez Garcia (2010). Rather than experiencing a transition from a U.S. to a Mexican school, Román González and Zúñiga (2014) argue that these students

> experience everyday ruptures when enrolling in Mexican schools, not only in terms of contents and materials, but also in school practices, forms and rates of evaluation, teaching styles, criteria for success or failure, types of pedagogical feedback, the role played by parents and other family members, school timetables, homework and/or other responsibilities.(282)

In spite of these vast differences in the way schools operate, there are almost no orientation programmes or Spanish as a Second Language classes to aid in the transition for the great majority of new immigrants (Jacobo and Jensen 2018).

There has also been a longstanding problem in Mexican schools of requiring birth certificates and citizenship documents with proper certification, translated into Spanish which in many cases have been impossible for returnees to acquire because they do not have the documents or the funds for translation or because they were unable to travel to government offices to get the official stamp. This has prevented some students coming from the U.S. to enrol in school. Mexican primary and secondary (middle) schools are now required to accept students as they present themselves with or without paperwork. However, reports continue that this is not always respected or perhaps even known in some parts of the country (Jacobo and Jensen 2018).

Although compulsory education in Mexico now extends to the completion of the *bachillerato* – or equivalent to high school – unlike the U.S., students are not automatically enrolled in a local school. They must apply and often must take tests to gain admission. There is no default enrolment. So, if a student arriving in Mexico from the U.S. does not know to apply he or she can be left without any means of attending upper secondary and, at the very least, be delayed in graduating.

The difficulty that students experience integrating into Mexican schools – when they are able to enrol – can also result in psychological harm. Zayas et al. (2015) have found that U.S. born children who accompanied their parents back to Mexico displayed symptoms of depression and negative self-esteem.

Other researchers report loss of a sense of belonging in school (Bybee et al. 2019), which can be particularly acute for the 1.5 generation (those young people who are returning to their birthplace after being raised in the U.S.), and can lead to heavy absences and dropping out (Hamann and Zuñiga 2011; Hirai and Sandoval 2016). Only about half of Mexico's students complete the *bachillerato,* or 12 years of schooling (OECD 2014), thus there is not the same social pressure to stay in school as in the United States. Moreover, extra-curricular and enrichment offerings are limited and most schools do not offer gifted programmes, special education services (i.e. Individualized Education Plans), counselling, or other support services (Santibañéz forthcoming). Lacking these services, many of the students facing the trauma of being relo-cated to a strange country have nowhere to turn for support.

An exception to the lack of resources for U.S. students arriving in Mexico is PROBEM (Programa Binacional de Educación Migrante). Established in 1976 by the Mexican government to address some of the needs of Mexican migrant stu-dents abroad (principally in the U.S.), it sponsors teacher and cultural exchanges and seeks to support Mexican students who have found themselves in US schools with weak support. In recent years, however, PROBEM has been tasked with helping Mexican origin students from abroad to integrate into Mexican schools. These offices, while coordinated nationally are the financial responsibility of the states and therefore vary widely in existence as well as the quality of services that they are able to provide. In the Mexican context PROBEM focuses largely on orienting arriving families as to how to enrol in school and "revalidate" the courses and credits students have acquired abroad so they can be appropriately placed at grade level. Most PROBEM offices in Mexico do not have resources to do much beyond easing the bureau-cratic burden of finding and enrolling in school (Jacobo and Jensen 2018).

It should also be noted that the Mexican Secretariat of Public Education has published and distributed 20,000 copies of the report by Zúñiga, Hamann, and Sánchez García (2009), *Alumnos transnacionales: Las escuelas mexicanas frente a la globalización*, which is a primer on the topic of transnational students. However, it is not clear how or when teachers actually come in contact with these materials.

Mexican public schools have also had a policy of offering English instruc-tion across basic education beginning in preschool since 2007, with the goal that all Mexican students completing their education would be bilingual. However, estimates are that less than half of Mexican English teachers have achieved the level of English proficiency necessary to adequately teach the language or to be able to interact meaningfully with students whose stron-gest language is English (Calderón 2015). Moreover, disproportionately these teachers reside in the private school sector, where 10% of Mexican stu-dents go to school (OECD 2017), not where most of these returning students will find themselves. The great majority of Mexican students have little or no access to a qualified English teacher; it is currently estimated that Mexico needs more than 300,000 English teachers to provide the instruction pre-scribed by Mexican educational policy (Calderón 2015).

Perhaps the Mexican public school system, colleges and universities can be excused for their failure to prepare their faculties for the huge numbers of "returned"[2] students, as the phenomenon is relatively new. For decades the migration flow was principally in the other direction. Nonetheless, the Mexican government has been aware for some time of the barriers its citizens face in educational institutions in the United States and has created programmes to help ease the transition into the U.S. education system. These have included transfer documents that show the courses and grades that students have received in Mexico, free Mexican textbook dissemination, online basic education available at community centres, and teacher exchanges. All of these programmes are potentially helpful to students, however none appears to have had a very large impact, probably because so few resources have actually been dedicated to implementing them (Gándara 2004).

In sum, whether the students we share are in the U.S. enrolled largely in English-only, segregated, low-performing schools where they consistently fall behind academically or they are in Mexican schools, with even fewer resources and no language support or orientation to schooling, we are routinely failing these students and jeopardizing both their and our own futures.

Addressing the challenges for the students we share

U.S. born students could be protected from the trauma of sudden displacement from their homeland through federal immigration policies designed to protect them. This was the intent of the aborted Deferred Action for Parents of Americans (DAPA) programme that President Obama announced in 2014. DAPA would have protected parents of U.S. citizen children from deportation and would have allowed them to work legally. This would have erased most of the fears of family separation for approximately 5 million children and stabilized the situation of the schools that educate these children. Unfortunately, 26 states sued the federal government saying that President Obama had overstepped his authority in creating the programme and the fifth circuit court of appeals struck it down. On appeal to the Supreme Court, a deadlocked Court (4-4) meant the fifth circuit ruling stood. And with the increasingly virulent anti-immigration policies of the Trump administration, little hope exists for a remedy for these families in the immediate future.

Bilingual programs for all

A critical response to the needs of the students we share is to recruit and train more truly bilingual and bicultural teachers on both sides of the border. If students were educated in the United States and in Mexico in both languages, their transitions would not be as difficult and wherever they find themselves they are likely to have superior educational outcomes as research has shown (Genesee et al. 2005; Valentino and Reardon 2015). In the United States, this could require little more than a serious campaign to recruit and train the teachers at the state level, as there is a large supply of bilinguals among college age students. The great majority of U.S. states –thirty-six– now award the Seal of Biliteracy to fluently bilingual high school graduates, with others actively considering it.[3] It is tangible evidence of a societal value for bilingualism and many employers indicate that it is something they too value and prefer for new hires across all sectors of the economy (Porras, Ee, and Gándara 2014). Having been launched in California in 2012, nearly 228,000 students of college age have been awarded the Seal as of 2018 (Spiegel-Coleman 2018) and this is in a state that until recently rarely provided bilingual instruction. Given the extraordinary response to the Seal of Biliteracy, a clear path for these already biliterate high school graduates to become teachers, combined with financial support to help them achieve this, could yield many new highly qualified bilingual teachers. California, a state committed to resisting the immigration policies of the Trump administration, is poised to undertake this challenge.

Texas, with the next largest population of students we share, has maintained its bilingual programmes in the elementary grades but is experiencing a shortage of bilingual teachers across the state (Swaby 2017). Most commentators attribute the problem to low pay compared to the hard work entailed and a state certification test that is poorly designed – two problems that Texas has been slow to correct. But it is also worth noting that Texas ends its bilingual instruction in the elementary grades, before most students have developed strong literacy skills. This policy almost certainly reduces the numbers of individuals who feel confident enough in their language skills to want to take on teaching in a non-English language. It would be relatively easy for Texas to adopt policies that increased the yield of bilingual teachers, but those policies run counter to the conservative politics of the state.

The solution to creating many more biliterate individuals in Mexico is not as easy to imagine. While there are many English-Spanish bilingual schools in Mexico, they are rarely public schools and they serve the more affluent families in large cities. But Baja California, in acknowledgement of the influx of English speaking students coming into the state in recent years, is on track to graduate 2,000 bilingual teachers in 2022 from its teacher education programmes (Mendoza 2018). Moreover, it is about to open its first public bilingual school in 2019 in Tecate. Not surprisingly, Baja California has a higher percentage of bilingual citizens than most of the rest of the country (Mexicanos Primero 2015). Moreover, a new effort is underway to launch the Seal of Biliteracy in the Tijuana area as a way of acknowledging the language skills of many students we share, and incentivizing the schools to help these students continue to develop their English skills. These students, as in the U.S., could be channelled into bilingual teacher preparation programmes. The Universidad Pedagógica Nacional (UPN) is poised to launch a programme geared toward those students from the US who find themselves in Mexico with strong English/Spanish skills. Hoping to enrol its first cohort of future bilingual teachers in 2020, the UPN is developing an intensive teacher preparation programme that would culminate in a *licenciatura* in two and a half years (González Monroy 2019)

In the past, one strategy to increase the numbers of bilingual teachers in the U.S. has been to create teacher exchanges with Mexico. However, this has had limited impact for a number of reasons: difficulty in identifying teachers with the requisite preparation and flexibility to teach abroad, difficulty in securing U.S. visas, the limitations of summer exchanges when regular school is on vacation, among others (Gándara 2004, 24). Ultimately, these exchanges are only able to include small numbers of teachers, which has a small and not necessarily lasting impact on the problem.

To address this, the University of California-Mexico Initiative of the Office of the President recently launched a "training of trainers" pilot programme at the US-Mexico border. This innovative project trains the faculty who train teachers in a binational, bilingual curriculum, preparing them to address the needs of the students we share. The teacher trainers (or "formadores") include faculty from Mexican and California universities and teacher colleges who jointly build the curriculum and then prepare the teachers in their institutions. The fundamental idea behind this project is to greatly multiply the impact, reaching many more teachers and teacher candidates than is possible with 1–1 exchanges (Alfaro and Gándara forthcoming).

Tapping parents as resources

Parents are a largely untapped resource in both the United States and in Mexico. While Mexican schools have somewhat different traditions than the U.S. with respect to parent involvement, many parents of "retornados" have been socialized in U.S. schools where they are expected to voice opinions and advocate for their children. Mexican schools can seize on this resource by identifying those parents who have had contact with these programmes and with U.S. schools and use them to lead efforts to help the Mexican schools to be more responsive to the needs of these students we share. Unfortunately, parents who have not been schooled in the U.S. often don't know how to go about doing it. Programmes such as PIQE (Parent Institute for Quality Education) that train immigrant parents to monitor their children's schooling experience and advocate for them have had significant success in raising the aspirations of both students and parents in the U.S. (Chrispeels, Bolivar, and Vaca 2008), and are being attempted in Mexico (Valladolid 2017). Many who previously thought post-secondary education was for someone else, now see this as a realistic goal for themselves.

A new vision of educational and economic opportunity for the students we share

Ultimately, forward thinking legislation must be initiated on both sides of the US-Mexico border that allows these students we share to continue their educations successfully in either or both countries. Ideally the United States and Mexico would create reciprocal agreements in which the two nations would cooperatively support the higher education of these youth without financial or bureaucratic barriers. A model for this exists at the Texas-Mexico border where Mexican students living near the border can access Texas universities at in-state costs and without bureaucratic barriers. In recent years several Mexican universities have proposed accepting students tuition-free that find themselves part way through their university educations in the U.S. when they are repatriated to Mexico. Discussions are ongoing about how, exactly, this can work. At the same time California has been a leader in providing state scholarships that cover tuition and expenses in its universities for students who graduate from the state's high schools with need regardless of their legal status. The state has also created a "Dream loan" fund for undocumented students who are not eligible for most federal or private loans. The Congressional Budget Office (2010) found that allowing "Dreamers"[4] to complete their postsecondary educations and remain in the United States to work would result in a significant reduction in the U.S. budget deficit adding revenues of about $2.1 billion over a ten-year period.

Mexico, too, would gain similarly from supporting the educations of youth who find themselves repatriated to that country with bilingual and bicultural skills and a desire to continue their educations. This can also include those who would choose to return to Mexico for the benefit of low cost access to higher education. The average education levels of both nations could be enhanced with such a strategy, and the ranks of highly qualified bilingual teachers could be significantly augmented. Unfortunately, current US immigration-education policy is not the product of either pragmatic self-interest or human compassion. However, this will change and both countries should be ready to implement human rights and education policies that better represent our shared self interest and our common humanity.

The demographic bust or bonus

The great irony of the anti-immigrant policies of the Trump administration is that the U.S. is, in fact, dependent on immigrants to fuel its economy now and into the future. The US birthrate has been declining for decades and is now well below replacement level. The only thing that keeps the overall population from dropping –and depressing economic growth– is immigration (Tavernise 2018). All of the population growth in the country is due to the children of immigrants. As the baby boom generation is reaching retirement age, without immigration, the U.S. would be looking at a shrinking cohort of young workers available to support the increasing share of the elderly. Mexico, however, has for decades experienced a much better age balance and still has a large advantage in youthful workers compared to the U.S., if their potential is realized. This is Mexico's "demographic bonus". But Mexican birth rates have continually declined since 1970, and by 2016 were only slightly above reproduction level at 2.16 per woman (Statista 2016).

In the near future the number of workers supporting each retired person will decline sharply in both countries and Mexico's demographic bonus will be over. The expectation of constant immigration of young people willing to work for low wages is coming to an end. Creating an environment that is hostile to immigration, as is currently the case in the U.S., is bad economic policy. The U.S. needs to invest in its existing human capital, especially its large and under-educated Latino population, and to attract more, not fewer, young and ambitious immigrants. Foreign students seeking to matriculate into U.S. universities have also declined precipitously, and the evidence suggests this is at least in part due to current anti-immigrant policies (Saul 2018). A rational and forward looking immigration system should be an immediate priority for U.S. policymakers. Similarly, the acknowledgement by Mexican policymakers that Mexico has become an immigrant receiving nation, with all the education policy infrastructure that entails, is necessary.

Looking to the future

Perhaps the most important thing that must happen first is that both nations come to see the students we share for the enormous potential, as well as the joint responsibility, they represent. This is a truly binational generation, with knowledge, understanding, and perspectives drawn from both sides of the border. Given the opportunity, they can be the new brokers of culture and communication that can help spur the economies of both Mexico and the United States. But legislators must find the will to reverse the U.S. immigration policies that are terrorizing many of these students and their families, support significant expansion of bilingual instruction, open greater access to higher education on both sides of the border, and provide financial support for binational students to complete their educations. Meantime, Mexico needs to acknowledge the asset it has in these students and provide educational programming suited to immigrant students who lack strong Spanish skills and are unfamiliar with Mexican schools. This should begin with better tracking of these students so that educators can be aware of their presence in their classrooms and know how they are faring. It must also include preparation of teachers who can communicate with and adapt instruction for them. The public schools in both Mexico and the U.S. need to step up to the challenge of providing the students we share with the kind of education that will allow them to flourish, whichever side of the border they choose to inhabit. If nothing else, self-interest demands that we do so.

Notes

1. Immigration and Customs Enforcement: the federal agency charged with policing immigration.
2. In Spanish these students are referred to colloquially as "retornados" or "returnees", even though they may have never set foot in Mexico before.
3. See sealofbiliteracy.org.
4. In the United States, those students who were brought to the country without papers at a young age, who have attended and successfully graduated from U.S. schools are known as "the dreamers."

Disclosure statement

No potential conflict of interest was reported by the author.

References

Alfaro, Cristina, and Patricia Gándara. Forthcoming. "Binational Teacher Preparation: Constructing Pedagogical Bridges for the Students We Share." Chapter 7 in *The Students We Share: Preparing US and Mexican Teachers for Our Transnational Future*, edited by Patricia Gándara, and Bryant Jensen. Albany: State University of New York Press.

American Immigration Council. 2018. "U.S. Citizen Children Impacted by Immigration Enforcement." https://www.americanimmigrationcouncil.org/sites/default/files/research/us_citizen_children_impacted_by_immigration_enforcement.pdf.

Annie E. Casey Foundation. 2017. *Race for Results*. AECF. https://www.aecf.org/m/resourcedoc/aecf-2017raceforresults-2017.pdf.

Berliner, David. 2006. "Our Impoverished View of Education Reform." *Teachers College Record* 108: 949–995.

Bialystok, Ellen, and Kenji Hakuta. 1994. *In Other Words*. New York: Basic Books.

Bybee, Eric, Erica Feinauer Whiting, Bryant Jensen, Victoria Savage, Alisa Baker, and Emma Holdaway. 2019. "Estamos Aquí Pero No Soy de Aqui": American Mexican Youth, Belonging and Schooling in Rural, Central Mexico." *Anthropology and Education Quarterly*. Forthcoming.

Calderón, David. 2015. "Public Policy for Learning English in Mexico." Chapter 3 in *Mexicanos Primero, "Sorry. Learning English in Mexico"*, 57–78. Mexico City: Mexicanos Primero.

Carnavale, Anthony, Megan Fasules, Michael Quinn, and Kathryn Peltier Campbell. 2019. "Born to Win, Schooled to Lose." Washington DC: Center on Education and the Workforce. Georgetown University. https://1gyhoq479ufd3yna29(7ubjn-wpengine.netdna-ssl.com/wp-content/uploads/FR-Born_to_win-schooled_to_lose.pdf.

Castillo, Andrea. 2017. "LA father Detained After Dropping Daughter Off At School May Be Deported," *Los Angeles Times*, July 17. http://www.latimes.com/local/lanow/la-me-romuloavelica-deportation-20170731-story.html.

Childtrends. 2018. "Immigrant Children." https://www.childtrends.org/indicators/immigrant-children.

Childtrends. 2019. "Trends in child poverty." https://www.childtrends.org/indicators/children-in-poverty#_edn2.

Chrispeels, Janet, José Bolivar, and Roberto Vaca. 2008. *Parent Institute for Quality Education High School Study*. Riverside: University of California.

Congressional Budget Office. 2010. "S. 3992 Development, Relief, and Education for Alien Minors Act of 2010. Cost Estimate." December 2, 2010. https://www.cbo.gov/sites/default/files/111th-congress-2009-2010/costestimate/s39921.pdf.

Cummins, James. 1996. "Negotiating Identities in the Classroom and Society." *Multicultural Education* 15: 7–11.,17.

Ee, Joy, and Patricia Gándara. 2019. "The Impact of Immigration Enforcement on the Nation's Schools." *American Educational Research Journal*.

Falicov, Celia. 2002. "Ambiguous Loss: Risk and Resilience in Latino Immigrant Families." In *Latinos Remaking America*, edited by Marcelo Suárez-Orozco, and Maria Paez, 274–288. Berkeley: University of California Press.

Frankenberg, Erica, Joy Ee, Jennifer Ayscue, and Gary Orfield. 2019. *Harming Our Common Future: America's Segregated Schools 65 Years After Brown*. Los Angeles: Civil Rights Project, UCLA. https://tinyurl.com/yyqyvcao.

Gándara, Patricia. 2004. *A Preliminary Evaluation of Mexican-sponsored Educational Programs in the United States: Strengths, Weaknesses, and Potential*. Davis: Institute for Education Policy, Law, & Government, University of California. https://www.civilrightsproject.ucla.edu/research/binational-u.s.-mexico/a-preliminary-evaluation-of-mexican-sponsorededucational-programs-in-the-united-states-strengths-weaknesses-and-potential/IME_Report_copy.pdf.

Gándara, Patricia. 2016. "Policy Report: The Students We Share." *Mexican Studies/Estudios Mexicanos* 32: 357–378. Berkeley: University of California Press.

Gándara, Patricia, and Frances Contreras. 2009. *The Latino Education Crisis*. Cambridge: Harvard University Press.

Gándara, Patricia, and Joy Ee. 2018. *The Impact of Immigration Enforcement on Teaching and Learning in the Nation's Schools*. Los Angeles: Civil Rights Project, UCLA. https://tinyurl.com/y9s7ygeg.

Gándara, Patricia, Julie Maxwell-Jolly, and Anne Driscoll. 2005. *Listening to Teachers of English Language Learners: A Survey of California Teachers' Challenges, Experiences, and Professional Development Needs*. Santa Cruz: Center for the Future of Teaching and Learning.

Genesee, Fred, Kathryn Lindholm-Leary, William Saunders, and Donna Christian. 2005. "English Language Learners in US Schools: An Overview of Research Findings." *Journal of Education for Students Placed at Risk* 10: 363–385.

Goldring, Rebecca, Soheyla Taie, and Minsun Riddles. 2014. *Teacher Attrition and Mobility: Results From the 2012–13 Teacher Follow-up Survey*. U.S. Department of Education. Washington, DC: National Center for Education Statistics.

Gonzalez, Roberto. 2011. "Learning To Be Illegal: Undocumented Youth and Shifting Legal Contexts in The Transition To Adulthood." *American Sociological Review* 76: 602–619.

González Monroy, Javier. 2019. Rector of UPN Baja California. Personal Communication. April 15, 2019.

Hamann, Edmund T., and Victor Zuñiga. 2011. "Schooling and The Everyday Ruptures Transnational Children Encounter in The United States And Mexico." In *Everyday Ruptures: Children and Migration in Global Perspective*, edited by Cati Coe, Rachel Reynolds, Diane Boehm, Julia Meredith Hess, and Heather Rae-Espinoza, 141–160. Nashville, TN: Vanderbilt University Press.

Hamann, Edmund T., Victor Zuñiga, and Juan Sánchez Garcia. 2008. "From Nuevo León to the USA and Back Again: Transnational Students in Mexico." *Journal of Immigrant and Refugee Studies* 6: 60–84.

Hamann, Edmund T., Victor Zuñiga, and Juan Sánchez Garcia. 2010. "Transnational Students' Perspectives on Schooling in the United States and Mexico: The Salience of School Experience and Country of Birth." In *Children and Migration: At the Crossroads of Resiliency and Vulnerability*, edited by Marisa Ensor, and Elzbieta Gozdziak, 230–252. New York: Palgrave Macmillan.

Hernandez, Donald, Nancy Denton, and Suzanne McCartney. 2009. "School-age Children in Immigrant Families; Challenges and Opportunities for America's Schools." *Teachers College Record* 111: 616–658.

Hirai, Shinji, and Rebecca Sandoval. 2016. "El Itinerario Subjetivo Como Herramienta de Análisis: Las Experiencias de Los Jóvenes Generación 1.5 Que Retornan a México." *Mexican Studies/Estudios Mexicanos* 32: 276–301. Berkeley: University of California Press.

Hopkins, Megan. 2013. "Building on Our Teaching Assets: The Unique Pedagogical Contributions of Bilingual Educators." *Bilingual Research Journal* 36: 350–370.

Jacobo, Monica, and Bryant Jensen. 2018. *Schooling for US-Citizen Students in Mexico*. Los Angeles: Civil Rights Project, UCLA. https://tinyurl.com/yxcaynrx.

Jensen, Bryant, and Patricia Gándara. Forthcoming. "The Students We Share and The Teachers We Need." In *The Students We Share: Preparing US and Mexican Teachers for Our Transnational Future*, edited by Patricia Gándara, and Bryant Jensen. Albany: State University of New York Press.

Kaiser Family Foundation. 2017. "Health coverage of immigrants. Fact sheet." https://www.kff.org/disparities-policy/fact-sheet/health-coverage-of-immigrants/.

López, Francesca. 2017. "Altering The Trajectory of The Self-Fulfilling Prophecy: Asset-Based Pedagogy and Classroom Dynamics." *Journal of Teacher Education* 68: 1–20.

López, Yara Amparo. 2018. Director, PROBEM, Ministry of Education, Baja California. Personal communication, July 30, 2018.

Mendoza, Miguel Angel. 2018. Secretary of Education, Baja California. Personal Communication July 16, 2018.

Mexicanos Primero. 2015. *Sorry. Learning English in Mexico*. Mexico City: Mexicanos Primero.

Minikwu, Joy. 2017. "Postville." Colorín Colorado. http://www.colorincolorado.org/article/lessons-postville-how-immigration-raid-changed-small-town-and-its-schools.

NCES. 2017a. "Nation's Report Card, Math." National Center for Education Statistics, U.S. Department of Education. https://www.nationsreportcard.gov/math_2017/#nation/achievement?grade=4 https://www.nationsreportcard.gov/math_2017/#nation/achievement?grade=8.

NCES. 2017b. "Digest of Education Statistics." Table 219.46. National Center for Education Statistics, U.S. Department of Education. https://nces.ed.gov/programs/digest/d17/tables/dt17_219.46.asp.

NCES. 2017c. "Digest of Education Statistics." Table 104.20. National Center for Education Statistics. U.S. Department of Education. https://nces.ed.gov/programs/digest/d16/tables/dt16_104.20.asp.

Newsday. 2016. "Donald Trump Speech, Debates, and Campaign Quotes." November 9, 2016. https://www.newsday.com/news/nation/donald-trump-speech-debates-and-campaign-quotes-1.11206532.

OECD. 2014. "Mexico. Education at a Glance 2014." http://www.oecd.org/education/Mexico-EAG2014-Country-Note.pdf.

OECD. 2017. "Mexico. Overview of the Education System." http://gpseducation.oecd.org/CountryProfile?primaryCountry=MEX&treshold=10&topic=EO.

Porras, Diana, Joy Ee, and Patricia Gándara. 2014. "Employer Preferences: Do Bilingual Applicants and Employees Experience An Advantage?" In *The Bilingual Advantage: Language, Literacy and the U.S. Labor Market*, edited by Rebecca Callahan, and Patricia Gándara, 234–257. Bristol, UK: Multilingual Matters.

Portes, Alejandro, and Lingxin Hao. 2002. "The Price of Uniformity: Language, Family and Personality Adjustment in The Immigrant Second Generation." *Ethnic and Racial Studies* 25: 889–912.

Potochnick, Stephanie, Jen-Hao Chen, and Krista Perreira. 2017. "Local-level Immigration Enforcement and Food Insecurity Risk Among Hispanic Immigrant Families with Children: National-Level Evidence." *Journal of Immigrant and Minority Health* 19: 1042–1049.

Rojas-Flores, Lisseth, Mari J. Hwang-Koo, and J. Judy London. 2017. "Trauma and Psychological Stress in Latino Citizen Children Following Parental Detention and Deportation." *Psychological Trauma: Theory, Research, Practice, and Policy* 9: 352–361.

Román González, Betsabé, and Victor Zúñiga. 2014. "Children Returning From The U.S. to Mexico: School Sweet School?" *Migraciones Internacionales* 7: 277–286.

Rumbaut, Rubén. 2014. "English Plus: Exploring the Socio-Economic Benefits of Bilingualism in Southern California." In *The Bilingual Advantage: Language, Literacy and the U.S. Labor Market*, edited by Rebecca Callahan, and Patricia Gándara, 182–209. Bristol, UK: Multilingual Matters.

Santibañez, Lucrecia, and Patricia Gándara. 2017. *Teachers of English Language Learners in Secondary Schools: Gaps in Preparation and Support*. Los Angeles: Civil Rights Project, UCLA.

Santibañéz, Lucrecia. Forthcoming. "Contrasting Realities: How Differences Between the Mexican and U.S. Education Systems Affect Transnational Students." Chapter 6 in *The Students We Share: Preparing US and Mexican Teachers for Our Transnational Future*, edited by Patricia Gándara, and Bryant Jensen. Albany: State University of New York Press.

Saul, Stephanie. 2018. "As Flow of Foreign Students Wanes, U.S. Universities Feel The Sting." *New York Times*, January 2, 2018. https://www.nytimes.com/2018/01/02/us/international-enrollment-drop.html.

Sánchez Garcia, Juan, and Edmund T. Hamann. 2017. "Educator Responses to Migrant Children in Mexican Schools." *Mexican Studies/Estudios Mexicanos* 32: 199–225.

Shan, Joy. 2018. "Asians Are The Fastest Growing Undocumented Group. And ICE Tends To Leave Them Alone." The California Sunday Magazine, *Los Angeles Times*, Section 9, July 25, 2018. https://story.californiasunday.com/sanctuary.

Spiegel-Coleman, Shelly. 2018. Liaison to the California State Department of Education. Personal Communication. August 12, 2018.

SRCD (Society for Research on Child Development). 2018. "Statement: The Science Is Clear: Separating Families Has Long-term Damaging Psychological and Health Consequences for Children, Families, and Communities." June 20, 2018. http://srcd.org/sites/default/files/documents/the_science_is_clear.pdf.

Statista. 2016. "Mexico: Fertility Rate From 2006 to 2016." www.statista.com/statistics/275413/fertility-rate-in-mexico/.

Steele, Jennifer, Robert Slater, Gema Zamarro, Trey Miller, Jennifer Li, Susan Burkhauser, and Michael Bacon. 2017. "Effects of Dual Language Immersion Programs on Student Achievement: Evidence From Lottery Data." *American Educational Research Journal* 54: 282S–306S.

Suárez-Orozco, Marcelo, and Carola Suárez-Orozco. 1995. *Transformations: Immigration, Family Life and Achievement Motivation among Latino Adolescents.* Palo Alto: Stanford University Press.

Swaby, Aliyya. 2017. "Texas School Districts Struggle To Recruit Bilingual Certified Teachers." *The Texas Tribune.* February 21. https://www.star-telegram.com/news/local/education/article134109659.html.

Tavernise, Sabrina. 2018. "U.S. Fertility Rate Fell To Record Low For Second Straight Year." *New York Times,* May 26, 2018. https://www.nytimes.com/2018/05/17/us/fertility-rate-decline-united-states.html.

The Economist. 2017. "Rhetoric and Reality." December 17, 2017. https://www.economist.com/united-states/2017/12/14/donald-trump-is-deporting-fewer-people-than-barack-obama-did.

Umansky, Ilana, and Sean Reardon. 2014. "Reclassification Patterns Among Latino English Learner Students in Bilingual, Dual Immersion, and English Immersion Classrooms." *American Educational Research Journal* 51: 871–912.

Valentino, Rachel, and Sean Reardon. 2015. "Effectiveness of Four Instructional Programs Designed To Serve English Learners: Variation By Ethnicity and Initial English Proficiency." *Educational Evaluation and Policy Analysis* 37: 612–637.

Valladolid, David. 2017. Director of PIQE. Personal communication, March 21, 2017.

Wong, Tom. 2017. *DACA Recipients' Economic and Educational Gains Continue to Grow.* Washington DC: Center for American Progress. https://www.americanprogress.org/issues/immigration/news/2017/08/28/437956/daca-recipients-economic-educational-gains-continue-grow/.

Zayas, Luis, Sergio Aguilar-Gaxiola, Hyunwoo Yoon, and Guillermina Rey. 2015. "The Distress of Citizen-Children With Detained and Deported Parents." *Journal of Child and Family Studies* 24: 3213–3223.

Zehler, Annette, Howard Fleischman, Paul Hopstock, Todd Stephenson, Michelle Pendzick, and Saloni Sapru. 2003. *Descriptive Study of Services to LEP Students and LEP Students with Disabilities.* Washington, DC: Development Associates.

Zong, Jie, Jeanne Batalova, and Jeffrey Hallock. 2018. *Frequently Requested Statistics on Immigrants and Immigration in the United States.* Washington, DC: Migration Policy Institute. https://www.migrationpolicy.org/article/frequently-requested-statistics-immigrants-and-immigration-united-states.

Zúñiga, Victor, Edmund T. Hamann, and Juan Sánchez García. 2009. *Alumnos transnacionales: Las escuelas mexicanas frente a la globalización.* Mexico, DF: Secretaria de Educación Pública.

Zuñiga, Victor, and Maria Vivas-Romero. 2014. *Divided Families, Fractured Schooling, in Mexico: Educational Consequences of Children's Exposition to International Migration.* Mexico: CEMCA, CNRS, ANR.

DACAmented in the age of deportation: navigating spaces of belonging and vulnerability in social and personal lives

Roberto G. Gonzales, Kristina Brant and Benjamin Roth

ABSTRACT

Heightened immigration enforcement in public spaces has brightened the boundaries of exclusion for undocumented immigrants in the United States. Yet, these immigrants simultaneously experience belonging and inclusion within the personal and social spheres of their lives. This article explores this tension among young people with Deferred Action for Childhood Arrivals (DACA). Drawing on interviews with 408 DACA beneficiaries in six states, our analyses underscore the significance of personal and social spheres as spaces of belonging. DACA expanded these spaces, helping respondents derive meaning, agency, and membership in their everyday lives. However, these personal and social spheres were at times disrupted by hostile and exclusionary contests to function as spaces of vulnerability. Respondents experienced the boundaries between belonging and vulnerability as unstable and, at times, ambiguous-as they navigated a state of social liminality. Ultimately, conflicting sociopolitical climates at the national, state, local and institutional levels have created this social liminality.

US immigration policy has dramatically disrupted long-established patterns of circular migration, increasing the number of undocumented migrants living in the United States (Massey, Pren, and Durand 2016). These immigrants have established roots in their communities, where many are also raising families. Of the country's estimated 10.5 million undocumented immigrants, more than 2.5 million have lived in the country since childhood. These young people are growing up under unprecedented levels of enforcement and a hostile anti-immigrant climate that have sown fear and anxiety in immigrant communities across the United States (Castañeda 2019). While scholars have long sought to understand the adaptation processes of the children of immigrants, immigration policy has become increasingly consequential in shaping how immigrant youth experience life in the United States.

Despite increasing levels of enforcement, undocumented immigrant youth develop attachments to people and places in their communities which endow them a sense of belonging (García 2019). While immigration scholars have traditionally relied on externally measurable markers of incorporation, immigrants' efforts to seek out spaces of refuge and support are noteworthy. Studying belonging, then, is a useful endeavour for understanding the ways in which conflicting contexts shape immigrants' daily lives.

On the surface, experiences of vulnerability and belonging appear to be separate realities for distinctly different groups of immigrants. Yet, the boundary between inclusion an exclusion is not always clear. While undocumented immigrants are excluded from certain spaces and denied privileges and rights, they can simultaneously experience belonging too. They can participate in community groups, employ others in their own businesses, serve as ministers, and defend the country in our local and national armed forces. As such, they are routinely excluded *and* included, and the terms of exclusion and inclusion can often change for them at different times, in different places, and in interactions with different people.

Undocumented immigrant youth have a unique relationship with belonging and exclusion. Since legal inclusion in K-12 schools helps them to integrate into the fabric of their communities, formative experiences of socialization allow undocumented youth to develop a sense of belonging in the United States, as well as expectations and aspirations rooted in American culture (Abrego 2006; Gonzales 2011). However, as they transition to adolescence, their undocumented status becomes much more consequential, enlarging spaces of vulnerability in their everyday lives and compelling them to navigate adulthood within similar legal constraints as their undocumented parents (Gonzales 2011, 2016).

Recent scholarship suggests that experiences of vulnerability and belonging are mediated by an array of factors, including race, social class, and educational attainment (Cebulko 2014; Patler 2014; Gonzales and Burciaga 2018). Additionally, the consequences of undocumented status can vary widely across geographies (Marrow 2011; Schmalzbauer 2014; Silver 2018). While young people living in places with more inclusive policies and supportive environments may have access to a greater number of public spaces of belonging, those living in places with more restrictive policies and harmful environments face greater vulnerability (García 2019).

On June 15, 2012, social positionality changed for many undocumented young people with the introduction of the Deferred Action for Childhood Arrivals (DACA) program, an administrative policy that offered temporary protection from deportation and work authorization to certain eligible youth

(Batalova et al. 2014). In addition to DACA's stated purpose, many states have passed additional legislation, helping DACA beneficiaries access essential benefits like driver's licenses or Medicaid. As of early 2018, more than 814,000 individuals had been granted DACA status.

Several studies have demonstrated the significant impacts of the DACA program (Abrego 2018; Gonzales et al. 2018; Martinez and del Carmen Salazar 2018). Since its inception, DACA has enabled young people to access better-paying jobs, health care, and the means of establishing credit through bank accounts and credit cards (Gonzales, Terriquez, and Ruszczyk 2014; Wong et al. 2016). In turn, these opportunities have provided benefici-aries an economic boost to better assist their families and communities (Wong et al. 2016). DACA has also helped beneficiaries enroll in new higher education programmes and return to programmes which they had previously been com-pelled to leave (Patler and Cabrera 2015; Gonzales et al. 2016, 2017). Access to work authorization has not only helped DACA beneficiaries better afford post-secondary education, it has also further motivated them to follow their edu-cational and career aspirations. In many states, DACA has provided beneficiaries with educational opportunities otherwise unavailable to undo-cumented immigrants, such as access to in-state tuition and professional licenses for specialized vocations (Gonzales et al. 2016).

However, due to DACA's temporary and partial nature, it is unclear whether DACA can fully endow its beneficiaries with durable forms of membership and a more permanent sense of belonging. As an administrative policy, DACA does not provide a pathway to citizenship, leaving beneficiaries vulnerable. In addition, only a small segment of the larger population of undocumented immigrants qualifies for DACA, leaving family and friends of beneficiaries entirely unprotected. As a result, DACA beneficiaries are impacted by their family members' and friends' vulnerability (Patler and Pirtle 2018).

While much of the existing research has explored how DACA beneficiaries navigate belonging and vulnerability at school and work (see Enriquez 2017 and Pila 2016 for notable exceptions), we turn instead to their private lives. Drawing on interviews with 408 DACA beneficiaries in six states, we consider how respondents experience familial, social, and community spaces under DACA. We find that personal and social spheres serve as important *spaces of belonging* in DACA beneficiaries' everyday lives. These spaces help young people create meaning, feel safe, and find community, particularly amid exclu-sionary and punitive measures. Yet, these personal and social spheres are not impervious to such harsh contexts. When outside forces encroach upon DACA beneficiaries' private lives, eliciting status-related challenges or deportation threats, personal and social spheres can become *spaces of vulnerability*. Belonging and vulnerability, therefore, coexist in DACA beneficiaries' private lives. While exclusionary contexts of reception increase the salience of per-sonal and social spheres as spaces of belonging, they also threaten to make these spheres spaces of vulnerability. As such, exclusionary contexts compel DACA beneficiaries to navigate a condition of *social liminality*, experiencing both inclusion and exclusion, and both belonging and vulnerability, in their private lives.

DACAmented in the age of deportation

Over the last decade, two measures have characterized US immigration policy. First, we have seen a continuation of the heavy immigration enforcement that began to accelerate in the late 1990s, resulting in record numbers of deportations. Second, DACA has provided a substantial boost for undocumented immigrant youth and their families. These measures are notable, as they were achieved through administrative means in the absence of federal immigration reform. Even more remarkable, as policies of exclusion and integration, they represent diametrically opposed philosophies regarding how to address the presence of an estimated 10.5 million undocumented immigrants in the United States. While immigration policy has opened up new forms of access and belonging to undocumented youth, it has also exacerbated vulnerability for their families and communities.

Hostile contexts sow seeds of vulnerability

Over the last decade, communities across the United States have seen an uptick in hostility towards non-citizens. Recent policy measures at the federal and local levels have taken an exclusionary stance towards newcomers, cracking down on efforts to integrate immigrants while ramping up levels of immigration enforcement. Taken together, these developments have placed strains on everyday life and have created a chilling effect in immigrant communities.

Since the 2016 presidential election, more Americans are reporting growing levels of stress related to national politics, with anxiety highest among Latin American origin immigrants (Chavez et al. 2019). Sharp divisions are emerging across a wide range of communities across the country, as growing anti-immigrant sentiment has resulted in outright hostility towards certain groups. Meanwhile, the charged political environment appears to be having a direct impact on young people who have become increasingly anxious with worry.

In addition, as immigration enforcement has extended efforts from the border to the country's interior through the Secure Communities Program and local 287(g) agreements, it has dramatically expanded its enforceable territory (Gonzales and Raphael 2017). Through DUI checkpoints, targeted activity in public spaces, and home raids, immigration enforcement has transformed the everyday lives of undocumented immigrants (Lopez et al. 2018).

These practices have resulted in the arrests, detention, and deportation of hundreds of thousands of undocumented immigrants, instilling a "palpable sense of deportability" and keeping immigrants fearful of the threat of removal (De Genova 2002, 439).

Menjívar and Abrego (2012) argue that increased immigration raids, apprehensions in community spaces, and mass detention and deportation inflict a form of "legal violence" upon individuals and families. Living under the threat of deportation has tremendous implications for physical and mental well-being (Castañeda et al. 2015; García 2018; Patler and Pirtle 2018; Del Real 2019). Daily perceptions of uncertainty and danger produce specific forms of fear and anxiety that have both physical and emotional effects (Willen 2007).

Fear of deportation also increases vulnerability to violent crime, as undocumented immigrants may avoid reporting such incidents to the police (Barranco and Shihadeh 2015). For many immigrant women, victimization in social and romantic relationships can reproduce legal violence in everyday life (Del Real 2018; García 2018). And while enforcement efforts generally target adult migrants, their effects are felt across entire families and communities (Dreby 2012; López 2015). Deportations of parents and spouses leave huge emotional and economic voids in family life, and fears of deportation have particularly negative effects on the health and well-being of children (Potochnick and Perreira 2010; Bean, Brown, and Bachmeier 2015).

Experiencing belonging in a time of enforcement

While undocumented immigrants are excluded from many aspects of the polity, they nevertheless form relationships and participate in their communities and other local spaces (García 2019). Recent scholarship posits that the lack of formal access may actually compel immigrants to seek out and create informal spaces of inclusion and membership (Reed-Denahay and Brettell 2008). These spaces provide alternative opportunities to foster a sense of belonging and buffer the negative implications of legal and political exclusion.

Regardless of their immigration status, undocumented immigrants often feel part of a community through their social relationships and cultural practices (Coutin 2003). We can view community membership, then, as a feeling that one has invested part of themselves to become a member, earning the right to belong. By deliberately uncoupling belonging from notions of formal citizenship, scholars have pointed out that immigrants often transcend the boundaries of territory and polity. Beyond the formal legal and juridical frameworks that shape possibilities for belonging and vulnerability are on-the-ground practices exhibited by immigrants and their social ties (Reed-Denahay and Brettell 2008).

Indeed, in certain places, one's immigration status can be more *or* less consequential. As enforcement efforts have transformed public places into spaces of vulnerability, policymakers and community members have made efforts to open new spaces of inclusion. For example, several cities have passed "sanctuary" laws, limiting cooperation with federal immigration enforcement agents to protect immigrants from deportation (Ridgley 2008). In addition, certain public bureaucrats, like police officers and health care professionals, have extended services to undocumented immigrants (Marrow 2009). Community-led worker centres provide aid, guidance, and stability to undocumented workers who find themselves in undesirable working conditions (Milkman 2011). And for young people, educational institutions (Nienhusser 2018), supplementary educational programmes (Zhou 2008), extra-family mentors (Portes and Fernandez-Kelly 2008; Smith 2008), and positive peer networks (Stanton-Salazar 2001) have opened spaces of access and participation to undocumented immigrant students. These examples highlight a range of spaces which are actively carved out to provide undocumented immigrants with support and a place to belong.

In addition to these spaces created by policymakers and local institutions, spaces of belonging also exist within personal relationships and community groups. Personal relationships – whether with neighbours, peers, family members, or romantic partners – can diminish loneliness, provide a sanctuary from external environmental factors, and bring new confidence. Local groups and activities can also connect people more deeply to their communities, provide opportunities for membership, and allow people to temporarily leave their immigration status behind.

As Bosniak (2006) contends, the boundary defining membership is at times sharp yet at other times fuzzy. It is within these fuzzy spaces that permeability exists between the borders of belonging and vulnerability (Goldring, Berinstein, and Bernhard 2007). Menjívar (2006) introduced the concept "liminal legality", to illustrate how such ambiguity endows immigrants with characteristics of both legal *and* non-legal statuses. This perspective provides a framework to assess the factors which mediate the relationship between immigration policies and immigrants' everyday decisions and actions, recognizing the movement that exists between these categories (Kubal 2013).

Contested contexts of reception

According to Portes and Rumbaut (2001, 2006), the experiences of vulnerability and belonging are structured by varying "contexts of reception". The context of reception – including the receiving government's policies, the society's response to newcomers, and the characteristics of one's own ethnic community – determines the extent to which immigrants can achieve integration (Portes and Rumbaut 2001, 313–314). Due to political grid-lock in Congress, local geographies have become a critical context shaping integration (Zúñiga and Hernández-León 2005). In the absence of federal immigration legislation, local and state action has resulted in an uneven land-scape of immigration policies, whereby locally crafted immigration policies tie one's residence to a multitude of local impediments and opportunities. As such, where one lives powerfully shapes experiences of vulnerability and belonging.

Building on these ideas, Golash-Boza and Valdez (2018) suggest that indi-vidual immigrants operate within various "nested contexts of reception" which provide different sets of challenges and opportunities. Golash-Boza and Valdez point out that undocumented immigrants are impacted not only by federal immigration policy but also by state, local, and institutional contexts. The interplay between these contexts determines the extent to which a person can experience inclusiveness. For example, favourable state laws in California and campus supports at the University of California suggest that DACA beneficiaries residing there should fare better than their counterparts in other states. However, despite inclusive state and institutional contexts, the federal context of mass deportation can undercut students' senses of belonging and increase their vulnerability.

Applying the nested contexts of reception conceptual framework to under-stand spaces of belonging and vulnerability, we explore the differential impacts these nested and oftentimes conflicting contexts have on community spaces and personal relationships. Amid exclusionary policies, spaces of belonging offer opportunities for immigrants to feel connected, seen, pro-tected, and included. However, these spaces are continually contested and renegotiated. The forms of belonging that exist in the grey spaces between inclusion and exclusion are conditional, partial, temporary, and revocable (Menjívar 2006). Any one of a number of factors can tip the balance either way. Therefore, many spaces imbue vulnerability *and* belonging. In some con-texts, local actors may provide spaces of access and inclusion for immigrants; in others, they may impose additional levels of restriction and exclusion. At any moment, inclusionary policies and practices can be overturned or cur-tailed, depending on the willingness of institutional agents and legislators. Even immigrants who have enjoyed spaces of inclusion can be apprehended, detained, and deported.

These observations raise important questions about how those with legally liminally statuses such as DACA beneficiaries experience personal and social spaces in their everyday lives. Can these social and personal spheres provide DACA beneficiaries a sense of belonging, even amid heavy immigra-tion enforcement? And can these private spheres insulate DACA beneficiaries from the more pervasive context of enforcement? If not, when and how do these more private spheres engender vulnerability?

Methodology

Our analyses draw from interviews conducted with 408 DACA beneficiaries from 2015 to 2019 in six states: Arizona, California, Georgia, Illinois, South Carolina, and New York. All respondents arrived to the United States before age 16; most migrated from Mexico (78 per cent), followed by countries in South America (7 per cent), Asia (5 per cent), Central America (4 per cent), the Caribbean (2 per cent), the Middle East (2 per cent), Africa (1 per cent), and Europe (1 per cent). Respondents represented a diverse cross-section of educational experiences: 33 per cent held or were pursuing a Bachelor's degree, 19 per cent held or were pursuing an Associate's degree, 14 per cent had attended some college but stopped out, 25 per cent had a high school diploma or GED with no postsecondary education, 4 per cent were still in high school, and 5 per cent had no formal schooling.

Interviews were comprehensive, covering respondents' migration journeys, childhoods in the US, K-12 and postsecondary education, work history, health and well-being, and experiences with DACA. Interviews were coded in stages. We first developed primary codes deductively using our interview protocol, focusing particularly on family, personal relationships, and community. We then conducted thematic analyses to identify patterns in respondents' experiences in these personal and social spheres. This process generated an inductive list of secondary codes, including themes such as "deepened friendships", "emotional support", "persisting uncertainty", and "mixed-status challenges". Our analysis enabled us to see when respondents' personal and social spheres endowed feelings of belonging, safety, and security, and when they, instead, enhanced feelings of vulnerability, fear, and anxiety.

Personal and social spheres as spaces of belonging and vulnerability

DACA beneficiaries navigate policy and sociopolitical contexts at the national, state, local, and institutional levels. As such, they confront an uneven landscape riddled with contradictions. They may experience inclusion at one level, but face exclusion at another. A young person may possess new rights and protections under DACA but struggle to achieve upward mobility in an exclusionary state context that denies post-secondary access to DACA recipients. Another beneficiary living in an inclusionary state may continue to face educational challenges at the institutional level if educational institutions do not provide the resources necessary to help DACA beneficiaries navigate higher education. And a beneficiary living in an inclusive state with positive local contexts can experience discrimination and fear when faced with an anti-immigrant federal administration.

Across our sample, DACA beneficiaries spoke of the important roles personal relationships and social spaces played in their everyday lives. These spaces – whether formed in romantic relationships, friendship circles, family bonds, or community groups – provided our respondents a sense of belonging and inclusion. Particularly when confronted with experiences that left them feeling vulnerable, our respondents sought out spaces where they could experience a sense of belonging. In these spaces, our respondents found crucial emotional and practical support, experienced momentary feelings of security and safety, and became empowered to persist despite exclusionary policies. In an environment that routinely strips undocumented immigrants of control over their economic, educational, and civic lives, their ability to exert control over their personal and social lives is critical to their continued sense of agency and personhood.

While our respondents sought out personal and social spaces to engender belonging despite exclusionary contexts of reception, the barriers of these spaces were not impervious to outside forces. Most DACA beneficiaries hold close relationships with undocumented immigrants who do not qualify for DACA themselves. While one's own relief from deportation can improve their sense of security, the vulnerability of friends and family members can pervade these social spaces. Additionally, since DACA status is both temporary and incomplete, beneficiaries continue to experience certain exclusions themselves. For this reason, we contend that harsh immigration policies and exclusionary contexts can transform personal and social spheres into *spaces of vulnerability*.

In the following sections, we first demonstrate how personal and social spheres can serve as spaces of belonging for DACA beneficiaries, particularly in the face of exclusionary contexts. We then consider how these exclusionary contexts can at times pervade beneficiaries' private lives, transforming their personal and social spheres into spaces of vulnerability. Finally, given that these spheres are dynamic and uncertain, we suggest that the coexistence of belonging and vulnerability within personal and social spaces produces *social liminality* in the lives of DACA beneficiaries. While personal and social spheres are necessary to provide meaning and belonging, even they cannot shield DACA beneficiaries from the threat of exclusion, blocked mobility, and deportation.

Carving out spaces of belonging

Both before and during DACA's implementation, our respondents experienced personal and social spheres as important *spaces of belonging*. Prior to DACA, when they faced exclusion from the workforce and a constant threat of deportation, personal and social spaces provided a sense of comfort, support, and safety in otherwise restrictive and limiting contexts. Yet even after DACA opened new educational and economic opportunities, respondents continued to face exclusionary contexts and hostile sociopolitical climates that compelled them to turn to partners, family members, friends, neighbours, and roommates for support.

When we met Marcos, he was 22 years old, working part-time while finishing a degree in aircraft maintenance at a local community college. Leaving Colombia at age eight, Marcos and his family landed in a small town in South Carolina. Living in the rural South, Marcos grew up witnessing visible racial resentment. He also noted the lack of diversity in his schools:

> [In] my graduating class, there were about four or five Latinos. So, it wasn't very diverse … it was in the country, kind of closer up to the mountains, so you get a lot of, for a lack of a better word, rednecks, a lot of racist comments … It was so hard to fit in when everyone else is not like you and [they] look at you like you don't belong there.

When Marcos graduated from high school, he was confronted by state policies that excluded undocumented students from its public universities and required DACA beneficiaries to pay out-of-state tuition while excluding them from state financial aid.[1] Due to the steep barriers shaping postsecondary access in South Carolina, Marcos was at a disadvantage navigating his next steps. However, he had formed strong bonds with a small group of friends and mentors who provided him support and a sense of belonging. During this time of need, Marcos turned to his support network, disclosed his undocumented status to them, and explained his dilemma. With their help, Marcos was able to access information and opportunities that enabled him to enroll in a two-year certificate programme at a local community college.

Isabel, on the other hand, grew up in New York City and in a context considered much more immigrant friendly. She felt supported in K-12 schools and she matriculated to a local college within the City University of New York (CUNY) system. Although Isabel could not access federal financial aid, as a student of CUNY she benefited from a 2001 New York State law that expanded eligibility for in-state tuition to include undocumented students.[2] Nevertheless, the relatively inclusive state and local contexts with their supportive institutional environments could not shield Isabel from the national context within which those state, local, and institutional contexts exist. Under the presidential administration of Donald Trump, which both threatened the future of DACA and revived public nativist sentiment, Isabel experienced significant fear and anxiety. She withdrew from activities and ceased disclosing her status to those around her. When we followed up with Isabel two years after the presidential election, she was feeling more optimistic. She had formed tight bonds with other undocumented and DACAmented peers that restored her sense of security and belonging.

> I surround myself with a lot of folks who are in the [immigrant rights] movement ... there are four of us who are like, we are family to each other. I feel like surrounding myself with people who understand what is going on, but can really assure you that things are going to be okay ... I'm with people who are organizing and mobilizing, who are telling me that things one day are going to be okay, and I believe them. We have each other's back.

For Isabel, this group of friends was essential to maintaining a sense of security and belonging, despite a national context which threatened her personhood. She believed that leaning into this social space would help her persist through the fearful period of Trump's presidency.

In the face of exclusionary laws and hostile social climates – whether at the national, state, local, or institutional levels – our respondents found comfort and safety in their personal and social spaces. These spaces – both formal and informal – provided respondents an opportunity to shield themselves from restrictive contexts and develop a sense of belonging and agency. However, for many of our respondents, these spaces also rendered them vulnerable.

The persisting threat of vulnerability

While personal and social spheres served as important spaces of belonging for our respondents, they did not always function as safe havens. Just as exclusionary contexts of reception compelled our respondents to carve out personal and social spaces in search of belonging, these spaces were not impervious to those very forces. Living under heavy public enforcement can take a toll even on one's private life. Under hostile contexts, personal and social spheres do not simply function as spaces of belonging; they can also function as *spaces of vulnerability*. Our respondents experienced vulnerability in their homes, local communities, and social relationships as these private spaces served as potential sites for arrest, detention, and deportation, either for them or their undocumented loved ones.

Take Malcolm, a 23-year-old DACA beneficiary living in the Bronx. With the work authorization Malcolm acquired through DACA, he was able to secure a better paying job which allowed him to more fully support his family. Feeling secure and optimistic, Malcolm eagerly accepted the role of head of household. He signed a lease for a bigger apartment in a safer neighbourhood, moving in his mother along with his wife, and their children.

Yet, Malcolm faced challenges in creating a safe home environment. Even though he was protected by DACA, his undocumented mother was legally unprotected and therefore vulnerable. Shortly after moving in, several sleepless nights and failed attempts to reason with noisy upstairs neighbours, prompted Malcolm to the police with a noise complaint.

> They used to throw dumbells [around] ... and my baby used to be scared all the time. He was three months old and he used to wake up crying ... I tried to talk to

them, and they were mean to me … The guys told me "since you called the police, I'm gonna call immigration and you are gonna have to leave."

Malcolm had hoped this apartment would provide a space where he and his family could feel safe, together, and at home. Yet his mother's undocumented status became a source of vulnerability for everyone, even in the privacy of his own apartment. Feeling stuck, scared, and unable to seek any recourse, Malcolm felt compelled to again move his family into another apartment. With little time to find a good fit, they landed in an even smaller and more expensive place. Malcolm felt as though he had little choice.

Whereas Malcolm's vulnerability extended from his mom's undocumented status, other respondents felt uneasy due to the partial protections of their DACA status. Recognizing the temporary and incomplete nature of their status, these respondents continued to feel susceptible to exclusionary policies and hostile social climates. When we interviewed 19-year-old Juan from Atlanta, the limitations of DACA, particularly within his own state context, had recently impacted his personal life.

In high school, Juan formed many close bonds, mostly with other Latino peers. He had a mixed-status friendship circle, but he noted that it was difficult for his American-born peers to understand his struggles lacking legal status in Georgia. Most notably, as an undocumented immigrant in the state, Juan faced steep obstacles to higher education. In 2010, the Georgia Board of Regents banned undocumented students from enrolling in its top public universities and denied them in-state tuition rates throughout the state. In 2017, Georgia passed the first anti-sanctuary campus bill in the country, barring private universities from protecting their undocumented students. Even in the context of DACA, these state laws severely limited his post-secondary prospects.

In his senior year of high school, Juan formed a serious relationship with a female classmate. Ultimately, though, the limitations of DACA status in Georgia drove a wedge between them. Unaware of the ways in which Juan's undocumented status continued to impede his educational trajectory, his girlfriend attributed his absence from higher education to a lack of motivation. As Juan recalled:

> She would always get on me about why I hadn't started [college]. I would tell her stuff like, "It's because I'm trying to save up money to go. It's not as easy as it is for you." She thought that she did more than me, and that I was not ambitious or motivated, just because I wasn't in [college] yet by spring semester of the year after I graduated.

As Juan's example illustrates, the legal barriers faced by DACA beneficiaries are often invisible to those on the outside, including friends and loved ones. The exclusionary context of Georgia not only narrowly circumscribed Juan's educational opportunities, it also limited his ability to fulfil normative expectations of dating (Pila 2016). By defining boundaries based on these expectations, Juan's girlfriend (perhaps unknowingly) drew a line, through which Juan was unable to cross due to persistent exclusions.

While restrictive laws and hostile social climates may have pressed respondents to seek refuge in familial and personal relationships, exclusionary contexts pervaded those very spaces they created to find belonging. Even with the protections of DACA, respondents routinely experienced private spaces and personal relationships as spaces of vulnerability. This is not to say that personal and social spaces ceased to provide a sense of comfort and belonging for respondents. But the broader contexts of their everyday lives shaped experiences of belonging *and* vulnerability.

Navigating social liminality

Despite the potential for external forces to produce fear and vulnerability, personal and social spaces remain important sources of belonging. In the context of exclusionary contexts, DACA beneficiaries' personal and social spheres can operate as both spaces of belonging and spaces of vulnerability simultaneously. Due to this duality, we contend that DACA beneficiaries experience a *social liminality* in their private relationships. While personal and social spheres provide DACA beneficiaries with everyday lives of belonging and meaning, these same spheres can also engender vulnerability due to the exclusionary contexts in which they are nested. As such, the line between spaces of belonging and spaces of vulnerability is fuzzy.

In their personal relationships, DACA beneficiaries continually navigate these liminal spaces. Take 18-year-old Miguel, for example. Growing up in an Arizona border town, Miguel's childhood and adolescence were punctuated by a context of heavy immigration enforcement. The public presence of Immigration Customs Enforcement (ICE) officers in communities throughout Tucson compelled his family to turn to each other for emotional support. While Miguel's friends motivated him to succeed in high school, his ineligibility from in-state tuition left him with no choice but to watch these friends move on without him after graduation. Facing steep barriers to higher education, his family support became even more important. Yet, like with others we have previously described, his familial ties also made him vulnerable.

When Miguel's brother was charged with trespassing and sent to a detention centre, this incident had an almost crippling effect on his family. Fearing further actions by ICE, they limited their activities and spent more time at home. The brother's deportation also sowed widespread stress and anxiety across the entire household, which manifested itself in strained well-being. In his brother's absence, Miguel took on added responsibilities in order to support his family. However, instead of fracturing the family, this incident brought them closer. They leaned on each other for emotional support.

> We were working together. We were trying our best to save enough money to pay his bail. It [made] us more aware of how fast someone could be out of your life without you realizing it. So, it got us closer, more together in an emotional sense.

In the face of a deportation threat that undermined their sense of safety, the detention of Miguel's brother simultaneously sowed vulnerability within his family and solidified their household as a place of support and belonging.

For many of our respondents, home was not always a place of sanctuary. But as with Miguel, vulnerability in one personal or social space compelled them to lean into another space to restore feelings of safety and belonging. Take Elisa, who moved to Georgia with her sister at age 15 to reunite with their mother. Soon after Elisa arrived, her mother married a white US citizen. Elisa's stepfather was verbally and physically abusive, creating a toxic home environment. Several flareups turned into major incidents in the household, with one of the three women incurring injury. The stepfather threatened to contact ICE if any of them were to call the police on him, using their legal vulnerability against them. To avoid the toxic environment of home, Elisa sought refuge at a local church with a large Latino community where she plugged in to its social and support structure. Elisa described her church community as a "space of safety and peace".

> I think that was my escape [from] everything that was going on, the people, the friends that I built there. Since they were Hispanic, I could connect with them because they would speak my language. It was so nice, [compared] to what I was living at home. I would rather be there all the time than being at home.

Not only did Elisa's church community provide her with emotional support and a sense of belonging and security, those relationships were also instrumentally supportive. When a church mentor heard about her difficulty at home, she helped Elisa find a job so that she could move out of her stepfather's house.

For our respondents, the threat of deportation sowed seeds of vulnerability in the personal and social spaces they had created to provide a sense of belonging and security. But while these hostile contexts infused vulnerability into these private spaces, they did not diminish the important role these spaces provided in imbuing meaning in our respondents' lives. For Miguel, it strengthened those bonds. In Elisa's case, vulnerability in her family life compelled her to seek support and belonging from other social spaces. In either case, our respondents' experiences highlight an important duality: within DACA beneficiaries' personal spaces, feelings of belonging and vulnerability coexist in liminal social spaces.

Conclusion

In this article, we have examined the tension between belonging and vulnerability in the everyday lives of DACA beneficiaries. While past research has explored this tension in schools and workplaces, we demonstrate its existence even in the very private spheres of beneficiaries' personal lives and social relationships. We find that the designations of *spaces of belonging* or of spaces of vulnerability in these personal and social spheres are not always clear. Just as DACA beneficiaries occupy a legally ambiguous position as undocumented immigrants who are temporarily afforded some rights and protections, their control over the most private areas of their lives is often shaded, and at times threatened, by hostile and exclusionary contexts. While personal and social spheres are often conceptualized as protected spaces where individuals hold agency and belonging, we find that the boundaries between belonging and vulnerability in these spheres can be fuzzy (Bosniak 2006). Extending Menjívar's (2006) liminal legality concept, we propose that the tension between belonging and vulnerability places DACA beneficiaries' personal and social lives in a state of *social liminality*.

While the tension that characterizes social liminality renders personal and social spheres more precarious, it does not minimize their importance. Our respondents demonstrate that bonds with family, friends, and communities can grow even stronger in the face of vulnerability. Nevertheless, it is important to note the limited reach of this belonging. Ultimately, the activation of this space as a space of belonging is often driven by fear – it can be a *reactive solidarity* fuelled by the need for protection rather than the need for companionship.

The impact of DACA has implications for defining spaces of belonging, spaces of vulnerability, and the boundaries that sometimes separate them. We find that DACA helps expand these spheres as spaces of belonging, but only to a certain extent, and in some situations more than others. Overlapping national, state, local, and institutional contexts of reception are capable of amplifying or muting the impact of legally liminal statuses like DACA. This observation is tied to structural and cultural characteristics of these localities, including racial diversity, the existence of racial animosity and anti-immigrant sentiment, the visible presence of ICE, and the integration between local law police and immigration controls. We do not think the conditioning influence of place means DACA's impact is minimal. Rather, we argue that the moderate and uneven effect of DACA on expanding belonging and reducing vulnerability reflects the overwhelming force of punitive enforcement measures. Forces of vulnerability – immigration enforcement, the impact of deportation on personal networks, experiences of discrimination, and social isolation – may differ in degree from one place to the next but are always present to some extent. While DACA may mute these direct threats temporarily, undocumented family members, friends, and partners remain unprotected.

The young men and women profiled here are part of a larger population of more than 2.5 million undocumented immigrants who have lived in the

United States since childhood. They are a sizable and vulnerable subset of the nation's foreign-born population. Without immediate and permanent policy intervention, this group remains at risk of becoming a disenfranchised underclass (Gonzales 2011). As long-term US residents, DACA beneficiaries possess social connections that endow a strong sense of belonging in their communities. They also possess the social capital and skills required to achieve upward mobility. Yet, their efforts are constantly thwarted by their lack of legal status.

The inevitability of integration for DACA beneficiaries is called into question precisely because the tension between vulnerability and belonging that characterizes their daily experience remains unresolved. While the ability to carve out spaces of belonging amid the dehumanizing experiences of liminal legality is laudable, it cannot fully counter the force of "illegality" as a master status. As Susan Coutin (2003, 193) warns, "Even if this space is in some ways subversive, even if its boundaries are permeable, and even if it is sometimes irrelevant to the individuals' daily lives, [it] can be deadly".

On September 5, 2017, the Trump administration terminated DACA, exposing DACA's limits in providing long-term relief for its beneficiaries. As we write, the future of DACA is being challenged in the court system, and Congress has yet to find a long-term solution for managing immigration. As DACA's fate is uncertain, so too are the futures of its beneficiaries. Ultimately, as a liminally legal status, DACA has limited inclusionary power. What undocumented young people need is a more permanent solution that could open new and enduring pathways to full integration. But DACA beneficiaries are also members of families and communities who are vulnerable because of their undocumented status. As such, even if DACA beneficiaries are provided a path to citizenship, a more complete sense of belonging and inclusion will continue to hinge on the immigration status of family and friends, as well as the community supports that structure everyday life. Social liminality is likely to persist for these young people if social relations remain vulnerable to immigration enforcement.

Notes

1. In 2007, the state legislature passed HB3620, excluding undocumented immigrants from receiving any form of student aid for higher education in South Carolina, including tuition assistance and scholarships. The following year, HB4400 was signed into law, making South Carolina the first state to prohibited undocumented students from enrolling in public colleges and universities in the state. Since the implementation of DACA, the state's Commission on Higher Education has lifted the restrictions of HB4400 for DACA beneficiaries.
2. Qualifying for the resident tuition rate is based on having attended and graduated from a New York high school or having received a GED in the state of New York.

Acknowledgements

We want to thank Alejandro Portes, Patricia Fernández-Kelly and the anonymous peer reviewers for very helpful comments and suggestions. We have presented earlier drafts of this research at the Harvard Inequality in America Initiative Workshop Series, the UCLA Latino Policy & Politics Initiative, and the Children of Immigrants in the Age of Deportation Conference at Princeton University, and we are particularly grateful to Mary Waters, Matt Barreto, and Patricia Gándara.

Disclosure statement

No potential conflict of interest was reported by the authors.

Funding

This work was supported by the John D. and Catherine T. MacArthur Foundation and the Bill and Melinda Gates Foundation.

References

Abrego, Leisy J. 2006. "'I Can't Go to College Because I Don't Have Papers': Incorporation Patterns of Undocumented Latino Youth." *Latino Studies* 4 (3): 212–231. doi:10.1057/palgrave.lst.8600200.

Abrego, Leisy J. 2018. "Renewed Optimism and Spatial Mobility: Legal Consciousness of Latino Deferred Action for Childhood Arrivals Recipients and Their Families in Los Angeles." *Ethnicities* 18 (2): 192–207. doi:10.1177/1468796817752563.

Barranco, Raymond E., and Edward S. Shihadeh. 2015. "Walking ATMs and the Immigration Spillover Effect: The Link Between Latino Immigration and Robbery Victimization." *Social Science Research* 52: 440–450. doi:10.1016/j.ssresearch.2015.03.003.

Batalova, Jeanne, Sarah Hooker, Randy Capps, and James D. Bachmeier. 2014. *DACA at the Two-Year Mark: A National and State Profile of Youth Eligible and Applying for Deferred Action*. Washington, DC: Migration Policy Institute.

Bean, Frank D., Susan K. Brown, and James D. Bachmeier. 2015. *Parents Without Papers: The Progress and Pitfalls of Mexican-American Integration*. New York: Russell Sage Foundation.

Bosniak, Linda. 2006. *The Citizen and the Alien: Dilemmas of Contemporary Membership*. Princeton: Princeton University Press.

Castañeda, Heide. 2019. *Borders of Belonging: Struggle and Solidarity in Mixed-Status Immigrant Families*. Palo Alto: Stanford University Press.

Castañeda, Heide, Seth M. Holmes, Daniel S. Madrigal, Maria-Elena Young DeTrinidad, Naomi Beyerle, and James Quesada. 2015. "Immigration as a Social Determinant of Health." *Annual Review of Public Health* 36: 375–392. doi:10.1146/annurev-publhealth-032013-182419.

Cebulko, Kara. 2014. "Documented, Undocumented, and Liminally Legal: Legal Status During the Transition to Adulthood for 1.5-Generation Brazilian Immigrants." *The Sociological Quarterly* 55 (1): 143–167. doi:10.1111/tsq.12045.

Chavez, Leo R., Belinda Campos, Karina Corona, Daina Sanchez, and Catherine Belyeu Ruiz. 2019. ""Words Hurt: Political Rhetoric, Emotions/Affect, and Psychological Well-Being Among Mexican-Origin Youth." *Social Science & Medicine* 228: 240–251.

Coutin, Susan B. 2003. "Cultural Logics of Belonging and Movement: Transnationalism, Naturalization, and U.S. Immigration Politics." *American Ethnologist* 30 (4): 508–526. doi:10.1525/ae.2003.30.4.508.

De Genova, Nicholas P. 2002. "Migrant 'Illegality' and Deportability in Everyday Life." *Annual Review of Anthropology* 31: 419–447. doi:10.1146/annurev.anthro.31.040402.085432.

Del Real, Deisy. 2018. "Toxic Ties: The Reproduction of Legal Violence Within Mixed-Status Intimate Partners, Relatives, and Friends." *International Migration Review* 53 (2): 548–570. doi:10.1177/0197918318769313.

Del Real, Deisy. 2019. "'They See Us Like Trash': How Mexican Illegality Stigma Affects the Psychological Well-Being of Undocumented and US-Born Young Adults of Mexican Descent." In *Immigration and Health (Advances in Medical Sociology, Volume 19)*, edited by Reanne Frank, 205–228. Emerald Publishing Limited: Bingley.

Dreby, Joanna. 2012. "The Burden of Deportation on Children in Mexican Immigrant Families." *Journal of Marriage and Family* 74: 829–845. doi:10.1111/j.1741-3737.2012.00989.x.

Enriquez, Laura E. 2017. "Gendering Illegality: Undocumented Young Adults' Negotiation of the Family Formation Process." *American Behavioral Scientist* 61 (10): 1153–1171. doi:10.1177/0002764217732103.

García, San Juanita. 2018. "Living a Deportation Threat: Anticipatory Stressors Confronted by Undocumented Mexican Immigrant Women." *Race and Social Problems* 10 (3): 221–234. doi:10.1007/s12552-018-9244-2.

García, Angela S. 2019. *Legal Passing: Navigating Undocumented Life and Local Immigration Law.* Oakland: University of California Press.

Golash-Boza, Tanya, and Zulema Valdez. 2018. "Nested Contexts of Reception: Undocumented Students at the University of California, Central." *Sociological Perspectives* 61 (4): 535–552. doi:10.1177/0731121417743728.

Goldring, Luin, Carolina Berinstein, and Judith Bernhard. 2007. "Institutionaling Precarious Immigrant Status in Canada." Paper presented at Con/founding refugee and forced migration studies, centre for refugee studies, York University, November 1–3.

Gonzales, Roberto G. 2011. "Learning to be Illegal: Undocumented Youth and Shifting Legal Contexts in the Transition to Adulthood." *American Sociological Review* 76 (4): 602–619. doi:10.1177/0003122411411901.

Gonzales, Roberto G. 2016. *Lives in Limbo: Undocumented and Coming of Age in America.* Oakland: University of California Press.

Gonzales, Roberto G., and Edelina M. Burciaga. 2018. "Segmented Pathways of Illegality: Reconciling the Coexistence of Master and Auxiliary Statuses in the Experiences of 1.5-Generation Undocumented Young Adults." *Ethnicities* 18 (2): 178–191. doi:10.1177/1468796818767176.

Gonzales, Roberto G., Basia Ellis, Sarah A. Rendón-García, and Kristina Brant. 2018. "(Un)authorized Transitions: Illegality, DACA, and the Life Course." *Research in Human Development* 15 (3-4): 345–359. doi:10.1080/15427609.2018.1502543.

Gonzales, Roberto G., Marco A. Murillo, Cristina Lacomba, Kristina Brant, Martha C. Franco, Jaein Lee, and Deepa S. Vasudevan. 2017. *Taking Giant Leaps Forward: Experiences of a Range of DACA Beneficiaries at the 5-Year Mark.* Washington, DC: Center for American Progress.

Gonzales, Roberto G., and Steven Raphael, eds. 2017. "Undocumented Immigrants and Their Experiences of Illegality." [Special issue] *Russell Sage Foundation Journal* 3 (4).

Gonzales, Roberto G., Benjamin Roth, Kristina Brant, Jaein Lee, and Carolina Valdivia. 2016. *DACA at Year Three: Challenges and Opportunities in Assessing Education and Employment, New Evidence From the UnDACAmented Research Project*. Washington, DC: American Immigration Council.

Gonzales, Roberto G., Veronica Terriquez, and Stephen P. Ruszczyk. 2014. "Becoming DACAmented: Assessing the Short-Term Benefits of Deferred Action for Childhood Arrivals (DACA)." *American Behavioral Scientist* 58 (14): 1852–1872. doi:10.1177/0002764214550288.

Kubal, Agnieszka. 2013. "Conceptualizing Semi-Legality in Migration Research." *Law & Society Review* 47 (3): 555–587. doi:10.1111/lasr.12031.

López, Jane Lilly. 2015. "Impossible Families: Mixed-Citizenship Status Couples and the Law." *Law & Policy* 37 (1-2): 93–118. doi:10.1111/lapo.12032.

Lopez, William D., Nicole L. Novak, Melanie Harner, Ramiro Martinez, and Julia S. Seng. 2018. "The Traumatogenic Potential of Law Enforcement Home Raids: An Exploratory Report." *Traumatology* 24 (3): 193–199. doi:10.1037/trm0000148.

Marrow, Helen B. 2009. "Immigrant Bureaucratic Incorporation: The Dual Roles of Professional Missions and Government Policies." *American Sociological Review* 74 (5): 756–776. doi:10.1177/000312240907400504.

Marrow, Helen B. 2011. *New Destinations Dreaming: Immigration, Race, and Legal Status in the Rural American South*. Palo Alto: Stanford University Press.

Martinez, Lisa M., and Maria del Carmen Salazar. 2018. "The Bright Lights: The Development of Oppositional Consciousness among DACAmented Latino Youth." *Ethnicities* 18 (2): 242–259. doi:10.1177/1468796817752495.

Massey, Douglas S., Karen A. Pren, and Jorge Durand. 2016. "Why Border Enforcement Backfired." *American Journal of Sociology* 121 (5): 1557–1600. doi:10.1086/684200.

Menjívar, Cecilia. 2006. "Liminal Legality: Salvadoran and Guatemalan Immigrants' Lives in the United States." *American Journal of Sociology* 111 (4): 999–1037. doi:10.1086/499509.

Menjívar, Cecilia, and Leisy J. Abrego. 2012. "Legal Violence: Immigration Law and the Lives of Central American Immigrants." *American Journal of Sociology* 117 (5): 1380–1421.

Milkman, Ruth. 2011. "Immigrant Workers, Precarious Work, and the U.S. Labor Movement." *Globalizations* 8 (3): 361–372. doi:10.1080/14747731.2011.576857.

Nienhusser, H. Kenny. 2018. *Implementation of Public and Institutional Policies for Undoc/DACAmented Students at Higher Education Institutions*. Los Angeles: UndocuScholars.

Patler, Caitlin. 2014. "Racialized Illegality: The Convergence of Race and Legal Status among Black, Latino and Asian-American Undocumented Young Adults." In *Scholars and Southern Californian Immigrants in Dialogue: New Conversations in Public Sociology*, edited by Victoria Carty, Rafael Luévano, and Tekle Woldemikael, 93–113. Lanham: Lexington Press.

Patler, Caitlin, and Jorge A. Cabrera. 2015. *From Undocumented to DACAmented: Impacts of the Deferred Action for Childhood Arrivals (DACA) Program*. Los Angeles: Institute for Research on Labor and Employment.

Patler, Caitlin, and Whitney Laster Pirtle. 2018. "From Undocumented to Lawfully Present: Do Changes to Legal Status Impact Psychological Wellbeing among Latino Immigrant Young Adults?" *Social Science & Medicine* 199: 39–48. doi:10.1016/j.socscimed.2017.03.009.

Pila, Daniela. 2016. "'I'm Not Good Enough for Anyone': Legal Status and the Dating Lives of Undocumented Young Adults." *Sociological Forum* 31 (1): 138–158. doi:10.1111/socf.12237.

Portes, Alejandro, and Patricia Fernandez-Kelly. 2008. "No Margin for Error: Educational and Occupational Achievement among Disadvantaged Children of Immigrants." *ANNALS of the American Academy of Political and Social Science* 620: 12–36.

Portes, Alejandro, and Rubén G. Rumbaut. 2001. *Legacies: The Story of the Immigrant Second Generation*. Berkeley: University of California Press.

Portes, Alejandro, and Rubén G. Rumbaut. 2006. *Immigrant America: A Portrait*. 4th ed. Berkeley: University of California Press.

Potochnik, Stephanie R., and Krista M. Perreira. 2010. "Depression and Anxiety among First-Generation Immigrant Latino Youth: Key Correlates and Implications for Future Research." *The Journal of Nervous and Mental Disease* 198 (7): 470–477. doi:10.1097/NMD.0b013e3181e4ce24.

Reed-Denahay, Deborah, and Caroline B. Brettell, eds. 2008. *Citizenship, Political Engagement, and Belonging: Immigrants in Europe and the United States*. New Brunswick: Rutgers University Press.

Ridgley, Jennifer. 2008. "Cities of Refuge: Immigration Enforcement, Police, and the Insurgent Genealogies of Citizenship in US Sanctuary Cities." *Urban Geography* 29 (1): 53–77.

Schmalzbauer, Leah. 2014. *The Last Best Place? Gender, Family, and Migration in the New West*. Palo Alto: Stanford University Press.

Silver, Alexis M. 2018. *Shifting Boundaries: Immigrant Youth Negotiating National, State, and Small-Town Politics*. Palo Alto: Stanford University Press.

Smith, Robert Courtney. 2008. "Horatio Alger Lives in Brooklyn: Extrafamily Support, Intrafamily Dynamics, and Socially Neutral Operating Identities in Exceptional Mobility among Children of Mexican Immigrants." *The Annals of the American Academy of Political and Social Science* 620 (1): 270–290.

Stanton-Salazar, Ricardo. 2001. *Manufacturing Hope and Despair: The School and Kin Support Networks of U.S.- Mexican Youth*. New York: Teachers College Press.

Willen, Sarah S. 2007. "Toward a Critical Phenomenology of "Illegality": State Power, Criminalization, and Abjectivity among Undocumented Migrant Workers in Tel Aviv, Israel." *International Migration* 45 (3): 8–38.

Wong, Tom K., Greisa Martinez Rosas, Adrian Reyna, Ignacia Rodriguez, Patrick O'Shea, Tom Jawets, and Philip E. Wolgin. 2016. *New Study of DACA Beneficiaries Shows Positive Economic and Educational Outcomes*. Washington, DC: Center for American Progress.

Zhou, Min. 2008. "The Ethnic System of Supplementary Education: Non-profit and For-profit Institutions in Los Angeles' Chinese Immigrant Community." In *Toward Positive Youth Development: Transforming Schools and Community Programs*, edited by B. Shinn, and H. Yoshikawa, 229–251. New York: Oxford University Press.

Zúñiga, Victor, and Rubén Hernández-León, eds. 2005. *New Destinations: Mexican Immigration in the United States*. New York: Russell Sage Foundation.

An imperfect realignment: the movement of children of immigrants and their families from the United States to Mexico

Rubén Hernández-León, Víctor Zúñiga and Sarah M. Lakhani

ABSTRACT
Over the past 15 years, hundreds of thousands of children of immigrants and their families have moved from the United States to Mexico pushed by different legal and economic expulsion factors. Using evidence from a multi-sited, twenty year-long study of Mexican migration to Georgia, we analyze the varied educational, linguistic, employment and family reunification experiences of children of immigrants in two communities of origin in central and northern Mexico. We draw from insights of the political sociology of international migration to contend that the movement of children of immigrants and their families to the parental homeland forces the realignment of people, state and territory that emigration initially disrupts. We also argue that this realignment is imperfect because children of immigrants, especially those who are U.S.-born and possess dual citizenship and their families continue to circulate between Mexico and the United States, employing mobility strategies and tapping resources located in both countries.

Introduction

Over the past 15 years, hundreds of thousands of children of immigrants and their families have left the United States for Mexico, many forced out by restrictive policies and punitive enforcement measures. Uprooted from their lives in the United States, these children of immigrants have suddenly become migrant children. But the minors who are part of this migratory flow have varied trajectories, legal status and socialization experiences. Some of them were born in Mexico and have spent most of their lives in the United States; others were born and raised in the United States and had never lived abroad until they moved to Mexico; and some others, with the benefit of dual nationality, have circulated between the two countries (Zúñiga and Giorguli 2018).

Using the migration of these children and adolescents and their families to Mexico as strategic research material, we ask: How do local communities, labour markets and government institutions in Mexico integrate newcomers and reintegrate long-absent members? How do return, first-time migrants and stay-at-home residents and households negotiate membership, inter-actions and resources for the newly arrived? Based on the insight of the pol-itical sociology of migration that emigration disrupts the alignment between people, state and territory (Waldinger and Soehl 2010; Morawska 2005), we argue that return migration forces a realignment between those who were abroad and are now back in the national territory, those who stayed behind, and the state. We contend that this realignment is imperfect and frac-tious as long-term absence creates social distance between returnees and stay-at-home individuals, on the one hand, and past migration endows some community members with characteristics and resources that connect them to another nation state and its population, on the other hand (e.g. dual nationality). Furthermore, we provide evidence suggesting that the inter-action between conditions of return, family resources and local responses, leads to a segmented integration/reintegration of children of immigrants into Mexico.

The empirical material for this article stems from a unique 20-year study of Mexican migration to a new destination in the U.S. South, Dalton, Georgia, and the more recent family flows to two sending communities, San Timoteo and Miramón (pseudonyms), in the states of Guanajuato and Zacatecas, respect-ively. We contribute to multiple, intersecting literatures on international migration, specifically to the scholarship on family return migration, deporta-tion and integration, and the cross-border mobility of children and adoles-cents to the parental homeland (Tsuda 2003; Veale 2014; Vadean and Piracha 2009; Chan and Tran 2011).

Framework

Return migration has long been a feature of the Mexico-U.S. migratory stream. Throughout its storied history, this flow has produced a steady return of circu-lar migrants and a series of intermittent mass expulsions (Alanís Enciso 2003). Over the past 15 years, hundreds of thousands of Mexican immigrant families, members of a long-term resident undocumented population in the United States, have been driven out of this country. Their move to Mexico has intro-duced a new component in the North American migratory system: a sojourn-ing population of more than half a million children and adolescents moving from the United States to Mexico. Mexican society and state institutions, especially schools, have been compelled to respond to the presence of migrant children in their midst (Hernández-León and Zúñiga 2016; Gándara 2016; Jacobo Suárez 2017).

The movement of immigrant families and their children from the United States to Mexico offers an opportunity to revisit how mass migration across international borders disrupts the alignment between people, state and territory (Su 2018). The initial disruption occurs when emigrants leave the national territory, temporarily, in some cases, and permanently, in others. This disruption stems not only from the exit of large numbers of individuals from the national territory but also from the fact that their exodus prompts the sending state to extend the protection of its citizens in the territory of the receiving state, albeit in a limited way (Waldinger 2015).

The disruptions that emigration produces also play out within the ranks of civil society (that is, not just in the relations between state and society). Absent from the national territory, emigrants grow roots in the country of destination, develop ties to its citizenry in the form of social capital and undergo powerful experiences of resocialization (Kim 2018; Gordon 1964). But emigrants do not sever relations with the country of origin. On the contrary, they remit money, call and visit home and make a variety of investments to reaffirm their belonging (Mahmud 2015). Still, the emigrant's absence has consequences; chiefly, the lack of participation in the everyday life of the places of origin. The result is a growing distance or divergence between emigrants and those left behind (Waldinger 2015).

Return migration forces a realignment between state, people and territory. In principle, those who were away come back to the national territory and reintegrate to the society and state institutions of the country of origin. In reality, the process of return and reintegration is imperfect and fractious for reasons intrinsic to the process of international migration. Return entails, after all, another border crossing, that is, a separate international migration and passage from one political jurisdiction to another. Returnees, state and stay-at-home citizens reunite and reconnect in the aftermath of a process of social change that has reshaped their relations, ideologies and identities. Initially, adult returnees and children who move for the first time to the parental homeland, especially (but not only) those forcefully expelled from the (former) receiving society, might experience their sojourn as form of dislocation and loss accompanied by a period of mourning (Román González, Cantú, and Hernández-León 2016). Those who are forcefully returned may be individuals with experiences in the criminal-justice system in the country of destination, suggesting that particular forms of return migration result from the U.S. government exporting downward assimilation to countries of origin (Olvera and Muela 2016; Rosen and Cruz 2018).

Soon after arrival, return migrants may come to the realization that neither state nor society welcomes them back with open arms. Stay-at-home family and community members may fear that returnees will lay claims on and

compete for scarce economic resources, may fear the ideas and cultural practices people bring from abroad, look down upon a "failed" migratory project
and suspect and stigmatize the reasons for and conditions of return (Wyman
1993; Golash-Boza and Ceciliano-Navarro 2019). Returnees themselves might
realize that, after a long absence, their social capital and networks have grown
cold, yielding limited benefits as they probe the labour market, and that
employers might not be so keen on hiring them, concerned about the
impact on workplaces (Hagan, Hernández-León, and Demonsant 2015).
These experiences can make feel returnees as strangers in their own land.

The institutions of the sending state (now the state to which former emigrants are returning to) might not have the experience, inclination and
resources to accommodate the needs of returnees, especially if large
numbers arrive in a short period. This is not just a matter of state capacity.
As the growing literature on transnational students in the Mexico-U.S.
context demonstrates (Boehm 2008; Giorguli and López 2009; Hamann and
Zúñiga 2011; Jensen, Giorguli, and Padilla 2018), returning children, U.S.-
born minors who are moving to Mexico for the first time, and pupils who
move repeatedly between the two countries, are an awkward fit with educational institutions designed to produce a mono-national, homogeneous citizenry. These institutions can set up obstacles to the formal and substantive
integration of these children and adolescents, rendering their experiences
invisible and their needs unattended (Jacobo Suárez 2017; Sánchez García
and Hamann 2016; Panait and Zúñiga 2016).

The fractious reintegration of return migrants does not stem from the
simple rejection of those long absent by the home state and society. Return
migrants are not the same emigrants who left the homeland, having been
transformed by the processes of migration and immigration. Central to this
transformation are the ties that returnees develop and retain with the
(former) receiving national society and that are not surrendered after migrants
come back to the country of origin. These connections, personified by the U.S.
citizen minors who are new to Mexico, are a reminder of the enduring connections returnees have to another national society. They are also a form of social
capital (Kim 2018), representing the possibility of remigration.

Methods

The empirical material presented in this article stems from fieldwork conducted in Dalton, Georgia, and two Mexican sending communities in the
states of Guanajuato and Zacatecas over a period of more than 20 years.
We began data collection in Dalton, where we fielded a survey of Latino
parents with children enrolled in Dalton Public Schools (n = 895, 468
women and 427 men), conducted semi-structured interviews and participant
observation in schools, neighbourhoods, restaurants, factories, soccer fields

and people's homes, in periodic visits to the city from 1997 to the mid-2000s. These surveys and interviews focused on the migratory trajectories individuals and families had followed to get to Dalton, the reasons why they had settled in this small city and their experiences of economic and social integration. During the first decade of research, our project also comprised a community development project and teacher exchange programme that sent Mexican instructors to Georgia schools, giving us insight into the reception of children of immigrants in the educational system.

We returned to Dalton in 2008 and 2009 to conduct semi-structured interviews with 58 young-adult children of immigrants (26 men and 32 women) in the early stages of their occupational careers. In 2011, we went back to the Carpet Capital to research the effects of the economic crisis and immigration enforcement on the decision to leave and return to Mexico, fielding 42 semi-structured interviews (not analyzed for this article). Our most recent fieldwork stint took place during the summer of 2018, when we interviewed immigrant entrepreneurs and activists, teachers, faculty and staff of the local college, elected officials and employees of the chamber of commerce, and members of the first, 1.5 and second generations, to assess the recovery of the local economy.

We began studying sending communities during the late 2000s, seeking to understand the transnational ties that connect Dalton to the homeland. From 2007 to 2009, we undertook three ethnographic fieldwork stints in the sending community of San Timoteo, Guanajuato, where we observed the patron saint festivities, the town's fair and other community activities, visited schools and nearby factories, and conducted interviews with local authorities, adult returnees, stay-at-home spouses and youths who had been deported. During these trips we were also able to observe the early effects of the Great Recession on the town as jobs and overtime became scarce in Dalton and remittances to the town began to decline. Starting in 2013, we went back to San Timoteo and also conducted ethnographic fieldwork in Miramón, Zacatecas, where we interviewed and interacted with return and retired migrants, deportees, and children, adolescents and young adults, some of whom had been born in the United States and were attending schools and were employed locally. In both communities, we also interviewed teachers at the towns' middle schools and observed agricultural and other economic activities.

The ethnographic and qualitative fieldwork we conducted in San Timoteo and Miramón is not strictly comparable as we undertook it during different moments of the Great Expulsion (Hernández-León and Zúñiga 2016). When we started collecting ethnographic data in San Timoteo, the state project of removing large numbers of undocumented immigrants was in its early stages and deportations appear to target individuals with criminal records. Ten years later, the deportation machine had cast a wider net, thanks in part to the collaboration between federal and local authorities. As a result, the fieldwork in Miramón captured a population of returnees composed of entire families, parents who had left children behind in the United States and minors who had reunited in the town with parents who had been forcibly removed (see below)

Children of Mexican immigrants in Dalton

Located deep in the southern Appalachia region, Dalton is the largest manufacturing hub of wall-to-wall carpet in the world. Dalton is the seat of Whitfield County and the economic centre of a five-county region in northwest Georgia, clustering carpet production and its auxiliary industries. Today, 85 percent of the carpets and rugs produced in the United States are manufactured in this region, with the industry employing nearly thirty thousand people in the state of Georgia (CRI 2017; Patton 1999).

Mexicans arrived in Dalton in massive numbers during the 1990s, directly from Mexico (primarily from the western and north-central historic region of emigration) and from U.S. gateway states (California, Illinois and Texas), turning the Carpet Capital into a destination for family migration and family reunification. The rapid growth of Latinos as a proportion of Dalton's total population is indicative of the dramatic transformation of the local demographic landscape. In 1990, Latinos were 6.5 percent of the total population. In contrast, by 2010 48 percent of local residents were Latino (American Fact Finder 2017; Hernández-León and Zúñiga 2000).

Dalton offered both a positive and a negative context of reception to children of immigrants, illustrating the contradictory nature of the societal and institutional responses to mass immigration. The leaders of the local urban regime – the owners and top managers of the carpet industry – saw immigrants as a vital addition to their workforce and contained nativist and xenophobic attacks. School leaders developed a progressive response to the dramatic transformation in the composition of the student body. Although these efforts did not unfold without controversy and contradictions, they symbolically and materially created a favorable context for children of immigrants (Hamann 2003). By 2001, the growing presence of Latino students had turned the local public school system into a majority-minority district, a trend that also emerged, albeit in a less pronounced way, in the neighboring school district of Whitfield County. In 2018, nearly 70 percent of the students enrolled in Dalton public school system were Latino, compared to about 43 percent in Whitfield (Georgia Department of Education 2018). As a corollary to these transformations, in 2017 the local state college became the first Hispanic Serving Institution in Georgia.

Many children of immigrants in Dalton were also migrant children, some born in Mexico and others in historic destinations of Mexican immigration, like California, moving subsequently to Georgia. In the interviews we conducted in 2008–2009 with 58 members of the 1.5 and second generations in Dalton, our subjects remembered the contradictory reception they encountered in schools. Recalling her first years in Dalton, Alma stated,

> In the beginning, you could feel a lot of hatred. You could feel the racism ... derogatory terms in schools by a lot of the students, but at the same time, you had all of these people that were welcoming, that were accepting, that wanted to help you and wanted to help you succeed.

Young men born and raised in California recounted stigmatization at the hands of teachers and principals in Dalton who, immediately upon arrival, labelled them as potential gang members. Despite the racialization our interviewees experienced at the hands of peers and some teachers and school officials, particularly during the early stages of Mexican settlement in Dalton, many of them explained that "things got better" as more immigrants arrived and became a large proportion of the student body. They also spoke of good relations with black peers and more tense interactions with white pupils, who often called them racial slurs.

Hernández-León and Lakhani (2013) have shown that despite these early experiences, children of Mexican immigrants are progressing steadily through the ranks of working- class and lower middle-class jobs. Armed with bilingual skills, they have entered the local labour market as cultural and linguistic brokers between the predominantly Spanish-speaking immigrant population and the English-speaking native population. Many of our young adult interviewees reported that being bilingual and, in some cases, biliterate, gave them an edge in the labour market, opening employment opportunities to them and highlighting the vital role of language as form of human and cultural capital in the process of integration.

However, young men and women have followed different occupational paths and, therefore, are applying their bilingual skills differently. Many men have joined their parents in the local carpet mills but have taken supervisory and mid-level managerial jobs, bridging the mostly white upper-managerial echelons and the immigrant-staffed assembly line. In contrast, many 1.5- and second-generation women have avoided the carpet mills, an environment they associate with sexual harassment. Instead, these women have utilized their bilingual skills in the service economy, filling roles designed to help businesses connect with Spanish-speaking customers (Hernández-León and Lakhani 2013).

At the same time, the high proportion of Mexican undocumented immigrants in Dalton exposed many families and children to the threat of deportation and the resulting experiences of trauma and dislocation (Hernández-León and Zúñiga 2016). A non-radom survey we fielded in 1998 showed that 80 percent of respondents were undocumented and only 20 percent had legal status. During the mid to late 1990s, the INS established checkpoints in the highways connecting Dalton to the region and conducted workplace raids in the local poultry plant and carpet mills (Hernández-León and Zúñiga 2005). After the

Republican takeover of the legislative and executive branches in the mid-2000s, the state of Georgia passed a barrage of anti-undocumented immigrant laws. While some of these laws merely replicated federal legislation targeting unauthorized adults, other provisions set their sights on the undocumented 1.5 generation. Different bills have excluded undocumented students from the benefits of in-state-resident tuition, a provision that in practice has prevented the approximately 4,000 DACA recipients in the Dalton region from receiving this form of assistance to make college more affordable (Foley 2017; Rose 2018). Other measures prohibited undocumented youth from attending Georgia's most selective public universities (Gonzales 2016).

In 2008, the Whitfield County Sheriff's Office signed a memorandum of understanding with Immigration and Customs Enforcement (ICE) to join the 287(g) programme. The 287(g) programme trained and deputized agents of the sheriff as ICE officials. Individuals arrested by sheriff deputies and detained in the local jail would be screened to check for their legal status using federal databases. Those found to be in the country without authorization would then be turned in to ICE. In June 2008, according to the local newspaper, the 287(g) became operational as a woman who had failed to appear on a charge of driving with a suspended license was found to be an undocumented immigrant and turned in to ICE (Sloan 2008). About the same time that 287(g) memorandum of understanding was signed, the Dalton Police Department (DPD) increased its traffic checkpoints in the city. Because the DPD did not have (and still does not have) its own detention facility and used the county jail, many undocumented immigrants arrested for traffic violations ended up in the hands of ICE.

Set up near factories, Latino neighbourhoods, soccer fields and other places frequented by immigrants, these checkpoints netted many as they went about their daily activities. These enforcement strategies coincided with the dramatic rise in unemployment as the Great Recession decimated carpet manufacturing, an industry closely pegged to housing and the construction sector in general, amounting to a programme to remove excess undocumented labour from the local economy (Capps et al. 2011). A dramatic slowdown in the growth of the Latino population in Dalton attests, albeit indirectly, to the effects of the crisis and draconian enforcement policies. Between 2010 and 2016, the Latino population only grew 1.4 percent, to reach 49.4 percent of the total population (American Fact Finder 2017). Dalton ceased to be a magnet of new immigration and started to push out people to other states in the region, like Tennessee, where undocumented immigrants perceived a less hostile environment, and to Mexico.

The context of return/move to Mexico

By the mid-2000s, hundreds of thousands of immigrants and their families began to move to Mexico, forced out by new interior enforcement strategies, the criminalization of migration, and the effects of the Great Recession of 2007-2009. During the 2005–2010 period alone, between 1 and 1.4 million people went back to Mexico (Hernández-León and Zúñiga 2016; Giorguli Saucedo and Gutiérrez 2012). Returning families have come back to different contexts, from depressed localities that continue to depend on rain-fed agriculture to dynamic cities embedded in the country's manufacturing export economy (Hagan, Hernández-León, and Demonsant 2015). As noted above, this flow of family return migration includes more than half a million minors, who have been welcomed with a patchwork of initiatives across states to facilitate their integration to schools and transition to the labour market (Gándara 2016; Hernández-León and Zúñiga 2016). The inadequate and contradictory nature of these initiatives are reflective not only of limited state capacity but also of the difficulty to realign state, (non-migrant) society, different categories of returnees and U.S.-born Mexican nationals who have arrived in Mexico for the first time.

Children of immigrants in communities of "origin"

San Timoteo, Guanajuato

San Timoteo is a small town of 1227 inhabitants (in 2010) located near the Gua-najuato-Michoacán state line in central-western Mexico, which has become a destination for members of the undocumented 1.5 generation, including some individuals who held and subsequently lost their U.S. permanent residency status. The U.S. policy to remove legal and undocumented immigrants after an entanglement with the criminal legal system in Georgia and other states put these children of immigrants into the deportation pipeline, ultimately resulting in their forced move to the parental homeland. During the second half of the 2000s decade, these young deportees – mostly males – had a visible presence in San Timoteo, where they gathered on street corners, playing dominoes and engaging in conversation. Most young deportees in the town – though not all of them – came from Dalton. Other deportees previously lived in California, Texas, Illinois, and other parts of Georgia.

Our observations and interviews in Dalton showed that some members of the 1.5 and 2nd generations formed and joined street gangs or crews. In turn, some of the adolescents and young adults who moved to San Timoteo seemed to have gang affiliations as well; they made their presence felt in town through tagging. During our fieldwork stints in the second half of the 2000s and then again in 2013, we noted that many walls, abandoned houses, and the modest plaza's gazebo were covered in graffiti including the names and emblems of local Mexican and Dalton street gangs. Many youths we spoke with claimed that local crews were affiliated with Dalton-based Mexican gangs.

According to the accounts provided by middle-school students residing in San Timoteo and Dalton, there used to be two gangs or crews, the *Arribeños* (the Highlanders) and the *Abajeños* (the Lowlanders), indicating San Timoteo's north and south divide along the street where the church and the plaza are located. These crews would fight with each other and with young males from neighboring towns during dances and other events. The same accounts described that many of the Abajeños moved to the United States with their parents, thus preempting the previous style of conflict and leaving the Arribeños as the sole crew in town. This crew has absorbed the remaining members of the Abajeños and functions now as an affiliate of a Dalton-based gang, the Caguamos, whose tags can be found all over San Timoteo.

In fact, the local crew no longer identifies by its old name and appears to have fully embraced the identity of the Dalton gang. Such a development is the outcome of a seemingly growing flow of deportees who have returned to San Timoteo and who are members of the Caguamos.[1] Many of these return migrants have been deported and barred from reentering the United States – some after having been detained by the anti-gang squad of the Dalton Police Department and later convicted of a range of felonies, including drug possession/trafficking and statutory rape. Several of them dress in full "cholo" attire, with baggy pants, loose shirts, and tennis shoes with long white tube socks. Crew cuts and tattoos adorn hands, arms, faces and torsos, to complement their look. Some of these deportees talked about having sojourned to Georgia either as children or as adolescents, not visiting San Timoteo in many years, and now feeling like strangers after the compulsory return to the hometown.

The homecoming of members of the Caguamos gang presented two challenges for residents of San Timoteo. The first challenge had to do with the returnees' economic reintegration to a locality with few and poorly paid employment opportunities beyond agriculture. Large assembly and manufacturing firms, which set up shop in the region in recent years, did not recruit these young adults. These companies followed a policy of not hiring job seekers with tattoos, gang attire, or prior drug consumption, which they could detect through blood and urine tests. During our fieldwork in San Timoteo, local authorities and residents repeatedly expressed concern about the limited chances these youngsters faced obtaining a gainful occupation and their dependence of remittances sent from Dalton and elsewhere in the United States.

Secondly, the arrival of young deportees threatened to create gang-style conflict for the control of territory in San Timoteo. In several individual and group interviews, middle school students, visiting youth from Dalton, and members of the Caguamos, recounted fights between the gang and youngsters from nearby hamlets who were passing through town. They described how San Timoteo was becoming a territorial turf to be defended against the incursion of youth from neighboring communities. The gang outlook is transparent in the words of a deported member of the Caguamos, who maintained that "in this town, we rule; nobody can come into our hood burnning rubber or blasting tunes."

Respondents also noted initiation rituals of new gang members, which included "getting jumped" by several older members of the group. Constant street fights and acts of vandalism prompted the political delegate to call the police, who detained several youngsters in the municipal jail. Interviews with youths and adults alike also revealed the existence of drug use, primarily marijuana. Although the evidence might suggest a spreading gang subculture in San Timoteo, teachers and other adult interviewees argued that some of these youngsters were merely "wannabe" kids who imitate rather than assume a full-blown gang identity. They underscored that many more children and adolescents were involved in the thriving brass bands of San Timoteo (which often financed their instruments with family remittances from the United States) than with a local crew or gang.

At the same time as some children and young adults were moving to San Timoteo, others were only beginning their migratory sojourn to the United States, particularly through family reunification. While conducting fieldwork in the town, we learned that even as the period of the Great Migration had drawn to a close (Hernández-León and Zúñiga 2016), men with families who had long sojourned alone to the United States were now moving their spouses and adolescent children to Dalton after securing lawful permanent residency for them. After spending childhood and early adolescence in the community of origin, these teenagers would replenish the ranks of the 1.5 generation in the Carpet Capital.

Miramón, Zacatecas

Miramón, a small town of 1,490 inhabitants (in 2010), located in the state of Zacatecas, has significant numbers of 1.5 and second generation youth, who have become members of what Zúñiga (2018) calls the 0.5 generation: children who have moved to the parental homeland after going through early socialization north of the border. Some of these migrant children were born in Dalton, while others were born in Mexico but left for the United States at a young age; both groups have spent many formative years in Dalton, where they attended school.

The immediate causes of their migration to Mexico are varied: some of them travelled with their mothers when the latter returned to help an ailing parent; others moved to the parental hometown with their families when a father or a mother was deported. Now in the parental homeland, these migrant children attend local schools – there are elementary, middle and technical high schools in town – and some adolescents are actively supporting their households. If in the 1990s and 2000s 1.5-generation migrant children experienced their sojourn to Dalton as part of a process of family reunification, in the 2010s their "homecoming" feels like a return to the old arrangement of the *casa dividida* (divided home), especially when fathers and older siblings re-emigrate to or remain in the United States. We also found evidence of a different type of *casa dividida*, in which deported fathers return and stay in Miramón, while their spouses and children remain in the United States. The expectation of these fathers is that once their children turn 21 years of age, they will be able to sponsor them as lawful immigrants.

Legal status looms large in the present and future of these youth (Zuñiga and Hamann 2013). Those who were born in Dalton and are U.S. citizens envision their lives as intertwined with the educational and employment opportunities available to them in Mexico *and* the United States. In contrast, those who were born in Mexico and resided in Dalton without authorization long for the time when they lived in the United States and hope for the uncertain possibility of a visa that takes them back to the place they once called home. This fundamental difference underscores the value of U.S. citizenship as institutionalized social capital giving access to cross-border mobility and economic resources (Kim 2018).

Citizenship and legal status (or lack thereof) are woven into the structure of opportunities and strategies that migrant parents develop and build for their children. We identified one of these distinct strategies while doing fieldwork in Miramón: Dalton-based families send their children to the hometown after they complete elementary school; the children spend between 1 and 3 years in Mexican schools in order to become literate in Spanish. Partly as a result of this strategy, as the teachers we interviewed reported, in Miramón's only middle school one-fourth of the students are U.S. born. When it is time to start high school in the United States, adolescents return to Dalton and continue their education there. Through this strategy, parents hope their dual-citizen children will be fully bilingual and biliterate, capable of operating in the labour markets of both Mexico and the United States.

In Dalton, we interviewed a young woman from Miramón whose experience fit these dynamics, even though the motives for her temporary return varied slightly. In this quote, Elvira responded to the questions posed by Sarah Lakhani (SL):

SL   How well would you say you speak Spanish and how well do you speak English?

Elvira   Very well, both of them. I would say I'm bilingual, but I'm also biliterate, meaning that I can read and write in both languages. I went to school in Mexico for four years, from the time in kindergarten up to 4th grade. Then in '98 we went back to Mexico, just to stay over there with the family and I was in middle school there for a year.

SL   So why did you guys go back to Mexico for a year?

Elvira Just to finish getting everything ready and organized and then come back over here with my father, but the year that I was there was very interesting also. I was in middle school and in Mexico English is a required class that you have to take. My teacher, who was also the principal of the school, was teaching the class and he was like, "Well, I know the language a little bit, but not as well as you do," so I started pretty much teaching the class. Yeah, it was very interesting being a 14-year-old teaching a class.

Having U.S. citizenship (or another legal status that allows for cross-border sojourns) enables strategies that promote socio-economic mobility, including transnational educational investments. However, the transnational strategies of children of immigrants and migrant children and their families defy the logic and practices of national school systems, which do not communicate with each other and are structured around the validation of national educational careers (Gándara 2016). The middle-school teachers we interviewed in Miramón frowned upon the cross-national educational strategies of migrant families and criticized migrant parents for moving their offspring repeatedly between schools in the United States and Mexico and for prioritizing the children's retention of the English language.

Social class is an equally important factor determining access to opportunities for children of immigrants in communities of origin. Children whose parents and grandparents own land and who managed to build a home in Miramón and accumulate some wealth using their savings and remittances, are afforded additional years of schooling in the United States and Mexico. Conversely, the children of migrants whose sojourns to the United States have not resulted in the accumulation of assets, such as a home, land, livestock and equipment, have to leave school and work to help support the family. Two vignettes created with ethnographic data we collected in late 2016 illustrate the very different paths of children of immigrants and former migrants currently residing in Miramón.

Miguel is 19 years old and was born in Miramón. He and his mother (and other siblings) joined his father in Dalton in 2002, when Miguel was five years of age. Three of his brothers were born in the United States. The family moved to Miramón when Miguel's father was deported in 2008. Miguel's aunts recounted the story that when he came back, Miguel stuffed his school diplomas in his pants and shoes, eager to keep proof of his academic achievements in Dalton. Miguel resumed his education in the local middle school and was a very good student with outstanding grades. He received four scholarship offers to continue high school in the capital city but none included a living stipend and funds for books and supplies.

Miguel's family was not in a financial position to support his educational pursuits: Miguel's father does not own land and works for others in town;

his mother runs a small grocery store out of two rooms in the family home. Consequently, Miguel stayed in Miramón and began working at a nearby Japanese assembly plant that produces wiring harnesses for cars. Miguel and his mother criticized the low wages and bad conditions at the factory, which eventually made him quit this job. At the time of our conversation, Miguel was working in agriculture, helping his father in the local bean harvest. Miguel stated vehemently that if he had U.S. citizenship, he would be working in construction in Atlanta or Dallas, installing steel rods in buildings, a job that could earn him as much as $40 an hour.

Contrast Miguel's experience with that of Leticia. Born in the suburbs of Atlanta in 1998, Leticia began her schooling in Dalton. She moved to Miramón with her mother when she was 10 years of age. Leticia completed the last two years of elementary school and all of middle school in Miramón to then return to Dalton to continue high school there. She finished 9th and 10th grades in Dalton and once again moved to Miramón, completing her schooling in the local technical high school. Leticia struggled with writing and reading Spanish but was supported by her grandfather, who read with her every afternoon, and by her teachers, who, knowing that she had studied in the United States, used her as a bilingual assistant.

Leticia finished high school with excellent grades. Following the advice of her teachers, Leticia applied to an English language certification programme at the Universidad de Zacatecas and is already working as an English teacher in the local elementary school while she completes the programme and obtains a full-time position. While her parents have planned for Leticia to return to and work in Dalton after she finishes the certification programme, she is taking steps towards a professional future in Mexico. Although her father recently returned to the United States (after losing his lawful permanent resident status) and her mother operates a taco stand in Miramón to make ends meet, Leticia's success appears to be anchored in the success and steady presence of her grandfather, who saved money from his sojourns in the United States, purchased agricultural equipment and owns land in Miramón.

Miguel and Leticia have similar experiences but different trajectories. Both have lived and attended schools in Dalton and Miramón and both are bilingual and bicultural. While in the United States, their families each lived in a mixed-legal-status situation: some members were citizens, some were lawful permanent residents, and others were undocumented. However, the fact that Leticia possesses dual citizenship and Miguel does not, powerfully differentiates their pasts and likely future trajectories. Sharing prior experiences of schooling in and ongoing ties to the United States, both Miguel and Leticia are candidates for remigration. Should they decide to re-emigrate, they will do so under very different circumstances. The unequal structure of opportunities they face is compounded by the social class standing of their respective families in Miramón. Despite his academic achievements in the United States and Mexico, Miguel is currently toiling next to his father on somebody else's land in rural Zacatecas. Propelled by her dual citizenship and her family's resources, Leticia is building a future as an English teacher with viable career possibilities on both sides of the border. Both of them are members of a new and large category of men and women with histories of cross-border mobility at a young age and whose likely trajectories are not tethered to a single nation-state.

Conclusion

We conclude by highlighting three contributions this article makes to the intersecting literatures of return migration, deportation and the movement of children of immigrants to the parental homeland. First, in the context of the Great Expulsion and mass migration of more than one million people from the United States to Mexico over the past decade and a half, we show that return and reintegration result in an imperfect and fractious realignment between returnees, the state and stay-at-home members in communities of origin. We argue that this fractious realignment reflects the contradictory experiences and forces implicated in the social process of international migration: multiple (intended and forced) border crossings, contested legal and social membership at home and abroad, immigration enforcement policies that spill over international boundaries, and transnational family strategies that challenge nationally oriented institutions.

We demonstrate, secondly, that children of immigrants are at the forefront of this process of imperfect realignment, which finds expression in the diversity of trajectories of integration and reintegration and the contradictory and limited institutional and societal responses they encounter in the parental homeland. Some children of immigrants, already in young adulthood, have forcefully moved to Mexico expelled by U.S. policies that effectively externalize downward assimilation to communities of origin. As young adults, many struggle as 'strangers in their own land,' unable to find occupational alternatives in the local rural economy and stigmatized by townspeople who suspect and see them as a source of social problems. Other children of immigrants have moved to Mexico as part of a process of family reunification, often following the deportation of a parent. After the initial uprooting and dislocation, these youths experience integration through schools and supported by family resources and strategies. Neither these children nor their families relinquish their formal and informal connections to the United States. On the contrary, U.S. citizenship, schooling and early socialization abroad and the remigration of parents and older siblings, update these minors' connections with localities in the Unites States, keeping open the chance to legally circulate between the two countries and take advantage of employment opportunities on either side of the border. But for those who lack or have more limited resources, the possibility of returning to the places they once called home seem more distant and costly.

Finally, our findings on the children of immigrants tentatively suggest a segmented integration into the parental homeland, a process that bears similarities with the segmented assimilation scholars have studied in the context of immigration (Portes and Zhou 1993). Multiple variables account for the segmented integration of children of immigrants, turned migrant children, into Mexico. Having come back as young adults in the aftermath of experiences of downward assimilation in the United States, older returnees have aged out of the opportunity of resocialization through the schools and are likely to be seen and treated as too dissimilar (Fitzgerald 2013) by stay-at-home community members. Their prospects for reintegration hinge on the economic context, employment opportunities and the family support networks they find upon return.

Younger returnees – including those who set foot in Mexico for the first time – are distinctly integrated through the public education system and the economic resources families have accumulated, often through inter-generational sojourning to the United States. Landless households and families whose return to Mexico happens in the aftermath of a failed migration project have limited resources; their children are likely to experience shortened educational careers and hastened transition to the labour market, often to the lower and more precarious echelons of the rural economy. In this context, U.S. citizenship and other types of documentation offering the chance to move legally across the border, become a powerful source of segmentation and social differentiation. Children with dual citizenship – just like emigrants of an earlier generation – might emerge as a distinct stratum, singled out by the possession of a highly prized kind of mobility capital.

Note

1. Not all returning Caguamos are deportees; some come to the town for extended visits during the summer.

Disclosure statement

No potential conflict of interest was reported by the authors.

References

Alanís Enciso, Fernando Saúl. 2003. "No cuenten conmigo: La política de repatriación del gobierno mexicano y sus nacionales en Estados Unidos: 1910–1928." *Mexican Studies/Estudios Mexicanos* 19 (2): 401–461.

American Fact Finder. 2017. "Race and Hispanic or Latino Origin: 2010. Dalton city, Georgia." https://factfinder.census.gov/faces/tableservices/jsf/pages/productview.xhtml?src=CF.

Boehm, Deborah A. 2008. ""For My Children": Constructing Family and Navigating the State in the U.S.-Mexico Transnation." *Anthropological Quarterly* 81 (4): 777–802.

Capps, Randy, Marc Ronseblum, Cristina Rodríguez, and Muzaffar Chisti. 2011. *Delegation and Divergence: A Study of 287(g) State and Local Immigration Enforcement*. Washington: Migration Policy Institute.

Chan, Yuk Wah, and Thi Le Thu Tran. 2011. "Recycling Migration and Changing Nationalisms: The Vietnamese Return Diaspora and Reconstruction of Vietnamese Nationhood." *Journal of Ethnic and Migration Studies* 37 (7): 1101–1117.

CRI. 2017. "Quick Facts about the Carpet Industry." *The Carpet and Rug Institute*. http://www.carpet-rug.org/carpet-statistics.html.

Fitzgerald, David Scott. 2013. "Immigrant Impacts in Mexico. A Tale of Dissimilation." In *How Immigrants Impact Their Homelands*, edited by Susan Eckstein, and Adil Najam, 114–137. Durham, NC: Duke University Press.

Foley, Elise. 2017. "Judge Sides with Dreamers over In-State Tuition in Georgia." *Huffington Post*. January 4. http://www.huffingtonpost.com/entry/georgia-daca-tuition_us_586d1d1ae4b0de3a08fa5bb4.

Gándara, Patricia. 2016. "Policy Report-Informe: The Students We Share-L@s Estudiantes que Compartimos." *Mexican Studies/Estudios Mexicanos* 32 (2): 357–378.

Georgia Department of Education. 2018. "Enrollment by Ethnicity/Race, Gender and Grade Level (PK-12)." https://app3.doe.k12.ga.us/ows-bin/owa/fte_pack_ethnicsex.entry_form.

Giorguli, Silvia, and Itzam Serratos López. 2009. "El impacto de la migración internacional sobre la asistencia escolar, ¿paradojas de la migración?." In *El Estado de la migración. Las políticas públicas ante los retos de la migración mexicana a Estados Unidos*, edited by P. Leite and S. E. Giorguli, 313–344. Ciudad de México: Consejo Nacional de Población.

Giorguli Saucedo, Silvia and Edith Y. Gutiérrez. 2012. "Children and Youth in the Context of International Mobility in Mexico." Paper presented at the Annual Conference of the Population Association of America, San Francisco, CA.

Golash-Boza, Tanya, and Yahaira Ceciliano-Navarro. 2019. "Life After Deportation." *Contexts* 18 (2): 30–35.

Gonzales, Roberto G. 2016. *Lives in Limbo: Undocumented and Coming of Age in America*. Berkeley: University of California Press.

Gordon, Milton M. 1964. *Assimilation in American Life: The Role of Race, Religion, and National Origins*. New York: Oxford University Press.

Hagan, Jacqueline M., Rubén Hernández-León, and Jean-Luc Demonsant. 2015. *Skills of the "Unskilled": Work and Mobility among Mexican Migrants*. Berkeley: University of California Press.

Hamann, Edmund T. 2003. *The Educational Welcome of Latinos in the New South*. Westport, CT: Praeger.

Hamann, Edmund T., and Víctor Zúñiga. 2011. "Schooling, National Affinity(ies), and Transnational Students in Mexico." In *Hyphenated Selves: Construction, Negotiation and Mediation of Immigrant Identity Within Schools – Transnational Dialogues*, edited by Saloshna Vandeyar, 57–72. Pretoria: Rozenberg Publishers/University of South Africa Press.

Hernández-León, Rubén, and Sarah Morando Lakhani. 2013. "Gender, Bilingualism, and the Early Occupational Careers of Second-Generation Mexicans in the South." *Social Forces* 92 (1): 59–80.

Hernández-León, Rubén, and Víctor Zúñiga. 2000. "'Making Carpet by the Mile': The Emergence of a Mexican Immigrant Community in an Industrial Region of the U.S. Historic South." *Social Science Quarterly* 81 (1): 49–66.

Hernández-León, Rubén, and Víctor Zúñiga. 2005. "Appalachia Meets Aztlán: Mexican Immigration and Intergroup Relations in Dalton, Georgia." In *New Destinations: Mexican Immigration in the United States*, edited by Víctor Zúñiga, and Rubén Hernández-León, 244–273. New York: Russell Sage Foundation.

Hernández-León, Rubén, and Víctor Zúñiga. 2016. "Introduction to the Special Issue: Contemporary Return Migration From the United States to Mexico—Focus on Children, Youth, Schools and Families." *Mexican Studies/Estudios Mexicanos* 32 (2): 171–181.

Jacobo Suárez, Mónica. 2017. "De regreso a 'casa' y sin apostilla: estudiantes mexicoamericanos en México." *Sinéctica* 48. https://sinectica.iteso.mx/index.php/SINECTICA/article/view/712.

Jensen, Bryant, Silvia Giorguli, and Eduardo Hernández Padilla. 2018. "International Migration and the Academic Performance of Mexican Adolescents." *International Migration Review* 52 (2): 559–596.

Kim, Jaeeun. 2018. "Migration-Facilitating Capital: A Bourdeusian Theory of International Migration." *Sociological Theory* 36 (3): 262–288.

Mahmud, Hasan. 2015. "Migrants' Remitting Beyond Altruism and Self-interest: A Study of Remitting Practices among Bangladeshi Migrants in Tokyo and Los Angeles." PhD diss. University of California, Los Angeles.

Morawska, Ewa. 2005. *International Migration Research. Constructions, Omissions and the Promises of Interdisciplinarity*. London: Routledge.

Olvera, José Juan, and Carolina Muela. 2016. "Sin familia en México: redes sociales alternativas para la migración de retorno de jóvenes deportados con experiencia carcelaria en Texas." *Mexican Studies/Estudios Mexicanos* 32 (2): 302–327.

Panait, Catalina, and Víctor Zúñiga. 2016. "Children Circulating Between the U.S. and Mexico: Fractured Schooling and Linguistic Ruptures." *Mexican Studies/Estudios Mexicanos* 32 (2): 226–251.

Patton, Randal. 1999. *Carpet Capital: The Rise of a New South Industry*. Athens, GA: University of Georgia Press.

Portes, Alejandro, and Min Zhou. 1993. "The New Second Generation: Segmented Assimilation and its Variants." *The Annals of the American Academy of Political and Social Science* 530: 74–96.

Román González, Betsabé, Eduardo Carrillo Cantú, and Rubén Hernández-León. 2016. "Moving to the 'Homeland': Children's Narratives of Migration From the United States to Mexico." *Mexican Studies/Estudios Mexicanos* 32 (2): 252–275.

Rose, Joel. 2018. "Why Employers in Georgia Are Watching the Immigration Reform Debate Closely." *National Public Radio*. February 19. https://www.npr.org/2018/02/19/585770437/why-employers-in-georgia-are-watching-the-mmigration debate-closely.

Rosen, Jonathan D., and José Miguel Cruz. 2018. "Overcoming Stigma and Discrimination: Challenges for Reinsertion of Gang Members in Developing Countries." *International Journal of Offender Therapy and Comparative Criminology* 62 (15): 4758–4775.

Sánchez García, Juan, and Edmund T. Hamann. 2016. "Educator Responses to Migrant Children in Mexican Schools." *Mexican Studies/Estudios Mexicanos* 32 (2): 199–225.

Sloan, Kim. 2008. "Whitfield County Georgia 287(g) Now Operational." *Dalton Citizen News*. June 11. Available at: https://ncvoiceblog.wordpress.com/2008/06/12/whitfield-county-georgia-287g-now-operational/.

Su, Phi Hong. 2018. "Cold War Coethnics: Nationhood and Belonging among Vietnamese Immigrants and Refugees in Berlin." PhD diss., University of California, Los Angeles.

Tsuda, Takeyuki. 2003. *Strangers in the Ethnic Homeland: Japanese Brazilian Return Migration in Transnational Perspective*. New York: Columbia University Press.

Vadean, Florin P., and Matloob Piracha. 2009. "Circular Migration or Permanent Return: What Determines Different Forms of Migration?" *Frontiers of Economics and Globalization* 8 (4287): 467–495.

Veale, Angela. 2014. "Complex Migrations, Migrant Child and Family Life Trajectories and Globalization." In *Child and Youth Migration Mobility-in-Migration in an Era of Globalization*, edited by A. Veale, and G. Dona, 1–20. London: Palgrave Macmillan.

Waldinger, Roger. 2015. *The Cross-Border Connection: Immigrants, Emigrants, and Their Homelands*. Cambridge, MA: Harvard University Press.

Waldinger, Roger, and Thomas D Soehl. 2010. "The Political Sociology of International Migration: Borders, Boundaries, Rights and Politics." In *The International Handbook of Migration Studies*, edited by S. Gold, and S. Nawn, 334–344. London: Routledge.

Wyman, Mark. 1993. *Round Trip to America: The Immigrants Return to Europe, 1880-1930*. Ithaca, NY: Cornell University Press.

Zúñiga, Víctor. 2018. "The 0.5 Generation: What Children Know About International Migration." *Migraciones Internacionales* 10 (1): 93–120.

Zúñiga, Víctor, and Silvia E. Giorguli. 2018. *Niñas y niños en la migración de Estados Unidos a México: la generación 0.5*. Ciudad de México: El Colegio de México.

Zuñiga, Víctor, and E. T. Hamann. 2013. "Understanding American-Mexican Children." In *Regarding Educación: Mexican-American Schooling, Immigration, and Bi-National Improvement*, edited by Bryant Jensen, and Adam Sawyer, 172–188. New York: Teacher College Press: Columbia University.

Hope turned sour: second-generation incorporation and mobility in U.S. new immigrant destinations

Helen B. Marrow

ABSTRACT

The number and size of "new immigrant destinations" (NIDs) in the United States grew quickly over the 1990s and 2000s, but Latino newcomers residing in them witnessed a profound negative turn in institutional and political reception after 2005. The present article takes stock of the causes and consequences of this shift, showing how intensifying enforcement and exclusionary policy-making at the federal and state levels after 2005 stoked anti-immigrant sentiment and institutional closure in many NIDs, especially in the South. Though the Latino "second generation" is just now beginning to come of age and to enter the workforce in NIDs, offering new opportunities for data collection and analysis going forward, the extant literature suggests that this shift has significantly weakened its prospects for structural incorporation and upward economic mobility, which are now strongly stratified by citizenship and legal status.

Introduction: the Latino second generation in new U.S. immigrant destinations

At the end of the twentieth century, the geographic dispersal of immigrants away from traditional urban gateways toward "new" rural and suburban destinations took many American immigration scholars by surprise (Gozdziak and Martin 2005; Singer, Hardwick, and Brettell 2008). By definition, "new immigrant destinations" (NIDs) have little prior historical experience with immigration, though some did host large shares of immigrants back in the early 1900s. Initially, most arrivals to new destinations were adult Mexican immigrant and Mexican American labourers who were "pushed" out of California and the U.S. Southwest by increased border enforcement and anti-immigrant sentiment, and "pulled" into growing construction, service, and manufacturing economies, during the 1980s and 1990s, often recruited directly by employers and contractors or indirectly through their own social networks (Hernández-León and Zúñiga 2003; Johnson-Webb 2003; Leach and Bean 2008).

Over time, these migrants began to send for family abroad, form new families, and have children in the United States. This was partially the result of maturing migration flows, including the "settling out" of both unauthorized immigrants and temporary agricultural labourers into local populations (Dunn, Aragonés, and Shivers 2005; Griffith 2008). But it was also due to changing political incentives that encouraged settlement, including the *Immigration Reform and Control Act (IRCA)* of 1986, which granted amnesty to long-term unauthorized residents and seasonal farmworkers, plus ongoing efforts to fortify the U.S.-Mexico border after the mid-1990s, which made it more costly for immigrants to return home thereafter (Massey, Durand, and Malone 2002; Massey 2008). By 2005, more than half of total Hispanic population growth in nonmetropolitan America already came from U.S. births rather than immigration (Johnson and Lichter 2008).

Scholars have faced several methodological challenges in constructing large, viable, representative samples of this "second generation" in NIDs, who are typically defined as U.S.-born individuals born to one or more immigrant parents (the true "second" generation) plus foreign-born youth who arrive early in life (the "1.5-generation"). One challenge is that NIDs tend to be smaller in size and more geographically dispersed than traditional gateways. Migration into NIDs also did not peak until the 1990s, which means many children did not arrive, or were not born, until recently. Contrast this with the model large-scale studies of the U.S. second generation (Portes and Rumbaut 2001; Kasinitz et al. 2008; Suárez-Orozco, Suárez-Orozco, and Todorova 2008; Telles and Ortiz 2008; Bean, Brown, and Bachmeier 2015; Luthra, Soehl, and Waldinger 2018) who were able to sample children from families who had arrived earlier (typically after 1965) and clustered in more densely populated metropolitan regions.

Consequently, most of the research on NIDs still centres on the adult first generation. Not only are there few studies which examine their second-generation children, but those that do typically utilize nonrandom and nonrepresentative samples, especially in places where immigrants are heavily concentrated. There is certainly value in focusing energy on such locales. For example, just eight percent of midwestern counties and 10 percent of southern counties accounted for over half of nonmetropolitan Hispanic population growth in each region, respectively, in the 2000s (Lichter 2012). Still, we know that such samples do not capture the full range of second-generation experiences across all NIDs, and that local area of settlement is likely correlated with various outcomes of interest in the second generation (Kasinitz et al. 2008).

In the present article, I call for more scholarship on the Latino second generation in new destinations. But given the focus of this special volume – "Children of Immigrants in the Age of Deportation: The Evidence and the Consequences" – I also wish to draw scholarly attention to an important shift that took place in many NIDs, especially southern ones, after 2005, that transformed their political and institutional receiving contexts from neutral, ambivalent, and sometimes even welcoming to decidedly hostile. Building on new studies that have already started to document the deleterious effects of this shift on immigrant adults, I argue scholars should begin tracing its downstream effects on their children, too.

In what follows, I start by explaining how this critical shift came about, initially stoked and inspired by the "symbolic politics" of *federal* debate over immigration in 2005–2006 and U.S. states' responses to it (Ovink, Ebert, and Okamoto 2016). I show how over time a host of restrictive laws and policies at the federal level combined with new exclusionary ones passed by politicians in various NID states, especially in the South, effectively "reversing" Latino immigrants' prior economic gains (Jones 2018) and "crystallizing" the symbolic and substantive boundaries between Latino immigrants and their U.S.-born neighbours (López-Sanders 2017). Next, I overview key findings from existing studies on the Latino 1.5 and second generation in NIDs, which have become more pessimistic in their prognostications over this time period. Though still few in number, these studies demonstrate how restrictive U.S. law and policy have weakened Latino youth's prospects for structural incorporation and upward economic mobility in NIDs, and exacerbated stratification by citizenship and legal status. I conclude by offering suggestions for how future research can collect more empirical data on the Latino second generation in NIDs and use the findings to link variations in outcomes to variations in legal and policy contexts across time and space.

Big events, crises, and shocks: reverse incorporation in new immigrant destinations

Due to spatial–temporal correlations between immigrants' period of entry, legal status, and settlement patterns at the end of the twentieth century, new immigrant destinations (NIDs) have relatively high proportions of unauthorized immigrants among their total foreign-born populations (Passel 2005; Passel and Cohn 2009). Consequently, lack of legal status is a salient characteristic of most NID communities not merely at an *individual* level, but also a *group* level. In a segmented assimilation model, this represents a forceful interweaving of negative governmental, economic, and social "contexts of reception" (Portes and Rumbaut 2014) facing immigrants in NIDs—especially rural NIDs where immigrants tend to be more heavily Mexican and more socioeconomically and linguistically disadvantaged (Torres, Popke, and Hapke 2006). Accordingly, even if some individual migrants have legal status or U.S. citizenship, high proportions of their families and surrounding coethnic communities do not, weakening the latter's ability to serve as protective resources (Portes and Rumbaut 2001). Alternately, in a revised assimilation framework, high rates of a group's unauthorized status lower its individual members' starting points for achieving economic success, social inclusion, and political representation. This shapes both the proximal and distal causal mechanisms underlying assimilation, simultaneously weakening immigrants' available capital in NIDs and hardening the rules and laws under which they must make their everyday decisions about work, education, and civic activity (Alba and Nee 2003; Marrow 2013).

Further, many NIDs experienced an acute negative turn in institutional and political receiving context after 2005 (Marrow 2011; 2017). The shift grew neither organically out of continued immigrant population growth in NIDs, nor out of isolated local shifts in public opinion. Rather, scholars now point to the high-profile political debate that took place at the *federal* level that year, which served to *activate* and/or *amplify* restrictive attitudes and behaviours at state and local levels (Ovink, Ebert, and Okamoto 2016; Jones and Brown 2019). In December 2005, the U.S. House of Representatives passed the *Border Protection, Antiterrorism and Illegal Immigration Control Act* (H.R. 4437), which proposed increasing penalties for employers who hired undocumented workers, dramatically extending fencing along the U.S.-Mexico border, and making unlawful presence a felony (as opposed to a civil offense). Though it ultimately died in the U.S. Senate and never became federal law, H.R. 4437 sparked a massive immigrant protest movement across the country that culminated between March and May 2006 (Portes and Rumbaut 2014), plus a wave of state-level restrictive policymaking that would intensify over the next several years (Ovink, Ebert, and Okamoto 2016).

While most of the 150 immigrant rights' marches associated with the former took place in large immigrant gateways, some also took place in new destinations like Omaha, Nebraska and Gulfport, Mississippi (Benajmin-Alvarado, DeSipio, and Montoya 2009). Scholars working on the ground in NIDs documented an immediate shift. Prior to the marches, for instance, Latinos in Greenville, South Carolina had perceived that they were "favored and wanted" over U.S.-born workers. Even as they suffered exploitation at work (Griffith 1995; Striffler 2005; Stuesse 2016), they were nonetheless viewed as "efficient" and "hard" workers, and employers referred to them as "God-sent people" (López-Sanders 2017). In a parallel covert ethnography of white and black South Carolinians, McDermott (2011b; 2016) concurred. Through 2005, whites in Greenville were largely "confused" about who Latinos were. Not only did they sometimes describe Latinos as "Greek, Indian, Chinese, White, and Black", alongside "Hispanic" and "Mexican"; their attitudes toward Latinos also leaned more paternalistic, compared to their more outwardly prejudicial attitudes toward blacks. Blacks were somewhat more hostile toward Latinos overall, with the exception of the black lower-middle class, who saw in them potential employment opportunities (McDermott 2011a).

However, close to 2,500 immigrants' rights protestors made their way through downtown Greenville on April 10, 2006, bringing traffic to a standstill (López-Sanders and Brown 2019). Although white bystanders observing the march were not visibly angry or impatient, McDermott did note "shock", "stony silence", and "stares" (2011b; 2016). In the midst of salient national media coverage of the marches, plus polarized federal political discourse over immigration (Hopkins 2010; López-Sanders and Brown 2019), she argued this was the key moment in which whites' formerly more diffuse and confused attitudes toward Latinos there quickly morphed into racialization, resentment, and threat. They began referring to all Hispanics as "Mexicans" and "illegals", and blacks' hostile reactions hardened further. Then, on April 26, less than three weeks after the initial march, white protesters, took to the streets in a nativist counter-protest organized by the South Carolina Council of Conservative Citizens (CoCC), burning Mexican flags and railing against Latinos as job stealers, fiscal sponges, linguistic threats, criminals, and terrorists. Even media portrayals of immigration began to shift. After 2005, English-language media in South Carolina would increasingly present "Mexicans" as a cultural threat, while its counterparts in other southern states would increasingly characterize "Hispanics/Latinos" as either criminals or hard workers, utilizing few alternative narratives (López-Sanders and Brown 2019; also Vaquera, Aranda, and Gonzales 2014; Brown, Jones, and Becker 2018). In 2009, McDermott returned to find both white and black South Carolinians angry and venting that "illegals" had taken their jobs.[1]

Latinos in NIDs felt these changes intimately. In the Greenville plant where López-Sanders (2017) worked, some were threatened with termination by their employers and managers if they dared to miss work to participate in the marches. U.S.-born workers also began talking about and querying their Latino immigrant coworkers openly about legal status, which made the latter feel humiliated, embarrassed, and fearful. "[White] Americans don't like us anymore", one told López-Sanders. So too did a Mexican immigrant in Winston-Salem, North Carolina tell Jones (2018):

> People that have been here even longer [than I] used to say that back in the 1990s when someone saw a Hispanic, the first reaction was curiosity. "Hey, how are you?" You know? It was "Good! Hey! So strange to see anyone here!" The treatment was different ... Hispanic ... has a negative connotation now. Hispanic is illegal unauthorized, poor, nothing to offer the society, criminal gangster (19).

Public and private discussion of Latino immigration shifted dramatically in rural eastern North Carolina, too, where upon returning in 2008, one white respondent told Marrow (2011) "the things I now hear being said [by whites] about Hispanics, you didn't even use to hear being said [by whites] about blacks". Another white resident even "joked" that the easiest way to "deal" with rising numbers of Hispanic newcomers might be to "line them up" in one of the area's large fields "and let the deer hunters take care of 'em (247-48)."

But the rapid shift in attitudes toward Latinos tells only part of the story. After the failure of H.R. 4437 in 2005, U.S. states also responded behaviourally. Ovink, Ebert, and Okamoto (2016) draw on Blumer's (1958) assertion that "big events" are key for developing and/or activating group prejudice by "set[ting] crucial issues in the arena of public discussion (3)." Using a subset of the State Immigration Legislation data set on all state-level bills related to policies regarding in-state tuition for going to college between 1996 and 2010, they found that, consistent with Blumer's expectations, it was not until *after* the failure of H.R. 4437 and the subsequent 2006 immigrant rights' protests that various U.S. states began to pass restrictive legislation toward undocumented immigrants in this domain. Also consistent with Blumer's expectations, the found that exclusive policymaking was most likely to come out of states with small shares of immigrants (i.e. "new destinations") and strong conservative voter constituencies (e.g. largely in the South).

Ovink et al. interpreted their results as suggesting that the "big event" of H.R. 4437s passage and failure introduced, made more salient, and significantly changed the meaning of the *national* debate over undocumented immigration in 2005. States' demographic and political characteristics then worked to *moderate* this main effect thereafter, such that the number of restrictive state bills surrounding in-state tuition increased noticeably in 2007–2008 nationwide, but *especially* in more conservative NID states, some of whom moved to eliminate unauthorized immigrants' access to higher education entirely (Flores and Chapa 2009; Yablon-Zug and Holley-Walker 2009).[2] Using a symbolic politics approach, Ovink et al. reason that politicians in NID states began putting forward restrictive bills after 2005 as one way of signalling to their constituents that they either agreed with, or were at least being attentive to, the failed federal legislation.

Several other exclusionary laws and policies toward immigrants, especially undocumented ones, gained momentum at the federal and state levels during this same time period (Quiroga, Medina, and Glick 2014; Browne, Reingold, and Kronberg 2018). Whereas interior immigration enforcement had been relatively lax in new destinations prior to 2005, it began ramping up after, especially in the South. As one example, "287(g)" refers to a programme named for Section 287(g) of the 1996 *Illegal Immigration Reform and Immigrant Responsibility Act* that allowed for state and local police to be "cross-deputized" through a variety of formalized "memoranda of understanding" so that they can better engage in the work of federal immigration enforcement (Provine et al. 2016; Armenta 2017a). While Florida and Alabama were the first states to sign 287(g) agreements, in 2002 and 2003, respectively, it wasn't until January 2006 that 67 local law enforcement agencies around the country began to join in, with North Carolina and Virginia taking the lead (Nguyen and Gill 2010; Coleman 2012; Marrow 2017).

In addition, after 2005 many states began passing tightening their requirements for obtaining driver's licenses and state identification cards. Some had already been experimenting with tighter regulations before 2005; for example, in late 2003 North Carolina passed legislation eliminating applicants' ability to present a Mexican national identification card (*matricula consular*) or any foreign birth certificate issued outside the United States as an adequate form of documentation for applying for a state driver's license (Marrow 2011, 218). However, following the failure of H.R. 4437 in 2005, and further buttressed by passage of the federal REAL ID Act in that same year—which would begin a gradual elimination of unauthorized immigrants' access to driver's licenses nationwide by institutionalizing the requirement of a social security number[3]— in August 2006 North Carolina passed the even more restrictive N.C. Senate Bill 602, known as the *Technical Corrections Act*. This bill further eliminated applicants' ability to use an individual tax identification number (ITIN) as an alternative to the social security number (Denning 2009). Consequently, just as state and local police were starting to cross-deputize *en masse*, many Latinos in North Carolina lost the ability to apply for and renew their state driver's licenses. Not surprisingly, fears of surveillance and deportation intensified (Gill et al. 2009; Marrow 2011; Jones 2018).

By the end of the decade, several states even began issuing restrictive "omnibus" bills targeting immigrants in multiple domains at once. A critical domain was employment. In the wake of H.R. 4437s failure, and this time buttressed by then President George W. Bush's expansion the federal *E-Verify* programme into all 50 states in 2007 (NILC 2011),[4] various states began to put forth policies, both stand-alone and as part of larger omnibus bills, trying to expand the programme's reach at the state level or make its usage mandatory (e.g. Marrow 2011, 248–50; Jones and Brown 2019). In South Carolina, for example, the *Illegal Immigration Reform Act (IIRA),* passed in 2008, expanded E-Verify into private workplaces with more than 100 employees. Though not mandatory and technically only applicable to new hires, local media coverage erroneously framed it as mandatory, and several employers, out of confusion, opted for early system implementation and retroactively submitted all their employees' information into the system. The "extent and rapidity" with which E-Verify had materialized into job loss "shocked" the Hispanic immigrant community in Greenville, South Carolina (López-Sanders 2017).

Indeed, López-Sanders argues heightened workplace enforcement and implementation of E-Verify are the two policy "crises" that have hurt Latinos in Greenville most harshly. During previous policy "shocks" in 2006 and 2007, Latinos had been partially successful at holding onto their "hardworker" identities for esteem and support. But once additional "changes in the law" took away their ability to work in 2008 and 2009,[5] they entered a "relentless downward spiral". Even members of formerly "thriving" communities she had observed as stable and upwardly mobile in 2005–2006, who had even been admired by U.S.-born community members for their resourcefulness and solidarity, now struggled with depression and isolation. One told her, "First came the rallies, but then the laws changed and things really got screwed up. [...] Many people lost their jobs. ... Not anymore, they don't want us anymore".

Jones (2018) agrees that the most impactful legacy of H.R. 4437 in southern NIDs is not merely the dramatic change in public sentiment, but its codification into formal law and policy at both the federal and state levels. Before 2006, Latinos' opportunities for building capital in Winston-Salem, North Carolina were still relatively plentiful—even though, of course discrimination, racism, and exploitation certainly existed, and even though legal status already stratified their employment opportunities and access to institutional resources, too. Specifically, banks still provided credit union loans, community colleges still provided adult English as a Second Language (ESL) courses, cooperatives still targeted Latinos for small business loans, and undocumented immigrants could still apply for work, driver's licenses, bank accounts, trailers, homes, and vehicles (Jones 2018). Often Latinos even encountered teachers, librarians, and other community members in NIDs who "helped" them navigate complex organizations and bureaucracies (Marrow 2011).

However, as more restrictive federal and North Carolina laws and policies were passed after 2006, what Jones calls "institutional and bureaucratic closure" set in. Suddenly, many of her Latino subjects could not do basic things like take out loans for credit or purchase cars. Their fears of surveillance by local police intensified, as did their perceptions of institutional and interpersonal mistreatment (also Fernández-Kelly 2019; Ribas 2016; Armenta 2017b). Many began to circumscribe their daily activities; some lost their jobs when they could not get to work. In just a few years' time, therefore, Latinos' economic, educational, and employment gains were "reversed", and the unauthorized were hardest hit. However, even their legal and U.S. citizen family members were impacted indirectly, such as when one welfare caseworker blocked a Latina's immigrant's U.S.-born, U.S.-citizen daughter from enrolling in both the Supplemental Nutrition Assistance Programme (SNAP) and the Special Supplemental Nutrition Programme for Women, Infants, and Children (WIC)—two programmes to which the child is legally entitled—because the mother did not have a social security number. "Many doors are closed to me now (19)," she told Jones.

To be sure, it would be an overstatement to say there were no local efforts to crack down on immigration in NIDs before 2005 (Lattanzi Shutika 2011; Luebke 2011; Winders 2013). But the failure of H.R. 4437 at the federal level still amplified state-level attention to such cases. For example, several anti-immigration efforts and discourses were already prominent in Alabama by the early 2000s, where Jones and Brown (2019) show local leaders worked to position Latinos as criminals, dependents, and inferiors, and pursued surveillance strategies based upon those frames (e.g. joining early 287(g) programmes). But starting in 2006, state politicians responded to the federal landscape by moving local anti-immigration policy-making consistently to the fore. The result was a "cascade of punitive, racializing policies that would culminate" in passage of the omnibus Alabama House Bill 56 in 2011 (541).

Implications of reverse incorporation for Latino youth

Though few studies have examined the impact of this shift on Latino youth directly, already the NID literature has become more pessimistic in tone. Prior to 2005, several studies of first-generation immigrants had documented enough economic stability and capital accumulation to be cautiously optimistic about their children's chances for achieving further upward mobility (Hernández-León and Zúñiga 2005; Striffler 2005; Marrow 2011). In Omaha, Nebraska, for instance, some 1.5- and second-generation Latino children had made substantial educational and occupational progress over the positions of their parents by 2004–2005 (Gouveia and Powell 2007). In Dalton, Georgia, second-generation Mexican Americans had effectively leveraged their educational credentials and bicultural and bilingual skills to access better jobs and make significant progress over the positions of their immigrant parents; by the late 2000s, some were employed in white-collar jobs in insurance firms and banks, while others were employed in supervisory and trainer positions in the immigrant-heavy carpet manufacturing niche (Hernández-León and Lakhani 2013). In New York City—a new destination for Mexicans even though a long-standing immigrant gateway—some second-generation Mexican young adults, especially women, had achieved upward economic mobility by the mid 2000s, many assuming "pink-collar" service sector positions like medical and legal secretaries or travel agents, which offered benefits and "clean work" (Smith 2005; n.d.). And in Greenville, South Carolina, McDermott (2016) still reasoned that the "prospects of a linguistically and culturally assimilated second generation" in Greenville, South Carolina were "strong", drawing on evidence she uncovered of their substantial structural integration with whites, plus positive institutional responses underway in area schools (also Jones-Correa 2008; Marrow 2011; Dondero and Muller 2012; Marschall 2017).

Taken together, revised assimilation scholars call such findings evidence of "short-distance" upward mobility (Alba and Nee 2003; Waldinger and Feliciano 2004). But the same studies simultaneously demonstrate how Latino youth's opportunities are stratified in NIDs by local economic context, citizenship, legal status, timing/cohort of arrival, and gender. Tellingly, the most successful youth appear to be members of *earlier* immigrant cohorts who have had the opportunity to obtain legal status or U.S. citizenship. The Mexican American young adults doing best in New York City, for instance, had immigrant parents who arrived during the 1980s and early 1990s, with greater opportunity to enter the country legally or legalize their status following IRCA (Smith n.d). By the time these youth reached early to mid-adulthood, they were doing much better than their counterparts whose parents had arrived later in the 2000s and 2010s and who—like many immigrants in other NIDs (e.g. Lattanzi Shutika 2011)—are more likely to be unauthorized and to lack similar opportunities to change status.

Scholars' prognostications have also become more guarded since 2006. Hernández-León and Lakhani (2013), for example, now suspect that the bilingual skills of upwardly-mobile Mexican Americans in Dalton, Georgia, may be valuable in part because these youth are still relatively unencumbered by coethnic competition, which could grow as children of later immigrant arrivals come of age and enter the workforce. They also worry that Dalton will continue to deindustrialize following the 2008 Global Recession, further constricting opportunity in carpet manufacturing where first- and second-generation Mexican men used to find plentiful jobs. In Omaha, Nebraska, Gouveia and Powell couched their optimism about second-generation Latinos' futures with an admonition that this path could be thwarted by a "growing climate of rejection toward Hispanics", which they already sensed was on the horizon. In both rural Montana (Schmalzbauer 2014) and "Allen Creek", North Carolina (Silver 2012; 2018), many Latino youth still consider their schools safe havens and have formed "special bonds" with their teachers, but they also feel structurally and geographically limited by their unauthorized status. After graduation, some in "Allen Creek" (a pseudonym) have joined their parents in local manufacturing plants or sought work in restaurants or domestic service, while their teachers, coaches, and employers have felt their "hands tied" from helping further. And in Washington state, the Latino youth most likely to be thriving by the late 2010s were U.S.-born and legal immigrants, whereas those without legal status, especially men, were encountering more barriers to completing primary education, moving on to higher education, and securing good jobs (Gonzales and Ruiz 2014).[6]

While few in number, these studies demonstrate how U.S. law and policy now stratify Latino youth's mobility pathways in NIDs much like they do in urban gateways (Abrego 2006; Gonzales 2015). Perhaps they even do so more acutely, given NID's high rates of unauthorized status and harsh restrictive turns since 2005. Research shows Latino youth in NIDs often have to serve as brokers, interpreters, teachers, and tutors for their parents and siblings. They often miss school to help their families and forego critical benefits and services (like free or reduced school lunch) to protect their family members from being discovered by immigration authorities. Deteriorating receptiveness has even increased interpersonal racism against them, making them "hyperaware" of legal status at very early ages and bringing on signs of acute stress, chronic anxiety, and fear of surveillance (Gonzales and Ruiz 2014; Schmalzbauer 2014). In turn, these health concerns have been linked to lower academic and work aspirations, and heightened senses of loneliness and isolation, among youth in a variety of NIDs (see Gándara 2019; Perreira, Fuligni, and Potochnick 2010; Perreira and Brietzke 2019; Spees, Perreira, and Fuligni 2017; Abrego and Schmalzbauer 2018).

Indeed, Dreby (2015) intimately demonstrates how restriction and enforcement have turned unauthorized status into a more consequential axis of social stratification since 2005, not merely for Latino adults but also youth. In 2009, she returned to New Jersey, a traditional gateway where she had conducted research for her first book in 2003. She was surprised to find that the experience of illegality felt qualitatively different in just six years. Mexican children there, plus those living in her comparison NID fieldsite of Ohio, now lived "hyperaware" of their own legal statuses plus those of their parents and siblings, years before social structures typically begin making them prohibitive. As in Montana and Washington, the youth showed signs of severe physical and emotional anxiety, stress, and sickness. Legal status now stratified almost everything about their lives, from day-to-day activities and contributions to household labour, to school performance and considerations about work and careers. It even stratified their identities; those without legal status felt most excluded not only from the United States but also Mexico. In both locales, Dreby reported a "culture of fear" had developed so intensely she deemed it a public health concern.

Of course, not all NIDs are the same, so the pathways to adulthood that 1.5- and second-generation Latino youth traverse will vary across them. Some NID states and localities have tried to push back against restrictive trends with more institute incorporative policies and laws. These do help "temper" (Cebulko and Silver 2016) and "mediate" (Martínez 2014) Latino youth's experiences of marginalization. In Colorado and Washington, for example, incorporative in-state tuition policies have helped some unauthorized Latino youth—notably, students who have been granted discretionary status, work permits, and temporary protection from deportation under the federal *Deferred Action for Childhood Arrivals (DACA)* executive order signed by then President Barack Obama in June 2012—get into college. DACA beneficiaries' experiences in such contexts are markedly more positive than those of DACA beneficiaries living in conservative southern states, where college-educated Latinos now experience great difficulty finding work if they are unauthorized (López-Sanders 2017), where DACA beneficiaries show signs of depressed aspirations (López-Sanders 2017), and where Latino youth feel more frustrated, excluded, and fearful of interacting with police and government officials (Cebulko and Silver 2016).

Conclusion

The Latino second generation is just now beginning to come of age and to enter the workforce in U.S. new immigrant destinations. While most scholarship still centres squarely on the adult first generation, the extant literature suggests that that H.R. 4437 functioned as a "big event" (Ovink, Ebert, and Okamoto 2016) that hardened public opinion against, plus initiated and amplified restrictive state and local restrictive policymaking toward, Latino immigrants in many NIDs, especially in the South. From a segmented assimilation perspective, this shift marked a distinct change in the modes of incorporation confronting first-generation Latino arrivals to NIDs, increasing in the possibility for economic stagnation, and possibly even downward assimilation (Portes and Rumbaut 2001; 2014), among their children (Dreby 2015; López-Sanders 2017; Jones 2018; Silver 2018). Similarly, from a revised assimilation perspective, it highlighted a re-assertion of "bright" boundaries (Alba and Nee 2003; Alba 2005) demarcating Latino arrivals and their children from the more established "native" social and cultural American "mainstreams" of many new destinations, where scholars had documented "blurrier" boundaries as recently as fifteen years ago (Marrow 2011; McDermott 2016).

Indeed, recent studies show that more Latino children in small towns and rural areas are already growing up poor and in more segregated neighbourhoods than two decades ago (Ellis, Wright, and Townley 2013; Crowley, Lichter, and Turner 2015; Lichter, Sanders, and Johnson 2015; Lichter, Parisi, and Taquino 2016). In this hostile context, Latino youth living in NIDs without legal status are especially likely to see their fortunes decline and feel they do not belong to the nation-state (Silver 2018, 149–52). The intensification of detention and deportation efforts has even left some of them to grow up alone (Saslow and Chavez 2018) or in newly single-parent households (Dreby 2012), simultaneously pushing many Latino leaders and activists in NIDs like Knoxville, Tennessee, who would otherwise advocate for them, underground (Shefner 2019). More immigrants and their children, both foreign- and U.S.-born, are even involuntarily returning to Latin America from NIDs as part of a growing "American diaspora" (Kanstroom 2012; also Golash-Boza 2015; Hagan, Leal, and Rodriguez 2015; Cardoso et al. 2016; Isaacs and Preston 2018).[7]

This suggests the time is ripe for collecting new, larger, and reasonably representative samples of 1.5- and second-generation youth in NIDs, and for integrating their results within the larger immigrant incorporation literature. For example, the present review shows that scholars working in NIDs already recognize, at least implicitly, that models of intergenerational incorporation must account for *temporal context* and *historical cohort*—the precise time periods in which immigrant arrive and/or their descendants are born— in addition to the traditional measure of *generation-since-immigration*

(Telles and Ortiz 2008; Jiménez 2010). Thus, new studies will do well to continue contextualizing findings on Latino youth's experiences and outcomes in NIDs in light of the "big event" of H.R. 4437s passage and failure in 2005, plus the various "shocks" and "crises" (López-Sanders 2017) that policymakers' responses to it have brought about, ranging from federal immigration raids and the rise of local cross-deputization agreements through the late 2000s, to federal and state closures to Latinos' opportunities to work, drive, go to school, and build capital.

Doing so could even contribute to the larger body of scholarship working to model the long-term negative consequences of restrictive law and policy on Latinos' lives, largely from the vantage point of traditional gateways. In Los Angeles, Bean, Brown, and Bachmeier (2015) have shown that a Mexican immigrant's unauthorized status, a political position manufactured by U.S. law, depresses not only their own educational attainment but also that of their children and even grandchildren, thereby contributing to cumulative intergenerational disadvantage and "working-class delay". The present review shows that Latino youth's experiences and opportunities in NIDs are also strongly stratified by citizenship and legal status, and that restrictive laws and policies passed since 2005 have arguably exacerbated this stratification, resulting in large financial losses and intense psychological and physical trauma among Latino families that some scholars argue are unlikely to ever be fully recouped—even in the second generation and perhaps even with the cushion of U.S. citizenship (López-Sanders 2017; Jones 2018). Thus, new studies will do well to continue following youth who are children of earlier immigrant cohorts to NIDs and/or who have obtained legal status or U.S. citizenship, in order to collect data not only on how their paths may have shifted (or not) in recent years, but also on how their experiences and outcomes compare to those of children of newer arrivals, children who lack legal status, and/or children who have come of age in the newer, more restrictive period.

Additionally, future studies would benefit from making geographical comparisons. While a few NIDs have taken positive steps like passing in-state tuition policies to expand access to higher education, instituting local sanctuary policies, or branding themselves as "welcoming" communities, Martínez (2014) still argues that such policies merely buffer, rather than overcome, the dominant landscape of restriction and enforcement now well entrenched against undocumented immigrants nationwide, which is becoming even harsher under the Trump Presidency. Further, inclusive efforts in NIDs currently pale in comparison to those in traditional destination states and cities such as New York and California. Thus, while a swing toward inclusion in NIDs is not unimaginable (see Pastor 2018 on California), it seems unlikely. More comparative research across NID types could help collect new empirical data on variations in Latino youth's economic, educational, and health outcomes across them in ways scholars could tie directly to variations in legal and policy contexts.

Notes

1. See Flores (2014) on a similar turn in the NID of Hazelton, Pennsylvania.
2. Over time, even states with larger immigrant population shares and/or more liberal voter constituencies, who had been initially more likely to push inclusive bills, began to back off.
3. Full compliance with the REAL ID Act in all 50 states would not be achieved until the end of the 2010s, due to state pushback over funding for the mandate.
4. E-Verify was initially established in 1991 to assist employers with the processing of determination employees' eligibility for work. But prior to 2007, it had only operated as a pilot program in several traditional immigrant gateway states like California and Texas (NILC 2011).
5. Her respondents attributed their difficulties to new laws and policies, *not* the Great Recession.
6. On gender, see also Hernández-León and Lakhani (2013) and Smith (2005).
7. Early research among youth returnees in Mexico shows that those who are U.S.-born, have U.S. citizenship, and come from families with greater class sources are faring best in Mexican schools, communities, and labor markets. In contrast, those who are unauthorized and have fewer class resources are faring worst and feel the most disconnected—not only from the United States but also Mexico (Hernández-León, Lakhani, and Zúñiga 2019; also Hernández-León and Zúñiga 2016; Zúñiga and Giorguli Saucedo 2019; Zúñiga and Hamann, forthcoming).

Acknowledgments

Special thanks for research leave provided by the Faculty Research Awards Committee at Tufts University, and to Natasha Kumar Warikoo, Laura López-Sanders, Alejandro Portes, Patricia Fernández-Kelly, Krista Perreira, Rubén G. Rumbaut, Jill Weinberg, and the anonymous reviewers at *E&RS* for feedback.

Disclosure statement

No potential conflict of interest was reported by the author.

Funding

This work is supported by Tufts University.

References

Abrego, L. J. 2006. "'I Can't Go to College Because I Don't Have Papers': Incorporation Patterns of Latino Unauthorized Youth." *Latino Studies* 4 (3): 212–231.

Abrego, L. J., and L. Schmalzbauer. 2018. "Illegality, Motherhood, and Place: Unauthorized Latinas Making Meaning and Negotiating Daily Life." *Women's Studies International Forum* 67: 10–17.

Alba, R. D. 2005. "Bright vs. Blurred Boundaries: Second-Generation Assimilation and Exclusion in France, Germany, and the United States." *Ethnic and Racial Studies* 28 (1): 20–49.

Alba, R. D., and V. Nee. 2003. *Remaking the American Mainstream: Assimilation and Contemporary Immigration.* Cambridge, MA: Harvard University Press.

Armenta, A. 2017a. *Protect, Serve, and Deport: The Rise of Policing as Immigration Enforcement.* Oakland: University of California Press.

Armenta, A. 2017b. "Racializing Crimmigration: Structural Racism, Colorblindness, and the Institutional Production of Immigrant Criminality." *Sociology of Race & Ethnicity* 3 (1): 82–95.

Bean, F. D., S. K. Brown, and J. D. Bachmeier. 2015. *Parents Without Papers: The Progress and Pitfalls of Mexican American Integration.* New York: Russell Sage.

Benajmin-Alvarado, J., L. DeSipio, and C. Montoya. 2009. "Latino Mobilization in New Immigrant Destinations: The Anti-H.R. 4437 Protest in Nebraska's Cities." *Urban Affairs Review* 44 (5): 713–735.

Blumer, H. 1958. "Race Prejudice as a Sense of Group Position." *Pacific Sociological Review* 1 (1): 3–7.

Brown, H. E., J. A. Jones, and A. Becker. 2018. "The Racialization of Latinos in New Immigrant Destinations: Criminality, Ascription, and Counter-Mobilization." *RSF: The Russell Sage Foundation Journal of the Social Sciences* 4 (5): 118–140.

Browne, I., B. Reingold, and A. Kronberg. 2018. ""Race Relations, Black Elites, and Immigration Politics: Conflict, Commonalities, and Context"." *Social Forces* 96 (4): 1691–1720.

Cardoso, J. B., E. Hamilton, N. Rodriguez, K. Eschbach, and J. Hagan. 2016. "Deporting Fathers: Involuntary Transnational Families and Intent to Remigrate Among Salvadoran Deportees." *International Migration Review* 50 (1): 197–230.

Cebulko, K., and A. Silver. 2016. "Navigating DACA in Hospitable and Hostile States: State Responses and Access to Membership in the Wake of Deferred Action for Childhood Arrivals." *American Behavioral Scientist* 60 (13): 1553–1574.

Coleman, M. 2012. "The 'Local' Migration State: The Site-Specific Devolution of Immigration Enforcement in the U.S. South." *Law & Policy* 34 (2): 159–190.

Crowley, M., D. T. Lichter, and R. N. Turner. 2015. "Diverging Fortunes? Economic Well-Being of Latinos and African Americans in New Rural Destinations." *Social Science Research* 51: 77–92.

Denning, S. R. 2009. "The Impact of North Carolina Driver's License Requirements and the REAL ID Act of 2005 on Unauthorized Immigrants." *Popular Government* 74 (3): Online supplement 1–14.

Dondero, M., and C. Muller. 2012. "School Stratification in New and Established Latino Destinations." *Social Forces* 91 (2): 477–502.

Dreby, J. 2012. "The Burden of Deportation on Children in Mexican Immigrant Families." *Journal of Marriage and the Family* 74: 829–845.

Dreby, J. 2015. *Everyday Illegal: When Policies Undermine Immigrant Families.* Oakland: University of California Press.

Dunn, T. J., A. M. Aragonés, and G. Shivers. 2005. "Recent Mexican Immigration in the Rural Delmarva Peninsula: Human Rights Versus Citizenship Rights in a Local Context." In *New Destinations: Mexican Immigration to the United States*, edited by V. Zúñiga and R. Hernández-León, 155–183. New York: Russell Sage.

Ellis, M., R. Wright, and M. Townley. 2013. "New Destinations and Immigrant Poverty." In *Immigration, Poverty, and Socioeconomic Inequality in the United States*, edited by S. Raphael and D. Card, 13–65. New York: Russell Sage.

Fernández-Kelly, P. 2019. "The Kid Paradox: Adaptation Practices among Immigrant Youths in the Age of Mass Deportations." *Ethnic and Racial Studies* 43 (1).

Flores, R. D. 2014. "Living in the Eye of the Storm: How Did Hazleton's Restrictive Immigration Ordinance Affect Local Interethnic Relations?" *American Behavioral Scientist* 58 (13): 1743–1763.

Flores, S., and J. Chapa. 2009. "Latino Immigrant Access to Higher Education in a Bipolar Context of Reception." *Journal of Hispanic Higher Education* 8 (1): 90–109.

Gándara, P. 2019. "The Students we Share: Falling through the Cracks on Both Sides of the US-Mexico Border." *Ethnic and Racial Studies* 43 (1).

Gill, H., M. T. Nguyen, K. Lewis Parker, and D. Weissman. 2009. "Legal and Social Perspectives on Local Enforcement of Immigration Under the 287(g) Program." *Popular Government* 74 (3): 2–18.

Golash-Boza, T. M. 2015. *Deported: Immigrant Policing, Disposable Labor and Global Capitalism*. New York: New York University Press.

Gonzales, R. G. 2015. *Lives in Limbo: Undocumented and Coming of Age in America*. Berkeley: University of California Press.

Gonzales, R. G., and A. Ruiz. 2014. "Dreaming Beyond the Fields: Unauthorized Youth, Rural Realities, and a Constellation of Disadvantage." *Latino Studies* 12 (2): 194–216.

Gouveia, L., and M. A. Powell. 2007. "Second-Generation Latinos in Nebraska: A First Look." In *Migration Information Source (January)*. Washington, DC: Migration Policy Institute. https://www.migrationpolicy.org/article/second-generation-latinos-nebraska-first-look.

Gozdziak, E., and S. F. Martin, eds. 2005. *Beyond the Gateway: Immigrants in a Changing America*. Lanham, MD: Lexington Books.

Griffith, D. 1995. "*Hay Trabajo*: Poultry Processing, Rural Industrialization, and the Latinization of Low-Wage Labor." In *Any Way You Cut It: Meat Processing and Small Town America*, edited by D. D. Stull, M. J. Broadway, and D. Griffith, 129–151. Lawrence: University of Kansas Press.

Griffith, D. 2008. "New Midwesterners, New Southerners: Immigration Experiences in Four Rural American Settings." In *New Faces in New Places: The Changing Geography of American Immigration*, edited by D. S. Massey, 179–210. New York: Russell Sage.

Hagan, J., D. Leal, and N. Rodriguez. 2015. "Deporting Social Capital: Implications for Immigrant Communities in the United States." *Migration Studies* 3 (3): 370–392.

Hernández-León, R., and S. M. Lakhani. 2013. "Gender, Bilingualism, and the Early Occupational Careers of Second-Generation Mexicans in the South." *Social Forces* 92 (1): 59–80.

Hernández-León, R., S. M. Lakhani, and V. Zúñiga. 2019. "An Imperfect Realignment: The Movement of Children of Immigrants and their Families to the Homeland." *Ethnic and Racial Studies* 43 (1).

Hernández-León, R., and V. Zúñiga. 2003. "Mexican Immigrant Communities in the South and Social Capital: The Case of Dalton, Georgia." *Southern Rural Sociology* 19 (1): 20–45.

Hernández-León, R., and V. Zúñiga. 2005. "Appalachia Meets Aztlán: Mexican Immigration and Inter-Group Relations in Dalton, Georgia." In *New Destinations:*

Mexican Immigration in the United States, edited by V. Zúñiga and R. Hernández-León, 244–273. New York: Russell Sage.

Hernández-León, R., and V. Zúñiga. 2016. "Introduction to the Special Issue: Contemporary Return Migration From the United States to Mexico – Focus on Children, Youth, Schools and Families." *Mexican Studies/Estudios Mexicanos* 32 (2): 171–198.

Hopkins, D. J. 2010. "Politicized Places: Explaining Where and When Immigrants Provoke Local Opposition." *American Political Science Review* 104 (1): 40–60.

Isaacs, A., and A. Preston. 2018. "Deporting the American Dream." *New York Times* (July 9).

Jiménez, T. R. 2010. *Replenished Ethnicity: Mexican Americans, Mexican Immigrants, and Identity*. Berkeley: University of California Press.

Johnson, K. M., and D. T. Lichter. 2008. "Natural Increase: A New Source of Population Growth in Emerging Hispanic Destinations." *Population and Development Review* 34: 327–346.

Johnson-Webb, K. D. 2003. *Recruiting Hispanic Labor: Immigrants in Non-Traditional Areas*. New York: LFB Scholarly Publishing, LLC.

Jones, J. A. 2018. "From Open Doors to Closed Gates: Intragenerational Reverse Incorporation in New Immigrant Destinations." *International Migration Review*, doi:10:1177/0197918318791982.

Jones, J. A., and H. E. Brown. 2019. "American Federalism and Racial Formation in Contemporary Immigration Policy: A Processual Analysis of Alabama's HB56." *Ethnic and Racial Studies* 42 (4): 531–551.

Jones-Correa, M. 2008. "Race to the Top? The Politics of Immigrant Education in Suburbia." In *New Faces in New Places: The Changing Geography of American Immigration*, edited by D. S. Massey, 308–340. New York: Russell Sage.

Kanstroom, D. 2012. *Aftermath: Deportation Law and the New American Diaspora*. New York: Oxford University Press.

Kasinitz, P., J. H. Mollenkopf, M. C. Waters, and J. Holdaway. 2008. *Inheriting the City: The Children of Immigrants Come of Age*. Cambridge, MA and New York: Harvard University Press and Russell Sage.

Lattanzi Shutika, D. 2011. *Beyond the Borderlands: Migration and Belonging in the United States and Mexico*. Berkeley: University of California Press.

Leach, M. A., and F. D. Bean. 2008. "The Structure and Dynamics of Mexican Migration to New Destinations in the United States." In *New Faces in New Places: The Changing Geography of American Immigration*, edited by D. S. Massey, 51–74. New York: Russell Sage.

Lichter, D. T. 2012. "Immigration and the New Racial Diversity in Rural America." *Rural Sociology* 77: 1–34.

Lichter, D. T., D. Parisi, and M. C. Taquino. 2016. "Emerging Patterns of Hispanic Residential Segregation: Lessons From Rural and Small-Town America." *Rural Sociology* 8 (4): 483–518.

Lichter, D. T., S. R. Sanders, and K. M. Johnson. 2015. "Hispanics at the Starting Line: Poverty among Newborn Infants in Established Gateways and New Destinations." *Social Forces* 94 (1): 209–235.

López-Sanders, L. 2017. "From 'God Sent' to 'God Damned': Nativist Shocks and Race Relations in New Immigrant Destinations. Paper presented at the Annual Meeting of the *American Sociological Association*, Montréal, Canada (August 13).

López-Sanders, L., and H. E. Brown. 2019. "Political Mobilization and Public Discourse in New Immigrant Destinations: News Media Characterisations of Immigrants During the 2006 Immigration Marches." *Journal of Ethnic and Migration Studies*, doi:10/1080/1369183X.2018.1556464.

Luebke, P. 2011. "Anti-Immigrant Mobilization in a Southern State." In *Being Brown in Dixie: Race, Ethnicity, and Latino Immigration in the New South*, edited by Cameron D. Lippard and Charles A. Gallagher, 261–278. Boulder, CO: First Forum Press.

Luthra, R. R., T. Soehl, and R. Waldinger. 2018. *Origins and Destinations: The Making of the Second Generation*. New York: Russell Sage.

Marrow, H. B. 2011. *New Destination Dreaming: Immigration, Race, and Legal Status in the Rural American South*. Stanford, CA: Stanford University Press.

Marrow, H. B. 2013. "Assimilation in New Destinations." *Dædalus: The Journal of the American Academy of Arts & Sciences* 142 (3): 107–122.

Marrow, H. B. 2017. "The Difference a Decade of Enforcement Makes: Hispanic Racial Incorporation and Changing Intergroup Relations in the American South's Black Belt (2003-16)." In *The Politics of New Immigrant Destinations: Transatlantic Perspectives*, edited by S. Chambers, D. Evans, An. M. Messina, and B. Fisher Williamson, 102–120. Philadelphia, PA: Temple University Press.

Marschall, M. 2017. "Immigrant Incorporation in Local Schools: School Policy and Practices in New Versus Established Destinations." In *The Politics of New Immigrant Destinations: Transatlantic Perspectives*, edited by S. Chambers, D. Evans, A. M. Messina, and A. Fisher Williamson, 248–276. Philadelphia, PA: Temple University Press.

Martínez, L. M. 2014. "Dreams Deferred: The Impact of Legal Reforms on Unauthorized Latino Youth." *American Behavioral Scientist* 58 (14): 1873–1890.

Massey, D. S. 2008. *New Faces in New Places: The Changing Geography of American Immigration*. New York: Russell Sage.

Massey, D. S., J. Durand, and N. J. Malone. 2002. *Beyond Smoke and Mirrors: Mexican Immigration in an Era of Economic Integration*. New York: Russell Sage.

McDermott, M. 2011a. "Black Attitudes and Hispanic Immigrants in South Carolina." In *Just Neighbors? Research on African American and Latino Relations in the United States*, edited by E. Telles, M. Sawyer, and G. Rivera-Salgado, 242–263. New York: Russell Sage.

McDermott, M. 2011b. "Anti-Immigrant Backlash in the Wake of Immigrant Rights Marches and the Recession." Paper presented at the Annual Meeting of the *American Sociological Association*, Las Vegas, NV (August 23).

McDermott, M. 2016. "Initial Reactions to Change in a New Immigrant Destination." Paper presented at the Annual Meeting of the *Midwest Sociological Society*, Chicago, IL (March).

National Immigration Law Center (NILC). 2011. "The History of E-Verify." https://www.nilc.org/wp-content/uploads/2015/12/e-verify-history-rev-2011-09-29.pdf.

Nguyen, M. T., and H. Gill. 2010. "The 287(g) Program: The Costs and Consequences of Local Immigration Enforcement in North Carolina Communities." Chapel Hill: The Latino Migration Project, Institute for the Study of the Americas and Center for Global Initiatives, University of North Carolina at Chapel Hill (February).

Ovink, S. M., K. Ebert, and D. G. Okamoto. 2016. "Symbolic Politics of the State: The Case of In-Statue Tuition Bills for Undocumented Students." *Socius: Sociological Research for a Dynamic World* 2: 1–15.

Passel, J. S. 2005. *Estimates of the Size and Characteristics of the Unauthorized Population*. Washington, DC: Pew Hispanic Center (March 1).

Passel, J. S., and D. Cohn. 2009. *A Portrait of Unauthorized Immigrants in the United States*. Washington, D.C.: Pew Research Hispanic Center.

Pastor, M. 2018. *State of Resistance: What California's Dizzying Descent and Remarkable Resurgence Mean for America's Future*. New York: The New Press.

Perreira, K., and P. Brietzke. 2019. "In the Eye of the Beholder: Perspectives on Acculturation from White and Black Americans In Emerging Hispanic Communities and Schools." *Ethnic and Racial Studies* 43 (1).

Perreira, K. M., A. Fuligni, and S. Potochnick. 2010. "Fitting In: The Roles of Social Acceptance and Discrimination in Shaping the Academic Motivations of Latino Youth in the U.S. Southeast." *Journal of Social Issues* 66 (1): 131–153.

Portes, A., and R. G. Rumbaut. 2001. *Legacies: The Story of the Immigrant Second Generation*. Berkeley and New York: University of California Press and Russell Sage.

Portes, A., and R. G. Rumbaut. 2014. *Immigrant America: A Portrait (4th Ed.)*. Berkeley: University of California Press.

Provine, D. M., M. W. Varsanyi, P. G. Lewis, and S. Decker. 2016. *Policing Immigrants: Local Law Enforcement on the Front Lines*. Chicago, IL: University of Chicago Press.

Quiroga, S. S., D. M. Medina, and J. Glick. 2014. "In the Belly of the Beast: Effects of Anti-Immigration Policy on Latino Community Members." *American Behavioral Scientist* 58 (13): 1723–1742.

Ribas, V. 2016. *On the Line: Slaughterhouse Lives and the Making of the New South*. Oakland, California: University of California Press.

Saslow, E., and M. R. Chavez. 2018. "'Are You Alone Now?' After Raid, Immigrant Families are Separated in the American Heartland." *Washington Post* (June 30).

Schmalzbauer, L. 2014. *The Last Best Place: Gender, Family, and Migration in the New West*. Stanford, CA: Stanford University Press.

Shefner, J. 2019. "An Emerging Resistance Infrastructure: How Tennesseans Respond to the Immigration Enforcement Regime." *Ethnic and Racial Studies* 43 (1).

Silver, A. 2012. "Aging Into Exclusion and Social Transparency: Immigrant Youth and the Transition to Adulthood." *Latino Studies* 10 (4): 499–522.

Silver, A. 2018. *Shifting Boundaries: Immigrant Youth Negotiating National, State, and Small-Town Politics*. Stanford, CA: Stanford University Press.

Singer, A., S. W. Hardwick, and C. B. Brettell, eds. 2008. *Twenty-First Century Gateways: Immigrant Incorporation in Suburban America*. Washington, DC: Brookings Institution Press.

Smith, R. C. 2005. "Racialization and Mexicans in New York City." In *New Destinations: Mexican Immigration to the United States*, edited by V. Zúñiga and R. Hernández-León, 220–243. New York: Russell Sage.

Smith, R. C. n.d. unpublished book manuscript in progress. *Horatio Alger Lives in Brooklyn, but Check His Papers*. Oakland: University of California Press.

Spees, L., K. M. Perreira, and A. Fuligni. 2017. "Family Matters: Promoting the Educational Adaptation of Latino Youth in New and Established Destinations." *Journal of Family Issues* 38 (4): 457–479.

Striffler, S. 2005. *Chicken: The Dangerous Transformation of America's Favorite Food*. New Haven, CT: Yale University Press.

Stuesse, A. 2016. *Scratching Out a Living: Latinos, Race, and Work in the Deep South*. Oakland: University of California Press.

Suárez-Orozco, C., M. Suárez-Orozco, and I. Todorova. 2008. *Learning a New Land: Immigrant Students in American Society*. Cambridge, MA: Belknap Press of Harvard University Press.

Telles, E. E., and V. Ortiz. 2008. *Generations of Exclusion: Mexican Americans, Assimilation, and Race*. New York: Russell Sage.

Torres, R. M., E. J. Popke, and H. M. Hapke. 2006. "The South's Silent Bargain: Rural Restructuring, Latino Labor and the Ambiguities of Migrant Experience." In *The New South: Latinos and the Transformation of Place*, edited by H. A. Smith and O. J. Furuseth, 37–68. Aldershot, UK: Ashgate Press.

Vaquera, E., E. Aranda, and R. G. Gonzales. 2014. "Patterns of Incorporation of Latinos in Old and New Immigrant Destinations: From Invisible to Hypervisible." *American Behavioral Scientist* 58 (14): 1823–1833.

Waldinger, R., and C. Feliciano. 2004. "Will the New Second Generation Experience 'Downward Assimilation'? Segmented Assimilation Re-Assessed." *Ethnic and Racial Studies* 27 (3): 376–402.

Winders, J. 2013. *Nashville in the New Millenium: Immigrant Settlement, Urban Transformation, and Social Belonging*. New York: Russell Sage.

Yablon-Zug, M. A., and D. Holley-Walker. 2009. "Not Very Collegial: Exploring Bans on Unauthorized Immigrant Admissions to State Colleges and Universities." *Charleston Law Review* 3: 101–117.

Zúñiga, V., and S. E. Giorguli Saucedo. 2019. *Niños y niños en la migración de Estados Unidos a México: La Generación 0.5* [Children Moving From the United States to Mexico: The 0.5 Generation]. Mexico: El Colegio de México.

Zúñiga, V., and E. T. Hamann. Forthcoming. "The 0.5 Generation: Children's Voices About 'Return' Migration From the United States to Mexico." *Journal of International Migration and Integration*.

Integrating Hispanic immigrant youth: perspectives from white and black Americans in emerging Hispanic communities and schools

Krista M. Perreira, Stephanie Potochnick and M. Priscilla Brietzke

ABSTRACT
Acculturation is bidirectional and includes not only the process of Hispanics adaptation to US culture(s) but also the process of US cultural adaptations to Hispanics. Our study examines the acculturation of non-Hispanic students, parents, and teachers in emerging Hispanic communities to Hispanic immigrant youth. This study utilizes focus-group data from the Southern Immigrant Academic Adaptation (SIAA) study – a multi-site, high school-based study conducted in North Carolina. We held 34 focus groups with 139 participants from two rural and two urban high schools. In each high school, at least five focus groups were conducted to include non-Hispanics: (1) black students, (2) black parents, (3) white students, (4) white parents, and (5) high school teachers. In each high school, we identified different modes of incorporation or receiving-community acculturation that included varying degrees of accommodation of heritage cultures and languages as well as cultural exchanges ranging from inclusionary to exclusionary.

Introduction

As the US Hispanic population began to settle outside of states with historically large Hispanic populations, multiple studies examined how Hispanic adolescents adapted or acculturated as they interacted with long-time residents in Emerging Hispanic Communities (EHC) (Ko and Perreira 2010 Green, Perreira, and Linda 2016; Brietzke and Perreira 2017; Silver 2018). However, there is another facet of acculturation that is largely neglected. Acculturation is, by definition, bidirectional which includes not only the process of Hispanic adaptation to US culture(s) but also the process of cultural adaptations to Hispanics made by existing cultural groups within EHCs (Berry 2003). New assimilation theories also highlight the bidirectional nature of assimilation processes and emphasize the possibility that immigrant-origin populations will influence the host society (Alba 2005; Orum 2005; Jiménez and Horowitz 2013).

Nevertheless, few studies of Hispanic adolescent adaptation have examined the ways in which EHCs adapt to or fail to adapt to new Hispanic residents. Our study addresses this gap by examining how non-Hispanic white and black students, parents, and teachers in North Carolina's (NC) high schools have acculturated to the Hispanic adolescents in their communities, most of whom are first (i.e. foreign-born with foreign-born parents) and second-generation (i.e. US-born with foreign-born parents) children of immigrants. Treating acculturation as a two-way process, our study aims to: (1) explore non-Hispanics' perceptions of and attitudes towards Hispanics across different population segments (i.e. adolescents, parents and teachers), (2) describe how non-Hispanic students, parents, and teachers interact with Hispanic newcomers in their schools and communities, and (3) understand the systems and structures that assist or deter Hispanics' adaptation to their communities.

We focus on NC as the fastest growing EHC between 1990 and 2000 when the Hispanic population settled in rural and urban areas throughout the state and grew 394 per cent from 76,726 to 378,963 (Guzmán 2001) We further focus on high school students in 2007–08 – a year in which the school enrolment of Hispanic foreign-born youth neared its peak. By 2007–08, approximately 33,000 Hispanic youth were enrolled in the state's high schools and 40 per cent of these Hispanic youth were foreign-born (US Census 2008). Nationally, both the adoption of local immigration enforcement agreements (called 287(g) agreements) and noncriminal removals by Immigration and Customs Enforcement (ICE) also peaked in 2007–08. Between 148,000 and 158,000 persons without criminal records (44–46 per cent of all deportations) were deported by ICE from the interior of the US (Rosenblum and McCabe 2014). Many communities within NC, an early adopter of 287(g) agreements, had become increasingly hostile towards immigrants (Gill 2010; Silver 2018). The high prevalence of noncriminal deportations through local immigration enforcement efforts left many youth and their families feeling particularly vulnerable.

Within this context, we argue that NC's schools were the most important institutional environment in the socialization and adaptation of Hispanic foreign-born and US-born youth (Kandel and Parrado 2006; Perreira, Fuligni, and Potochnick 2010). Schools exposed youth to different cultural groups, shaped co-ethnic interactions, and influenced youth's beliefs about what society and persons outside of their family expect from them. Schools also provided opportunities for parents and teachers from different cultures to interact. Moreover, policies and practices within schools established norms and expectations that influenced how newcomers were welcomed (or not) by peers, parents, and teachers from different cultural backgrounds.

To understand the context of reception for Hispanic youth, we argue that it is essential to understand the attitudes, behaviours and practices of non-Hispanic students, parents, and teachers in the school system. Although federal and state-level policies shape the institutional landscapes of the US, schools refract these policies and create microcontexts for reception which reflect the availability of resources across schools, the racial/ethnic and socioeconomic composition of each school, and the history of racial/ethnic relations in each school and its surrounding community.

Theoretical considerations

Three theoretical frameworks inform our analysis – acculturation theory, new assimilation theory, and theories on prejudice and intergroup relations. We anchor our research in Berry's (2003) conceptualizations of acculturation as a bi-directional process and the recognition that modes of incorporation (i.e. institutional and cultural reactions to immigrant groups) can shape immigrant assimilation (Portes and Rumbaut 2001). Using Berry's framework, we classify schools along two dimensions – degree of cultural inclusion by non-Hispanic US-born natives and degree of accommodation of heritage cultures and identities. Arrayed along these two dimensions, the modes of incorporation adopted by schools and the individual acculturation strategies adopted by students, parents, and teachers within a school can vary tremendously. First, schools can combine accommodations to facilitate the maintenance of heritage cultures by newcomers with substantial opportunities for cross-cultural interactions that facilitate learning and understanding of host community cultures. Second, schools can pursue cultural inclusion without accommodation, expecting newcomers to give up their cultural heritage as they embrace and adopt the values of the dominant cultural group in the receiving community. Third, schools can promote cultural separation with accommodations to facilitate cultural maintenance. Newcomers may be allowed to maintain their cultural heritage while also being discouraged from interacting with the dominant cultural group due to neighbourhood socioeconomic segregation, linguistic classroom segregation, or overt racial/ethnic discrimination. Lastly, schools can expect newcomers to give up their cultural heritage and adopt the behaviours and practices of the dominant group while also excluding them from full participation in the civic life of the receiving communities. In some cases, these exclusions may be forced or codified by law.

Complementing Berry's work, new assimilation theory argues that adaptations of immigrants to their new homes will be shaped by "institutional mechanisms of monitoring and enforcement" that either "brighten" or "blur" social boundaries between racial/ethnic groups (Alba 2005). Boundaries can become bright when institutional mechanism (e.g. local immigration enforcement efforts, English-only laws) strengthen the power and authority of one group while diminishing another. Boundaries can become blurred when institutional mechanisms (e.g. translated public documents) promote equal rights, mutual respect, shared understanding, and shared control. Blurred boundaries provide opportunities for newcomers to modify the cultural mainstream, whereas brightened boundaries limit these opportunities and change might only be possible through collective resistance (e.g. the Civil Rights Movement).

These institutional mechanisms can be shaped by historical race/ethnic relations and community prejudices (Fussell 2014). The threat hypothesis suggests that white and black Americans will view Hispanics, especially immigrants, as either a cultural, political, or economic threat. The threat perception may be amplified in communities where Hispanic populations have grown rapidly and/or where there is greater competition for scarce resources (e.g. jobs). The contact hypothesis takes a more positive view of intergroup contact, suggesting that positive interactions between groups will decrease prejudice and promote mutual understanding, cooperation, and respect. Thus, positive attitudes towards Hispanic newcomers should grow over time and the context of reception should become more welcoming or accommodating. Previous research in NC supports both viewpoints (McClain et al. 2007; Marrow 2008; O'Neil and Tienda 2010; Watson and Riffe 2012).

Based on these theoretical considerations, we hypothesize that the attitudes, behaviours, and practices of students, parents, and teachers will reflect varying degrees of accommodation and cultural inclusion which either brighten or blur social boundaries in each school. Furthermore, the degree of accommodation and cultural inclusion will vary across schools depending on the availability of resources in each school, the racial/ethnic and socioeconomic composition of each school, and the history of racial/ethnic relations in each school and its surrounding community. Schools in urban areas with higher SES whites and fewer resource constraints will feel less threatened by Hispanic newcomers and will be more inclusive and accommodating of different cultural viewpoints. In contrast, schools in rural areas with lower SES white and black Americans and greater resource constraints will feel more threatened by Hispanic newcomers and will tend to be less inclusive or accommodating.

Methods

Data

This study utilizes focus-group data from the Southern Immigrant Academic Adaptation study (SIAA) – a study of nine high schools randomly selected from urban-rural strata with a probability proportional to the number of Hispanic students enrolled in 9th grade (see **online supplement** for additional details). From among these nine high schools participating in the study, two rural and two urban schools were randomly selected to participate in the focus group arm of the study. The four schools selected represented four of the five school districts participating in the study and reflect the diverse geographic settlement of Hispanics in North Carolina. Across the schools, we held 34 focus groups with 139 non-Hispanic participants in 2007–08. In each school, at least seven focus groups were conducted with non-Hispanic: (1) teachers, (2) black female adolescents, (3) white female adolescents, (4) black male adolescents, (5) white male adolescents, (6) black parents, and (7) white parents.

We organized student and parent focus groups by sex and race/ethnicity to facilitate open conversation about stereotypes and racial dynamics (Hollander 2004). All focus groups followed an open-ended discussion guide and most were conducted by a research team member of the same racial background (see **online supplement**). Focus groups lasted between 45 and 90 min and were digitally recorded and transcribed. Participants received $15 gift cards for participating.

Schools and participants

According to data from the NC Department of Public Instruction (2017), the four schools in which focus groups were conducted differed substantially along several dimensions (Table 1, **Panel A**, data rounded to protect school identities). In particular, there were clear racial and economic differences between rural and urban schools. School 1 was an urban magnet school attracting white families into a more racially/ethnically mixed community. School 2 was urban, majority white, and had few Free and Reduced-Priced Lunch (FRPL) students. School 3 was rural and our poorest school with a relatively large white population and 70 per cent FRPL students. School 4 was rural, majority black with 60 per cent FRPL students. Consequently rural-urban location differences intersected with race and class differences across schools. Among 9th-grade Hispanic students enrolled in these schools (see **online supplement**), school climates were evaluated most positively by Hispanic students in School 1, reports of encouragement by adults were highest in School 2, and perceptions of discrimination were highest in Schools 3 and 4.

Table 1. School characteristics and focus group demographics, by school.

	Total		School 1		School 2		School 3		School 4	
	Panel A. 2007–08 School characteristics[a]									
School Size	–	–	$N = 1500$		$N = 2000$		$N = 500$		$N = 600$	
Hispanic growth 2000–15	–	–	Low		Medium		High		High	
% Hispanic	–	–	10%		15%		20%		25%	
% White	–	–	45%		55%		50%		25%	
% Reduced lunch	–	–	40%		25%		70%		60%	
Student/teacher ratio	–	–	18:1		15:1		16:1		22:1	
Teacher turnover	–	–	10%		15%		20%		40%	
Graduation rate: All	–	–	70%		80%		65%		60%	
Graduation rate: Hispanics	–	–	50%		70%		55%		35%	
Graduation rate: LEP	–	–	35%		75%		20%		25%	
	Panel B. Focus group demographics, by school, frequency (%)[b]									
	N	(%/M)	N	(M/%)	N	(M/%)	N	(M/%)	N	(M/%)
Sample N	139	100%	31	100%	40	100%	36	100%	32	100%
Male	46	33%	11	35%	14	35%	11	31%	10	31%
Mean student age	–	16	–	15	–	15	–	16	–	16
Mean adult age	–	40	–	48	–	47	–	41	–	41
Born in NC**	89	64%	17	55%	16	40%	31	86%	25	78%
Race**										
White	64	47%	15	48%	25	64%	13	38%	11	35%
Black	62	46%	14	45%	14	36%	16	47%	18	58%
Other	5	4%	–	–	–	–	3	9%	2	6%
Parent college graduate	14	52%	4	50%	4	57%	3	43%	3	60%
Employed	63	45%	15	48%	20	50%	13	36%	15	47%

**$p < 0.05$ fisher's exact test. Note(s): M = Mean; [a]Data in Panel A are from the North Carolina (NC) Department of Instruction 2007–2008. To protect participating schools and students from deductive disclosure, data in Panel A have been rounded. [b]Nine schools were randomly selected for participation in the study based on the proportion of Hispanics enrolled in 9th grade. From these nine schools, two rural (school 1 and 2) and two urban schools (school 3 and 4) were randomly selected to participate in the focus groups arm of the study.

Table 1, **panel B** describes focus group participants. Age ranges for students were 13–18, and for parents and teachers 24–57. Most participants (64 per cent) were born in NC and identified as non-Hispanic white (47 per cent) or black (46 per cent). Participants had diverse immigration views, according to preliminary questionnaires (see **online supplement**). They were evenly divided between those who felt immigrants strengthened the country (35 per cent); burdened the country (30 per cent); and, had no opinion (32 per cent). Though not statistically significant, participants from rural (School 3 and 4) versus urban (Schools 1 and 2) schools viewed immigrants more negatively.

Analysis

The research team conducted preliminary analysis concurrently with data collection (Miles and Huberman 1994). Following each focus group, we discussed what we learned and generated an iterative list of emerging themes and codes. Then, we coded transcripts independently using Atlas.ti Version 6.0 and compared and reconciled coding and identified important subthemes. Next, we identified and mapped conceptual links between themes, examined variations and patterns in each theme across schools, and evaluated patterns and variations within themes by race, gender, and population segment (teachers, parents, and students). Each layer of analysis lent a greater degree of complexity and different viewpoints.

Our research team consisted of US-born and foreign-born Hispanics and non-Hispanic Blacks and Whites. Although the language used by some focus group participants was distressing and hurtful to team members, the team valued the opportunity to understand other perspectives. The portrait that emerges is at times uncomfortable and yet provides important insights into the reception that Hispanic youth encounter.

Results

To learn how participants were adapting to the growing Hispanic population, our focus group discussions sought participants' descriptions of their community's *attitudes* towards Hispanics, *behaviors* or interactions with Hispanics, and information on school practices or *accommodations* for Hispanics (Berry 2003). These three factors worked together to define acculturation strategies adopted by peers, parents, and teachers and how Hispanic students were incorporated into school in each receiving-community. *Attitudes* reflected beliefs about Hispanics degree of threat to their communities, ability to function successfully in their communities, and expected ways of behaviour. *Behaviors* reflected depictions of interpersonal interactions with Hispanics and widespread practices that shaped these interactions. *Accommodations* reflected descriptions of formal and informal systems (e.g. physical/organization structure of the school; school policies/programmes; and resource allocations) that could assist or deter Hispanic adaptation.

Our analysis (organized by school) revealed substantial variation in the strategies of immigrant incorporation adopted within each school. Though no school could be characterized as pursuing a high degree of cultural inclusion without accommodation or cultural exclusion with accommodation, Figure 1 shows that the degree of cultural inclusion and accommodation of heritage cultures varied tremendously within schools. At the same time, it shows that cultural inclusion appeared to go hand in hand with accommodation.

School 1: cultural inclusion with accommodation

School 1, our most inclusive and accommodating school, is characterized as striving towards multiculturalism. Set in an urban community, many of its students, parents, and teachers had relocated from other states, drawn by the low cost of living and employment opportunities in business, healthcare

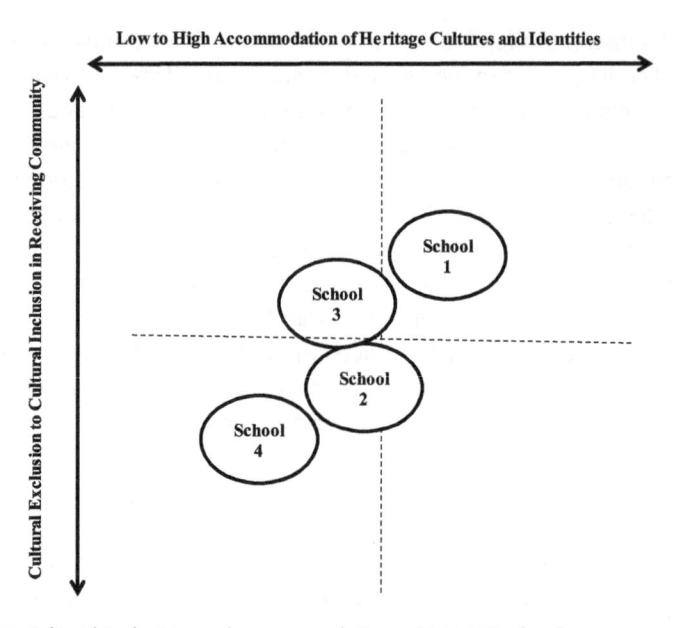

Figure 1. Cultural inclusion and accommodation within NC schools.

and education. According to parents, job availability and affordable housing reduced racial tensions in the city as every racial/ethnic group benefited from economic growth. Neighbourhoods, however, remained ethnically/racially separated. Moreover, parents and teachers believed that district school choice policies perpetuated racial/ethnic separation, as families gravitated towards racially/ethnically homogenous schools. Participants viewed their high school as an exception. It was large, racially/ethnically and economically diverse, and strived to be culturally aware and inclusive.

Community
Exemplifying the strong sense of connection, the safe learning environment, and the diversity valued in the school, two black parents stated:

> R1: This is really a great school, safe environment … They have a lot of opportunities. [School 1] is keeping up with the day, what's going on with technology and everything.

> R2: [My daughter] has a course in foreign language, and she's learning Spanish, Korean. She's learning like four different languages and I just think that's awesome.

Attitudes
Teachers, parents, and students in School 1 generally expressed positive attitudes towards Hispanics and some viewed the Hispanic community as both culturally and socioeconomically diverse.

R3 (*AA parent*): You know those Hispanic men, they will get out there and work and take care of the family … They coming for a better life. They learn how to hustle and bustle.

R2 (*White Parent*): I think that we have to divide the conversation into the professional Hispanic community, of which there are lawyers, bankers, and doctors. … There's also a large, unserved, underclass, which is not part of that same socioeconomic level.

Interactions

Though they valued the mixed racial/ethnic school composition, racial/ethnic interactions were limited. Students explained that this racial/ethnic separation was partially the result of course structures. Hispanic students in their school were placed in English as a Second Language (ESL) and remedial courses, sometimes located in isolated trailers. According to teachers, these courses often took up much of Hispanic students' schedules, leaving little room for electives and sports where they could interact with other students. Students felt that lack of shared classes prevented them from making Hispanic friends. The racial/ethnic separation in the city's and school's social structure trickled down into participants' informal interactions. At lunch time, according to black male students, Hispanic students *"just, like, disappear"*.

As described by a group of black female students, however, black and Hispanic students may have interacted somewhat more than white and Hispanic students due to their shared socioeconomic and minority backgrounds.

R2: I've never seen them [whites and Hispanics] interact …

R4: I think a lot of the Hispanics get along with the African Americans 'cause they think they can identify with us more than the Caucasians. I'm not sure why. I think cause we're all minorities in a sense, so they feel they're equal to us, more so than with Caucasians.

Accommodations

Overall, parents and teachers were proud of the school's efforts to meet their growing Hispanic community's educational needs. These included a well-regarded ESL programme, a website in Spanish, translators and translated materials available for non-native English speakers and their parents, and remedial courses to support students not meeting grade-level requirements. The school had invested in these resources for several years.

At the same time, the use of Spanish by Hispanic students was frowned upon and raised suspicions that Hispanic students were either speaking badly about other racial/ethnic groups, attempting to be disruptive, or attempting to force other groups to accommodate them. These concerns were summarized best by a group of black female students:

> R3: ... They'll be speaking English and if you piss them off, they'll turn around and start speaking Spanish! That makes me feel like they're talking about me.

> R4: I think it's disrespectful to speak another language if you do speak English.

Additionally, the resources expended to support Spanish-speakers were seen as taking away from resources to support other students:

> R1: I feel that they're being treated like they're handicapped ... [teachers] end up doing their work for them ... .Teachers hurt other students by taking extra time to help [Hispanics] ...

Consistent with these beliefs and attitudes, participants in this school also believed that Hispanics in their community should put more effort into learning English, socializing with people outside of their group, and applying themselves academically.

As a context of reception, participants described a high school that was making a concerted effort to meet students' need for education, while struggling to socially integrate them. Partially resembling Berry's notion of a multicultural context, from the top down, the school sought to integrate Hispanic youth into their community by providing culturally-sensitive educational support, which they hoped would facilitate this process. However, the lack of opportunities for daily interaction with non-Hispanics reduced the cultural inclusiveness of the school. Additionally, concerns expressed about Hispanic students' use of Spanish in school highlighted the limits of support for accommodating the maintenance of cultural heritages. Conflicted feelings regarding whether Hispanics were an asset or burden on the community reflected the potential to view acculturation as a zero-sum game where accommodating the maintenance of heritage cultures could be costly.

School 2: cultural separation with passive accommodation

School 2 was striving to build racial/ethnic cohesion amidst a legacy of racial/ethnic and socioeconomic segregation. In fact, when asked to describe their school, teachers and students alike described it with a single word – "*segregated*". Like school 1, school 2 was set in an urban area where a low cost of living and job opportunities had attracted new residents from other states as well as immigrant populations from both Latin America and Asia.

Community
Some parents and teachers praised the school for its racial/ethnic and socioeconomic diversity as well as its high academic quality. They lauded the racial/

ethnic change, indicating that it promoted *cultural mixing* and opportunities to learn and understand different cultures. As noted by one black parent, *"with the influx of Latinos and blacks and Asians ... Kids will have to be exposed to other cultures and start learning about other cultures"* (R3).

However, most parents and teachers rarely spoke of the school's diversity in positive terms. They worried that growing racial/ethnic diversity in the school and surrounding neighbourhoods was upsetting a historical balance in what had been a predominately white school. They worried that administrative turnover and the hiring of many young, new teachers would reduce the quality of education at the school. They worried about increased absenteeism, students falling asleep in class, inappropriate and abusive language, and disengaged parents. They expressed concern that Hispanic immigrant students would drain public resources and lead to violence, gangs, poorer quality public education, and segregated schools.

Attitudes

At least one participant in each focus group expressed the desire for stricter immigration control or wished that foreign-born Hispanic students would return to their home countries. For example, a group of white male students indicated that *"the Border Patrol needs to do a better job"* (R3) and should *"put a huge stone wall ... like the Great Wall of China"* (R2). Negative attitudes were not limited to Hispanics. *"They [Teachers]"*, commented one black Female student (R5), *"think black or Hispanic equals violence"*.

Despite the presence of these negative attitudes, some teachers and students believed that racial/ethnic tensions were not high. Summarizing this sentiment, one teacher (R8) stated:

> It's not really tensions. I mean, everyone gets along, and that's why we're saying it's like a family ... .Even in your own family ... you love each other, but sometimes you get on each other's nerves ... .That's what happens a lot of times with these kids.

Interactions

Nevertheless, teachers and students indicated that there were few opportunities for positive racial/ethnic interactions at school. As discussed by teachers and students, the segregation embodied by the school was rooted in the school's historical design. Built in the Jim Crow system, the building had standard facilities for whites and separate, lower quality facilities (e.g. restrooms, drinking fountains, and cafeterias) for blacks. Though the practice of segregating facilities in schools is no longer legal, these separate facilities remained. Teachers and students noted that, over the years, as more Hispanic students attended the school, they began using the separate, *"lower-quality"* facilities as spaces to socialize with other Hispanic students. Reflecting on this practice, a group of white female students remarked:

> R2: I don't even know why, but all the Spanish kids use [the small cafeteria]—

> R3: Yeah, the school used to be segregated … .that's why there's little and big cafeterias … The bathrooms over there were for the black people and then the ones down with the full-length mirror were for the white people. It [segregation] still happens. I think Hispanics all just want to be together. It's not like the Hispanics or the Latinos can't come in the big cafeteria.

Practices limiting racial/ethnic interactions in the school and promoting separation were also present in the classroom structures and the structures of extracurricular activities. As described by one black student (R3), *"Honors classes tend to have more white people … Lower class blacks and Hispanics … tend to be in the lower classes"*. Similarly, a white parent (R1) commented that his daughter told him not to put his son in a regular class because *"that's the lowest level class, and that's all the blacks"*. Although black and white students indicated that they mixed at sporting events, they also indicated that few Hispanic students engaged in these events, in school leadership or in school clubs. According to one teacher (R6), students were *"scared to push themselves together and to push themselves into getting to know one another"*.

Accommodations

Despite the on-going segregation, both students and teachers wanted their school to become more integrated and inclusive of Hispanic students. However, they did not know how best to achieve this and there was little accommodation or support for the maintenance of Hispanic students' heritage cultures and languages. For instance, students noted it was a common practice for teachers to forbid students from speaking Spanish in class.

Several teachers and parents felt that providing Hispanic students and parents with more Spanish-language materials would remove an incentive to learn English. For this reason, according to one teacher (R3), the school had not invested in a translator or in teacher training to help students better understand the experiences of their immigrant students. Instead, teachers and parents strongly emphasized the need for Hispanic students and their families to learn English quickly, be grateful for the work that they have, and legalize their status. As a group of white parents summarized:

> R3: When the immigrants were coming in from Europe, … they knew they had to come here and learn the language. That helped them, you know, become American. I think really we bend over backwards to a point where I think it's a problem. I think it's costing the tax payers a lot of money and resources.

R4: If they're gonna be here, there needs to be a way that they can integrate into the community rather than just come here and still be with their own kind.

Accordingly, the school required full English immersion for new students and did not allow students to enrol in ESL classes until they had been at the school for at least two years. The school had also applied for, but not yet received, a grant to offer ESL classes to parents.

Overall, school 2, in contrast to school 1, resembled more of a pressure cooker. With few school- or community-based systems to facilitate cultural exchange and only passive accommodations for language or cultural maintenance, Hispanic youth and their families bore the burden of learning to fit in on their own.

School 3: cultural inclusion with limited accommodation

School 3 is best characterized as a melting pot, close to boiling over. Described as *"small"* and *"overcrowded"*, School 3 was set in a racially diverse, poor, rural town that most families had lived in for generations. The small town offered ample factory and agricultural jobs but few activities for adolescents to enjoy. Both black and white participants indicated that white farmers controlled town and school governance. Few Hispanics or blacks were considered town or school leaders.

Community

According to focus group participants, the Hispanic population began moving into and settling in the county in the early 1990s. Prior to this time, the Hispanic population had primarily consisted of migrant labourers who lived seasonally in camps outside of town and interacted little with local residents. All focus groups – teachers, parents, and students – uniformly associated the increasing presence of Hispanics in the town with rising gang activity, drugs, and violence. They discussed recent cases of shootings in the town and fights in the school. Some of these fights were within the Hispanic community; others were between black and Hispanic students. Because of concerns about gang colours and symbols, the school had adopted clothing restrictions and had a security guard. Furthermore, our focus group of black parents thought that the school needed a metal detector. At the same time, teachers believed that recent tragedies at the school (the murder of two Hispanic students), were helping to bring the community together. As summarized by one teacher, *"I think that our [student] body as a whole, with the tragedies we have suffered in the last 3 or 4 years, that our kids come together as a whole"*.

Attitudes

Violence and the increasingly visible presence of Hispanics in the town and high school made some community members feel threatened. As one black female student (R3) explained, *"They [Mexicans] are everywhere, in all the halls at school. If I turn right, they're there, or right there, or in front of you ... They be like trying to take over".* At the same time, most focus group participants lauded the Hispanic newcomers for their strong family and religious values, standing up for one another, and willingness to do the *"dirty"* or *"hard"* jobs that others in town were unwilling to do. For example, a white parent (R2) commented,

> My husband actually has two Hispanic employees. They've been there a long time working for him. And he thinks highly of them .... And really, a lot of your farmers and people like that, they want people who are going to work hard .... My husband will tell you, that of his employees, they're probably the hardest working.

Interactions

Because the school was relatively small with limited resources and no advanced placement classes, classrooms were racially/ethnically integrated. Hispanics rarely attended separate ESL classes, many were US-born and/or spoke primarily English, and they interacted with non-Hispanic students on a daily basis. However, race/ethnic interactions in the classroom were not always positive. Black parents noted that their children were sometimes *"treated disrespectfully"* and faced discrimination in the process of selecting kids to participate in prestigious activities or to win awards. In their focus group, black female students indicated that some teachers were *"prejudiced against black people (R2)"*, *"You want to learn, but you feel like they ain't trying to teach you (R3)"*. They felt that white students received special treatment and that teachers *"talked down"* to *"people of color"*. White male students also spoke with frustration about teachers and students who were *"judgmental"* or *"stereotyped"* Hispanic and black students. Commenting on this, one white male (R4) said,

> People make fun of what they don't understand. They don't understand why they [Hispanics] came. Some people think that because they're Hispanic, they're bad people. Some of the Hispanic kids are really cool. You just have to get to know them. The same with black people.

Accommodations

When asked about what could be done to improve their school, teachers emphasized the need for more ESL resources for students and trained translators who could reduce the reliance on the use of fellow students as translators. Teachers also felt it was important to provide an opportunity for students to take pride in their ethnic identity and had arranged a Hispanic cultural celebration at the school. As explained by one teacher (R2), *"When you're involved in their [Hispanic] culture, it makes the classroom environment more smooth. You try to see what's going on with them to make the classroom environment more enjoyable and you have less discipline problems".*

Students from every focus group in this school commented that they *"liked"* the Hispanic Heritage celebration, had *"learned something"* from it and, in the case of black students, gained empathy indicating that *"Some of what they went through, we went through (R3)".* White female students thought that there should be more cultural celebrations because *"everyone likes to feel included, to feel like part of a group (R6)".* Students, teachers, and parents also mentioned that they or someone they knew was trying to learn Spanish.

Nevertheless, as in School 1, efforts to seek cultural understanding and make accommodations for the growing Hispanic community had limits. Students were upset by the use of Spanish and by overt displays of ethnic pride. For example, one black female student commented, *"I get mad when … I feel like they're talking about me [in Spanish]. If you're going to say something, say it in my language".* While a white male student commented, *"We show our American pride, but we don't blow it up in their face".* Furthermore, white parents complained that Hispanic students required additional attention in school, which took *"time out from [their] child"* and *"affected [their] child's opportunity to learn"* (R2). Lastly, teachers expressed a desire to see Hispanic students adapt to the existing culture and speak in English more rapidly. They lamented that they *"have to constantly ask students not to speak Spanish!"* (R1).

Overall, School 3 might be best characterized as a boiling pot. The Hispanic population had grown more rapidly than in the urban school districts where schools 1 and 2 were located. This led some participants to characterize the high rate of growth of the Hispanic community in School 3 as a *"takeover"* that threatened the town's existing cultural fabric. At the same time, the rurality and poverty of the school forced daily racial/ethnic interactions throughout the community and limited the resources available to invest in services (e.g. translation services) to assist newcomers. This led to empathy, efforts to promote cultural understanding and Spanish-language acquisition, and inter-racial/ethnic dating in some cases. In other cases, it led to racial/ethnic tensions, vocal concerns about racial/ethnic discrimination and bias, as well as physical violence.

School 4: cultural exclusion without accommodation

Located in a rural, agricultural community, focus group participants characterized School 4 as being small, poor, and with a largely black student body, which had been historically marginalized. Among the focus group participants with deep, local roots in NC, Hispanic newcomers to the community were seen as a burden that the school did not have the resources to accommodate. In every focus group, people reflected on the difficult financial and social climate that students, parents and teachers faced. In the decades preceding our study, factory closings in the town left behind limited job opportunities, mainly in agriculture. This created competition for the few desirable retail and service jobs in the area.

Community

School 4 and its surrounding community was largely viewed as marginalized with an increasing minority presence. As a result, according to one white parent (R1), white families were moving: *"It's gotten decidedly more Latino, and well even, even a little more black. A lot of the [white] people I know have moved away from here ... We may have laws against segregation, but that doesn't mean people don't segregate themselves anyway".* Another black parent (R1) echoed this, *"[The whites] send all their kids to [a different public school] or to private schools, so they don't have to mingle with the black students".*

Parents believed that the resources in the school declined as the percentage of whites in the school declined. Teacher turnover had increased and many of the teachers were less-experienced substitutes who, according to students, would *"leave at the end of the semester"* and, according to parents, *"don't care".* Commenting on the high teacher turnover, one teacher (R2) said,

> The number one reason why people [Teachers] leave is really not about the money ... It's about them not having support from the administration, or not having support of their coworkers, or their peers. Then going into the classroom feeling isolated, feeling alone.

Black students characterized the school as *"boring"*, *"cheap"*, and without opportunities. White students characterized the school as *"poor, very poor"* and *"underprivileged".* They characterized the teachers as *"mean"* and *"racist"* telling Hispanic students to *"Talk in English, now"* without appreciating that they are just learning English. They commented that the town lacked tax revenue for the school and the school lacked basic supplies and books. Both groups of students discussed how the school was *"low performing"* and in danger of being shut down.

Attitudes

There were highly palpable racial/ethnic tensions in the school. Attitudes of white parents were particularly negative toward undocumented Hispanic immigrants who they perceived as taking advantage of public assistance programmes and breaking laws without repercussions. Students were aware of the racial tensions that existed among adults, had adopted them, and also perceived the growing Hispanic presence as a threat. A group of white male students commented:

R1: They [Hispanic immigrants] come over here, they're taking advantage of our social security, food stamps, and stuff, and programs like that because they want to live off the government for free.

R3: The elderly ... most of them are racist ... , and I'm racist to a point. I'm racist against some black people, because they try to act like something they're not.

R2: I'm a racist person against Hispanics, because I don't like them coming over here and trying to steal our country from us.

Black parents and students also expressed concern that Hispanics were "taking over". At the same time, they expressed appreciation for their work in agriculture and empathized with Hispanics who shared their experiences of racism in the community. A black male student (R1) expressed this empathy saying, " ... *So it's like we're both [blacks and Hispanics] trying to be accepted at the same time".*

Interactions

Racial/ethnic tensions in the community manifested as racial/ethnic segregation in the school. Parents, teachers, and students commented on how each racial/ethnic group in the school "rarely meshed". According to black parents, Hispanic students segregated themselves by country of birth but sometimes connected with black students.

R2: Hispanic kids, they don't mingle a lot of them, because Mexicans don't like Guatemalans, Guatemalans don't like Mexican. So, they don't hang with one another ... .But they hang with all the blacks ... .They date the black girls ... .

According to black male students, Hispanics students had adopted stereotypical views of blacks and whites which strained relationships. For example, one black student (R1) commented, "They [Hispanics] probably be like, that's a black dude. He's not that smart ... That's a white boy. They know everything".

Accommodations

In this community with high levels of racial/ethnic conflict and low levels of resources, accommodating Hispanic students was not a priority. The teachers noted that there was only one ESL teacher in the school and Hispanic students had to rely on *peer tutoring* by other Hispanic students when they could not understand the teacher. As in school 2, accommodation was seen as a costly zero-sum game. One white parent (R1) explained,

... So we start taking a bunch of resources to help that [Hispanic] kid ... So while the teacher's over there for the 19th time ... trying to explain to Jose that $2 + 2 = 4$ ... that extra time that she spends away from my child ... [My] child there has nothing to do.

In contrast, black parents focused on the need to improve the quality of resources in the school more generally and improve communication with all parents.

In thinking about what the school needed to assist with their growing Hispanic population, teachers emphasized:

R2: If we could get some more finances and hire some assistants to be in the classrooms with the teachers, and some more who did have bilingual skills. That would be good.

R1: Bilingual teachers. If we are going to continue having a high population of Latino students, all of the teachers should be trained in Spanish –all of the teachers. We should at least have conversational Spanish.

More generally, teachers agreed that the school needed to improve communication with students, provide more discipline, and give students more incentive to try harder.

Both black and white students believed that, in addition to more resources, students and teachers needed to challenge racial/ethnic stereotypes and see change as an opportunity for cultural understanding and Spanish language acquisition. For example, one white male student commented (R2), " ... it's [growth of Hispanic population] actually good 'cause ... I've learned a lot more out of different cultures from different races ... I've learned a little Spanish ... ". Sharing the same sentiment, a black female student (R2) said, "To me, it's a positive thing ... It's good, like educated, to learn another culture, another language, especially by a different country".

Though there were signs of the potential for change, the overall incorporation strategy adopted by School 4 was one of exclusion. Blacks, whites, and Hispanics attended the same school and shared the same classrooms but, unlike in school 3, rarely interacted. While there appeared to be a normative view that Hispanics were hardworking, participants expressed beliefs that Hispanics were unwelcome and contributing to the town's economic decline. Feeling impoverished and burdened by a history of exclusion and racism, participants' accounts point to a school that lacked the resources and collective will to accommodate the growing Hispanic segment of the town's population.

Discussion

As suggested by Berry's framework (2003), our research revealed substantial variability across schools in their degree of cultural inclusion and accommodation of cultural heritages. However, none of our schools combined high inclusion with low accommodation or low inclusion with high accommodation. The two urban schools tended to provide more accommodations for Hispanic students than the rural schools. Yet they had distinct approaches to cultural inclusion/exclusion. Among the urban schools, School 1 was viewed as inclusive, whereas School 2 was viewed by parents, teachers, and students as "segregated". Students of different racial/ethnic groups attended the same school but had limited contact with one another. Hispanic newcomers' customs and traditions were accommodated but not integrated into the school or broader community. Similarly, among the rural schools, School 3 could be characterized as inclusive though the high degree of racial/ethnic interactions sometimes led to physical conflicts. On the other hand, School 4 had an entrenched, historical pattern of racial/ethnic separation that was extended to include Hispanic newcomers. Moreover, the broader community perceived Hispanic newcomers as a threat to their way of life.

Consistent with Alba (2005), we also identified a variety of institutional practices, student behaviours, and teacher behaviours across the schools that brightened rather than blurred racial/ethnic boundaries, reduced Hispanic newcomers influence in schools, and potentially inhibited their assimilation. In School 1, Hispanic students in ESL classes were physically located in trailers set apart from the rest of the school. In School 2, separated restrooms and cafeterias built during the Jim Crow era had become a safe haven for Hispanics. In School 3, the use of Spanish and overt displays of ethnic pride had become sources of resentment and suspicion among students, and sometimes, teachers. In School 4, English-only classroom requirements and a lack of translation services prevented communication between Spanish-speaking parents and students and English-speaking teachers, parents, and students. Because of these brightened boundaries, Hispanic newcomers had limited opportunities to actively participate in the civic life of the school and community. Both racial/ethnic isolation and defensive mainstream hostility inhibited cross-cultural learning between Hispanic newcomers and long-time non-Hispanic black and white residents.

Additionally, we found that not all members of each school or community reacted to Hispanic newcomers in the same way. Comparing racial/ethnic group responses to Hispanic newcomers across schools, we found that blacks expressed political solidarity with Hispanics while also perceiving an economic threat from Hispanics. They repeatedly commented on their shared minority status and Hispanics' willingness to engage in the agricultural jobs that blacks had left behind. At the same time, they worried about school resources being re-directed towards Hispanic students and whites privileging Hispanics in service sector jobs. The attitudes of whites differed by socioeconomic status and location, which were intertwined. Higher SES whites in our urban areas expressed little sense of economic threat from Hispanic newcomers, but also limited social interaction with Hispanics in their schools or communities. They talked about Hispanics using stereotypical and sometimes unintentionally demeaning tropes. Lower SES whites in rural areas, by contrast, expressed a strong sense of both cultural and economic threat. It was only some of the younger generation of students (rather than parents or tea-chers) that seemed to value the potential for cultural exchanges and inter-actions that could enrich their lives.

Differences in schools' modes of incorporation (Portes and Rumbaut 2001) partially reflected the availability of resources in the schools and the intersec-tion of rural location, poverty, and race/ethnicity. Because funding for public schools is tied to local property taxes, the urban schools had more resources available to accommodate Hispanic newcomers than the rural schools. They had higher percentages of white students than the rural schools, lower teacher turnover, lower percentages of students receiving free/reduced price lunches, and lower percentages of Hispanic students. In the rural schools where the influx of foreign-born Hispanic students was greater, poverty higher, and patterns of racial/ethnic segregation more entrenched, there was both less capacity and less commitment to accommodating heri-tage cultures or facilitating cross-cultural exchanges.

Though ten years have passed since these data were collected, the patterns identified in these schools and their surrounding communities have endured, even as the Hispanic population in these school and communities has become predominately US-born. The youth of the schools in each of our sites are now the adults responsible for the civic lives of their communities. Newspaper and public opinion reports suggest a stronger commitment to accommodating immigrants and racial/ethnic minorities in urban areas of North Carolina and con-tinued fears about the economic and social impact of Hispanic newcomers in more rural areas (Watson and Riffe 2012; Gergen and Martin 2015; PRRI 2015). The rural areas of North Carolina, including those in this study, voted overwhel-mingly in favour of Donald Trump and the immigration policies he espoused during his presidential campaign (Politico 2016). In contrast, to facilitate the "suc-cessful integration" of immigrants more urban areas in NC have adopted "wel-coming city" initiatives and/or terminated their 287(g) programmes.

Overall, this study demonstrates that modes of incorporation vary substan-tially across schools even within a single state. The modes of incorporation within each school reflect differences in the availability of resources across schools, the racial/ethnic and socioeconomic composition of each school, and the history of racial/ethnic relations in each school and its surrounding community. However, because rural location, race/ethnic, and social class across our schools are highly intertwined, we are not able to disentangle the influence of each on modes of incorporation within schools. To better understand the influence of these factors, future research should encompass many more schools with greater variation in rural-urban location, racial/ethnic composition, and socioeconomic composition. Our research is also limited to four schools at a single point in time. We do not have longitudinal data from the non-Hispanic students, parents, and teachers in the school to evaluate whether these differences in modes of incorporation are maintained or change over time or to evaluate their effects on the socio-cultural assimilation of Hispanic youth in the South. Future research should also aim to collect longitudinal data on the attitudes, behaviours, and practices in schools and the socio-cultural assimilation of Hispanic youth. The adaptation of immigrants and their children does not take place in a vacuum. As we develop federal, state, and local policies and practices, we must remember that our choices will not only shape the futures of immigrants and their children but also the future of our entire community.

Acknowledgements

We gratefully acknowledge funding from the Russell Sage Foundation (RSF 88-06-07), the Russell Sage Visiting Scholar programme, and the Carolina Population Center for training support (T32 HD007168) and for general support (P2C HD050924). We also thank Rachel Osbourne, Tia Palermo, Kathleen Shannon, and Tasia Smith for their assistance with data collection. Finally, the authors would like to thank participants in the Children of Immigrants in New Places of Settlement Conference for their helpful suggestions.

Disclosure statement

No potential conflict of interest was reported by the authors.

Funding

This work was supported by National Institutes of Health: [grant number P2C HD050924,T32 HD007168]; Russell Sage Foundation: [grant number 88-06-07].

References

Alba, Richard. 2005. "Bright vs. Blurred Boundaries: Second-Generation Assimilation and Exclusion in France, Germany, and the United States." *Ethnic and Racial Studies* 28 (1): 20–49.

Berry, John. 2003. "Conceptual Approaches to Acculturation." In *Acculturation: Advances in Theory, Measurement, and Applied Research*, edited by Kevin M. Murphy, Pamela Balls Organista, and Gerardo Marin, 17–38. Washington, DC: American Psychological Association.

Brietzke, M. Priscilla, and Krista Perreira. 2017. "Stress and Coping: Latino Youth Coming of Age in a New Latino Destination." *Journal of Adolescent Research* 32 (4): 407–432.

Fussell, Elizabeth. 2014. "Warmth of the Welcome: Attitudes Toward Immigrants and Immigration Policy in the United States." *Annual Review of Sociology* 40: 479–498.

Gergen, Christopher, and Stephen Martin. 2015. "How Not to Handle N.C.'s Immigrant Boom." *Charlotte Observer*, December 5.

Gill, Hannah. 2010. *The Latino Migration Experience in North Carolina: New Roots in the Old North State*. Chapel Hill: University of North Carolina Press.

Green, Matthew, Krista M. Perreira, and Ko Linda. 2016. "Schooling Experiences of Latino/a Immigrant Adolescents in North Carolina: An Examination of the Relationships between Peers, Teachers, and Parents." In *Immigration and Education in North Carolina: The Challenges and Responses in a New Gateway State*, edited by Xue L. Rong, and Jeremy Hilburn, 53–80. Boston, MA: Sense Publisher.

Guzmán, Betsy. 2001. *The Hispanic Population: Census 2000 Brief*. Brief. Washington, DC: Census Bureau.

Hollander, Jocelyn. 2004. "The Social Contexts of Focus Groups." *Journal of Contemporary Ethnography* 33 (5): 602–637.

Jiménez, Tomás, and Adam Horowitz. 2013. "When White Is Just Alright: How Immigrants Redefine Achievement and Reconfigure the Ethnoracial Hierarchy." *American Sociological Review* 78 (5): 849–871.

Kandel, William, and Emilio Parrado. 2006. "Hispanic Population Growth and Public School Response in Two New South Immigrant Destinations." In *The New South: Latinos and the Transformation of Place*, edited by Heather A. Smith, and Owen Furuseth, 111–134. Aldershot, UK: Ashgate Press.

Ko, Linda K., and Krista M. Perreira. 2010. "'It Turned My World Upside Down': Latino Youths' Perspectives on Immigration." *Journal of Adolescent Research* 25 (3): 465–493.

Marrow, Helen B. 2008. "Hispanic Immigration, Black Population Size, and Intergroup Relations in the Rural and Small-Town South." In *New Faces in New Places: The Changing Geography of American Immigration*, edited by Douglas S. Massey, 211–248. New York: Russell Sage Foundation.

McClain, Paula D, Monique L. Lyle, Niambi M. Carter, Victoria M. DeFrancesco Soto, Gerald F. Lackey, Kendra Davenport Cotton, Shayla C. Nunnally, Thomas J. Scotto, Jeffrey D. Grynaviski, and J. Alan Kendrick. 2007. "Black Americans and Latino Immigrants in a Southern City: Friendly Neighbors or Economic Competitors?" *Du Bois Review: Social Science Research on Race* 4 (1): 97–117.

Miles, Matthew, and Michael Huberman. 1994. *Qualitative Data Analysis: An Expanded Sourcebook*. Thousand Oaks, CA: Sage Publications.

North Carolina Department of Public Instruction. 2017. *North Carolina School Reports Cards*. Raleigh, NC: North Carolina Department of Public Instruction.

O'Neil, Kevin, and Marta Tienda. 2010. "A Tale of Two Counties: Natives' Opinions Toward Immigration in North Carolina." *International Migration Review* 44 (3): 728–761.

Orum, Anthony. 2005. "Circles of Influence and Chains of Command: The Social Processes Whereby Ethnic Communities Influence Host Societies." *Social Forces* 84 (2): 921–939.

Perreira, Krista M., Andrew Fuligni, and Stephanie Potochnick. 2010. "Fitting In: The Roles of Social Acceptance and Discrimination in Shaping the Academic Motivations of Latino Youth in the U.S. Southeast." *The Journal of Social Issues* 66 (1): 131–153.

Politico. 2016. "2016 North Carolina Presidential Election Results." *Politico*, December 13.

Portes, Alejandro, and Rubén G. Rumbaut. 2001. *Legacies: The Story of the Immigrant Second Generation*. Berkeley, CA: University of California Press.

PRRI (Public Religion Research Institute). 2015. *American Values Atlas*. Washington, DC: PRRI.

Rosenblum, Marc, and Kristen McCabe. 2014. *Deportation and Discretion: Reviewing the Record and Options for Change*. Washington, DC: Migration Policy Institute.

Silver, Alexis. 2018. *Shifting Boundaries: Immigrant Youth Negotiating National, State and Small-Town Politics*. Stanford: Stanford University Press.

U.S. Census. 2008. *Selected Characteristics of the Native and Foreign-Born Populations: 2008 American Community Survey 1-Year Estimates*. Washington, DC: U.S. Census Bureau.

Watson, Brendan, and Daniel Riffe. 2012. "Perceived Threat, Immigration Policy Support, and Media Coverage: Hostile Media and Presumed Influence." *International Journal of Public Opinion Research* 25 (4): 459–479.

The value of reproduction: multiple livelihoods, cultural labor, and immigrants in Iowa and North Carolina

David Griffith

ABSTRACT

In the US South and Midwest, early immigrant populations consisted primarily of young, Latinos recruited to work in low-wage jobs. After six or seven years, family members from Mexico and Central America began joining early arrivals, changing the character of immigrant interactions with host residents and institutions. While many natives viewed the single men as migrant workers, important for economic services, the arrival of women and children stimulated ambivalent reactions in North Carolina and Iowa rural communities. This suggests that native perceptions of immigrants can be traced, in part, to immigrants' roles in local economies, including their participation in multiple livelihoods and their deployment of cultural labor. The contradiction between anti-immigrant sentiments and the need for immigrant labour can be understood as a reaction to increasingly precarious economic conditions facing both natives and immigrants in the twenty-first century and the changing values of productive and reproductive economies.

Introduction

Like many new immigrant destinations, Marshalltown, Iowa and Eastern North Carolina traced the origins of recent immigration to wage labour recruitment (Griffith 2005, 2008).[1] In Midwest meatpacking communities, recruitment of primarily Mexican workers began in the late 1980s and early 1990s, at the same time poultry and seafood companies began recruiting Mexican and Central American workers in Eastern North Carolina (Ribas 2017; Steusse 2016; Striffler 2005; Stull, Broadway, and Griffith 1995). In seafood, Mexican women were recruited as temporary, legal guestworkers carrying H-2B visas. By contrast, beef, pork, and poultry plants recruited large numbers of young, single men, who found housing in working-class neighbourhoods, small towns, and rural trailer parks, largely socially isolated from much of the native population. The seafood workers, living in company housing at or near the seafood plants, were similarly isolated.

The growing use of immigrant and foreign-born contract labour in the food industry occurred as a result of industrial restructuring and changing immigration policy. The 1986 Immigration Reform and Control Act (IRCA) was written and passed during the 1970s and 1980s dismantling of labour unions, a process common among Iowa Beef Processors (IBP), Hormel, and other large food producers and epitomized by Reagan's firing of the unionized air traffic controllers in 1981 (Griffith 1993; Kalleberg 2011). As multiple authors have discussed, these developments were the culminations of geographical shifts in food production from cities to rural areas and from North to South in search of cheaper supplies of labour and land in close proximity to livestock raising facilities, most of which were integrated into production regimes through subcontracts (Broadway 1995; Hage and Klauda 1988; Skaggs 1986). By the time that single young immigrant women and men arrived in Iowa and North Carolina to work in the food industry, these developments were far advanced.

During initial years of immigration, Iowa and North Carolina natives related to these immigrants and guestworkers as temporary residents, as they had been relating to Latino migrant farmworkers who passed through Iowa to detassle corn and North Carolina to harvest tobacco. Individuals interviewed in city governments, businesses, and other local institutions in Iowa and North Carolina nearly always referred to them as *migrants* (Grey 1999). Many expressed the view that as long as they were there to work, they were not a drain on community resources. This implied that the costs of their maintenance during unproductive periods of their lives, and their reproduction, had not and would not be borne locally. This is indeed the case with guestworkers, who are contracted for work as adults, after their maintenance and reproductive costs have been paid by their home communities, work in host countries without their families, and return home if injured or disabled (Griffith 2006).

In both Marshalltown and Eastern North Carolina, however, natives' views toward immigrants changed as women and children joined those who had arrived six or seven years earlier. By the early twenty-first century, and especially with the release of the 2000 census, it was becoming obvious that the immigrant communities in both states had changed from productive *workers* to productive and reproductive *families*. In short, these immigrants began to establish reproductive economies along with their contributions to the productive economy. This was accompanied by increasing immigrant social activism, the establishment of new immigrant businesses, and more frequent interaction with local institutions, especially schools, churches, health care centres, and law enforcement.

This article discusses these developments in light of changing U.S. rural economies and in particular the growing importance of multiple livelihoods under deteriorating economic conditions. It argues that migration, settlement, nativist reactions to immigrants, and immigrant entrepreneurship and social movements in new U.S. destinations reflect the precarious economic conditions that more and more people have been facing. Economic precariousness, further, is not confined to immigrants, but affects families from a variety of backgrounds, most evident in rising income inequality and declining or stagnating wages among individuals with low levels of education (Saez and Zucman 2016). I argue here that critical social forces related to income inequality, and to stagnating and declining incomes, are the rise in contract labour and combining self-employment with wage labour in multiple livelihood households.

Methods and data

This article is based on two initial studies in the rural U.S. Midwest and South conducted early in the twentieth century, from 2003 to 2010, and subsequent research in North Carolina to the present. Key findings from the first two studies—one on the impact of immigrants on rural communities in Georgia, North Carolina, Iowa, and Minnesota and the second on immigrant entrepreneurship in Iowa and North Carolina—have been published (Griffith 2005, 2008), as have some results from some of the subsequent work (Griffith 2009; Contreras and Griffith 2012). However, the principal theoretical arguments presented here were developed in the context of more recent (2013-present) research in rural North Carolina with insights from a project on managed migration between Guatemala and Canada and Mexico and the United States (Griffith 2014, 2017; Griffith, Preibisch, and Contreras 2018).

Each of these studies used a combination of methods, beginning with open-ended interviewing and structured observations using check lists and cultural mapping protocols, using findings from these early interactions with human subjects to develop more structured interviewing tools, and returning to select individuals, businesses, households, and other entities for more in-depth data collection. For example, the two initial studies generated contacts with individuals who then participated in oral history interviews for a study of Latino leadership in Eastern North Carolina, whose results are archived at https://digital.lib.ecu.edu/collection/latinoleadership.aspx. The author continues to visit the households and businesses of guestworkers, immigrant entrepreneurs, and native Latinos on a regular basis, in both North Carolina and Mexico.

While the more structured instruments were administered to larger samples, from around 100–200 individuals, pure random or representative sampling was impossible due to a variety of barriers: employer refusals of access to guestworkers; undocumented immigrants' fears; the mobility of the population, etc. Nevertheless, these larger samples allowed us to confirm which sentiments and behaviours discovered in early interviews and observations were widely shared. While we discuss both Iowa and North Carolina below, the discussion is biased toward the information from North Carolina, where research continues.

Productive and reproductive economies in migration theory

It has been well established in the social scientific literature that migration beginning as labour migration—that is, as an economic phenomenon—gradually develops into something more socially and culturally complex (Castles, De Hass, and Miller 2014; Massey et al. 1987). This complexity includes the development of ethnic enclaves, transnationalism, elaboration of social networks, and migration industries of coyotes (labour smugglers), identity support (tax IDs, documents), housing and transportation alternatives, language services, and so on (Hernandez-Leon 2013). Literature on new U.S. immigrant destinations, particularly rural areas, has raised questions about whether or not these processes are occurring differently in these locations than they have in California, New York, Texas, and other traditional immigrant destinations, where immigrant populations tend to concentrate in urban areas.

As noted earlier, migration into Eastern North Carolina and Iowa were the result of active labour recruitment by the food industry. Most of this occurred through a process of reaching out to migrant farmworkers and other foreign-born populations, including refugees, and subsequently engaging in network recruiting among current workers, resulting in some transnational ties as well as ties to other immigrant destinations in the United States (Grey and Woodrick 2002). Yet the settlement and incorporation of immigrants in both settings became more complex, and that complexity involved, primarily, the growth of immigrant reproductive economies with ties to local business development and activism.[2]

Migration scholars have long noted that one of the economic consequences of international labour migration has been that the costs of reproducing the labour force are borne by the migrants' home communities and countries, while the benefits of the labour accrue to the receiving businesses and economies (Meillassoux 1972; Pessar 1982; Griffith 1985). The migrants' home regions do not receive the highly productive labour of the workers who leave, yet they absorb the responsibilities of caring for unproductive children and elderly and less productive workers who stay. In short, the sending communities subsidize the receiving economies.

While these arguments were developed by examining relations between sending and receiving regions, my argument here is that, with the local growth of reproductive economies, these relationships change. In receiving settings, reproductive economies are as liable to complement or undermine productive economies as subsidize them, at times creating value themselves. I argue further that this occurs primarily in economies where individuals, families, and household groups engage in multiple livelihoods, with several income streams coming from a range of economic activities. Some of these activities may take place in the formal economy, as waged and salaried jobs, while others may take place in the informal sector as self-employment or labour that yields income in forms other than cash (e.g. scavenging, gardening, foraging) or may involve tapping into social support networks, whether formal (e.g. federal nutrition assistance) or informal (e.g. loans from relatives). Most importantly for work on the children of immigrants, the birth of children and the elaboration of reproductive economies facilitate and, in some cases, encourage engagement in multiple livelihoods, as this can provide flexibility with regard to child care and other domestic responsibilities. These behaviours grow with increasing economic insecurity and precariousness (Sassen 2014; Sharma 2006; Golding and Landolt 2013).

Further, when these processes occur at times of increasing anti-immigrant sentiments and state attempts to managed migration more comprehensively, tensions are likely to develop among those experiencing precarious and insecure economic conditions—conditions enhanced in the rural United States, where communities routinely witness business closures, deteriorating infrastructure, the flight of youth, environmental degradation, and shrinking tax revenues. Viewed through the lens of economic precariousness, the changes occurring in rural new immigrant destinations, including relations between immigrants and natives, can be considered extensions of the neoliberal practices and policies of privatization, commodification, and proletarianization that have destabilized local economies around the world. Indeed, their prevalence in locations that routinely send migrants to the United States, such as Mexico and Central America, stimulated much of the migration that has underwritten transnationalism, which, viewed through a material rather than cultural lens, has become a platform for extending multiple livelihoods across diasporas.

The political economics of separation

Early in the twenty-first century, rural Iowa and North Carolina were experiencing a brief wave of, if not immigrant acceptance, at least tolerance. Scattered developments in both states seemed destined to coalesce and overwhelm anti-immigration forces that included the Clinton Administration's 1994 strategy of "prevention through deterrence" and Bush and Obama deportation campaigns (Loyd and Mountz 2018; Massey 2018). Progressive-minded school officials in Marshalltown founded a bilingual programme in one of the local elementary schools, and lawyers with Legal Aid in North Carolina threatened to sue the state Department of Public Instruction if they did not begin providing Limited English Proficient (LEP) programmes to immigrant children—both developments indicating increased institutional interest in and support for growing immigrant populations. Centres to welcome immigrants were established at the University of Northern Iowa and the University of North Carolina at Greensboro. In many rural communities, local natives praised the revitalization efforts of immigrant businesspeople as they moved into storefronts abandoned by native merchants after the rise of box stores.

Not all was positive. These changes were accompanied by increased anti-immigration voices in the two states calling for English-only laws, partnerships between sheriffs' departments and Immigration and Customs Enforcement (ICE), and other legal mechanisms nearly as draconian as those passed in Arizona and Alabama but subsequently deemed impossible to enforce. These voices have fluctuated over time, often nearly silenced as racist, yet recent scapegoating at the national and international levels has lent additional legitimacy to anti-immigrant sentiments, leading to increased bullying in schools, confrontations in public spaces, racialized policing of immigrant spaces, and consequent incarcerations and deportations (Massey 2018; Gándara 2018).

In Iowa, over time, funding for the Welcoming New Iowans Center dried up even as immigrant and refugee groups continued to arrive in the state. Today the state has a strong Republican base; many of its residents, supporting Trump, resent immigrants. While North Carolina still has its Welcoming New North Carolinians at University of North Carolina (UNC)-Greensboro, other campuses have stepped back from supporting new immigrant programmes, leaving advocacy to the immigrants themselves—many of them youth (e.g. https://www.thetimesnews.com/news/20181014/new-north-carolinians).

In both Iowa and North Carolina, immigrant workers remain critical to the states' labour forces and economies, yet political action has grown increasingly nativist and negative. How do pro-capitalist interests reconcile the contradiction between the need for immigrant wage labour and the intolerance of immigrants? Again, we see this in a preference for single immigrant workers at the same time we witness increasing tolerance for separating families at border crossings and the inept politics surrounding the fate of the children of immigrants granted temporary sanctuary, recently revoked, under the Deferred Action for Childhood Arrivals Act (DACA).

The nativist preference for productive workers over reproductive people is evident among employers, politicians, and U.S. citizens who generally oppose immigration yet support the importation of *nonimmigrant* guestworkers (Ruhs and Martin 2008). Donald Trump is among those politician-employers who opposes immigration yet actively hires foreign contract workers for his resorts and his vineyards, recently doubling the number of H-2B temporary work visas (Fahrenthold 2018). Similarly, Craig Lang, the Iowa farmer who hired Cristhian Rivera, the Mexican national who murdered Mollie Tibbetts, was widely reported to have been a "prominent Republican" who was the former head of Iowa Farm Bureau (KKCI News, August 22, 2018). However, instead of focusing on Lang's dependence on Mexican nationals for his dairy farm's labour force, the coverage focused on problems with the e-verify system and the ability of immigrants to engage in identity theft to access employment (Fox New, August 22, 2018). In short, it aimed its criticism at the system and immigrant criminal behaviour rather than businesses that hired the undocumented.

Immigrant resistance

Immigrants have not been passive recipients of hostility or resentment, but instead, in both Iowa and North Carolina, struggle to settle with and without legal documents. They have done this in a variety of ways, but relying on the public-school system and other state and local institutions, as well as churches and ethnic organizations, have facilitated their resistance. Connecting with these local institutions, as noted above, occurred coinciden-tally with the growth of an immigrant reproductive economy. Again, the mere presence of children significantly alters the social dynamics between immi-grant and native communities and within immigrant families. Moreover, immigrants and others experiencing precarious economies often highly value reproductive labour and its yields of productive children, well-being, and happiness (Griffith, Preibisch, and Contreras 2018; Johnston et al. 2012).

The children of immigrants have played important roles in assisting in settling and assimilation, often among the most fluent in English in their households and responsible for translating for parents at medical centres, in courts of law, and in everyday settings such as yard sales, flea markets, and grocery stores. Occupying these roles, they often mature more quickly than they otherwise would have and experience pressures that children who are not immigrants or the children of immigrants rarely experience (Gonzales 2016). For example, a Latina woman whom I hired as a research assistant demonstrated the speed at which immigrant youth often must mature: Carmen (pseudonym), migrated from Pauhuatlán, Puebla at 14 to live with her aunt in Atlanta, Georgia before moving to Durham, North Carolina at 16, where a number of individuals from her home town have settled. She enrolled in high school and began learning English in English as a Second Language (ESL) classes, but after two years still had mastered only a rudimen-tary knowledge of the language.

Carmen was 18 when she began working for me, part-time, and, even though still attending high school, combined work for me with two other part-time jobs in Durham fast food restaurants, living with friends from

Pauhuatlán in a minimally-furnished apartment. Around the time she turned 19, her mother, Doña Eusebia, migrated from Pauhuatlán to Durham with Carmen's younger brother, age 10, and younger sister, age 14. The four of them found an apartment together, Carmen's brother and sister enrolled in the Durham public schools, and Doña Eusebia founded an informal business making lunches for workers from Pauhuatlán, each day exchanging a new lunch box for the previous day's box.

Shortly after Doña Eusebia's arrival, tensions developed between her and Carmen. In Carmen's view, Doña Eusebia entertained her clients in the evening far too frequently, and paid too little attention to either of her two younger children. Eventually, Doña Eusebia moved to Atlanta to be with her sister, the aunt whom Carmen had lived with, and Carmen moved into a smaller apartment with her two younger siblings, assuming principal care for them. "*Mi vida ha cambiado totalmente*," ("My life has totally changed") she told me, adding that she had encouraged her mother to move, viewing her as a bad influence on her siblings. A short time later, Carmen's sister, at only 15, became pregnant.

Carmen is an exceptional young woman. Despite being undocumented, she continues to hold multiple jobs, has finished high school, and now has two children herself with a young immigrant construction worker from Pauhuatlán. She and her partner have benefited from the fact that entrepreneurs from Pauhuatlán have established bakeries and other small businesses in Durham where they can meet and talk with others from their home community, that there are Pauhuatlán soccer clubs, and that the city is in an area—the Durham, Raleigh, Chapel Hill Triangle—that is more tolerant of immigrants than many other areas in North Carolina. Carmen's need to mature rapidly is not uncommon among children and young adult immigrants, as they are enlisted to assist with child care, the establishment of informal businesses, and other attributes of the immigrant experience. Those who cannot mature as rapidly as someone like Carmen, unfortunately, often become involved in substance abuse, unsafe sex, crime, and other deleterious behaviours to cope with additional responsibility (Garcia 2008).

In the remainder of this article, I discuss a few ways that immigrant families struggle to stay in North Carolina, where my research continues. I also engage the larger debate mentioned earlier: that of the roles of immigrants in increasingly precarious economies. Here I discuss two methods with which immigrants assert their right to stay: 1) the formation of ethnic associations; and 2) immigrant entrepreneurship, which often results in families engaging in multiple livelihoods. Both entail connections to U.S. institutions—schools, health care centres, churches, businesses, government agencies, etc.—that assist with the reproduction of families and communities.

Cultural labor: ethnic activism and immigrant settlement

At least since the turn of the twenty-first century, North Carolina's immigrants have been involved in advocacy for their rights in many ways. Among the first and most enduring organizations has been the *Asociación de los Mexicanos de Carolina del Norte* (AMEXCAN), which was founded by and is still operated by Juvencio Rocha Peralta (Peralta, Griffith, and Contreras 2014). Established in 2001, AMEXCAN assists Mexicans, Central Americans, and other Latinos in Eastern North Carolina by acting as a liaison between Latino immigrants and their consulates; providing information about jobs, schooling, and other opportunities; co-hosting celebrations of Latino culture; seeking funding to address problems facing Latinos (e.g. diabetes, discrimination); acting as a strong advocate for immigrant rights; providing internships to local college students; and developing workshops on various issues of interest to the health and welfare of the local Latino immigrant populations (e.g. nutrition, prenatal and child health, domestic violence, entrepreneurship). Juvencio himself has been locally praised for his work in a number of venues, in 2017 receiving East Carolina University's award for outstanding community outreach and engagement, which was one of a long line of awards from local institutions, governments, and organizations.

Unfortunately, AMEXCAN has suffered from chronic problems with funding, relying on local institutions for free office space, venues for its workshops, and volunteer services. Some of these problems derive from a lack of cooperation with other, larger organizations such as La Raza or the Latino Credit Union, while others can be traced to little sustained native commitment to a non-African American ethnic organization in Eastern North Carolina. Yet, in part because of its chronic struggle with funding, AMEXCAN conforms to James Coleman's (1988) definition of social capital, able to marshal its social capital at strategic moments yet also capable of remaining dormant for long periods. This social capital consists of connections with local institutions, particularly Pitt Community College and East Carolina University (mediated by faculty interested in immigration issues), with local churches, with African American ethnic organizations, with the Mexican consulate in Raleigh, and with local media outlets.

Following the election of Donald Trump and a rise in local anti-immigrant expression, AMEXCAN called attention to increased bullying of Latino students in local schools. This occurred, first, by assembling Eastern North Carolina residents—natives and immigrants—in a local church one evening to share experiences and discuss methods of dealing with discrimination and, second, developing a workshop to teach students how to deal with bullying in school (Botex 2017). This kind of response to discrimination against immigrants is quite typical of AMEXCAN. Depending on support from the local community and various institutions, Juvencio has managed to draw on local clergy, educators, and others to assist him in such organizational efforts.

Like many small organizations with leaders reluctant to share power, however, AMEXCAN spawned other ethnic organizational activities when some members broke from AMEXCAN to found their own organization. After an internal dispute over the disposition of funding regarding a project involving encouraging increased outreach among Latino *promatoras de salud* (health advisors), several Latino mothers left AMEXCAN to found a Latino youth organization called *Jóvenes en Acción* (Youth in Action).[3] The organization consisted primarily of the founders' teenaged children and their friends, and its goal was to encourage leadership and entrepreneurship among Latino youth and to perform highly visible community service—cleaning public parks and other public spaces—that would demonstrate to the wider community that they were an asset rather than a drain on community resources. The youth in *Jóvenes* constituted the principal audience for a workshop on entrepreneurship held in April 2011, as part of a USDA-funded research project on immigrant entrepreneurship in rural new destinations (Contreras et al. 2012). For the workshop lunch, their mothers prepared traditional Mexican cuisine for participants, instructors, and organizers, and the parents remained throughout the workshop, as interested in the information provided as their children.

Other ethnic organizations, however, have not been nearly as successful. During a brief period around 2010, an organization emerged that called itself *Mujeres sin Fronteras* (Women without Borders) in the rural countryside of Wayne and Greene Counties, both of which import large numbers of Latino farmworkers during the summer months. *Mujeres* was an organization formed by around half a dozen female farmworkers who claimed to represent farmworkers across all of Eastern North Carolina. Their connections with two youth-oriented organizations, Migrant Education and Duke University's Student Action for Farmworkers (SAF), enabled them to access a variety of goods and services. They were assisted by volunteers—mostly area undergraduate college students and professors—who offered them free labour (one student's in the form of a summer internship) and solicited donations on their behalf.

During its brief life, *Mujeres* managed to engage teams of student and faculty workers, partnering with Migrant Education staff and SAF personnel, to achieve three concrete objectives: 1) building and stocking a chicken coop and greenhouse in the yard of the leader; 2) organizing a clothing drive for farmworkers, which *Mujeres* planned to distribute to increase their legitimacy in the farmworker community; and 3) establishing a booth at a local flea market to sell eggs from the chickens and produce from the greenhouse to finance *Mujeres* activism. For its part, *Mujeres* offered to assist in organizing workshops for farmworkers to teach them about farm safety issues, nutrition, diabetes, and other issues. Eventually, however, it became obvious that what had originally begun as about half a dozen women working together devolved into one astute Latino woman, Dolores, using her status as a farmworker and mother of migrant children to receive goods and services for herself. She shared none of the proceeds from the sales of eggs and produce with others in the organization and sold the donated clothing from her flea market booth rather than distributed it to farmworkers. Her hoarding led to the disintegration of *Mujeres*.

These examples illustrate the appeal of what we can call cultural labour in defending and promoting immigrants' rights. Like social capital, cultural labour depends on (ethnic) group membership and trust, and involves drawing on cultural heritage and shared history to marshal the participation of both members of ethnic communities and others who sympathize with their plights. Juvencio and Dolores have relied extensively on trust, which Juvencio continues to use for the benefit of the wider Latino community (if occasionally attempting to husband resources) and Dolores may have abused but, in the process, contributed to the missions of Migrant Education and SAF. Despite that Dolores was ultimately somewhat of a con artist, in her defense, several small conferences and events were organized on behalf of *Mujeres* and, at each of these, she was able to educate locals about the plights facing farmworkers in Eastern North Carolina. Although poorly educated, Dolores was quite an articulate and emotional speaker, speaking in a soft voice and even tone about the suffering and sacrifice of farmworkers in the region.

Similar observations could be made about Juvencio and AMEXCAN. Although the women who founded *Jovenes* broke from him in a dispute over funding, Juvencio has managed to raise awareness about issues facing immigrants across Eastern North Carolina. Local newspapers regularly seek him out for quotes when anything involving immigrants receives media attention, such as the militarization of the Mexico-U.S. border at the arrival of Central Americans in November 2018.

As forms of cultural labour, these and other efforts to organize immigrants and enlighten natives about their plights enable the elaboration and reproduction of Latino culture in Eastern North Carolina. While Latinos are by no means culturally homogeneous, the deployment of cultural labour has enabled some homogeneity with local Spanish-speaking radio programmes, talk shows, and other media. These have been organized by Hondurans, Mexicans, Mexican-Americans, Guatemalans, Puerto Ricans, Cubans, and others, many of whom occupy positions in social services, health care, education, and legal services directed toward Spanish speakers. Many of their stories are included in the Latino leadership archive mentioned earlier. Many too depend on the entrepreneurial skills of their founders and supporters, who work to access resources from multiple sources to keep the organizations going at that minimal level needed to marshal social capital during times of crisis.

Furthering cultural labor: immigrant entrepreneurship

Latino immigrants have established many new businesses across North Carolina, most serving primarily immigrants but a few, particularly in the skilled
construction and mechanical trades, catering to a wider clientele. Focusing
on four North Carolina rural counties and one metropolitan county with
high concentrations of immigrants—two in Western North Carolina and
three in the East—we collected information from 128 entrepreneurs/
businesses that fell into five categories. Table 1 shows the distribution of
businesses by business sector and by county, using pseudonyms for the counties but giving their general locations in the state.

Almost two-thirds (63%) of the businesses visited fall into those categories
that are most common among immigrant entrepreneurs—general convenience stores and restaurants or food stands. Many of the convenience
stores also provide services, such as money transfers or referrals to immigration attorneys and local clinics, and sell as wide a variety of products as, say, a
Family Dollar: clothes, shoes, baptismal blankets, votive candles, pots and
pans …. Services include beauty salons, tax services, computing/ communication services, immigration/ travel services, auto mechanics, and construction (painting, roofing, masonry, heating and air conditioning, etc.). Other
businesses include furniture stores, light manufacturing, laundries, and book
or music stores. Combined with labour contracting and human smuggling,
these immigrant-owned businesses can be considered part of the migration
economy—or those economic sectors and government services and agencies,
including ICE and their sheriff-department partners, that depend on continued immigration to survive and flourish (Steusse and Coleman 2014). Table
2 shows the types of goods and services these businesses provide, many of
which qualify as parts of the informal/ underground economy.

The names of businesses often reflect the origins of the owners (e.g. La
Tienda Michoacana), and although most are owner-operated, each business
tends to generate additional jobs outside of the owner's family. In so far as
these jobs promote specific cultural histories, they can be considered cultural
labour. In any case, they are sources of employment within the Latino community. Bilingual Latino youth are the most common employees hired, putting

Table 1. Inventory of Latino Businesses Contacted by County (totals not 100% are due to
rounding error).

County/ Total interviews	Stores	Food	Services	Clothing	Other
Merwin/ 35 [rural, eastern]	42% [14]	28% [10]	11% [4]	11% [4]	8% [3]
Bartram/ 39 [semi-rural, east central]	33% [13]	31% [12]	23% [9]	0	13% [5]
Lawson/ 22 [rural, western mountains]	32% [7]	14% [3]	9% [2]	18% [4]	27% [6]
Wright and Bly/ 19 [rural, western foothills]	21% [4]	42% [8]	10% [2]	5% [1]	21% [4]
Beloit/ 13 [metro, eastern]	46% [6]	31% [4]	15% [2]	0	7% [1]
Total [128]	**44 (34%)**	**37 (29%)**	**19 (15%)**	**9 (7%)**	**19 (15%)**

Table 2. Types of Goods and Services of Immigrant Businesses.

Types of Products	Variations	Examples
Nostalgia Products	Processed/ Prepared	Oaxacan tortillas; Honduran sauces; Latino baked goods; tooled leather.
	Natural	Cactus leaves; tomatillas; spices.
Ceremonial Products	Religious	Votive candles; baptismal blankets; images of the Virgin of Guadalupe; wedding dresses.
	Secular	Quinceañera dresses; birthday cakes.
Entertainment Products	Live	Performed music; arranged dances; theatre performances; billiards; cockfights; boxing/ sporting events; prostitution; alcoholic beverage/ drug sales.
	Electronic	Dish antennae installation; Spanish-speaking television playing in stores; video games.
	Other media	DVDs; books/ comic books; games.
Work-Related Products	Services	Income tax service; accounting; legal advice.
	Goods	Box lunches; hard hats, work boots & gloves.
Migration Industry Products	Communication	Phone cards; internet services; packaging/ shipping.
	Financial Services	Wire transfers; money orders; check-cashing/ loan services.
	Transportation	Bus ticket sales; courier services.
Health & Beauty Products	Services	Hair cutting/ styling; manicures/ nail decorating; tattooing; curing (herbal, conventional medical); nutritional advice.
	Goods	Herbal remedies; lotions; shampoos; Mexican prescription pharmaceuticals sold over-the-counter.
Repackaged Products (sifted into comfortable cultural settings)	From Retail Giants (e.g. Sam's Club)	Snacks (e.g. chips in individual bags); canned/ dry goods; packaged meat products.
	From distributors	Frito-Lay/ snack products; local dairy products; eggs.
Products Related to Trust	Common cultural background	Health care/ curing; referrals to health care centres with bilingual staff; child care services.
	Communication	Translation services.
	Legal issues	Referrals to lawyers, consular staff, immigration specialists.

these businesses more or less on par with other sources of teen employment (e.g. fast food/ restaurant work, clerks, cleaning staff).

Many of these businesses are often owned, managed, and staffed by women. Self-employment among immigrant women, several Latino women reported, has been a way that they can care for children while generating income for the family. Even when the principal business person is male, women and children provide so many support services to immigrant businesses that immigrant entrepreneurship is deeply intertwined with the immigrant reproductive economy.

In a broader sense, these businesses have become part of struggling rural communities' attempts to revitalize their economies and reproduce them-selves in the wake of native population loss, the impacts of box stores on local merchants, and generally deteriorating, precarious economic conditions. Many immigrant businesses have moved into commercial districts of rural counties—country road strip malls, the downtowns of small communities, etc.—that have been abandoned by native merchants. We encountered several other venues of Latino businesses in our research as well, including an increasing share of stalls and food stands at county flea markets. Most flea markets operate between one to three days per week, and several of the Latino businesspeople we encountered at flea markets follow a circuit that includes two or three different flea markets in either neighbouring or more distant counties, making it possible to combine flea market sales with other jobs. Some entrepreneurs incubated their business acumen in flea markets before moving into storefronts. Most of the produce sales in rural flea markets have been entirely or nearly entirely Latinized, as have most of the cooked food stands and stalls.

In addition to the flea markets and formerly abandoned storefronts and offices, Latino entrepreneurs have set up temporary structures and stands in parking lots, usually selling produce or cooked food. Some store owners have outfitted vans with shelves to travel on weekends to Latino neighbourhoods or labour camps, selling products ranging from phone cards and snacks to clothing, blankets, boots, and produce. Finally, a number of Latinos operate businesses out of their homes, including one photographer and one artist, signalling a move into the visual arts.[4]

One key way in which many Latino artisans, craftsmen, and people skilled at trades like carpentry become entrepreneurs is through subcontracting. This dovetails with recent labour market trends in many fields that utilize immigrant labour. Subcontracting takes a variety of forms, from crews on construction sites who provide specialized services (e.g. framing, hanging and taping sheetrock, providing electrical services) to labour contracting and temp agencies who place people in companies but continue to serve as the employer of record, shielding the firms utilizing the workers' labour from compliance with labour and immigration laws.

Once largely restricted to the farm, construction, and garment labour markets, subcontracting has become more and more popular across the U.S. economy and now characterises large segments of the so-called gig economy (e.g. Uber drivers, consulting social scientists). This is reflected in recent figures on the growth of 1099-Misc forms issued by the IRS as compared to W-2 forms. Dourado and Koopman (2015) reported that 1099-Misc forms, or those issued to people for nonemployee compensation (usually contract work) increased by 22% from 2000 to 2015, while W-2 forms declined by 3.5%. Proponents of subcontracting argue that these arrangements allow capitalist enterprises to remain flexible, expanding and contracting their labour forces with fluctuations in demand for their products, just as garment manufacturers could hire and fire multiple seamstresses as fashion cycles changed as often as the hems of ladies' dresses. Although subcontractors can consider themselves entrepreneurs, being technically self-employed, these relations often become highly exploitative (Rosenblat 2018).

Subcontracting does allow immigrant artisans and craftsmen to teach their trades to their children, however. As such, they can fill in the gaps in opportunity for those without papers and even without proper schooling, allowing children of immigrants to drop out of school and still find work if bullying occurs or with threats of ICE raids. Unfortunately, in some households I have encountered, parents have encouraged their children to leave school to contribute to the family income as soon as they become capable of earning, again speeding up maturing.

Conclusion: new immigrants, new destinations, new economics

New immigrant destinations reflect many of the same social and economic developments we witness among populations incorporated into capitalist political economies in largely low-wage, lesser-skilled, and subservient, often hazardous positions. Although jobs in meatpacking, poultry processing, construction, and other sectors now targeted by immigrants have been unionized in the past and some are still represented by unions today, most such wage labour employment has deteriorated, providing ever more precarious livelihoods and ever more fluid, mobile populations, with the sources of the perceived and real flux coming from multiple social sectors. Failing to achieve security and still tied to immigrant diasporas, many new immigrants in new destinations suffer from incomplete, segmented, or otherwise uneven assimilation even while they attempt to settle in places like Iowa and North Carolina, raise their children, and forge their own identities.

Part of adjusting to new destinations has involved engaging both existing local institutions such as health care centres and schools and new, emerging "economies" that have been forged by immigrants themselves or are typical of new economic relations developing in many areas of the world. These include, for example, the informal economy, which has been a part of economic formations across time, as well as newer formations such as the gig economy, the sharing economy, the migration economy, the barter economy, and so on. None of these are complete economies, but are instead parts of larger economic formations that engage more or fewer people in different class, social, or cultural positions depending on trajectories of political economic growth and decline.

The economic developments taking place with these new economies both resemble the economics of many natal communities of immigrants in sending countries, where combining multiple livelihoods is the norm, and increasingly characterise areas, like Iowa and North Carolina, whose economies are transforming, changing from formerly "good" manufacturing jobs in sectors like meatpacking and textiles to poorly-paid work in the food industry, tourism, services, and so forth. These changes have altered relations between productive and reproductive economies in ways similar to the incorporation of indigenous others into expanding North American capitalism, which often results in the maintenance of alterity to prevent assimilation and effective class-based resistance (Wolf 1982; Kingsolver 2007).

How, in new immigrant destinations, have such processes been cushioned or softened, even as they contribute to uneven assimilation? The above observations suggest that the process of immigrant settlement and resistance to deportation involves engagement with institutions and that, among all institutions, those involved with reproducing society and community—schools, health care centres, churches, etc.—provide the most critical liaison functions between immigrant populations and the wider society. As such, they complement the cultural and reproductive labour that immigrants marshal and deploy to construct the conditions of permanent settlement, in the process establishing a reproductive economy with ever more and ever deeper links to the productive economy.

Once this occurred, political forces representing anti-immigrant sentiments strengthened their efforts to separate immigrants from schools and other public institutions, denying access to them to people living in the country without documents. These processes are extremely disruptive to reproductive economies and a cornerstone of exploitative labour relations that separate productive from reproductive labour, as with guestworker programmes (Griffith 1987). As efforts to cut off immigrants from public resources and deportation efforts increase, more and more employers of immigrants have been lobbying for guestworker programmes to gain access to legal, temporary, foreign contract labour. Not only do these programmes separate productive from reproductive labour, they also bind workers to single employers without free access to the labour market, approximating, in many worker advocates' minds, slavery and indentured servitude. Separating children from their parents at the border as a deterrent is therefore little more than yet another phase in a long tradition of separating productive from reproductive labour—from the settings and protections of reproduction— that have been the source of slavery, human trafficking, and guestworker programmes. Among the principal methods immigrants have to resist these efforts is, quite simply, to reproduce.

Notes

1. After Nancy Foner (2003), I use the term immigrants to refer to the foreign-born who have come to Iowa and North Carolina to live and work, rather than migrants, although I realize that transnational ties and continued mobility often means that these same people may become migrants; however, migrants in Iowa and North Carolina tends to carry pejorative meanings, associated with migrant farmworkers.
2. Considering reproductive and productive economies separate economies is more analytical than real, as the two are deeply intertwined in daily practice. Yet, for our purposes here, we consider reproductive economies as those oriented toward the maintenance and reproduction of human groups rather

than the creation of goods and services, most of which are considered commodities, for sale or consumption, which falls within the productive economy.

3. This is a pseudonym because tensions still exist between parents of this youth group and AMEXCAN.

4. The interest in visual arts among Latino entrepreneurs has included at least one foray into filmmaking. Wilmington, NC has a film industry that has struggled over time but has remained operating, producing shows for cable television, films, and spawning theatres throughout the city and beyond. It may have been the influence of Wilmington's film industry across eastern North Carolina that encouraged one particularly enterprising Latino entrepreneur to produce a film, *Lágrimas del Corazon* (Tears of the Heart), available on DVD, which is set mostly in eastern North Carolina and stars member of his family along with some fairly well-known Mexican actors.

Acknowledgements

Many thanks to the multiple individuals who agreed to be interviewed for this paper, and to the National Science Foundation (grant #0722468), the U.S. Department of Agriculture, and the University of North Carolina Sea Grant College Program for providing funding for the research upon which this paper is based. Thanks also to Alejandro Portes and Patricia Fernandez-Kelly for organizing the conferences where this work was originally presented and offering comments on earlier drafts. Finally, many thanks to three anonymous reviewers, and to Amanda Eastell-Bleakley of Ethic and Racial Studies, for their helpful comments on an earlier draft of this article.

Disclosure statement

No potential conflict of interest was reported by the author.

Funding

This work was supported by National Science Foundation, Division of Social and Economic Sciences [Grant Number 0722468]; University of North Carolina Sea Grant College Program; United States Department of Agriculture.

References

Botex, Shelia. 2017. "Workshop Addresses Bullying against Hispanics." The Daily Reflector, Greenville, NC. March 2. (www.reflector.com; accessed March 23, 2017).

Broadway, Michael. 1995. "From City to Countryside: Recent Changes in the Structure and Location of the Meat- and Fish-Processing Industries." In *Any way They cut it: Meat Processing and Small-Town America*, edited by D. Stull, M. Broadway, and D. Griffith, 17–40. Lawrence: University Press of Kansas.

Castles, Stephen, H. De Hass, and M. Miller. 2014. *The Age of Migration*. New York: Palgrave.

Coleman, James. 1988. "Social Capital in the Creation of Human Capital." *American Journal of Sociology* 94: 24–36.

Contreras, Ricardo, Kim Larson, John Pierpont, David Griffith, and Juvencio Rocha Peralta. 2012. "Capacity Building in the Latino Community: Lessons From the Promatora Project in Eastern North Carolina." *Practicing Anthropology* 34 (4): 19–24.

Contreras, Ricardo, and David Griffith. 2012. "Managing Migration, Managing Motherhood: The Moral Economy of Gendered Migration." *International Migration* 50(4): 51–66.

Dourado, E., and C. Koopman. 2015. *Evaluating the Growth of the 1099 Work Force.* Fairfax, VA: Mercatus Center, George Mason University.

Fahrenthold, David. 2018. Trump's Mar-a-Lago Club in Florida seeks to hire 78 foreign workers. Washington Post, July 10. Accessed 13 January 2019. https://www.washingtonpost.com/politics/trumps-mar-a-lago-club-in-florida-seeks-to-hire-40-for eign-workers/2018/07/05/5ef094b8-8099-11e8-bb6b-c1cb691f1402_story.html

Gándara, Patricia. 2018. The students we share: falling through the cracks on both sides of the U.S.-Mexico Border. Paper presented at the conference, Children of Immigrants in an Age of Deportation, Princeton University, October 27.

Garcia, Victor. 2008. "Problem Drinking among Transnational Mexican Migrants." *Human Organization* 67 (1): 12–24.

Golding, Luin, and Patricia Landolt. 2013. "The Social Production of Non-Citizenship: Intersecting Trajectories of Precarious Legal Status and Precarious Work." In *Producing and Negotiating Non-Citizenship*, edited by L. Goldring, and P. Landolt, 154–174. Toronto: University of Toronto Press.

Gonzales, Roberto. 2016. *Lives in Limbo: Undocumented and Coming of age in America.* Berkeley: University of California Press.

Grey, Mark. 1999. "Immigrants, Migration, and Worker Turnover at the Hog Pride Pork Packing Plant." *Human Organization* 58 (1): 16–27.

Grey, Mark, and A. Woodrick. 2002. "Unofficial Sister Cities." *Human Organization* 61 (4): 364–376.

Griffith, David. 1985. "Women, Remittances, and Reproduction." *American Ethnologist* 12 (4): 676–690.

Griffith, David. 1987. "Nonmarket Labor Processes in an Advanced Capitalist Economy." *American Anthropologist* 89 (4): 838–852.

Griffith, David. 1993. *Jones's Minimal: Low-Wage Labor in the United States.* Albany: SUNY Press.

Griffith, David. 2005. "Rural Industry and Latino Immigration and Settlement in North Carolina." In *New Destinations of Mexican Immigration in the United States: Community Formation, Local Responses, and Inter-Group Relations*, edited by Victor Zúñiga, and Rubén Hernández-Leon, 50–75. New York: Russell Sage Foundation.

Griffith, David. 2006. *American Guestworkers: Jamaicans and Mexicans in the U.S. Labor Market.* University Park, PA: Penn State University Press.

Griffith, David. 2009. "The Moral Economy of Tobacco." *American Anthropologist* 111 (4): 432–442.

Griffith, David. 2008. "New Midwesterners, New Southerners: Immigration Experiences in Four Rural U.S. Settings." In *New Faces in New Places: The Changing Geography of American Immigration*, edited by Douglas Massey, 179–210. New York: Russell Sage Foundation.

Griffith, David, ed. 2014. *(Mis)Managing Migration.* Santa Fe, NM: School of Advanced Research.

Griffith, David. 2017. Multiple Livelihoods, Multiple Sources: Labor along North Carolina's coastal plain. Final report to the UNC Sea Grant College Program.

Griffith, David, Kerry Preibisch, and Ricardo Contreras. 2018. "The Value of Reproductive Labor." *American Anthropologist* 120 (2): 224–236.

Hage, David, and Paul Klauda. 1988. *No Retreat, no Surrender: Labor's war at Hormel.* New York: William Morrow.

Hernandez-Leon, Ruben. 2013. "Conceptualizing the Migration Industry." In *The Migration Industry and the Commercialization of International Migration*, edited by T. Gammeltoft-Hansen, and N. Nyber Sorensen, 21–42. New York: Routledge.

Johnston, Barbara, E. Colson, D. Falk, G. St. John, J. Bodley, B. McCay, A. Wali, C. Nordstrom, S. Slyovics, and On Happiness. 2012. *American Anthropologist* 114 (1): 6–18.

Kalleberg, Arne. 2011. *Good Jobs, Bad Jobs: Polarization and Precarious Employment Systems in the United States.* New York: Russell Sage Foundation.

Kingsolver, Ann. 2007. "Farmers and Farmworker: Two Centuries of Strategic Alterity in Kentucky's Tobacco Fields." *Critique of Anthropology* 27 (1): 18–32.

Loyd, Jenna, and Alison Mountz. 2018. *Boats, Borders, and Bases.* Berkeley: University of California Press.

Massey, Douglas. 2018. Creating the Exclusionist Society: From the War on Poverty to the War on Immigrants. Paper presented at the conference, Children of Immigrants in an Age of Deportation, Princeton University, October 27.

Massey, Douglas, Rafael Alarcón, Jorge Durand, and Humberto González. 1987. *Return to Aztlan.* Berkeley: University of California Press.

Meillassoux, Claude. 1972. "From Production to Reproduction." *Economy and Society* 1 (1): 93–105.

Peralta, Juvencio, David Griffith, and Ricardo Contreras. 2014. "A History of Activism: The Organizational Work of Juvencio Rocha Peralta." In *(Mis)Managing Migration: Guestworkers' Experiences in North American Labor Markets*, edited by D. Griffith, 211–224. Santa Fe, NM: School of Advanced Research Press.

Pessar, Patricia. 1982. "The Role of Households in International Migration." *International Migration Review* 2 (16): 342–364.

Ribas, Vanessa. 2017. *On the Line: Slaughterhouse Lives and the Making of the New South.* Berkeley: University of California Press.

Rosenblat, Alex. 2018. *Uberland: How Algorithms are Rewriting the World of Work.* Berkeley: University of California Press.

Ruhs, Martin, and Philip Martin. 2008. "Numbers vs. Rights: Trade-Offs and Guest Worker Programs." *International Migration Review* 42 (1): 249–265.

Saez, E., and G. Zucman. 2016. "Wealth Inequality in the United States Since 1913." *Quarterly Journal of Economics* 131 (2): 519–578.

Sassen, S. 2014. *Explusions.* Cambridge, MA: Harvard University Press.

Sharma, N. 2006. *Home Economics: Nationalism and the Making of 'Migrant Workers' in Canada.* Toronto: University of Toronto Press.

Skaggs, Jimmy. 1986. *Prime Cut: Livestock Raising and Meatpacking in the United States: 1907–1983.* College Station: Texas A&M University Press.

Steusse, Angela. 2016. *Scratching out a Living.* Berkeley: University of California Press.

Steusse, Angela, and Mathew Coleman. 2014. "Automobility, Immobility, Altermobility: Surviving and Resisting the Intensification of Immigrant Policing." *City & Society* 26 (1): 51–72.

Striffler, Steve. 2005. *Chicken: the Dangerous Transformation of America's Favorite Food.* New Haven, CT: Yale University Press.

Stull, Donald, Michael Broadway, and David Griffith. 1995. *Any Way They Cut It: Meat Processing and Small Town America.* Lawrence: University Press of Kansas.

Wolf, Eric. 1982. *Europe and the People Without History.* Berkeley: University of California Press.

Infrastructures of repression and resistance: how Tennesseans respond to the immigration enforcement regime

Meghan Conley and Jon Shefner

ABSTRACT
This paper addresses challenges faced by immigrants in two Tennessee locales, Nashville and Knoxville, focusing on Latino immigrant communities and the institutions to which they have responded during the period spanning the 2005 passage of the Sensenbrenner Bill and the Trump administration. We examine how the K-12 school system has reacted to draconian legislation and review the ways in which law enforcement affects the lives of immigrants and their children. We also investigate ways in which immigrants have circumvented or embraced political mobilization, responding to barriers and seizing occasional opportunities.

Introduction

Of interest to the study of immigrant children in the age of mass deportations are the ways in which local populations mobilize to resist or espouse policies designed to exclude newcomers. How has immigrant-rights mobilization manifested itself in the past dozen years? How does resistance infrastructure operate in new destinations? How do hardships and threats, or hostility affect immigrant children and children of immigrants? Not enough research has been conducted on such questions. Some exceptions include Conley's (Forthcoming) work, which examines organizing efforts of regional and state groups in developing movement infrastructure in the *Nuevo South*. Another exception is Stuesse (2016) who gives attention to issues of race and labour in the US Southeast, particularly how the influx of immigrant workers complicates labour organizing opening and sometimes shrinking avenues for political expression.

In this paper, we build on such efforts to examine patterns of repression and resistance involving immigrants in Knoxville and Nashville, Tennessee. We discuss political reactions to the growth of immigrant communities, focusing pri-marily on schools and colleges and their response to the enforcement system. We then turn attention to expressions of resistance in the same sites. Finally, we note Tennessee's contradictory environment of reform, as city governments face pressure from immigrant rights action while county and state governments largely follow the anti-immigrant ethos of the federal government.

Data and methods

In our study of political mobilization on behalf of immigrants and their children in Tennessee, we used a combination of qualitative research methods from 2006 to the present, including participant observation, interviews, and docu-ment analysis. Sites of observation included protests, organizational meetings of advocates and social movement actors, and public meetings convened by local government. We interviewed immigrants who have been directly and indirectly affected by enforcement in Knoxville, as well as local immigrant rights advocates, including leaders and participants, public school teachers and school support staff, faith-based allies, and social service providers. We also analyzed newspaper articles, organizational memos, and policy state-ments from advocacy and service groups; press releases from federal immigra-tion authorities, and internal documents from local law enforcement agencies. The latter were obtained through open records requests.

Shefner (2016) discusses how social science research is conducted within a spectrum of relationships to political standpoint, from community based par-ticipatory action research, to public sociology as a form of advocacy, to a "normal science" model in which the researcher examines politically relevant issues with no effort to affect the conditions being investigated. Work for this article was conducted under a variety of points along that continuum, ranging from conventional science procedures to collaboration with activists, and the organization of educational activities to better serve new destination immi-grants. At all stages, this research was conducted with attention to multiple perspectives and insuring triangulation.

Background

Despite increased focus on new destinations (Furuseth and Smith 2006; Lippard and Gallagher 2011; Marrow 2011; Mohl 2003), research on immigrant rights mobilization continues to focus on places with a long history as end-points for newcomers. This is insufficient because political movements may differ in places long accustomed to immigrant populations by comparison to those where even small numbers of recently arrived foreigners cause tremor and anxiety. Such variations affect the wellbeing of youngsters as they are most vulnerable to hostile responses on the part of enfolding populations and public officials seeking to augment constituency support. For that reason, there is much to be learned by examining processes of repression and political responses in novel points of immigrant arrival.

Migration to new destinations in the US Southeast began in earnest in the 1990s, but substantial flows to Tennessee lagged behind those directed to neighbouring states. As Alabama, Georgia, and North Carolina implemented increasingly aggressive anti-immigrant policies, foreign-born Latinos and Asians went scattered to other states, including Kentucky and Tennessee. In 1990, Tennessee's foreign-born population was only 1.2 percent—about 75,000 people. By 2013 it had grown to 5 percent—302,000 residents. In other words, the foreign-born population in Tennessee grew over 300 percent between 1990 and 2010, making it one of 16 states in which the proportion of foreigners rose by one third or more during that period (Blau and Mackie 2016). Most immigrants in Tennessee have settled in six counties, two of which are anchored by Nashville and Memphis.

Like other immigrants, foreign-born Latinos set roots in Tennessee and across the *Nuevo South* for its relatively high economic growth and low cost of living compared to other regions. Diminishing opportunities in older destinations (Durand, Massey, and Capoferro 2006; Gouveia and Saenz 2000; Marrow 2005) contributed to the same trend. Finding homes in small towns and big cities, recently arrived workers secured employment in poultry and other food processing plants, and in auto manufacturing and agriculture (Nagle, Gustafson, and Burd 2012). As industrial restructuring and technological change routinized work and reduced required skills, the demand for low-wage and low-skill labour increased. Firms moved to "rural areas in the South and Plains states to take advantage of lower land and labour costs and diminished union presence" (Nagle et al. 2012, 20). These newly relocated industries may have weathered the 2008 Great Recession better than others. Although Latino workers in the South experienced rising unemployment rates earlier than elsewhere, they also exhibited lower rates of joblessness than the general population. Ironically, their rapid return to work may have reflected a weakened leverage, as Latinos felt pressure to compromise by working fewer hours and for paltry wages (Nagle et al. 2012).

Immigrant rights movements in established and new destinations

Large nationwide protests followed the introduction of the 2005 Sensenbrenner bill, which threatened to criminalize unlawful presence and subject social service agencies and humanitarian organizations to prosecution for aiding unauthorized immigrants, without providing opportunities for them to adjust their status. Protestors were outraged by the bill's enforcement-centered approach and Congress' failure to enact humanitarian policy reforms.

Costanza-Chock (2008) calls the response to Sensenbrenner "the largest wave of mass mobilizations in U.S. history." Marches, with turnout estimates exceeding 3.7 million (McCann et al. 2016), occurred despite substantial risk to participants, especially immigrants, and were often aided by community organizations and labour networks (Milkman and Terriquez 2012).

Okamoto and Ebert (2010) find that foreign-born populations are less likely to protest in some cases; other researchers note how "certain contexts provide aggrieved actors with thicker and more diverse support networks" than others (Nicholls, Uitermark, and van Haperen 2016, 1038). On the other hand, Nicholls (2014: 23) notes that immigrant rights mobilization defied theory with the movement's willingness to organize, despite "inhospitable political and discursive environments."

Subtle differences in mobilization occurred across locations. Immigrants themselves became main organizers and participants most often in established areas (Heyman, Morales, and Nuñez 2008; Martinez 2011; Corrunker 2012; Enriquez 2014). Okamoto and Ebert (2010: 551) observe that "the occurrence of *any* protest event was less likely in ... new immigrant destinations." Research such as that conducted by Nicholls et al. (2016) focuses on Los Angeles, Washington, DC, Arizona, and other cities covered by national outlets like the *New York Times*. As a result, it sheds little light on variations occurring in new immigration sites; instead it confirms that enduring networks and organizational experience facilitated political activity in older, more seasoned areas.

Immigrant youths leading *DREAM* demonstrations in states like Alabama and Georgia came from external locations with longstanding activist infrastructures and were supported by networks and organizations in the same places (Heredia 2016). Zepeda-Millán (2016) draws attention to ways in which well-known Latino community members acted as brokers to help mobilize in response to the Sensenbrenner threat in Fort Meyers, Florida (a Southern destination, but not new). Such political expressions demonstrated that "immigrants' lives are actually filled with all kinds of assets that may not seem overtly political in their routine functions, but that can in fact be activated by communities for political purposes" (Zepeda-Millán 2016, 24).

We contend that the hostility noted by other researchers is exacerbated in new destinations, where support networks for mobilization are less fully elaborated than those in established destinations. This intensifies conditions faced by immigrant children and their parents. In the next sections, we examine hardships suffered by newcomers in schools and universities. We also give attention to the enforcement system in Tennessee, and to emergent strategies of resistance.

Schools and law enforcement

Schools are the single most important formal institution in most children's lives, but they are especially significant among immigrant youngsters, as they provide both opportunities and obstacles to social incorporation. The impact of schools is magnified when immigrant families are under attack, as they have been for much of this millennium. Educational settings may provide resources for students and families, but they can also harbour conflict and contradiction, as the diverging intents of local and federal governments are played out in school districts and individual schools. The role of law enforcement in the lives of immigrant families may seem less obvious than that of schools but it is, in fact, of paramount import. In our research we document efforts to protect immigrant parents and their offspring even as law enforcement authorities impose great harm on them. In both schools and law enforcement we see how substructures of repression are built, but also how they are resisted.

Schools operate as platforms for inequality and penalization but also contestation and struggle . The Supreme Court's 1982 ruling in *Plyler v. Doe* (1982) guaranteed all children in the US the right to free public K-12 education. That law, however, does not always translate into equal access to high-quality instruction or to fair outcomes, especially with respect to immigrant children. Students with limited English proficiency, identified as English Language Learners (ELLs), trail behind English proficient students in math and reading (Bohon and Conley 2015). Similarly, children from immigrant families are disadvantaged by barriers to parental involvement compared to those with US-born parents (Gonzalez et al. 2013). Finally, immigrant children confront other institutional hurdles such as lack of bilingual and bicultural school personnel, a paucity of in-language resources, and inadequate ELL curriculums (Bohon, Macpherson, and Atiles 2005; Singer 2004).

Overburdened schools are ill-prepared to accommodate the needs of immigrants and their kids. Following the Latino population boom in Tennessee, 10 percent of all kindergarteners in that state will be Latino within the next three to five years. Such youngsters are more likely to come from impoverished homes and live in linguistic isolation. Among immigrant children ages 5–9, 36 percent live in households in which no one over the age of 13 speaks English well. This rises to 44 percent among children ages 0–4 (Nagle et al. 2012). In 2013 and 2014, after the influx of unaccompanied minors from El Salvador, Guatemala, and Honduras, an investigation revealed that immigrant youths in Tennessee and thirteen other states had been systematically denied enrollment in their neighbourhood schools, kept out of school for extended periods due to excessive paperwork, and deflected to alternative education programmes (Burke and Sainz 2016).

The Supreme Court's ruling in *Plyler v. Doe* does not guarantee a right to attend public institutions of higher education. The rising cost of tuition makes college unattainable for many, but undocumented and *DACAmented*[1] youth in the state of Tennessee confront additional obstacles upon graduation from high school. Unlike more than twenty states that provide in-state tuition to undocumented graduates and DACA recipients; Tennessee students in those categories pay out-of-state tuition, which can be as much as two- to three times higher than in-state tuition (Tennessee only allowed in-state tuition to US-born Tennessee-resident children of unauthorized immigrants in 2014). Despite support from the previous governing board at one of the state's university and community college system, and from then-Governor Bill Haslam, Tennessee's General Assembly refused to enact legislation to provide in-state tuition for undocumented and/or DACAmented students (Hooker et al. 2015). Noting this denial, board member Barbara Prescott stated, "When we do not allow in-state tuition to these undocumented students we really are denying them access" (Tamburin 2017).

Undocumented and DACAmented immigrants are also prohibited from receiving federal grant money for higher education. Tennessee offers a number of aid programmes to reduce the cost of advanced studies, including *Tennessee Promise*, which extends two years of free access to formal instruction beyond high school to all state residents, and the *Hope Scholarship*, which provides financial awards to offset the costs of public higher education. The requirements of such programmes, however, bar access to undocumented and DACAmented youth. Lacking legal status, they are not able to qualify as residents of Tennessee, regardless of how long they have lived there. Only a few colleges and universities in the state work with private funders—such as MPower Financing—that extend loans to undocumented and DACAmented students without citizen co-signers.

In response, the Tennessee Immigrant and Refugee Rights Coalition (TIRRC), a statewide advocacy organization, mounted a legislative push for "tuition equality" to expand access to higher education for DACAmented and undocumented students. In 2017, after multiple failures, yet another tuition equality bill (SB1014 / HB0863) was introduced by a Republican Senator and a Republican Representative. It would have allowed public universities to exempt students from paying out-of-state tuition, provided that they graduated from a Tennessee high school or obtained a GED in the same state. The bill would not have applied to undocumented or DACAmented individuals. All the same, it ultimately failed in committee.

Access to education for immigrant children is also limited by real and perceived threats from the immigration authorities. Rumours of Immigration and Customs Enforcement (ICE) raids and checkpoints in the wake of Trump's 2017 executive order on interior enforcement—which significantly expanded deportation priorities—unsettled immigrant families, with school districts reporting substantial impacts on students' attendance and well-being (Samuels 2017). After an ICE raid on a meatpacking plant in East Tennessee, the superintendent of the neighbouring school district—where most of the affected families reside—reported more than 500 youngsters absent from school the following day, by comparison to the district's average number of 75 student absences.

The executive order's implementation memorandum also rescinded directives on existing policy, raising additional uncertainties about enforcement priorities in schools. Of special concern was the ambiguous scope of the Sensitive Locations Memo, which established in 2011 that ICE would not conduct arrests, interviews, searches, or surveillance in places of worship, hospitals, and schools. Trump's cessation of DACA, and pronouncements by the nation's Attorney General, John Kelly, that the Department of Homeland Security (DHS) would no longer "exempt classes or categories of removable aliens from potential enforcement" (Kelly 2017), raised concerns that ICE would target undocumented youths in schools.

DHS ultimately affirmed guidelines against enforcement in sensitive locations. Nevertheless, ICE flouted the spirit of its own policy, detaining unauthorized immigrants as they left a church hypothermia shelter in Alexandria, Virginia (Hernandez 2017) and a father as he dropped off his daughter at school in Los Angeles (Castillo 2017). To our knowledge, Tennessee has not experienced violations of the Sensitive Locations Memo but, according our observations and interviews, the enforcement climate puts youngsters at risk. In East Tennessee and beyond, students and educators report disturbing incidents since the 2016 presidential election, including aggressions such as white students chanting "Trump, Trump, Trump!" at them as they passed by in the hallways. One student received death threats in class, via text message, from the very same gang he escaped in Central America. Because of Trump's attacks on asylum seekers, that student was afraid to attend an upcoming court hearing, worried that his application would be denied and he would be deported. His teacher received no guidance and therefore did not know whether to counsel the youngster to attend the hearing or avoid it. Another teacher reported that her students, undocumented themselves or children of undocumented parents, repeatedly asked whether they should stay home from school to avoid potential contact with immigration agents. In a different case, an undocumented high school student, arrested on a misdemeanor, was transferred to a detention centre in Louisiana, where he missed five weeks of schooling before he was released on bond and allowed to return to Knoxville.

Because educators and advocates across Tennessee are concerned about students' access to education, they have developed tactics to address institutional, social, and legislative barriers at both K-12 school and colleges while, at the same time, subverting repressive actions on the part of the authorities. Their aim is to and create a welcoming environment (see also Marrow 2005; Williams 2015). Following the 2016 presidential election, TIRRC pushed for, and won, a school board resolution from the Metropolitan Nashville Davidson County Board of Public Education designating the Metro Nashville Public School system (MNPS) as a "safe zone" for students and families "threatened by immigration enforcement and targeted by bullying." Approved in

December 2016, the resolution affirmed its 'intent ... to ensure equal access to education regardless of ... immigration status.'

That the resolution signals *intent*, rather than containing a direct and timely course of action, was not lost on educators and community organizers in Knoxville, who drafted their own school board resolution. Nashville community leaders and TIRRC staff pushed for concrete measures to implement the safe zone policy. In Knox County, an informal network of educators, inspired to address the needs of immigrant students and their parents, led the way in crafting the initial document. Its goal was to compel Knox County Schools to provide "know your rights" (KYR) training for kids and families, require mandatory training for school staff, especially front-office personnel, on immigration-related matters, and prohibit the sharing of students' personal information without a judicial warrant or parents' permission.[2] Efforts to bring this resolution to the school board have largely stalled, however, and organizers have turned their attention to mitigating the impacts of enforcement experiences on youthful populations. Still, the desire to implement proactive policies in schools continues to motivate teachers and other advocates in Knox County. Groups have sought piecemeal reforms that do not require approval from the school board or the Knox County Schools System. Another effort includes coalition building to encourage the Knox County Schools Strategic Plan to hire bilingual English/Spanish mental health counsellors.

Educators have also pushed to broaden awareness of immigration-related matters among students, parents, teachers, and administrative personnel through expanded anti-harassment policies and in-service training. At one Knox County high school, the principal noted a disturbing number of student absences in the weeks immediately following Trump's election and issued a letter to parents in English, Spanish, and Arabic assuring that the school shares no personal information with anyone, reiterating their commitment to providing students with a safe space, and making clear "that everyone, regardless of race, nationality, or documentation is welcome." In other schools, teachers have less support and are left to their own devices as they try to educate themselves on immigration issues and support youngsters in the face of hostility from peers and omnipresent enforcement. Some teachers have even decided to serve as emergency contacts for their undocumented students; others have completed paperwork to become temporary legal guardians of young people in the event of their parents' deportation.

The makeup of the student population appears to influence schools' responses. Teachers in Knoxville with sizeable immigrant and/or marginalized students have been in a better position to champion the provision of resources to families and push for responses from administrators, the school board, and other public officials. After the 2016 presidential election, a community school[3] partnered with local immigrant advocacy organizations, including Centro Hispano and AKIN (Allies of Knoxville's Immigrant Neighbors) to offer KYR training, a discussion of potential impacts of the incoming administration on immigrants and their children, and guidance on talking with youngsters about fears related to immigration enforcement.

With the explosion of prosecutorial discretion at the federal level and the expansion of state or local policies of cooperation with federal immigration authorities, educators have organized to help develop action plans for families facing possible deportation. Following implementation of the executive order on interior enforcement, they began to address concrete needs among those facing raids and detentions. One "family preparedness" workshop attracted more than 40 families, including 100 children. It provided organizational training and notarization of documents related to medical and school records; temporary guardianship in the event of a parent's deportation; and power of attorney for assets such as bank accounts and homes. Similar events have been scheduled at schools and other locations, although they are not officially sanctioned by Knox County Schools. Such initiatives were made possible by earlier efforts on the part of Centro Hispano, AKIN, and others to develop a consolidated network of advocates and interpreters willing to assist immigrants in various capacities. The events also helped attract new volunteers, including lawyers and public notaries, creating networks that immigrants may rely on in later struggles.

Law enforcement in the lives of immigrant children

In Tennessee, the enforcement system's profile has expanded alongside political efforts to criminalize immigration, with major impacts upon immigrant children and the children of immigrants. Approximately 5.1 million children in the United States live with at least one undocumented parent, and 20 percent of those minors are themselves unauthorized (Capps, Fix, and Zong 2016). Young people witness enforcement actions against parents and adult siblings; experience discriminatory policing practices; share household fears of arrest and incarceration, and often avoid contact with officers even when facing danger. The escalation in real or perceived threats of law enforcement under the new administration is not lost on youngsters, who feel heightened levels of anxiety as a result (Kamenetz 2017; Vargas and Ibarra 2017).

One event illustrates the effects of these pressures on children in Knoxville. In March 2017, a student reported to a tutor that his neighbourhood—a small community of predominantly immigrant families—had been terrorized by strangers the previous night. Another resident in the same community reached out to one of the authors of this paper, Megan Conley. As a steering committee member of AKIN, and a facilitator of the group's rapid response network, she helped organize a team to record the events of the previous evening. A group of four men had occupied the neighbourhood for three hours, banging on doors and windows, rifling through mailboxes, and photographing license plates. No one called the police; some suspected that the perpetrators were immigration enforcement agents. Mothers reported that their children were terrified, dreading that their parents would be taken. Some were wary of sending their sons or daughters to school the next day frightened that they would be detained while the children were away, leaving no one to care for them.

Given the state's heavy handed approaches, it is easy to see why immigrant families in Tennessee fear the authorities. In 2006, the Highway Patrol was trained to enforce immigration law. Later that year, newspapers documented a surge of federal raids across the state targeting businesses with unauthorized immigrant employees, striking terror in families, children in particular. By 2007, arrest numbers in five southern states doubled those of the previous year (Connolly 2007). At that time, Tennessee legislators introduced 45 anti-immigrant bills, which Latino leaders decried as "psychological warfare" (Alapo 2007). By the end of session, five legislative proposals remained active, menacing employers who "knowingly" hired unauthorized immigrants with the loss of their business licenses; criminalizing the transportation of unauthorized immigrants; disallowing the "driving certificate" programme; designating the Tennessee Highway Patrol as immigration enforcer; and prohibiting use of the taxpayer identification number as proof of identity (Humphrey 2007).

Such actions had chilling effects on crime reporting; immigrant women with children were reluctant to denounce or seek aid for domestic abuse, worried that sons and daughters would be taken away. According to not-for-profit organizations that work with the state's growing Latino population, fear of deportation and language barriers also dampened reports (Trevizo 2008). At the same time, increasing detentions overwhelmed the court system. By 2010, immigration judges in Tennessee could not keep up with their caseloads (Ross 2010). In 2010 the anti-immigrant climate was confirmed again when the legislature entertained proposals making it a felony to violate identification laws when voting—previously such a violation would have elicited only a charge of perjury (West 2010).

As in other places, anti-immigrant sentiment and actions contributed to political careers, becoming a central theme in the 2006 Tennessee Senate race, with eventual victor Bob Corker challenging his rivals' anti-immigrant pedigrees. US Representative Zach Wamp vocally supported 287(g), a form of police-ICE collaboration that deputizes local law enforcement agencies (LEAs) to implement aspects of federal immigration law. Anti-immigrant stances were reinforced by the actions of local Republican John Duncan, who in 2010 sought to deny citizenship to US-born children of unauthorized immigrants (Collins 2010). By 2018, anti-immigrant language punctuated the campaigns of every Republican primary contestant for higher office.

Similar levels of politicization characterized local government activities. In 2009, Knox County Sheriff Jimmy "JJ" Jones actively pursued the 287(g) programme. The application was not reviewed until 2012, and by that time 287(g) was no longer a priority for the Obama administration. In 2013, when the Knox County Sheriff's Office (KCSO) application for 287(g) was formally denied (after more than fourteen months of sustained community opposition by AKIN and other groups), the Sheriff was unequivocal in his condemnation of the federal government, which in his view:

> "shirk[ed] its responsibilities for providing safety and security to its citizens by denying Knox County the 287(g) corrections model ... Hopefully, the denial of this program will not create an influx of illegal immigrants who think that without this program they will be able to break the law and then be less likely to be deported. ... I will continue to enforce these federal immigration violations with or without the help of U.S Immigration and Customs Enforcement (ICE). If need be, I will stack these violators like cordwood in the Knox County Jail until the appropriate federal agency responds."

Other jurisdictions in Tennessee provided contrast to Knox County, largely because the four largest cities in Tennessee are governed by Democratic and liberal administrations, while surrounding county governments are Republican and conservative. In Davidson County, Sheriff Daron Hall, whose department received 287(g) authority in 2007, declined to renew the program in 2012. Nevertheless, in five years of operation under 287(g), the Davidson County Sheriff's Office (DCSO) deported more than 10,000 individuals, leaving numerous children stranded. Even the DCSO acknowledged that the vast majority of those arrests were for misdemeanors (DCSO 2009; Kee 2012). The American Civil Liberties Union (ACLU) of Tennessee and TIRRC documented several civil rights violations in Davidson County's execution of 287(g) (Kee 2012).

One horrific case was that of Juana Villegas, who at nine-months pregnant was arrested in Davidson County in front of her children, jailed, and held in shackles throughout her labour up to the birth of her child. Afterward, her newborn was taken from her, and her family was not immediately able to locate the infant. Villegas was also denied adequate medical care and developed a breast infection due to the forced separation from her baby and the jail's refusal to provide a breast pump or anti-inflammatory medications. In 2011, a federal judge in Tennessee ruled that the Davidson County jail had demonstrated "deliberate indifference" to Villegas' suffering and medical needs; Davidson County later settled a civil lawsuit over her treatment for nearly half a million dollars (Preston 2013).

In Knoxville, the City Mayor and City Police Chief have publicly welcomed immigrants, stating that police officers are "not required by law to be ICE agents and we will not voluntarily be ICE agents" (Witt 2017). Such declarations were part of a nationwide push by the US Conference of Mayors to stand in solidarity with immigrants and in support of immigration reform. By contrast, the Knox County Sheriff's Office reapplied for and received 287 (g). The programme became fully operational in 2018. The benefits of the City Mayor's statement are therefore symbolic: since Knoxville's jail is located in Knox County, everyone arrested by city police ultimately ends up under KCSO jurisdiction. Although city police do not technically engage in immigration enforcement through direct participation in 287(g), they take part indirectly when arresting people for citable offenses (like driving without a license) and transporting them to the County jail.

In the streets and elsewhere

Despite legislative trends toward criminalization, there has been notable resistance—both active and passive—to anti-immigrant policies across Tennessee. Social movement activity supporting immigrants and their families has ranged from the streets to the legislature, from religious organizations to businesses. For example, the unfriendliness of Tennessee's anti-immigrant laws towards businesses has been denounced by the Hispanic Chamber of Commerce (Alapo 2007). The Nashville Music Association Union, Tyson Foods, and the National Pork Producers Council have lobbied for immigration reform to raise caps on worker visas (Tennessean 2010). Non-profit legal groups like Mid-South Immigration Advocates and the Community Legal Center act on behalf of immigrants in detention and provide them with a variety of low-cost legal services that increase the likelihood of their release. Responses have also differed depending on which institution is involved. Earlier we described some of the actions pursued in the educational system. Here we give a brief glimpse of other activities, largely in Knoxville, where we have organized and participated.

Like people throughout the US, Tennesseans were involved in the 2006 protests fuelled by the Sensenbrenner Bill. TIRRC mobilized large numbers of activists across the state. Ten thousand marched in Nashville and 2,000 in Knoxville in early March, that year. Such demonstrations were held in anticipation of Senator Arlen Specter's "guest worker" legislation (Alapo 2006). A different form of mobilization occurred at the University of Tennessee from March 31 through April 1, as dozens of academics joined with hundreds of service providers (lawyers, nurses, teachers, librarians, and journalists) in a hybrid conference that not only addressed scholarly questions regarding new-destination immigration, but also gave service providers skills to meet the needs of vulnerable immigrants and their children (Ansley and Shefner 2009). Days later, many of the same community members marched alongside immigrants through downtown Knoxville, culminating in a demonstration of 2500 protesting federal attacks outside a government building (Kenner 2006). The Highlander Research and Education Center, a renowned social movement school and centre of activism, played an important role in organizing that protest. Mobilization in Knoxville continued into the spring, with over 600 immigrants and their supporters rallying at a TIRRC-organized "Day Without Immigrants." Participants emphasized the need for comprehensive immigration reform and highlighted the contributions of immigrants and their families to the American economy (Ferrar 2006).

Knoxville has a variety of organizations dedicated to immigrant issues but, as in many new destinations in the US Southeast, such groups have focused primarily on immigrant integration, civic engagement, service provision, and promotion of diversity and cultural acceptance (Conley Forthcoming). HoLa Hora Latina, for example, organized the first Hispanic Heritage Festival nearly two decades ago, and this yearly event now draws an exponentially increasing audience. Organizations like Centro Hispano, Latino Task Force, and the Office of Hispanic Ministry of the Catholic Diocese of Knoxville promote education and integration for Latino immigrants and their children, including adult instruction and child development classes; English classes, and seminars on everything from civic engagement to financial planning. Other organizations, like Catholic Charities Immigration Services, provide legal screenings and counsel for immigrants who are victims of violence.

Other groups, such as the *Comité Popular de Knoxville* and AKIN, are comprised entirely of volunteers who work more explicitly on defending and securing the rights of immigrants and their families. The Comité, a group of unauthorized immigrants, emerged in 2012 in coordination with a regional push toward organizing neighbourhood defense committees through the efforts of entities like TIRRC and the Southeast Immigrant Rights Network (SEIRN). Following the massive mobilizations around Sensenbrenner, regional and state immigrant rights groups in the Southeast recognized that future organizing efforts were unsustainable absent strong, immigrant leaders and infrastructure (Conley Forthcoming). As a result, they turned to developing grassroots leadership in immigrant communities to address issues of local concern, such as state-level restrictionist policies. In Knoxville, the Comité crystalized around opposition to the Knox County Sheriff's pursuit of 287(g), before KCSO's first application was denied by the Obama administration. Activists with the Comité have developed a regular broadcast programme through a local community radio station, which they use to educate vulnerable immigrants on strategies to avoid the reach of the criminal justice system. More recently, the Comité's leadership has stepped back from public organizing out of fear of the Trump administration's enforcement regime, although some leaders continue to be involved through more discreet platforms, such as providing direct support to families of detained immigrants.

AKIN has existed in various forms since the mid-2000s and its members were originally linked to TIRRC, the state-wide immigrant rights organization. In 2012, AKIN formalized as an autonomous organization because of its desire to harness local capacity to address local needs and direct independent campaigns, particularly around 287(g). Over the years, AKIN and the Comité have partnered on a variety of events—sharing *posadas* as well as campaigns, hosting informational sessions and designing civil disobedience demonstrations. Immigrant children participate in all such activities. In contrast to many organizations that work with immigrants in Knoxville, AKIN is engaged in explicitly political work, which is facilitated by its status as an unincorporated organization largely comprised of US citizens and established lawful permanent residents.

AKIN has helped shepherd a number of affiliated organizations and programmes, including networks of educators, faith leaders and laity, and autonomous ally groups in adjacent cities of Alcoa/Maryville and Oak Ridge. It has also cultivated a Speaker's Bureau of experts, including faith leaders and immigrants of varying citizenship and documentation statuses. These experts speak before community organizations, neighbourhood associations, and faith groups on a variety of immigration-related issues, including criminalization and mass incarceration, racism and racialization, and immigration history, politics, and policies.

The Welcoming Immigrants Faith Network in Knoxville works closely with AKIN to establish a spectrum of sanctuary practices, from coordinating space for a physical shelter within one local church; to providing accompaniment for those who must attend immigration hearings across the state; to providing transportation for those who must travel to Nashville to submit biometrics; to offering food and other assistance to those left behind by detained and/or deported family members. Recent developments have led AKIN to monitor and provide community support at ICE check-ins. After a raid in Bean Station, ICE released 32 of 86 workers detained on immigration violations, but required them to regularly report to the ICE office in Knoxville. After consulting with organizers and affected families, Meghan Conley worked with faith leaders to organize community witnessing at each check-in point. Since then, faith leaders have established a regular presence at the ICE office. Each Wednesday, as immigrants report to the ICE office, witnesses stand in song, prayer, or silent meditation, holding a large banner—*Ama a tu prójimo* [love thy neighbor]. When requested, witnesses stand in line with families to accompany them through the check-in.

Conclusion

Our goal in this article has been to provide a richly textured description of the political context enfolding immigrant children and their families in Knoxville and Nashville, Tennessee, two points of recent destination for newcomers, mostly from Mexico and Central America. We contend that a necessary step to properly assess barriers faced by immigrant youngsters is to grasp the character and magnitude of repressive and exclusionary actions taken by federal agents and state politicians seeking support from local constituencies.

We drew attention to differences in the capacity and effectiveness of immigrant rights mobilization in established and newer areas of immigrant destination, arguing that, in the former, a longer history of contestation and resistance has built organizational networks that enable groups and individuals to rapidly and compellingly confront cruel actions on the part of state and federal authorities. Such has been the case in places like California, Arizona, and Washington, among others. In new areas of immigrant destination, such as Alabama, Georgia, and Tennessee—the location where our research took place—the rapid growth of the foreign-born population and the comparative absence of long-term organizers and grassroots organizations fighting for immigrant rights makes opposition and resistance more difficult and complicated. Without the resources available in more established locations to defend the rights of immigrants, politicians and immigration authorities are in a better position to implement draconian measures that negatively affect the wellbeing of immigrant families and, especially, their children.

Given such circumstances, the advances made by civic organizations in Tennessee are surprising and worthy of note. By establishing bonds with activists in other states, entities like AKIN have been able to provide an abundance of services that range from educational programmes, to legal referrals, and a profusion of resources—including the notarization of guardianship agreements for people at risk of deportation, accompaniment to court hearings, and quiet advocacy on behalf of children and parents—all improving the ability of persons and communities to protect unauthorized immigrants.

Tennessee is different from much of the US currently enduring the Trump administration because of its contradictory political field in a new destination context. How these contradictions play out in the near future will have a great deal to do with how extreme federal immigration policy becomes; the responses of states and locales; and how immigrant rights resources further consolidate. Pro-immigrant rights infrastructure in Tennessee has strengthened since 2005. Groups have become more flexible and innovative, even in the absence of adequate assets.

Nevertheless, despite the growing strength of immigrant rights organizing, the situation is dire because of measures taken by the state legislature. Moderate beacons of hope in local city governments are tempered by the realities of being surrounded by red counties in a deeply red state. In 2017, the Tennessee legislature passed an anti-sanctuary law, HB 2315, which prohibits state and local governments from enacting any type of sanctuary policy, including measures that limit police-ICE collaboration with immigration detainers. These and other similar deeds limit the extent to which organizers are able to mitigate immigration enforcement at the local level where government and local jurisdictions are more sympathetic to immigrants. In other words, there is a yawning divide between the harsh and often arbitrary actions being taken by federal authorities and more benign approaches taken by local governments. Although immigrant rights groups continue to push for pro-immigrant policies at the state and local levels, much of their attention has focused on ameliorating the effects of mass detentions and deportations spurred at the federal level. Against such a background, it is not surprising that many immigrants, especially those with tenuous status, have largely receded from the political landscape of public organizing.

Schools are as important as the political context in which immigrants must seek survival and progress. We presented a detailed account of educational terrains in Nashville and Knoxville, arguing that schools are both facilitators of immigrant integration and places where the repressive arm of the state connects with vulnerable populations in search of opportunity. Our account of increasingly punitive legislation affecting the capacity of youngsters to move along integrative paths or face harsh exclusion is a reminder of political dimensions surrounding education from the elementary to the advanced stages. Especially significant, in that respect, is the emotional and physical impact that harsh policies of exclusion have upon immigrant workers and, especially, their children. When youngsters are too scared to attend school; when they fear that their parents might be deported while they are away, trying to learn; when mothers feel impotent to seek medical care or protection from domestic violence; when qualified students are unable to move along educational paths because of their undocumented status, the scene has been set for the creation of an excluded population of people *in* the society but not *of* the society (Glazer 1964). Frightened children will grow into disaffected adults. Many will be deported but most of them will remain in the United States—will they learn to see America as their home or as the place where their ambitions were stalled? Only time will tell.

Notes

1. *DACAmented* students obtain protection from Deferred Action for Childhood Arrivals (DACA), Obama's 2012 executive order granting temporary status and work authorization to certain unauthorized youth. DACA recipients often refer to themselves as DACAmented to signify that their status is dependent on the whims of the executive branch and that they do not have the same rights as other visa holders.
2. The Family Educational Rights and Privacy Act of 1974 (FERPA) enables schools to share information with select entities, including law enforcement, without authorization from parents and without requiring parents to be notified.
3. Community schools are a Knox County initiative to make K-12 schools a centralized source of community resources, providing on-site medical and dental services, academic enrichment programmes, and cultural events.

Disclosure statement

No potential conflict of interest was reported by the authors.

References

Alapo, Lola. 2006. "Immigration rally to focus on new bills – Hundreds expected to take part in effort toward legal reform." *Knoxville News Sentinel*, March 17.

Alapo, Lola. 2007. "Transitioning Together." *Knoxville News Sentinel*, June 24.

Ansley, Fran, and Jon Shefner, eds. 2009. *Global Connections and Local Receptions: New Latino Immigration to the Southeastern US*. Knoxville: University of Tennessee Press.

Blau, Francine, and Christopher Mackie, eds. 2016. *The Economic and Fiscal Consequences of Immigration*. Washington, DC: National Academies Press.

Bohon, Stephanie, and Meghan Conley. 2015. *Immigration and Population*. Cambridge: Polity.

Bohon, Stephanie, Heather Macpherson, and Jorge Atiles. 2005. "Educational Barriers for New Latinos in Georgia." *Journal of Latinos and Education* 4 (1): 43–58.

Burke, Garance and Adrian Sainz. 2016. "Migrant Children kept from Enrolling in School." *Associated Press*, May 2.

Capps, Randy, Michael Fix, and Jie Zong. 2016. "A Profile of US Children with Unauthorized Immigrant Parents." Fact Sheet. *Migration Policy Institute*. Washington, DC.

Castillo, Andrea. 2017. "Immigrant arrested by ICE after dropping daughter off at school, sending shockwaves through neighborhood." *LA Times*, March 3.

Collins, Michael. 2010. "Duncan gaining support for bill." *Knoxville News Sentinel*, August 7.

Conley, Meghan. Forthcoming. *Immigrant Rights in the Nuevo South: Enforcement and Resistance at the Borderlands of Illegality*. Philadelphia: Temple.

Connolly, Daniel. 2007. "CBU event preps immigrant families – Parents, kids are invited to learn about college." *Memphis Commercial Appeal*. September 24.

Corrunker, Laura. 2012. "'Coming Out of the Shadows': DREAM Act Activism in the Context of Global Anti-Deportation Activism." *Indiana Journal of Global Legal Studies* 19 (1): 143–168.

Costanza-Chock, Sasha. 2008. "The Immigrant Rights Movement on the Net: Between Web 2.0 and Comunicación Popular." *American Quarterly* 60 (3): 851–864.

Davidson County Sheriff's Office. 2009. *287(g) Two-Year Review*. Nashville, TN: Davidson County Sheriff's Office.

Durand, Jorge, Douglas Massey, and Chiara Capoferro. 2006. "The New Geography of Mexican Immigration." In *New Destinations: Mexican Immigration in the United States*, edited by V. Zúñiga, and R. Hernández-León, 1–20. New York: Russell Sage.

Enriquez, Laura E. 2014. "'Undocumented and Citizen Students Unite': Building a Cross-Status Coalition Through Shared Ideology." *Social Problems* 61 (2): 155–174.

Ferrar, Rebecca. 2006. "Immigrants rally for rights, locally." *Knoxville News Sentinel*, May 2.

Furuseth, Owen, and Heather Smith. 2006. *Latinos in the New South: Transformations of Place*. Burlington: Ashgate.

Glazer, Nathan. 1964. "Ethnic Groups in America." In *Freedom and Control in Modern Society*, edited by Monroe Berger, Theodore Abel, and Charles H. Page, 158–173. New York: Van Nostrand.

Gonzalez, Lauren, L. DiAnne Borders, Erik Hines, Jose Villalba, and Alia Henderson. 2013. "Parental Involvement in Children's Education: Considerations for School Counselors Working with Latino Immigrant Families." *Professional School Counseling* 16 (3): 185–193.

Gouveia, Lourdes, and Rogelio Saenz. 2000. "Global Forces and Latino Population Growth in the Midwest: A Regional and Subregional Analysis." *Great Plains Research* 10 (Fall): 305–328.

Heredia, Luisa Laura. 2016. "More Than DREAMs." *NACLA Report on the Americas* 48 (1): 59–67.

Hernandez, Arelis. 2017. "ICE raids under Trump spark fear in Maryland, Virginia." *The Washington Post*, February 17.

Heyman, Heyman, Maria Morales, and Guillermina Nuñez. 2008. "Engaging With The Immigrant Human Rights Move Movement In A Besieged Border Region: What Do Applied Social Scientists Bring To The Policy Process?" *Napa Bulletin* 31: 13–29.

Hooker, Sarah, Margie McHugh, and Angelo Mathay. 2015. *Lessons From the Local Level: DACA's Implementation and Impact on Education and Training Success.* Washington, DC: Migration Policy Institute.

Humphrey, Tom. 2007. "Immigration legislation." *Knoxville News Sentinel*, June 24.

Kamenetz, Anya. 2017. "I have children crying in the classroom." NPR, March 9.

Kee, Lindsay. 2012. *Consequences & Costs: Lessons Learned From Davidson County, Tennessee's Jail Model 287(g) Program.* Nashville, TN: The ACLU of Tennessee.

Kelly, John. 2017. *Enforcement of the Immigration Laws to Serve the National Interest.* Washington, DC: Department of Homeland Security.

Kenner, Randy. 2006. "City streets flooded in sea of red and white – crowd marches downtown for immigration reform." *Knoxville News Sentinel*, April 11.

Lippard, Cameron, and Cameron Gallagher, eds. 2011. *Being Brown in Dixie: Race, Ethnicity, and Latino Immigration in the New South.* Boulder: First Forum Press.

Marrow, Helen. 2005. "New Destinations and Immigrant Incorporation." *Perspectives on Politics* 3 (4): 781–799.

Marrow, Helen. 2011. *New Destination Dreaming: Immigration, Race, and Legal Status in the Rural American South.* Stanford: Stanford University Press.

Martinez, Lisa. 2011. "Mobilizing Marchers in the Mile-High City: The Role of Community -Based Organizations." In *Rallying for Immigrant Rights*, edited by K. Voss, and I. Bloemraad, 123–141. Berkeley: University of California Press.

McCann, James A., Katsuo A. Nishikawa Chávez, Marisa Plasencia, and Harper Otawka. 2016. "The Changing Contours of the Immigrant Rights Protest Movement in the United States: Who Demonstrates Now?" *Forum (2194–6183)* 14 (2): 169–190.

Milkman, Ruth, and Veronica Terriquez. 2012. "We Are the Ones Who Are Out in Front: Women's Leadership in the Immigrant Rights Movement." *Feminist Studies* 38 (3): 723–752.

Mohl, Raymond. 2003. "Globalization, Latinization, and the Nuevo New South." *Journal of American Ethnic History* 22 (4): 31–66.

Nagle, Nicholas N., Randy Gustafson, and Charlynn Burd. 2012. *A Profile of the Hispanic Population of the State of Tennessee.* Knoxville, TN: University of Tennessee Center for Business and Economic Research.

Nicholls, Walter. 2014. "From Political Opportunities to Niche-Openings: the Dilemmas of Mobilizing for Immigrant Rights in Inhospitable Environments." *Theory & Society* 43: 23–49.

Nicholls, Walter, Justus Uitermark, and Sander van Haperen. 2016. "The Networked Grassroots. How Radicals Outflanked Reformists in the United States' Immigrant Rights Movement." *Journal of Ethnic and Migration Studies* 42 (6): 1036–1054.

Okamoto, Dina, and Kim Ebert. 2010. "Beyond the Ballot: Immigrant Collective Action in Gateways and New Destinations in the United States." *Social Problems* 57 (4): 529–558.

Preston, Julia. 2013. "Settlement for a Shackled Pregnant Woman." *The New York Times*, October 17.

Ross, Janell. 2010. "Immigration court in TN can't keep up with caseload." *The Tennessean*, February 24.

Samuels, Robert. 2017. "After Trump's immigration order, anxiety grows in Florida's farm fields." *The Washington Post*, February 25.

Shefner, Jon. 2016. "How Community Collaboration Transformed the Research Question in a Study of Knoxville's Green Economy." In *Qualitative Research Ethics in Practice*, edited by Martin Tolich, 147–158. Walnut Creek, CA: Left Coast Press.

Singer, Audrey. 2004. *The Rise of New Immigrant Gateways*. Washington, DC: Brookings Institution.

Stuesse, Angela. 2016. *Scratching Out a Living: Latinos, Race, and Work in the Deep South*. Berkeley: University of California Press.

Tamburin, Adam. 2017. "College system endorses in-state tuition for undocumented students." *The Tennessean*, March 31.

Tennessean. 2010. "TN firms lobby for amnesty." *The Tennessean*, July 30.

Trevizo, Perla. 2008. "Immigrants face domestic violence fears – Language barriers, uneasiness about deportation keep many Hispanic women from reporting abuse." *Chattanooga Times Free Press*, March 5.

Vargas, Edward, and Vickie Ibarra. 2017. "U.S. Citizen Children of Undocumented Parents: The Link Between State Immigration Policy and the Health of Latino Children." *Journal of Immigrant Minor Health* 19 (4): 913–920.

West, Phil. 2010. "Law could require proof of citizenship – Senate divided on bill some say amounts to profiling." *Memphis Commercial Appeal*, May10.

Williams, Linda M. 2015. "Beyond Enforcement: Welcomeness, Local Law Enforcement, and Immigrants." *Public Administration Review* 75 (3(May/June)): 433–442.

Witt, Gerald. 2017. "Knoxville Mayor: KPD Officers aren't ICE Agents." *Knoxville News Sentinel*, March 21.

Zepeda-Millán, Chris. 2016. "Weapons of the (Not So) Weak: Immigrant Mass Mobilization in the US South." *Critical Sociology* 42 (2): 269–287.

The integration paradox: contrasting patterns in adaptation among immigrant children in Central New Jersey

Patricia Fernández-Kelly

ABSTRACT

I report findings from research conducted among immigrant children and children of immigrants in Princeton and Trenton, New Jersey—including unaccompanied minors and those protected by *Deferred Action for Childhood Arrivals* (DACA). On the basis of participant observation and extended interviews, I investigate the role played by human and financial resources, advocacy organizations, kin and friendship networks, and religiosity in the capacity of young people to resist downward mobility. Demographic factors and class-related dynamics prove to be decisive factors shaping the self-image of immigrant children. The paper provides a theoretical framework accounting for variations in young people's power to adjust in hostile environments.

Introduction

How are immigrant youths addressing the pressures of vilification, reduced channels for upward mobility, and possible deportation?[1] I set out to answer that question through an exploratory study that includes participant observation and 68 extended interviews with mostly Central American students in the Princeton and Trenton areas. Emerging results shed light on the ways in which various categories of individuals are using available resources to confront seemingly insurmountable difficulties. The relevant question guiding this project is not whether punitive measures against undocumented and insufficiently documented kids and their parents will affect them negatively—all signs point in that direction—but whether variations at the local level will lead to different adaptive mechanisms and, in turn, disparate outcomes in education and employment. I highlight *toponomic*, that is, spatially situated reserves, symbolic as well as physical, in the development of identities, viewpoints, and attitudes. I present a theoretical framework for the assessment of differences in young people's capacity to adjust in hostile environments.

At the centre of my argument lies a paradox of sociological interest: experience and logic suggest that, like all youths, immigrant children will face promising futures in locations characterized by tolerance and educational and material resources of high quality; living in safe neighbourhoods with good schools and good jobs enhances their self-image and thus facilitates social and economic advance. My research, however, shows a different landscape: economically depressed environments marked by reduced educational and employment opportunities can also provide avenues for empowerment when two conditions are met, that is, when (a) immigrants form a substantial proportion of the population and (b) they share with most residents a common class position or racial filiation. Young people arriving from Central America into affluent settings face psychological and social challenges that are quite different and may be greater than those being confronted by similar youngsters in urban environments with a substantial number of co-ethnics and low-income residents (See also Foner and Simon 2015). Being part of a small group of outsiders submerged in a prosperous milieu magnifies deficits and causes anxiety, even paralysis; by contrast, residing in places characterized by attenuated class differences and a diversified population induces a kind of comfort, a sense of possibility not available in other locations.

In Princeton, a wealthy university town with a long history of liberal advocacy, children of immigrants and immigrant children benefit from a large resource base that includes well-financed schools and sympathetic advocates. Nevertheless, and despite efforts on the part of local authorities and volunteers, wide chasms in social class, national origin, and linguistic capability have had an isolating effect that potentially impedes their successful integration.

By contrast, in Trenton—a predominantly black and impoverished city—immigrant children have at their disposal assets of lesser quality but, in schools and public spaces, they are surrounded by large numbers of immigrants—some of whom own small businesses—and young African Americans who spin narratives of struggle and vindication. Discourses focusing on contestation and resistance are prevalent among immigrant children in that setting, as are religious notions of resignation and salvation. In other words, significant variations in outlook are connected to differences in the resource base of the two locations *but also* to demographic thresholds and social-class convergence. Undocumented and insufficiently documented immigrants face demolishing forces at the aggregate level but they succeed or fail in local spaces.

The paper is divided into four sections. I first describe methods and locations. The second section includes a brief review of relevant sources, followed by a theoretical framework connecting different kinds of assets to categories of youngsters and their ideational leanings. The third section contains a sampler of illustrative cases. In the conclusion I recapitulate the argument and consider a small number of practical implications.

Research approach and locations

Between April 2017 and June 2019, I conducted participant observation among immigrant youths in middle schools and high schools; community colleges and universities; places of employment and churches in Central New Jersey, with Princeton and Trenton as anchoring points. I had extended conversations with 68 young people ranging in ages between 14 and 25. Selection criteria were restricted to age and residence in Mercer County. The sample is almost equally divided between young men and women and, although it was not constructed by aleatory means, it is illustrative of youthful populations in the area. All those included trace their origins to Mexico and Central America but nearly all (61) hail from Guatemala. Only ten are legal residents or citizens of the United States. The others are individuals protected by DACA (Deferral Action for Childhood Arrivals), undocumented minors or asylum seekers awaiting resolution of their cases from the immigration authorities. Approximately one third consists of individuals without any kind of documentation. Thirty-five youngsters reside with their families in the Trenton-Ewing area; 20 live with their families in Princeton, Kingston, West Windsor, and Lawrenceville. Thirteen arrived as unaccompanied minors and now share quarters with other immigrants.

Initial interviews lasted two hours on the average and, in most cases, I followed with subsequent interactions. I focused on four subjects: (a) biographical and demographic profile; (b) economic resource flows; (c) social networks; and (d) general outlook on success and failure. I compiled notes and produced summaries containing points of singular interest, narrative patterns, and similarities and differences by comparison to other interviews. Fernández-Kelly (2012) offers additional details about this methodological approach. In addition to participant observation and interviews, my study included dialogues with educators, leaders in community organizations, advocates, and public officials. I also made use of archival materials, newspapers, and social media outlets.

As research locations, Princeton and Trenton may be seen as points in a continuum of tolerance/hostility towards immigrants; they lay bare conditions diluted in larger metropolitan centres with more complex government structures, and a longer experience as points of reception for newcomers. Princeton, a wealthy university town organically connected to New York, was founded long before America came into existence. It boasts approximately

25,000 residents (not counting university students), 67 per cent of who are white; 15.4 Asian; 6.1 per cent African American and 8.4 per cent Hispanic (US Census Bureau 2017a; Widner 2017). In other words, nearly 3,000 Hispanics reside in that city. When including people of the same background in nearby demarcations such as Kingston, Hamilton, and Lawrenceville, the number may be three times larger. That population tends to be young and it includes a significant number of unaccompanied minors living alone. Approximately 40 such youngsters are enrolled at Princeton High School.

Mexicans from the remote southern state of Oaxaca began arriving in Princeton in the 1980s and soon after became visible in construction sites, landscaping companies, hotels and restaurants. Some have created businesses which operate legally despite the undocumented status of their owners.[2] While Mexicans have been around for a longer period of time, it is Guatemalans who constitute the largest immigrant group in Princeton. They started arriving in the 1990s propelled by a genocidal war in their home country and, more recently, by gang-related violence; many are indigenous people of Mayan filiation for whom Spanish is a second language. Almost all are undocumented. Nassau Street, Princeton's central artery, features numerous places of commerce, including fancy jewellry stores, and expensive restaurants, all of which employ undocumented immigrants.

Princeton is explicitly defined by its governing authorities as a *welcoming city*. Public agencies—including the Office of Human Resources, and the Police Department—in collaboration with grassroots organizations have put in place programmes to foster hospitality and help immigrants gain access to necessary services. Soon after the 2016 presidential election, hundreds of yard signs bearing welcoming messages in English, Spanish, and Arabic sprung up like mushrooms throughout the city as evidence of a favourable disposition towards inclusivity. Teachers and administrators at the local high school stretched out their job definitions to ensure the safety of students without papers. Citizens banded together to shelter residents facing possible deportation.

Only 13 miles away from Princeton is Trenton but the contrast between the two cities could not be sharper. Beginning in the second half of the nineteenth century, Trenton became a point of destination for several generations of European immigrants who found work in an expanding industrial sector. The city was once the world's first producer of commercial ceramics (Crown and Rogers 2000). Nevertheless, by the end of the 1970s, as economic globalization took hold, thousands of factories had closed down and jobs had been relocated to foreign locations. Industrial decline accelerated even as African Americans from southern rural states arrived seeking a better life. Rapid demographic change paralleled losses in formal employment. What had been a prosperous reflection of the American Dream became an exemplification of urban decay.

Trenton is home to 84,000 residents—half of them black (US Census Bureau 2017b); less than 14 per cent are white but, significantly, nearly 34 per cent are Hispanic, mainly Guatemalans and Mexicans but also Ecuadorians, Colombians and Peruvians. Most are undocumented or insufficiently documented people. The Chambersburg district—inhabited by Germans, Bohemians, and Moravians in the nineteenth century, and more recently by the descendants of Irish and Italian immigrants—is now solidly Hispanic, dotted with small stores bearing Spanish names. Latino restaurants have replaced the Sicilian-owned eateries that for a long time stood as unique tourist attractions.

By contrast to Princeton, Trenton is an impoverished city buffeted by long-term disinvestment. In the 1960s the city's motto, *"What Trenton makes, the World Takes,"* reflected pride in a gritty industrial identity. Now, decrepit buildings dappled with graffiti, boarded-up structures, and empty lots bear witness to abandonment. No convention centres or resorts exist in Trenton. Some hotels flourish nearby, in places like Bordentown, Robbinsville, and Hamilton but there are none in the city proper. And, although Trenton holds rank as New Jersey's capital, the governor's mansion, Drumthwacket, is not in that city but in Princeton, another sign that Trenton is not a favoured residential choice for those with money and status.

Although situated in close proximity, Princeton and Trenton represent two separate environments with varying political climates and resources that differ in terms of quantity and quality. They are ideal spaces to assess disparities in the effects of context of reception on the lives of immigrant children. How do youngsters perceive and act upon educational and employment opportunities? How do they imagine their place in the larger society and their future as citizens or outcasts? These are questions I address in the next sections.

Research background

Over the past two decades several major studies have deepened knowledge about adaptation patterns in the fastest growing segment of America's youthful population, ages 24 or under. One-fourth of that segment encompasses immigrant children or children of immigrants (Hagan 2008; Hagan, Leal, and Rodríguez 2015; Donato and Sisk 2015). Scholars have also focused on the large-scale displacement of settled immigrants and new arrivals from traditional areas of concentration in the West and Southwest toward new destinations in the Midwest, East, and South. Works documenting that transition, include Douglas S. Massey's *New Faces in New Places* (2010); *Global Connections and Local Receptions* by Fran Ansley and Jon Shefner (2009); and *New Destinations: Mexican Immigration in the United States,* edited by Victor Zuñiga and Rubén Hernández León (2006).

There are also studies of immigrant youngsters living in America during the first half of the twentieth century (Chinn 2008; Brown 2018), but burgeoning interest in their recent counterparts dates back to the mid-1990s when the *Children of Immigrants Longitudinal Study* (CILS) was spearheaded by Alejandro Portes and Rubén Rumbaut. That project, spanning more than ten years, included three surveys and ethnographic research centred on a large sample of second-generation immigrants and their families in Florida and California. The result was a comprehensive portrait of life trajectories among immigrant youths, most of whom had roots in Latin America and the West Indies (Portes and Rumbaut 2014).

That and other projects show that the experience of second-generation immigrants varies significantly in terms of national provenance and race (see also Adsera and Tienda 2012; Tienda and Haskins 2011; and Yoshikawa 2011). While Cuban exiles and their offspring followed paths of upward mobility in South Florida, Haitians and Jamaicans in the same area faced heightened risks of school abandonment and incarceration. Children of Mexicans in San Diego illustrated processes of stagnant mobility and high levels of residential segregation. Portes and Zhou (1993) distilled such findings into the concept of *segmented assimilation*, which draws attention to the heterogeneous outcomes of migration (See also Zhou 1997).

Related studies uncovered factors that enable children in impoverished and stigmatized groups to succeed in education and employment. Fernández-Kelly (2008), for example, found that reducing the capacity of impoverished children to interact with peers outside the family, in combination with strong narratives highlighting ethnic identity, protect youngsters and enable them to reach unexpected levels of success in education and employment. Kasinitz, Waters, and their colleagues (2010) discovered that in New York immigrant children benefit from preexisting narratives of success and related resources forged by the Civil Rights Movement. Lee and Zhou (2015) documented differential rates of economic and educational success by placing emphasis on *hyperselectivity* and *stereotype promise*. They found that class position in country of origin is a determining factor increasing the probability of successful adaptation among Asian immigrants. Their characterization as a "model minority" further improves their odds of successful incorporation.

More recently, authors have turned their attention with force to the effects of punitive policies. Dreby and Enriquez (2015) exhaustively describes the erosion of kinship ties and subsequent family collapse caused by deportations. Gonzales (2011) offers gut-wrenching descriptions of young people trying to make sense of their position in American society when lacking the fundamental documents that would enable their integration. Menjívar (2006) describes feelings of confusion, and reduced socioeconomic alternatives, induced by states of social liminality among Salvadorans and

Guatemalans in the United States. De Parle (2019) lays out a multi-genera-tional picture of migrants, emphasizing the devastating effects of family sep-arations on both parents and their children (see also Chaudry et al. 2010; and Dreby and Enriquez 2015).

Such writings demonstrate that immigrant integration does not happen in a linear fashion but through recurrent interaction between foreign-born youngsters, other immigrants, and their native-born counterparts in schools, workplaces, and other public spaces. Equally relevant is the effect of legal, economic, and ideational resources on the capacity of immigrant children to navigate steady courses of upward mobility in the receiving society. Study after study affirms the critical significance of context of reception.

I extrapolate from those predicates to construct a synthetic framework that connects and contrasts material and social resources with ideational leanings among immigrant children. That schema is summarized in Table 1.

Typologies are part of the sociological stockpile. Robert K. Merton's use of classificatory schemes in the study of Social Structure and Anomie (Merton 1938) and Discrimination and the American Creed (Merton 1976) still resonate today. Similar tools have been applied in immigration research, dating back to Robert Park's study of cultural conflict and marginality (1928), passing through William Petersen's general typology of migration (1958), and culminating in classic works by Berry (1997; 2005) (see also Iredale 2008 and King 2012). Most are taxonomies of immigrants themselves—professionals, middlemen minorities, labour migrants, etc. or categorizations relevant to cultural amalga-mation. Berry (1997), for example, was among the first to offer a typology con-necting cultural context and individual behavioural developments. Such instruments have enhanced migration studies but they have not consumed possibilities.

The typology presented here adds to earlier efforts by drawing attention to the relationship between (a) types of material and social resources embedded in particular settings and (b) ideational leanings, not culture. The underlying claim is that fluctuations in the relationship between the two factors best explains different responses to pressures such as stigma, risk of deportation, family sep-aration, and uncertain legal status. *Ideational leanings* refer to attitudes, aspira-tions, explanations, and expectations expressed in conversational narratives and collected as data by the researcher.[3] The typology is therefore a stylized

Table 1. Hypothesized relation between outcomes and resources in a sample of immigrant children.

	Advocacy	Material supports	Tolerance	Ideational leanings
Achievers	+	+	+	Aspiration
Stayers	−	+	+	Resignation
Insurgents	−	−	+	Contestation
Skidders	−	−	−	Withdrawal

representation of hypothesized relationships between various kinds of assets and categories of youngsters. It is not an exhaustive account but an analytical instrument to facilitate understanding—a cudgel rather than a stiletto.

Several terms anchor the typology. *Advocacy* refers to active involvement on the part of *external* partners, individuals as well as organizations, bent on expanding prospects for young people. Advocates meet regularly with undocumented students, represent them before institutions such as schools and courts; they also seek educational and financial assets on their behalf. They constitute what Mark Granovetter (1973) called *weak ties,* supplementing information available to families, and providing assistance on vital matters, including college applications. *Material supports* comprise monetary enhancements, including financial aid and scholarships, but also employment opportunities for students and their families. *Tolerance* denotes perceptions on the part of immigrant youngsters, not impressions held by members of other groups. Politicians, clerics, or teachers may engage in efforts to create accepting environments but gaps produced by social distance, linguistic limitations, and social segregation may foil their expectations. The crucial point then is whether the young people under consideration perceive their surroundings as hospitable or not. Especially significant are perceptions of racial discrimination and exclusion.

The typology sorts out ideational leanings found among the four categories of youngsters. It analytically distinguishes storylines that young people in my sample deploy when making sense of their circumstances (see also Deaux 2011; Wiley and Deaux 2011; and Bloemraad, Sarabia, and Fillingim 2016). Ideational leanings are not mechanically connected to a single group; instead, they represent alternative discourses found to a greater or lesser extent in each of the four categories. Thus, Achievers tend to focus on hope and aspiration but often mesh those feelings with elements of anger and frustration drawn from cultural repertoires more frequently found among Insurgents and Skidders. In the same vein, youngsters in the last two categories express hopes of inclusion and achievement, although their stories are permeated by elements of discontent and contestation.

Ethnographic account

I use participant observation, and verbal interactions to pinpoint the meanings that social actors impose on their actions and enfolding conditions. In that respect, ethnographic research is not only about observed facts but also about the accurate representation of ways in which actual persons in tangible places make sense of their experience. The cases presented are illustrative of circumstances surrounding, and outlooks found, among immigrant youngsters in Central New Jersey. I use no composites. Although the names are fictitious, the persons are real, each case representing an instance in the typology presented earlier.

Achievers

These are individuals swiftly advancing along educational and occupational paths despite legal and economic barriers. In the pursuit of their goals, such youngsters rely on the advocacy of mentors, counselors, and organizations, which provide financial support and valuable information. They tend to reside in hospitable spaces, mostly devoid of intense surveillance or fear of detention. In such environments, immigrant children can develop narratives that buttress hope and high aspirations. A case in point is 20-year old Osvaldo Del Cid, Jr. whose story is sketched below:

> Osvaldo lives with his mother, Marina, who is 42, and his 12-year old brother, Erwin, in a modest but well-appointed home in Ewing, a city minutes away from Trenton. Mildred, Osvaldo' sister, is 24. She lives nearby with her boyfriend, Mario, and their three-year old daughter, Noemi. The family entered the US with legal visas but didn't leave when they expired. Osvaldo and Mildred were able to attain protected status under DACA and have once renewed their permits, although they worry daily about the possible termination of the program.[4] They live in limbo but forge ahead to honor the memory of their father, Osvaldo Del Cid, Sr., who first arrived in New Jersey in 2001.

> Osvaldo Sr. had grown up in Jalapa, Guatemala, a farming community where his own father had acquired some status as a land owner. His ambition far surpassed his eight-grade education. Once in the United States, he worked hard in construction and then started a small landscaping firm which he legally incorporated in 2010. Eight years earlier he had gone back to Guatemala to make arrangements for his wife and children to join him in his adopted land. Back in the US, his tiny business prospered and he altered the terms of his firm's incorporation to ensure that his wife appeared as the owner. Marina helped her husband but mostly she took care of her kids and prepared *tacos* and *tamales* for sale to supplement the family's income. Erwin, the youngest child, came into the world in 2006, a full American by birth. The family's settlement and advance was aided by the presence of relatives and friends living in the same area. Marina's brother had resided in New Brunswick for nearly a decade when she first arrived. Her husband had two cousins in Ewing.

> Osvaldo Jr. was brought by his parents to the United States when he was only five. He grew up in a large family and bilingual, although English is his preferred language. His father sought a way to acquire green cards for his wife and children but the means were not available to adjust their status. Although they paid thousands of dollars to *notarios* and lawyers, they remained in the margins but also expectant and patient in their search of opportunity. As a token of their ambition, Osvaldo's parents had given him a middle name evoking a solid English connection; a middle name crafted after Stewart, the appellative of the famous actor whom they had watched in American movies back in their home town; except that they didn't know how to spell the word, so Osvaldo ended up with *Estywer* which, phonetically, sounds close enough. Small gestures tell big stories.

Early in 2013, Osvaldo Sr. bought new equipment for his business, ready to make that year a time of growth. That summer, while trimming a tree in the yard of a Princeton University professor, a falling branch killed him instantly. He was only 38 years old. In addition to the colossal loss of her husband, Marina was held responsible for the accident—the Occupational Safety and Health Administration (OSHA) found that Osvaldo' death had involved small violations to rules governing landscaping firms and, technically, she was the firm's owner. Even as she buried her husband, Marina faced fines and training obligations to avoid similar mishaps in the future. She went from loyal housewife to independent entrepreneur.

Ironically, the tragic event that left him without a father, connected Osvaldo Jr. to new resources, both financial and human. Horrified by the accident, a neighbor made a call on behalf of the family to LALDEF (Latin American Legal Defense and Education Fund), a grassroots organization founded in 2004 by Princeton activists to advocate and educate on behalf of immigrants in Central New Jersey.[5] LALDEF represented Marina before the OSHA authorities, securing a reduction in fines; it also procured the required training for her to take full ownership of her small business; it reached out to Osvaldo to provide support as he transitioned to college.

With renewed determination, the boy worked hard at school, got a job, wrote for the school's newspaper, and joined the tennis club in his senior year. He graduated with a 3.5 GPA and above-average SATs. Throughout that period he prepared college applications under the supervision of a LALDEF volunteer. In 2017 he was accepted as a first-year student at The College of New Jersey. He beamed with pride—to get an education from that institution had been his dream. He had played by the rules, done his job, and honored his father's legacy. Osvaldo concluded his first year of college with a 3.4 GPA bolstered by a B+ in statistics. He is majoring in sociology.

Things are going well for Osvaldo, largely because of his spirit and resilience but also because of his fortuitous connection to a grassroots organization prepared to buttress his aspirations. His story illustrates the experience of undocumented children whose resource base is large as a result of local government initiatives and the presence of volunteer organizations in the areas where they reside. Their lives are not easy and they often experience high levels of frustration and anger because of their marginal status. All the same, they are in a position to nurture ambition.

Stayers

These are youngsters who may benefit from tolerance and even acceptance but lack strong advocacy sources or material supports. They may be unable to pursue educational goals because of the need to support themselves or others through employment in low-paying jobs. A paucity of information and limited linguistic ability present additional barriers to steady mobility.

Under such circumstances, Stayers are apt to develop narratives focused on resignation and forbearance. Children in that category expect not to gain full membership in the larger society but they see survival as a realistic goal. Below is an illustrative case:

> Marcos González left his small village in Southern Mexico in 2001 expecting to open up new routes for his children, Fernando and Ramiro, who were seven and five at the time. Originally from Putla in the southern state of Oaxaca, Mexico, Marcos and his wife, Amelia, knew many people in Princeton. Starting in the 1980s, Putlecans had created small businesses in that city, mostly grocery stores and landscaping firms. One family had even bought a food and catering outfit right in the heart of town; proudly, they had plastered a sign on the front window reading "English Spoken Here." With such compatriots in the area, Marcos thought it would be no trouble finding a job and he was right. Unfortunately, wages were low and it was difficult to make ends meet. Twice, a boss refused to pay him; Marcos didn't report him for fear of being deported. He forged ahead, working as a busboy and dishwasher at a local restaurant and later in construction and landscaping. Amelia made food to peddle at social events.

> The two boys did well in school. Fernando, the older sibling, liked classes and received good and passing grades but he never quite excelled. The reason was simple: he was never able to give full time to his studies; his father often took him to work. Especially in high school, Fernando struggled to combine paid employment and educational demands. As a child he had dreamed about becoming a doctor. As a teenager he scaled down aspirations to meet blunt realities. It was also true that Ramiro, his younger brother, was emerging as the academic star in the family. After graduating from high school, Fernando postponed his educational goals to work with his father full time. Their goal was to pool financial resources to ensure that Ramiro could attend a good college. They succeeded: in 2016, Ramiro was accepted at the University of Pittsburgh where he is majoring in Political Science. After graduating, he hopes to become an actuary.

> Fernando is proud of his younger brother and, especially, of having contributed to Ramiro's success. His own aspirations, however, have shrunk. Lacking external resources, both human and material, he has had to rely on paid employment to survive. "There's always a job for someone willing to bust his ass," he told me recently, "I suppose I'll always be busting my ass as a worker ... so be it!"

Fernando's trajectory exposes some of the compromises young, undocumented people are forced to make. Torn between the need to subsist and the hope to advance, they often opt for the former, postponing goals and becoming part of the vast web of service providers in a bifurcated economy where richer people can buy their labour at a small price. Young men like Fernando represent a growing population of children of immigrants without regular status, whose aspirations have been arrested. They live as part of American society but they are not of the society. Their insufficiently documented status and separation from viable resources virtually guarantee that they will not gain full incorporation into their adopted nation. As they ponder their circumstances, such youngsters are prone to see themselves as people resigned to their fate; people trying to make the best out of a bad deal.

Insurgents

These are individuals facing diminished levels of advocacy and meagre material resources in contexts characterized by toleration. Insurgents are more likely than others to rely on ideational narratives centred on opposition, resistance, and vindication. Some use religious faith and values to explain misfortune and legitimize confrontational action. The journey undertaken by Leiser Castro illustrates such conditions.

> In the summer of 2008, Leiser was looking forward to his eighth-grade graduation at the high school he attended in Guatemala City. He had even bought a tuxedo for the much anticipated prom. At a time of joy he was also harboring monstrous fears. His father was gravely ill and without money to pay for a doctor. Even more terrifying was the looming presence of two gangs: *Toles* and *Guatucos*. They were at war and everyone knew of the crimes they committed in the name of honor and territory—thefts, rapes, intimidation and, worse, killings. Leiser was popular in school and got good grades; he had a reputation as a caring, charismatic kid, which may have been the reason why he was approached by the leader of the *Guatucos*. "We like you," he told Leiser, "We need you. We can give you money to take care of your father; we can give you a car; we can give you respect … and all you have to do is kill whomever we tell you to kill." Leiser knew immediately what the options were: to accept the offer and become a murderer or to decline and be murdered. He was only fifteen.

> Such were the thoughts that floated in his mind that summer day as he thought about his forthcoming graduation. Then his cell phone rang. It was his paternal uncle calling from Trenton. He had been living in that city for five years and had often asked his nephew to join him. Now, unexpectedly, he had decided to return to Guatemala the following month. Leiser felt panic rushing through his body—he had been contemplating escape to the US to live with his uncle while looking for a job. He might as well act now. Less than 48 h later, Leiser was on his way to New Jersey. A group of *coyotes* financed his journey expecting to be paid with interest after he settled in America. He traveled in buses. He walked for long stretches in Mexico. Twice he was jumped by thieves who thought he might be carrying money. Four times he faced death in the Arizona Desert. Almost a month later, he arrived in his uncle's apartment, a small, cramped space shared with other immigrants. Soon after, Leiser moved out into a rented room in Princeton. He found a job as a dish washer in a local restaurant and showed up at Princeton High School. He also joined the Assemblies of God in Trenton and made it a habit to attend multiple worship services. He became part of the Young Voices of Faith in his congregation.

After graduating from Princeton High School, with a lackluster GPA of 2.5, and still not fluent in English, Leiser enrolled at Mercer County Community College (MCCC), hoping to get a degree in visual arts. He wants to be a filmmaker. His aspirations are high but circumstances conspire against him. For nearly ten years he has had to support himself and send remittances to his family in Guatemala. He works at an expensive restaurant where two things are true: his manager values Leiser's diligence and frequently asks him to work overtime— this means higher earnings but less time for school. Now 24, he feels stuck but not defeated. He has a mentor who made it possible for him to receive financial aid to pursue his education at MCCC. His teachers think he has talent. Yet he despairs. "By the time I get done with my education," he tells me somberly, "I will be an old man." It is hard to look into the future when dragging your feet in a swampy present.

And still, despite frustration and anxiety, Leiser can't give up because of a promise he made to God while facing starvation in the Arizona Desert. "Twice the *migra*[6] passed me by and they didn't see me; I was there but God Almighty made me invisible. I owe it to God to make the best of myself; to honor his name, and pay back for my life."

Leiser's religious fervour is emblematic of narratives found among undocumented youngsters who have faced massive obstacles and whose capacity to overcome hinges on stories of struggle and affirmation. In Leiser's case, it is a Christian outlook that keeps him strong. In many other instances, found mostly in Trenton, it is the black experience of endurance and triumph that excites the minds of young Latinos without papers. Marino Pérez, a junior at Trenton High School, said it most poignantly one lustrous afternoon in the fall of 2017. We were chatting about his belief system. "Life is rough," he told me,

People disrespect you because you look different, you talk different; they know maybe you don't have papers and that gives them permission to fuck with you like you're nothing … but I keep moving 'cause I know that black people have been in a place worse than [mine] and they survived. The Civil Rights Movement, yeah, Martin Luther King—we study all that in school. And I think, if those people made it, I can make it. I know who I am and I know where I'm going.

Others, like Diego Beltrán, also a junior at Trenton High School, find respite in knowing that they are not alone. He explains: "Trenton can be a hard city but Latinos like me are changing it, making it better. We got the culture and the food and the *cojones* to turn this city into our city." Diego is referring to the constellation of Hispanic businesses and the multiplicity of restaurants now bearing Spanish names like *Rinconcito Latino, Guatepan, Guatelinda Restaurant,* and *El Chapin*; places of work owned by people like him; catering to people like him. He knows racial discrimination is real but he doesn't feel much of it because his friends are from Guatemala and they speak Spanglish, just like him.

In other words, living in spaces shared with people from the same background, who face similar challenges, provides a kind of comfort despite overwhelming barriers, legal, economic, and social. Lee and Zhou (2015) make a similar point when underscoring the significance of immaterial ethnic resources that buttress educational outcomes among the children of Asian immigrants from poor and working-class backgrounds; co-ethnic role models play a decisive role in bolstering the images of struggling youngsters. Moreover, black students at Trenton High School, who form the majority, can engage in discriminatory behaviour but they can hardly lord over Guatemalans—both populations have felt in the flesh similar kinds of disrespect from outsiders. The potential for romance and solidarity is as real as that of conflict and dissention.

Skidders

I use that term to shine light on the experience of youngsters facing extreme dearth of resources—including advocacy and material supports—and heightened levels of prejudice and hostility. Such youngsters tend to depart from established paths for educational attainment and gainful employment. They are less capable of articulating narratives based on hope and effort, gravitating towards withdrawal, isolation, and exit. Such is the case of two children born to Alma Del Cedro:

> Alma Del Cedro left Pénjamo (Guanajuato), Mexico, in 2000, escaping an abusive husband who threatened her with bodily mutilation during an alcoholic tirade. She took her three children. The eldest, Esteban, was eight years old; his brother, Luis, five; and the youngest, Lucy, only two. They arrived without papers in Trenton—where Alma's sister lived—and were never able to adjust their legal status. The city was undergoing rapid demographic change: Latinos were now a sizable population. Alma soon found work at one of the few factories left in the area. She was the only support of her family and the shifts were long, so she hardly ever saw her kids. For more than three years she lived with her sister; Alma didn't earn enough to rent an apartment.

> This made for an uncomfortable situation, especially as the children grew older and bristled at authority, chasing freedom. Esteban began showing worrisome signs—he hated school, mostly because he couldn't speak English and his teachers said he was disruptive. He was diagnosed with Attention Deficit Disorder, a familiar occurrence among impoverished children. That made him feel even more different and not in a good way. He knew he wasn't wanted. He started peddling drugs in middle school and graduated to thievery in high school. He wanted money to help his mother but, along the way, he became an addict. After dropping out of school in his senior year, he took to the streets and meddled with a posse of equally disaffected youngsters. That he had no papers was not a problem; most of his cronies were undocumented too. In 2016, he was caught in a burglary and sent to prison for three years. This was a relief to his mother; she no longer had to worry about where Esteban spent his nights. He will be deported after completing his sentence.

Luis, Amelia's younger son didn't fare much better. He's never been in jail but he also dropped out of Trenton High School in his senior year. That is because he wanted to earn some serious money to support his girlfriend who was pregnant. For the last seven years, Luis has been working in construction. He and his girlfriend now have three children; they live with his mother in an expensive but ramshackle apartment owned by a woman from Mumbai. He cannot afford to live on his own. Only Lucy, Alma's youngest child, has escaped the cycle of poverty and dysfunction. She is currently completing her first year as a college student at Rutgers.

I sit quietly at the kitchen table in Alma Del Cedro's tiny apartment. Crumpled laundry accumulates in one corner. Dirty dishes await washing. Across from me sits Luis trying to decide whether to take an early shift at the construction site where he has worked for the last two weeks or call it quits. I ask him whether he has considered enrolling in Community College to get a vocational degree and, eventually, a better job. It's not too late, I say. A look of disbelief passes through his young face: "going to school at my age is a waste of time," he responds, "it's always been a waste of time, even when I was younger; time spent in school is time spent away from money. It ain't worth it. We, my brother and me, we're hood, we play by the rule of the streets; we know what it takes to survive and it ain't school."

Luis is voicing feelings emerging in sub-sectors formed by undocumented youths. Without advocates and resources; unable to assess the merits of formal education; mired in financial need and living in isolation, people like Luis are reliving the experience of disaffected African Americans and possibly spinning a new cycle of inter-generational immiseration.

Conclusion

In this paper I aimed to make sense of the variegated experience confronted by undocumented children in two different settings. I underscored *toponomic* factors, that is, spatially situated resources such as advocacy, material supports, and perceived levels of tolerance to account for coping strategies and emerging outcomes in a sample of youngsters in Central New Jersey. I presented a typology connecting categories of immigrant children, embedded resources, and ideational leanings to illustrate the effects of context upon heterogeneous responses in populations sharing a common experience.

Conditions surrounding undocumented or partially undocumented youngsters in Princeton and Trenton vary significantly. In Princeton High School, Hispanic students face high levels of internal segregation and are tracked into courses less demanding than those set aside for a majority of white, more affluent students. Teachers struggle to support undocumented pupils but they acknowledge monumental problems, including high levels of clinical depression, attempted suicides, and early pregnancies. Social isolation, linguistic limitations, and a yawning social distance vis-à-vis the surrounding population diminishes the potential effects of policies designed by the local government to boost the prospects of immigrants and their children.

In Trenton, where most students attending high-school are African American or Latino, separation in terms of race exists but class distinctions are less acute. This may be leading to a paradoxical outcome: a greater capacity on the part of undocumented youngsters in Trenton to develop stronger identities and more positive self-valuation than those in Princeton.

In both Trenton and Princeton, immigrant youngsters tend to be part of families that live modestly but not all are poor. Many reside with parents who own small businesses. Others are part of a thriving informal economy not reflected in official data. Such families are able to provide their children with some resources. In the two locations, as well, immigrant children tend to be part of social networks whose members share a common experience and are therefore practiced at offering and receiving support. The exchange of favours and information often provide youngsters without full legal status with effective ways to navigate employment and social terrains.

Finally, the uncommon hostility towards immigrants and refugees that has characterized the Donald J. Trump administration has had an unanticipated consequence—the emergence of citizen networks aiming to shelter immigrant children and their families. Not long ago, progressive voices clamored for immigration reform. Now they are also demanding protection for undocumented Americans regardless of whether the nation can fix its broken immigration laws or not. While immigrants are being targeted for draconian treatment at the federal and state levels, residents in local spaces are banding together to offer protection and solidarity to immigrant families. That may yet create the proper microclimate to forestall social and economic decline among youngsters seeking full inclusion in American society.

Notes

1. For a glimpse of the draconian policies currently shaping the conditions youngsters in my study are confronting, see Bennett and Memoli (2017); Brané and Schlanger (2018); Dickerson (2018); Leal and Rodríguez (2015); Reilly (2017); Shear and Baumgaetner (2018), and Waters (2015).
2. As evidence of the divided character of the American State, the Internal Revenue Service provides identification numbers to businesses legally formed by undocumented immigrant even as the Department of Homeland Security seeks in earnest to deport them.
3. That is by contrast to "culture," a term generally used to designate "way of life."
4. DACA (Deferred Action for Childhood Arrivals) was implemented by President Barack Obama in 2010 through executive order to provide relief to children brought into the United States at an early age by undocumented parents. The act was rescinded in 2017 under the Trump administration, although its reinstatement or final dissolution is currently being litigated in federal courts.

5. LALDEF operates a community centre in Trenton, Casa de *Bienvenida / Welcome House*. It offers adult education courses, English-as-a-second-language classes, assistance to victims of domestic violence, mentoring to students in transition to college, tax preparation advice, legal referrals, and community ID cards. The author serves as chair of the board of trustees at LALDEF.
6. An abbreviation of *migration,* used to designate the border patrol.

Acknowledgement

I am deeply grateful for the advice provided by Jennifer Lee regarding the title and content of this paper. I am also in debt to four anonymous reviewers whose recommendations significantly strengthened my argument.

Disclosure statement

No potential conflict of interest was reported by the author.

References

Adsera, Alicia, and Marta Tienda, eds. 2012. *Migrant Youth and Children of Migrants in a Globalized World, Annals of the American Academy of Political and Social Science.* Vol. 643(September). New Delhi: SAGE.

Ansley, Fran, and Jon Shefner. 2009. *Global Connections and Local Receptions: New Latino Immigration to the Southeastern United States.* Knoxville, TN: University to Tennessee Press.

Bennett, Brian, and Michael A. Memoli. 2017. "The White House has found ways to end protection for 'Dreamers' while shielding Trump from blowback." *Los Angeles Times.* February 16. http://www.latimes.com/politics/la-na-pol-trump-daca-20170216-story.html.

Berry, John W. 1997. "Immigration, Acculturation, and Adaptation." *Applied Psychology: An International Review* 46: 5–68.

Berry, John W. 2005. "Acculturation: Living Successfully in Two Cultures." *International Journal of Intercultural Relations* 29: 691–712.

Bloemraad, Irene, Heidy Sarabia, and Angela Fillingim. 2016. "Staying Out of Trouble" and Doing What is "Right" – Citizenship Acts, Citizenship Ideals, and the Effects of Legal Status on Second-Generation Youth." *American Behavioral Scientist* 60 (13): 1534–1552.

Brané, Michelle, and Margo Schlanger. 2018. "This is what's really happening to kids at the border." *The Washington Post* (May 30). https://www.washingtonpost.com/news/monkey-cage/wp/2018/05/30/this-is-whats-really-happening-to-kids-at-the-border/?noredirect=on&utm_term=.dd6c63b7a58a.

Brown, Rosellen. 2018. *The Lake on Fire.* Louisville, KY: Sarabande Books.

Chaudry, Ajay, Randolph Capps, Juan Pedroza, Rosa Maria Castañeda, Robert Santos, and Molly M. Scott. 2010. "Facing our Future: Children in the Aftermath of Immigration Enforcement. Urban Institute. http://www.urban.org/UploadedPDF/412020_FacingOurFuture_final.pdf.

Chinn, Sarah E. 2008. *Inventing Modern Adolescence: The Children of Immigrants in Turn-of-the-Century America.* New Brunswick, NJ: Rutgers University Press.

Crown, Cathleen, and Carol Rogers. 2000. *Images of America: Trenton*. Charleston, NC: Arcadia Publishing.

Deaux, Kay. 2011. "An Immigrant Frame for American Identity." *Applied Developmental Science* 15 (2): 70–72.

DeParle, Jason. 2019. *A Good Provider is One Who Leaves: One Family and Migration in the 21st Century*. New York, NY: Viking.

Dickerson, Caitlin. 2018. "Detention of Migrant Children has Skyrocketed to Highest Levels Ever." *The New York Times* (Sept 12). https://www.nytimes.com/2018/09/12/us/migrant-children-detention.html.

Donato, Katharine M., and Blake Sisk. 2015. "Children's Migration From Mexico and Central America to the United States: Evidence From the Mexican and Latin American Migration Projects." *Journal of Migration and Human Security*. http://jmhs.cmsny.org/index.php/jmhs/article/view/43.

Dreby, Joanna, and Laura E. Enriquez. 2015. *Everyday Illegal: When Policies Undermine Immigrant Families*. Oakland, CA: University of California Press.

Fernández-Kelly, Patricia. 2008. "The Back Pocket Map: Social Class and Cultural Capital as Transferable Assets in the Advancement of Second Generation Immigrants." *Annals of the American Academy of Political and Social Science* 620: 12–36.

Fernández-Kelly, Patricia. 2012. "Making Sense of the Other: Ethnographic Methods and Immigration Research." In *International Handbook of Migration*, edited by Steven J. Gold, 539–552. Oxfordshire, UK: Routledge.

Foner, Nancy, and Patrick Simon, eds. 2015. *Fear, Anxiety, and National Identity: Immigraton and Belonging in North America and Europe*. New York, NY: Russell Sage Foundation Press.

Gonzales, Roberto G. 2011. "Learning to Be Illegal: Undocumented Youth and Shifting Legal Contexts in the Transition to Adulthood." *American Sociological Review* 76 (4): 602–619.

Granovetter, Mark. 1973. "The Strength of Weak Ties." *American Journal of Sociology* 78 (6): 1360–1380.

Hagan, Jacqueline M. 2008. *Migration Miracle: Faith, Hope, and Meaning on the Undocumented Journey*. Cambridge, MA: Harvard University Press.

Hagan, Jaqueline M., Leiser Leal, and Nestor Rodríguez. 2015. "Deporting Social Capital: Implications for Immigrant Communities in the United States." *Migration Studies* 3 (3): 370–392.

Tienda, Marta and Ron Haskins. 2011. "Immigrant Children: Introducing the Issue." *The Future of Children*, 21(1): 3–18.

Iredale, Robyn. 2008. "The Migration of Professionals: Thories and Typologies." *International Migration* 39 (5): 7–26.

Kasinitz, Philip, John H. Mollenkopf, and Mary Waters. 2010. *Inheriting the City: The Children of Immigrants Come of Age*. New York, NY: Russell Sage Foundation Press.

King, Russell. 2012. "Theories and Typologies of Migration: An Overview and a Primer." *Willy Brandt Series of Working Papers in International Migration and Ethnic Relations* 12 (3): 1–43.

Leal, Leiser, and Nestor Rodríguez, eds. 2015. *Migration in an Era of Restriction*. New York, NY: Springer.

Lee, Jennifer, and Min Zhou. 2015. *The Asian American Achievement Paradox*. New York, NY: Russell Sage Foundation Press.

Massey, Douglas S. 2010. *New Faces in New Places: The Changing Geography of American Immigration*. New York, NY: Russell Sage Foundation Press.

Menjívar, Cecilia. 2006. "Liminal Legality: Salvadoran and Guatemalan Immigrants' Lives in the United States." *American Journal of Sociology* 111 (4): 999–1037.

Merton, Robert K. 1938. "Social Structure and Anomie." *American Sociological Review* 3 (5): 672–682.

Merton, Robert K. 1976. "Discrimination and the American Creed." In *Sociological Ambivalence and Other Essays*, 189–216. Glencoe, IL: The Free Press.

Park, Robert E. 1928. "Human Migration and the Marginal Man." *American Journal of Sociology* 33 (6): 881–893.

Petersen, William. 1958. "A General Typology of Migration." *American Sociological Review* 23 (3): 256–266.

Portes, Alejandro, and Rubén Rumbaut. 2014. *Immigrant America: A Portrait*. Oakland, CA: University of California Press.

Portes, Alejandro, and Min Zhou. 1993. "The New Second Generation: Segmented Assimilation and its Variants." *Annals of the American Academy of Political and Social Sciences* 530: 74–96.

Reilly, Katie. 2017. "Here's What President Trump Has Said About DACA in the Past." *TIME* (September 5). http://time.com/4927100/donald-trump-daca-past-statements/.

Shear, Michael D., and Emily Baumgaetner. 2018. "Trump Administration Aims to Sharply Restrict New Green Cards for Those on Public Aid." *The New York Times* (Sept. 22).

US Census Bureau. 2017a. "Quick Facts: Princeton, New Jersey." https://www.census.gov/quickfacts/princetonnewjersey.

US Census Bureau. 2017b. "Quick Facts: Trenton, New Jersey." https://www.census.gov/quickfacts/trentoncitynewjersey.

Waters, Mary C. 2015. "The War on Crime and the War on Immigrants: Racial and Legal Exclusion in 21st Century United States." In *Fear, Anxiety and National Identity: Immigration and Belonging in North America and Europe*, edited by Nancy Foner, and Patrick Simon. New York, NY: Russell Sage Foundation Press.

Widner, Ralph. 2017. "Princeton Residents." Review Draft. Council for Princeton Future. (Unpublished).

Wiley, Shaun, and Kay Deaux. 2011. "The Bicultural Identity Performance of Immigrants." In *Identity and Participation in Culturally Diverse Societies: A Multidisciplinary Perspective*, edited by Assaad E. Azzi, Xenia Chryssochoou, Bert Klandemans, and Bernd Simon, 49–68. Hoboken, NJ: Blackwell/ Wiley.

Yoshikawa, Hirokazu. 2011. *Immigrants Raising Citizens: Undocumented Parents and Their Young Children*. New York, NY: Russell Sage Foundation Press.

Zhou, Min. 1997. "Segmented Assimilation: Issues, Controversies, and Recent Research on the New Second Generation." *International Migration Review* 31 (4): 975–1008.

Zúñiga, Victor, and Ruben Hernandez-Leon. 2006. *New Destinations: Mexican Immigration in the United States*. New York, NY: The Russell Sage Foundation Press.

Coming of age before the great expulsion: the story of the CILS-San Diego sample 25 years later

Cynthia Feliciano and Rubén G. Rumbaut

ABSTRACT
California was transformed by immigration in the 1980s. In 1991, a representative sample of children of immigrants and refugees was drawn from 8th/9th graders in San Diego's public schools. These CILS respondents were followed for nearly 25 years, from early adolescence to their late thirties, combining surveys with in-depth qualitative interviews. The educational and cultural integration of this segment of the new second generation has been largely positive. These adult children of immigrants – from Mexico, the Philippines, Vietnam, Cambodia, Laos, China, India and elsewhere – have above average educational attainments and mainly think of themselves as mainstream Americans, outcomes produced in an inclusive multiethnic context with a strong and accessible public higher education system. But in the current national context of accelerated deportations and exclusions, and a continuing retreat from investments in public education, the future for the next generation of immigrants' children is far from certain.

The study of "the new second generation", arguably the most consequential legacy of contemporary immigration to the United States, is now more than a quarter century old, and has generated a vibrant field of study. The incorporation trajectories of the adult children of the new immigration have been the subject of vigorous debate: are they not only "assimilating" into the American "mainstream" but exhibiting a "second-generation advantage" relative to native-born peers, or experiencing "downward assimilation" or "second-generation decline"? (e.g. Alba and Nee 2003; Gans 1992; Kasinitz et al. 2008; Portes and Zhou 1993). Previous studies have provided insight into the socio-economic trajectories and cultural adaptations of the growing second generation population in adolescence and *early* adulthood (Haller, Portes, and Lynch 2011; Kasinitz et al. 2008; Portes and Rumbaut 2001; Rumbaut 2008). However, existing research is limited because studies have focused mainly on children of immigrants in their teens (in the 1990s) or mid-twenties (in the early 2000s), even as it is taking longer than in the past to complete higher education and other adult transitions (Settersten, Furstenberg, and Rumbaut 2005). Existing studies were also largely carried out prior to the punitive "age of deportation" that has come to mark the present period.

In this study, we draw from our latest follow-up to the Children of Immigrants Longitudinal Study (CILS) in San Diego, which provides a unique longitudinal view spanning nearly 25 years of the life course of our respondents (1991–2016), from their early teens to their late thirties. It enables us to more fully analyze processes of socioeconomic attainment and cultural incorporation among children of immigrants born in the late 1970s, who grew up during a notably inclusionary period for immigrants and refugees in San Diego and in the U.S. (which contrasts sharply with the context under which many children of immigrants throughout the country are coming of age today); in a state (California) that had invested in a well-planned system of accessible and affordable public colleges and universities; in an era of widening income inequalities in which the prospects of social mobility of immigrants' children have hinged on their levels of education more than ever before; and who navigated the Great Recession just as they were turning 30. As an indicator of socioeconomic attainment, we focus on educational attainment, arguably the most important indicator of long-term socioeconomic success (Tamborini, Kim, and Sakamoto 2015). While prior studies have examined educational attainment in early adulthood (e.g. Borgen and Rumbaut 2011; Rumbaut 2008), we note that over half of our respondents were still attending school in their mid-twenties, and 39 per cent attended postsecondary school into their thirties. As indicators of cultural incorporation, we examine the degree to which respondents identify as American and consider themselves part of the American mainstream. Finally, we consider whether and to what degree the current era of immigrant exclusion and expulsion has impacted them.

California and the new second generation

Waves of international migrants since the 1960s have transformed and will continue to transform the United States, and especially California. Indeed, recent estimates indicate that almost all of the growth of the U.S. working-age population between now and 2060 will consist of immigrants and their children (Vespa, Armstrong, and Medina 2018). In Southern California, the importance of children of immigrants for the overall workforce cannot be overstated. Even with recent immigration shifts to "new destinations", since the 1970s more immigrants have settled in Southern California than in any other metropolitan region of the world. Southern California is home to the largest concentrations of Mexicans, Salvadorans, Guatemalans, Filipinos,

Koreans, Japanese, Taiwanese, Vietnamese, Cambodians, and Iranians outside of their respective countries of origin, and to sizable contingents of many others (Rumbaut 2004, 2008). More than half of the nearly 40 million people living in California today are immigrants or their US-born children.

The demographic transformation of California has proceeded so rapidly that it is hard to recall that Southern California itself had only relatively recently become a "new destination". From 1920 to 1960, "Los Angeles was the whitest and most Protestant city in the United States" (Wiener 2008). By the end of the 1980s, however, fully *a third* of all the 19.8 million immigrants in the U.S. had settled in California – and immigrants from eight of the top 10 origin countries had established their primary settlements in California, a pattern that remains – with Los Angeles the principal destination. Indeed, by 2000 California (the largest of the 50 states by far) had already become a "majority-minority" state. From 1980 to 2017, California's Asian population grew from 5 per cent to 15 per cent, and the Latino population grew from 19 per cent to 39 per cent. Thus, our respondents came of age in a context that became increasingly diverse and multicultural throughout their lives.

The newcomer population is enormously diverse in terms of both national and social class origins. By far the most *and* the least educated groups in California and the United States today are immigrants, and the highest *and* the lowest poverty rates are similarly found among immigrants and refugees. Group characteristics interact with external contexts of reception to form the conditions within which immigrants' children adapt to American society (cf. Portes and Rumbaut 2001). But thus far studies have not been able to fully explore the adaptation of children of immigrants as it unfolds over the life course from adolescence to middle adulthood, even as the size of the adult second generation has grown, in sharply different and changing contexts of incorporation. This generational succession will continue to expand in the coming decade – during a quasi-revanchist period which has been marked by nativist backlash and growing xenophobia (cf. Kanstroom 2007). Since 2001, over 5 million people have been deported, leaving behind several million spouses and children, many of whom are U.S. citizens.

The context: a great inclusion?

The period spanning approximately the quarter century from 1965 to 1990 has been arguably the most inclusive era in American immigration history, certainly when focused on the governmental *context of reception* at the federal level. Immigrants and refugees during this "Great Inclusion" – which saw a sharp shift in their national origins to Asia and Latin America – benefited from the *1965 Immigration Act* (whose chief strength was its appeal to egalitarianism in the spirit of the Civil Rights movement, and its repeal of the blatantly racist immigration policy that had been in place for decades); the resettlement of hundreds of thousands of Cold War refugees from Cuba after the 1959 Revolution, and even more from Vietnam, Laos and Cambodia after the end of the Indochina War in 1975, for whom the U.S. assumed a historic responsibility; the passage of the *Refugee Act of 1980* (which finally conformed US law with the UN's definition of "refugee") – 1980 was the peak year of US refugee resettlement in US history, and more refugees were resettled in the US during the decade of the 1980s than in any other; the amnesty provisions of the *Immigration Reform and Control Act of 1986* (which legalized the status of 2.7 million undocumented immigrants); and the tripling of immigrant visas to the highly skilled by the *1990 Immigration Act*.

Two Supreme Court decisions during this period strongly affirmed an inclusionary context of reception: *Lau v. Nichols* (1974) and *Plyler v. Doe* (1982). In *Lau*, the Court unanimously ruled that the lack of supplemental language instruction in public school for students with limited English proficiency violated the 1964 Civil Rights Act; the school district was required to provide LEP students with "appropriate relief". The *Lau* ruling was followed by the passing of the Equal Educational Opportunities Act of 1974, which required school districts to take "appropriate action" to overcome barriers to equal participation of all students. In another landmark case in 1982, the Court ruled in *Plyler v. Doe* that public schools were prohibited by the Fourteenth Amendment from denying the children of undocumented Mexican immigrants access to a public education. *Plyler* specifically forbade public schools from adopting policies that would deny students the right to a public education based on their immigration status or that of their parents (Olivas 2012). It was during this era that our respondents' parents immigrated to the United States.

To be sure, the "Great Inclusion" was not uniformly so throughout our respondents' formative years, and "contexts of reception" are not one-size-fits-all; they vary by national origin and immigration status, by states and localities, by accessible opportunity structures and the "warmth of the welcome", by historical contexts. Many of these newcomers, for example, had no co-ethnic communities formed by previous migrations to the U.S. or California (such as the refugees from Vietnam, Cambodia and Laos), but received significant public assistance as refugees. The Mexican case has always been unique, and the experiences of this group are shaped by its long and deep history in the United States – from the annexation of nearly half the territory of Mexico (including California) in a war of aggression by the U.S. in the mid-nineteenth century to their racial segregation for a century afterwards, including forced mass "repatriations" (Balderrama and Rodríguez 2006). This history has shaped "generations of exclusion" among Mexican-Americans (Telles and Ortiz 2008) as well as the "Latino threat narrative", fuelling fears about Mexican immigrants, long a staple of U.S. public discourse (Chavez 2008). The threat narrative contributed to the landslide passage, in November 1994, of California's anti-Mexican-immigrant *Proposition 187*.[1] This was followed in 1998 by *Proposition 227,* a California initiative which eliminated bilingual education in the public schools, despite the Supreme Court's decision in *Lau v. Nichols.*

Yet Proposition 187 was never implemented (it was found unconstitutional, in part because it violated the Supreme Court's ruling in *Plyler*), Proposition 227 was later repealed, and Republicans became a minority party in California. In the 2016 presidential election, Hillary Clinton beat Donald Trump by more than 4 million votes in California alone. State legislation in the twenty-first century has helped create a far more inclusive climate in California – for all immigrants, undocumented or not – than in the rest of the country.

After 2000, California passed the most far-reaching laws in the country aimed to assist with immigrant integration, particularly those whose undocumented status blocks them from opportunity. This "California package" of state laws on immigrant integration "goes well beyond any benefits envisioned in federal proposals on immigration reform, and toward a new conception of *de facto* state citizenship that operates in parallel with formal citizenship at the national level" (Ramakrishnan and Colbern 2015).[2] Those changes occurred with relatively little political rancour – remarkable given the heated national debate about illegal immigration (Mason 2015). In a March 2018 PPIC survey, a solid majority of Californians (61 per cent) supported the state taking action to protect undocumented immigrants. While immigration continues to divide partisans, it unites most Californians across the state (Bonner 2018).

The setting: San Diego, California

Paradoxically, San Diego is California's oldest city, founded in 1769, yet it feels new, reflecting the fact that it started growing rapidly only after World War II (the site of the largest U.S. Navy and Marine Corps bases in the Pacific, many returning veterans settled there after the war), and notably after the 1960s with accelerating internal and international migration. It is California's second largest city, surpassing Detroit in 1982 to become the 6th largest city in the U.S., yet it was also known as "the largest small town in America" for its overwhelmingly White, Navy-town feel, conservative politics and relative lack of ethnic diversity. No longer.

San Diego County's population has grown steadily in recent decades, and numbers more than three million people. The foreign-born population in the region grew very rapidly during the 1980s, and increased by another 41 per cent in the 1990s. Situated on the Mexican border, the

San Diego-Tijuana corridor has been the largest international border crossing in the world, as well as a principal path for undocumented migration
from Mexico (until the militarization and fencing of the border after
1993). The location of the U.S. Navy base there long ago led to the formation of one of the three largest Filipino communities in the country
(the other two are also in California), given the exceptionally high rate of
Filipinos in the U.S. Navy (indeed, by the 1970s there were more Filipinos
in the U.S. Navy than in the Philippine Navy). The selection of Camp Pen-
dleton (Marine Corps) as one of four military camps for the resettlement of
Vietnamese refugees who fled after the fall of Saigon in 1975 helped make
San Diego a principal area of Vietnamese as well as Cambodian, Lao and
Hmong refugee resettlement, peaking during the 1980s. And the establishment of the University of California campus in San Diego in the mid-1960s
and the region's subsequent economic expansion also attracted many professional immigrants, especially from Asian countries, greatly diversifying
the area's ethnic composition (Rumbaut 2008).

For the children of immigrants and refugees, socioeconomic success
hinges on access to public colleges and universities – which are affordable
and available in San Diego, with many community colleges, the flagship
state university campus, and the UCSD campus. California's system of public
higher education is based on a three-tier "master plan" adopted by the legislature in 1960. Under the plan, the top eighth of the state's graduating high
school seniors would be able to enter one of the University of California
(UC) campuses, the top third would be able to enter one of the California
State University (CSU) campuses, and the community colleges would accept
all applicants – a crucial springboard for lower income students, many of
whom are children of immigrants. Today, more than 2.1 million students
are enrolled in the state's 115 community colleges; eligible students can transfer to the CSU or UC systems to complete bachelor's degrees. The 23 CSU campuses, which annually award about half of the state's bachelor's degrees and a
third of its master's degrees, enrol more than 480,000 students. And nearly
240,000 students are enrolled in the 10 UC campuses, which award most of
California's doctoral degrees.

In view of the striking population transformations described above, it is
accurate to say that California's future – and San Diego's – will be shaped
by how the second generation of adult children of immigrants is incorporated in its economy and society. Virtually every aspect of that
process will be affected by the extent of their attainment of post-
secondary education. Immigrants and their children will be key to the
growth of the U.S. labour force in the coming decades, with the fastest
growing occupations requiring college degrees; in California, there are
already not enough eligible college graduates to meet demand
(Johnson and Reed 2007; Pastor 2018).

The study: the children of immigrants longitudinal study (CILS) in San Diego

We analyze survey and qualitative data drawn from the Children of Immigrants Longitudinal Study (CILS) in San Diego, a unique panel study which has followed for almost 25 years a representative sample of young people from immigrant families, from the end of junior high school through their late thirties. The baseline sample consisted of children attending 8th or 9th grades in all San Diego public schools in 1991–92 who were either foreign-born (coming to the United States before age twelve), or of foreign parentage (born in the U.S. of immigrant parents) – i.e. either 1.5- or second generation.[3] The study used a school-based sampling frame[4] to accurately capture the population of immigrants' children in San Diego before they could legally drop out of school. Reflecting their proportions in the larger community, the largest ethnic groups were of Mexican, Filipino and Vietnamese origin, with smaller groups of Cambodians, Laotians, Hmong, Chinese (from the PRC, Hong Kong, Taiwan), Asian Indians, and other Latin American and Asian nationalities. Almost half were U.S. citizens by birth; most others had become naturalized citizens. Because the data are limited to a sample drawn in Southern California in fall 1991, the findings cannot be generalized beyond this. However, San Diego was and remains a principal site of contemporary immigrant and refugee settlement.

Data collection and sample

Respondents were surveyed four times (T1, T2, T3, and T4). The first survey was carried out in 1992 at the end of junior high (14.2 years old on average); the second in 1995 toward the end of senior high (17.2 years old); the third in 2001–03 (24.2 years old). That third phase of data collection obtained surveys from 1,480 respondents (in 2001–02) from whom a representative subsample of 134 was drawn with whom in-depth, open-ended qualitative interviews were conducted about a year later. More than twelve years later (2014–16), this subsample of 134 was systematically tracked, and a full fourth wave of surveys and in-depth qualitative interviews were conducted with 112 respondents, who averaged 37.2 years old. Logistic regressions comparing the 112 interviewed at T4 and the full T1 baseline sample showed no sample attrition bias on any key characteristic (age, gender, generation, GPA, family SES, etc.)[5]

The third and fourth data collection periods took longer due to the difficulties of tracking, locating and surveying this very mobile population, most of whom were no longer residing in their parents' homes. At T4, they were located not only in California (86 per cent) but all over the country, from Alaska to Texas, New York City, Chicago, Baltimore and Atlanta, as well as Mexico. Three were homeless; two were in group quarters (a state prison, a rehab centre).

The flexible interview format at T4 allowed us to delve deeply into the most important aspects of each person's experiences, while collecting standard survey data comparable to earlier survey responses. We combined data collected through closed-ended responses with existing CILS longitudinal data, analyzing it using descriptive statistics. We analyzed the interview data in Dedoose, a software programme for analyzing qualitative and mixed-methods data, using the constant-comparison method, in which we coded responses into conceptually similar categories, and compared within and across groups by key attributes to discern patterns (Boeije 2002).

Background characteristics of the sample

The sample's national origins reveal much about their parents' class origins and time of arrival. The two largest groups, Mexicans and Filipinos, came earlier than the others, most arriving in the 1970s. The refugees from Vietnam, Cambodia and Laos arrived predominantly in 1980 (the peak year of refugee resettlement in U.S. history) or in the early 1980s – with the Vietnamese also reflecting a sizeable first wave who arrived in 1975 after the fall of Saigon. The Chinese and Indians arrived mainly in the 1980s. The pre-1982 years of arrival for the overwhelming majority of the Mexican immigrants and the passage of IRCA in 1986 ensured the legalization of their status before the CILS sample was drawn. As a result, our sample has virtually no undocumented respondents or parents – a crucial characteristic.

Half of the respondents' mothers and 40 per cent of their fathers had less than a high school education; the least educated were the Hmong, Cambodian, Lao and Mexican parents. Only 14 per cent of the mothers and 23 per cent of the fathers had college degrees; the most educated came from India, the People's Republic of China, and the Philippines. In between were Vietnamese refugees and immigrants from Hong Kong and Taiwan. In San Diego, their children grew up in neighbourhoods that varied sharply by poverty rates, and closely tracked the parents' levels of education. A third lived in areas of concentrated poverty (census tracts where the 1990 poverty rates exceeded 50 per cent); only a third lived in tracts with poverty rates below 15 per cent. Over half were homeowners.

Over half of our respondents were foreign-born – i.e. members of the "1.5" generation (although the majority of them came as pre-school age children). The rest were born in the U.S. of two foreign-born parents (32 per cent) or of one foreign-born parent and one U.S.-born parent (13 per cent). Slightly more than half of the respondents are women (54 per cent), slightly less than half are men. When they were growing up in San Diego, 71 per cent lived in 2-natural-parent homes. Less than half of the Cambodians lived in 2-natural-parent families (a legacy of the "killing fields" of the late 1970s), as did 58 per cent of the Mexicans and 66 per cent of the Vietnamese, compared to over 90 per cent of the Indian, Chinese, Hmong and Filipinos and 83 per cent of the Lao.

Findings

The T4 CILS survey and in-depth interviews collected data on a wide range of outcomes, including language, religion, political views and behaviours, ethnic identities, transnational ties, family formation, arrests and incarceration, cultural practices, occupation and work histories, earnings and household income, student debt, and much more. We consider here only a few selected outcomes.

Bachelor's degree attainment

To show how the immigrants' children in middle adulthood have fared socio-economically, we focus on a key indicator: the attainment of a bachelor's degree. We focus on education, rather than occupational or other economic outcomes, because degree attainment maps so strongly onto other measures of SES. For example, 95 per cent of respondents who attained a bachelor's degree and *all* respondents who attained a graduate or professional degree were employed in middle-to-high status occupations[6] in middle adulthood, compared with only one-quarter of those with less than a bachelor's degree. Moreover, as we discuss below, the process of educational attainment can be followed through the life course and linked to the opportunity context in California.

Table 1 presents data on the percentage of respondents in our sample who earned a bachelor's degree or more, by national origin. We also include comparisons to a similar sample of adult children of immigrants (aged 30–39) from

Table 1. Percent with bachelor's degree or higher, by national origin.

	CILS-San Diego, T4 sample		Current Population Survey[a]	
	BA/BS or more	n	BA/BS or more	n
Overall	**52.7**	112		
Non-Hispanic White 3rd+ generation[b]	–	–	43.1	231
Mexican[b]	39.4	33	23.5	116
Filipino[c]	51.9	27	47.9	85
Vietnamese[c]	78.6	14	54.9	45
Cambodian-Lao-Hmong[c]	26.7	15	35.2	19
Chinese[c]	84.6	13	81.8	45
Indian[c]	100.0	4	95.3	16
Other 1.5/2nd/2.5[c]	33.3	6	48.5	530

[a]Percentages below are weighted population estimates based on a combined dataset from the years 2010–2015, for those ages 30–39; n is the sample size.
[b]CPS estimate is for San Diego County.
[c]CPS estimate is for the Southern California 6 county region.

the Current Population Survey, for San Diego County and the Southern California region, at about the same time period. These comparisons are important because Southern California, and San Diego in particular, has a more highly educated population than the United States overall, stemming from the availability of relatively affordable public higher education (historically), and an economy reliant on high-skilled workers. We also note that the educational attainment of Mexican-origin respondents, in particular, is notably greater in San Diego than in the greater Los Angeles region, suggesting that San Diego is a destination for more selective immigrants than enclaves such as East Los Angeles and Santa Ana. A similar positive selectivity appears to be the case for Vietnamese in San Diego, compared to enclaves like Westminster and Garden Grove in Orange County.

Table 1 shows that our respondents fare favourably in terms of educational attainment, relative to the similar non-Hispanic White population in San Diego. Overall, 53 per cent of our sample had completed at least a bachelor's degree by their late 30s (this includes 20 per cent who had completed an advanced degree). By comparison, only 43 per cent of similarly-aged non-Hispanic Whites in San Diego completed a bachelor's degree.

However, educational attainment varies widely by national origin. Although sample sizes in both the CILS and, for many groups, the CPS, are small, patterns of group difference are clear. Adult children of immigrants from China, India, and Vietnam earn bachelor's degrees at extraordinary rates, and Filipinos and others also surpass the national average. None of the Cambodians had earned a bachelor's degree by their late 30s, nor had two-thirds of the Lao – not surprising given their low socioeconomic origins – although the Hmong did much better than expected. Given their similarly low SES origins, however, the attainment of a bachelor's degree or more by Mexican-origin respondents (39 per cent) is notable as this percentage is only slightly lower than that among native-parentage Whites of comparable age in San Diego (43 per cent) or nationally (40 per cent).

For most CILS respondents, but especially for those who attained bachelor's degrees or higher, public higher education was key. In fact, 72 per cent of those who attained a bachelor's degree or higher earned their highest degree (whether a bachelor's, master's, or professional degree) at a California public university. Delving further into the often complex educational paths taken towards higher degrees, we found that a remarkable 95 per cent of those who attained a bachelor's degree or higher attended at least one public institution of higher education (including California community colleges) along their journey to their eventual highest degree. For example, Leo,[7] who migrated at age 3 from Mexico, and now works as a systems engineer, earned a master's degree from a California State University at the age of 30. His journey through higher education began at a community college, which he perceived as more accessible for him than today:

> I got awarded [a grant]—this was back when money was a little bit more available—and … I mean, it was just like, wait a minute, I get to go to school … it gets paid for, and plus they give me a little stipend for books … And then, the first two or three years got me through … the grants, the job on campus … I just thought, okay I can do this. And that's when counselors and mentors at my JC started saying, hey, you gotta really think about what you're gonna do … and I ended up transferring to [CSU] …

Leo later reflects on whether economic opportunities have improved since the recession:

> I think it's gotten worse … Cause like I said, the key is education. To me. And … education has been just gutted. In the sense of like grants and subsidies … like when I was going … I ended up paying like $900, $1000 … for like a quarter. And now … I hear stories where it's like a couple thousand.

Like nearly all of our upwardly mobile respondents, Leo's experience and perspective illustrates how the educational attainment of the CILS respondents was inextricably linked to the accessible California public higher education system during the time they were attaining their degrees. This finding points to positive outcomes along a main dimension of socioeconomic achievement. We further discuss its implications below. But we turn next to cultural indicators of integration.

Identifying as American

We have focused elsewhere on our findings showing a range of ethnic self-identifications among immigrants' children in middle adulthood, varying between and within national-origin groups (Feliciano and Rumbaut 2018, 2019). While the majority of immigrants' adult children express ethnic self-identities reflecting attachments to their home countries/origin culture (69 per cent), a significant minority (30 per cent) indicate no real connection to their ethnic background – with some indicating they were really "just" American and others indifferent towards ethnic or national identity labels altogether. Notably, we see a similar breakdown in the percentages who maintain linguistic connections: 71 per cent considered themselves bilingual, while another 29 per cent reported speaking only English.

Among the largest group of respondents (37 per cent) who expressed a strong ethnic identity as central to their sense of self, most *also* identified as American. For example, thirty-six-year-old Isabella emphasized her American identity along with her Mexican identity:

> [My identity as Mexican American] is very important because my family is from Mexico and . . . they came here to be better, you know, for that American Dream … I'm proud … to say that I'm Mexican, but I was born here, so I am American.

Similarly, 1.5- generation Anh recognized her dual identities: "[Identifying as Vietnamese] is very important because it's a huge part of me … [being

Vietnamese American] is really important too … I do all the stereotypical American things". Respondents who were actively trying to maintain aspects of their national-origin culture also saw no contradiction in ethnic maintenance and Americanism. For example, Houa, a 1.5 generation Hmong-American woman explains:

> I want [my children] to have a conscious of, okay, my parents are these type of people. They come from here … so I mix the culture, a little bit here, a little bit there … But then now we are … American … we're trying to fit in like everyone else. Trying to make a living, like everyone else. We're also American.

Similarly, 1.5 generation Noi explains that she began to feel more American after the 9/11 attacks. "But I don't feel like I'm less … Lao. But I feel like I'm more American … I mean, I'm really happy that I'm an American. A Lao-American".

As is clear in the excerpts above, respondents often brought up their Americanness organically. These findings indicate that ethnic and American identities are not zero-sum. Respondents who maintained identities rooted in their home countries also identified as American and saw no contradictions in maintaining both identities.

Part of mainstream America

Respondents were asked explicitly whether they considered themselves part of mainstream America, and most responded affirmatively (69 per cent). Feeling part of the American mainstream did not vary substantially by education, family socioeconomic background, or immigrant generation. However, the few non-citizens ($n = 8$) felt more outside of the American mainstream than their U.S. citizen peers. Also notable is that almost all of the respondents who had married White Americans considered themselves fully part of mainstream America.

As suggested above, we found no relationship between feeling part of the American mainstream and having a strong ethnic identity rooted in the home country. For example, Nancy, a pre-school teacher, maintains a strong identity as Mexican-American, has married a Mexican-American man, and maintains several Mexican cultural practices, including bilingualism (although she speaks English with her children), but also sees herself in the American mainstream:

> We celebrate a lot [on] Fourth of July, Labor Day, we usually … put up a flag, and it means a lot to us. Especially now that my brother's in the military … that makes us really proud that he's serving his country …

Others defined the American mainstream as American cultural practices: because they did what most Americans do, they felt part of the mainstream. For example, Emma who is married to a White American man and has an infant daughter, uses her Chinese immigrant mother's cultural practices as a counterpoint to explain why she is a mainstream American:

> ... we cook American or Mexican ... But my mom at home ... she only cooks Asian. She ... doesn't like burgers or fries or any of that stuff so. And she shops at the Asian markets and I shop at Von's ...

A small minority ($n = 10$) indicated that they were decidedly not part of the mainstream, though not because of their ethnic or national origins. Some deemed themselves outsiders because of unique situations, such as homelessness ($n = 2$) or incarceration ($n = 1$), or simply because they did not keep up with the latest American trends.

Respondents who provided a qualified response – they felt partly in and out of the mainstream, in some ways but not others (22 per cent) – often noted that mainstream America varied by context. Vietnamese-born Kim Cuc, for example, states astutely that in San Diego she is part of the American mainstream, but not everywhere:

> I've been to states like Texas and Florida where they see you as like an alien ... as though they've never seen an Asian person in their life. Where here ... you see people from all walks of life ... [In] big urban areas, I feel more mainstream but in isolated areas I don't.

Similarly, second-generation Gloria notes, "I think in certain parts I wouldn't be part of the mainstream. Just because there's not a lot of ... Mexican population there. So you kinda feel out of place ... "

Gloria's perspective was more common among Mexican-origin respondents than those from some other backgrounds. Moreover, among the Mexican-origin respondents, most who did not feel fully part of the mainstream referenced culture or race/ethnicity as factors, which was less common for those from other national-origin groups. Mexican-born Claudia, for example, asserts, "I just think we should be part of mainstream Amer ... we are part of the mainstream America, but we're underrepresented".

Yet it was not only Mexican respondents who suggested that minorities were not currently accepted as mainstream Americans. Rina, who was born in Panama and identified as Afro-Latina, put it this way: "I definitely don't consider myself part of the American mainstream ... when I think mainstream, I still think ... White Anglo Saxon Protestant ... and everything outside of that ... is not". This view, while not the most common, suggests a feeling of not being fully accepted as American, akin to that expressed by racial minorities in other studies (Waters 2001).

Deportation knowledge and experiences

We asked respondents in middle adulthood whether they had any knowledge of anyone who had been deported or nearly deported. Overall, more than half of the sample (54 per cent) knew of no one who had such experiences. But 20 per cent *did* know of a close family member or friend who was deported, and another 26 per cent of a more distant relative or acquaintance. In one rare instance, a deportation resulted in a violent outcome, as one respondent's sister was murdered in Mexico after she was deported. Not surprisingly given recent deportation patterns, over one-third of Mexican-origin respondents had *close* relatives or friends who had been deported – as did half of the Cambodians and a third of the Lao. By contrast, *none* of the Vietnamese, Chinese or Indians reported that they knew of any close family member of friend who had been deported, and substantial majorities of these groups, as well as Indians and Filipinos, knew no one, even distantly, affected by deportation.

The qualitative data reveal a principal pattern of disengagement with the issue of deportation, even among those who had distant knowledge of deportation cases, as illustrated by Vanna, who was born in the U.S. of Cambodian parents:

> I've heard friends that have family members that are afraid of [deportation]. But I've never really personally known anyone … it's not something that really crossed my mind to really get involved with knowing about.

In another example, the way second-generation Mexican-origin Ana recounts one deportation case suggests a lack of concern with the issue, "The only person I can think of is one of my best friend's former coworkers. That's about it … I know he was caught driving under the influence … and so he got deported (laughs)".

However, a few who were aware of distant stories felt strong sympathy for deported immigrants and their families. For example, Mexican-American Nancy, mentioned above, explains:

> I'm putting myself in the shoes of the mother, the children, [often] it's the husband that is deported. And this affects the whole family … especially the children. They miss their father. The whole family's torn apart … He's probably the main breadwinner. And now the mom has to go out and … look for employment. However, she has no experience … it's really sad.

Cambodian-born Sena had several close friends and family members who were deported. Her reactions to each situation varied based on whether she thought their infractions warranted such a penalty. Regarding the deportation of a few friends prior to 9/11, she states, "I don't like it, but, what they did was uncalled for and unacceptable". However, she perceived more recent deportations as unfair:

> Everything just changed [after 9/11] … It was heartbreaking … to know that your friends and relatives are back over there for something they didn't do majorly … They didn't kill nobody … It was over little minor stuff …

These deportations, which included her son's father and a cousin, led to fears that this could happen to her:

> you don't know what else gonna happen … They'll probably like, uncitizenize me and send me back … if I do something stupid, you know? … now they're saying that they can change your status from citizen to non-citizen and send you back to where you come from. I'm like, 'that's not right.' You can't do that … Why?

Sena's case illustrates that even among adult children of immigrants who came of age in more inclusive contexts, the current era of deportation – which began well before Trump's election – can deeply influence their sense of security, depending upon their social location. However, most adult children of immigrants in our sample (none of whom are undocumented) are detached from the most affected communities, contributing to their own feeling of inclusion.

Discussion and conclusion

The latest outcomes of the adult children of immigrants in our study, born in the late 1970s and coming of age in San Diego in the 1990s, must be considered within a particular historical, social, political, economic, demographic and geographic context – a context that was far more inclusive than that in which many children of immigrants throughout the country today are coming of age. The socioeconomic and cultural integration of this segment of the new second generation, who were part of arguably the most inclusive immigration era in U.S. history, in a state in which more than half of the state's population consists of immigrants and their children, has been largely positive.

In terms of educational attainment, the higher than average educational attainments among these adult children of immigrants are particularly remarkable given the modest class backgrounds and harsh migration histories of many of their immigrant and refugee parents. This positive outcome was shaped by the accessibility of affordable public higher education in San Diego and in California, and is illuminated by recent national studies. The Commission on the Future of Undergraduate Education (2016) completed a comprehensive portrait of U.S. postsecondary education, including public and private universities. Educational attainment is increasing over time across all income quartiles, but the gap in educational economic inequality is widening. In the 1979–1982 birth cohort (born at about the same time as the CILS respondents), only 9 per cent of students from families in the lowest income quartile had completed college, in contrast to 54 per cent of those in the upper income quartile. The 54 per cent achieved by the children of the more affluent families is almost identical to the 53 per cent achieved by the T4 CILS sample during 2014–2015, despite the much lower socioeconomic background of the CILS parents.

If higher education is the central pathway to intergenerational mobility, do different colleges shape upward mobility outcomes differently? Using data from 1999 to 2013, Chetty et al. (2017) show that the colleges promoting the most intergenerational income mobility – measured by both access and success outcomes – were mid-tier *public* institutions, including UC/CSU California colleges and universities, precisely the institutions attended by our most educated respondents.

The logical policy conclusion from such robust data is to invest in public higher education, not to disinvest. Yet state funding in public higher education since the financial crisis (from 2008 to 2016) has gone in the opposite direction: a national reduction in funding of −18 per cent. Of the largest 15 states, California shows the *lowest* negative change in per-student funding of higher education (−3 per cent) – well below the national average. But other large states have *disinvested* massively in public higher education, deeply cutting per-student funding by half or more. Our CILS findings in California point to the crucial role of public colleges and universities in providing a structure of educational opportunities for an economy that increasingly demands more college-educated workers.

In terms of cultural measures of integration, a key outcome that has been the subject of contentious debate is whether immigrants' children consider themselves American. Our findings show that respondents with the strongest ethnic attachments also identify as American. Moreover, a large majority consider themselves fully part of the American mainstream. Some respondents were keenly aware of the role of context in shaping their perceptions, indicating that they would not be accepted as fully American outside of the super-diverse multicultural California context in which most still live. But the main pattern that emerges, as it did with language (over two-thirds are bilingual), is that at least for this California sample, identity and belonging are not either/or zero-sum games, but additive rather than subtractive adaptations.

Even within the largely inclusive context of Southern California, contexts of reception vary by national-origin. While a minority even among the Mexican-origin respondents, more of the Mexican respondents than other groups felt that they could not fully be accepted as part of the American mainstream – reflecting historical legacies of racial exclusion (Telles and Ortiz 2008) as well as the persistence of a "Latino threat narrative" (Chavez 2008) that, while noticeably louder today under the Trump administration than it was during the formative years of our respondents, has long pervaded U.S. society. Further, while most adult children of immigrants across national-origin groups, including Mexicans, have largely been insulated from the threats of the current deportation regime, Mexicans (as well as Cambodians) more often had significant others or friends who were deported. These experiences shaped them in different ways. Some who saw loved ones or friends deported for minor infractions felt vulnerable themselves, even as U.S.

citizens, while others who deemed deportation as a suitable punishment for a serious criminal offense were unaffected. Existing studies suggest that the rising number of deportations, especially for non-violent offenses, lead to fear and insecurity among a broader swath of children of immigrants coming of age today (Dreby 2015).

Overall, while our California-based study of a sample of children of immigrants and refugees drawn over a quarter century ago suggests that the story of the new second generation is largely one of successful integration across a number of dimensions, a key question moving forward is whether similar outcomes are likely to be repeated in the future, in different contexts of inclusion and opportunity. We argue that an inclusive multiethnic context with a strong and accessible public higher education system was key to shaping the positive integration of the CILS respondents. However, with a current national context characterized by a Great Expulsion of immigrants and a Great Exclusion of refugees and asylees, and a continuing retreat from investments in public education by most states, the future for the next generation of children of immigrants is far from certain.

Notes

1. Proposition 187 would have denied health care, public education, and social services to undocumented immigrants and their children in California and required government employees to report suspected undocumented immigrants to authorities.
2. The "California Package" is the term used by Ramakrishnan and Colbern (2015) for an array of policies giving undocumented immigrants access to in-state tuition and child health benefits, professional and driver's licenses, and low-cost auto insurance. Most recently California declared itself a "sanctuary state."
3. The larger CILS study included a South Florida sample (followed through T3) not used here.
4. See Portes and Rumbaut (2001, 2005) for further information about the original CILS sample.
5. The sole exception was national origin, which was by design. The T3 in-depth interviews intentionally included a larger Chinese sample to facilitate ethnic comparisons.
6. Middle to high status occupations are those that rank above the median according to the Duncan Socioeconomic Index (SEI).
7. All names are pseudonyms.

Acknowledgments

The authors thank Dr. Linda Borgen and Alma Nidia Garza for research assistance, the Russell Sage Foundation and Spencer Foundation for research funding, and the anonymous reviewers and editors for their helpful feedback.

Disclosure statement

No potential conflict of interest was reported by the authors.

Funding

This work was supported by grants from the Russell Sage Foundation and the Spencer Foundation.

References

Alba, Richard, and Victor Nee. 2003. *Remaking the American Mainstream: Assimilation and Contemporary Immigration*. Cambridge, MA: Harvard University Press.

Balderrama, Francisco E., and Raymond Rodríguez. 2006. *Decade of Betrayal: Mexican Repatriation in the 1930s*. Albuquerque: University of New Mexico Press.

Boeije, Hennie. 2002. "A Purposeful Approach to the Constant Comparative Method in the Analysis of Qualitative Interviews." *Quality and Quantity* 36 (4): 391–409.

Bonner, Dean. 2018. "Do Californians Support State Action on Immigration?" *Public Policy Institute of California*, May 14.

Borgen, Linda and Rubén G. Rumbaut. 2011. "Coming of Age in 'America's Finest City': Transitions to Adulthood among Children of Immigrants in San Diego." In *Coming of Age in America: The Transition to Adulthood in the Twenty-first Century*, edited by M. C. Waters, Patrick J. Carr, Maria J. Kefalas, and Jennifer Holdaway, 133–168. Berkeley: University of California Press.

Chavez, Leo. 2008. *The Latino Threat: Constructing Immigrants, Citizens, and the Nation*. Stanford: Stanford University Press.

Chetty, Raj, John N. Friedman, Emmanuel Saez, Nicholas Turner, and Danny Yagan. 2017. "Mobility Report Cards: The Role of Colleges in Intergenerational Mobility." NBER Working Paper No. 23618.

Commission on the Future of Undergraduate Education. 2016. *A Primer on the College Student Journey*. Cambridge, MA: American Academy of Arts and Sciences.

Dreby, Joanna. 2015. *Everyday Illegal: When Policies Undermine Immigrant Families*. Berkeley: University of California Press.

Feliciano, Cynthia, and Rubén G. Rumbaut. 2018. "Varieties of Ethnic Self-Identities: Children of Immigrants in Middle Adulthood." *RSF: The Russell Sage Foundation Journal of the Social Sciences* 4 (5): 26–46.

Feliciano, Cynthia, and Rubén G. Rumbaut. 2019. "The Evolution of Ethnic Identity from Adolescence to Middle Adulthood: The Case of the Immigrant Second Generation." *Emerging Adulthood* 7 (2): 85–96.

Gans, Herbert J. 1992. "Second Generation Decline: Scenarios for the Economic and Ethnic Futures of the Post-1965 American Immigrants." *Ethnic and Racial Studies* 15 (2): 251–270.

Haller, William, Alejandro Portes, and Scott M. Lynch. 2011. "Dreams Fulfilled, Dreams Shattered: Determinants of Segmented Assimilation in the Second Generation." *Social Forces* 89 (3): 733–762.

Johnson, Hans P. and Deborah Reed. 2007. "Can California Import Enough College Graduates to Meet Workforce Needs?" *California Counts: Population Trends and Profiles* 8 (4). https://www.researchgate.net/publication/234573098_Can_California_Import_Enough_College_Graduates_to_Meet_Workforce_Needs_California_Counts_Volume_8_Number_4

Kanstroom, Daniel. 2007. *Deportation Nation: Outsiders in American History*. Cambridge: Harvard University Press.

Kasinitz, Philip, John H. Mollenkopf, Mary C. Waters, and Jennifer Holdaway. 2008. *Inheriting the City: The Children of Immigrants Come of Age*. New York, Cambridge: Russell Sage Foundation, Harvard University Press.

Mason, Melanie. 2015. "California Gives Immigrants Here Illegally Unprecedented Rights, Benefits, Protections." *Los Angeles Times*, August 11.

Olivas, Michael A. 2012. *No Undocumented Child Left Behind: Plyler v. Doe and the Education of Undocumented Schoolchildren*. New York: New York University Press.

Pastor, Manuel. 2018. *State of Resistance: What California's Dizzying Descent and Remarkable Resurgence Mean for America's Future*. New York: The New Press.

Portes, Alejandro, and Rubén G. Rumbaut. 2001. *Legacies: The Story of the Immigrant Second Generation*. Berkeley and New York: University of California Press and Russell Sage Foundation.

Portes, Alejandro, and Rubén G. Rumbaut. 2005. "Introduction: The Second Generation and the Children of Immigrants Longitudinal Study." *Ethnic and Racial Studies* 28 (6): 983–999.

Portes, Alejandro, and Min Zhou. 1993. "The New Second Generation: Segmented Assimilation and Its Variants." *The Annals of the American Academy of Political and Social Science* 530: 74–96.

Ramakrishnan, Karthick S., and Allan Colbern. 2015. "The California Package: Immigrant Integration and the Evolving Nature of State Citizenship." *Policy Matters* 6: 3.

Rumbaut, Rubén G. 2004. "Ages, Life Stages, and Generational Cohorts: Decomposing the Immigrant First and Second Generations in the United States." *International Migration Review* 38 (3): 1160–1205.

Rumbaut, Rubén G. 2008. "The Coming of the Second Generation: Immigration and Ethnic Mobility in Southern California." *The Annals of the American Academy of Political and Social Science* 620 (1): 196–236.

Settersten, Richard A., Frank F. Furstenberg, and Rubén G Rumbaut. 2005. *On the Frontier of Adulthood: Theory, Research, and Public Policy*. Chicago: University of Chicago Press.

Tamborini, Christopher R., Chang Hwan Kim, and Arthur Sakamoto. 2015. "Education and Lifetime Earnings in the United States." *Demography* 52: 1383–1407.

Telles, Edward E., and Vilma Ortiz. 2008. *Generations of Exclusion: Mexican Americans, Assimilation, and Race*. New York: Russell Sage Foundation.

Vespa, Jonathan, David M. Armstrong, and Lauren Medina. 2018. "Demographic Turning Points for the United States: Population Projections for 2020 to 2060." Current Population Reports, P25-1144.

Waters, Mary C. 2001. *Black Identities: West Indian Immigrant Dreams and American Realities*. Cambridge, MA: Harvard University Press.

Wiener, Jon. 2008. "City of Fear." *The Nation*, June 11.

The changing U.S. Latinx immigrant population: demographic trends with implications for employment, schooling, and population Integration

Richard Durán

ABSTRACT

This paper provides descriptive information regarding the composition of the Latinx population of the United States. I note differences in educational attainment and occupational mobility confirming findings by other authors– Latinix individuals continue to experience a stalled mode of incorporation in America. The paper also discusses policy implications, giving special attention to the changing character of the American economy. For Latinix people to advance socially and financially, they will need greater access to specialized technical skills. Without deliberate action on the part of government, the prospects seem dismal. Limited progress in educational institutions and the labour market threatens the future of children and grandchildren of Latinx immigrants.

Introduction

Cycles and patterns of Latinx origin immigration to the U.S. and migration within the U.S. have had a profound effect on the demographics of the country and its economic prosperity and social stability (Leal and Trejo 2011; Taylor 2015). As we near one-quarter of a new century in a world fraught with ethnic/racial and economic discord, the United States is facing yet another watershed moment in its history – one in which the settlement and well-being of immigrant generation Latinx inhabitants, and most principally their children, will play a more central role in the social and political cohesion of the country and its future economic prosperity (Murdock et al. 2015). This paper examines associations between Latinx population size over time, its educational attainment, readiness to meet national workforce needs, and the unequal distribution of wealth between Latinx individuals and the White non-Latinx population at large. The chapter concludes with a discussion of the efforts by progressive groups in the U.S. to implement a renewed social contract between American institutions and immigrant background communities with implications for the children of Latinx immigrants far into the future.

General Latinx population trends

The vast majority of Latinx immigrant background persons in the U.S. arrived in the post-World War II period. Demographers (e.g. Taylor 2015; Dimock 2019), and civil rights advocates alike (e.g. Dimock 2019), have found it useful to characterize the generations involved as "Boomers" – born 1946–1964, "Generation X" – born 1965-80, "Millennials" – born 1981–2018; and now, "Generation Z"– born after 2018. Census data reveal a differential acceleration in population growth of Latinx persons over the white non-Latinx portion of the population over these generations. This growth is most dramatic for Millennials, and is projected to continue for Generation Z.

Population projection data from the U.S. Census Bureau (March 2018) shows that 66 per cent of the growth in the U.S. population from 2016 to 2060 will be due to increases in Latinx persons representing the Millennial generation, and Generation Z and their children. This dramatic population growth contrasts sharply with an estimated 17 per cent drop in the non-Latinx white population over the same generational span. While these data are projections and subject to many sources of estimation error, the trend is clear and deserves further attention given its economic, educational, and sociopolitical implications. Latinx people will play a crucial role in the political and social evolution of the United States.

Population projection estimates produced in 2018 by the US Census Bureau (op. cit.) indicate that the U.S. will no longer have a majority non-Hispanic white population by the year 2045 (Frey 2018a). Indeed, this threshold was reached in 2018 by the states of Hawaii, California, New Mexico, and Texas, and the District of Columbia (Nittle 2018). In 2045, based on the sources cited above, it is estimated that non-Hispanic whites will constitute a minority 49.7 per cent of the total U.S. population, compared to 24.6 per cent Hispanics, 13.1 per cent blacks, 7.9 per cent Asians and 3.8 per cent multiracial populations.

The growth of the Latinx and non-white portions of the U.S. population will continue, and will exceed that of white non-Latinos well past mid-century. As shown by census figures (U.S. Census Bureau, op. cit.), current projections are that in 2060 non-Hispanic whites will constitute 44.3 per cent of the U.S. population, Hispanics 27.5 per cent, Blacks, 13.5 per cent, and Asians 8.8 per cent, with under 10 per cent constituting multiracial or other category ethnic/racial populations (Frey, op. cit.).

The dynamics of the U.S. demographic shift heading into the second half of the present century are very much driven by a small set of critical interacting factors that affect not only the well-being of Latinx persons, but ultimately, the well-being of the country as a whole. First, the continued immigration of persons from Latin America will contribute to the rise of the Latinx population in the foreseeable future. It is true that the immigration rates of individuals from countries such as Mexico are declining in the aftermath of the great recession of 2007 and the antagonistic impact of restrictive federal immigration policies under the Trump administration. Nevertheless, the reducing numbers of immigrants from Mexico is paralleling rapid increases in immigration from Central American countries (Pew Research Center 2015).

A second factor contributing to the dynamics of the U.S. population shift is that Latinx population growth is fueled by the higher fertility rate of the Latinx portion of the population compared to the rest of U.S. residents (Taylor 2015). Although there is evidence that Latinx immigrants are showing lower fertility rates than in the past, their sheer numbers, coupled with the fact that second and third generation Latinx immigrant persons are already present in large numbers, and are younger than whites, may lead to a higher fertility impact, marked by a continuing growth in the percentage of Latinx persons in the U.S. population into 2060 (Frey 2018a).

A third factor underlying the dynamics of U.S. population shift is the rapid aging of the U.S. white non-Latinx population compared to Latinx persons and other racial/ethnic subgroups. Not surprisingly, as shown by data from the National Center for Health Statistics of the Centers for Disease Control (2018), this differential aging is also coupled with a higher mortality rate overall for the White non-Latinx population compared to the Latinx portion of the population (Sáenz and Johnson 2016). When the lower fertility rate of White non-Latinx persons is considered, the upshot is that white non-Latinx persons are a declining proportion of the total U.S. populations into the middle of this century, while Latinx persons are a growing proportion (Sáenz & Johnson, op. cit.; U.S. Census Bureau, March 2018).

Overviewing this shift, and considering the continuing growth of other "minority" communities of colour in the U.S. into mid-century, Frey (2018b) points to major social policy issues. Regarding the implications of this trend, he states:

> Minorities will be the source of all of the growth in the nation's youth and working age population, most of the growth in its voters, and much of the growth in its consumers and tax base as far into the future as we can see. Hence, the more rapidly growing, largely white senior population will be increasingly dependent on their contributions to the economy and to government programs such as Medicare and Social Security. This suggests the necessity for continued investments in the nation's diverse youth and young adults as the population ages (Frey 2018b).

Put simply, U.S. non-Hispanic whites are aging more rapidly and dramatically than other demographic groups in the country, and are becoming a smaller portion of the U.S. population that can contribute to the economy via the workforce.

General Trends in Employment Workforce and Education Needs with Implications for Latinx Immigrants

As pointed out by Frey (op. cit.) and others, the impact of the population trends cited on the composition of the US labour force will be dramatic, and noticeable in terms of Latinx peoples' contribution to the workforce age population well into the future. There is, however, one caveat: traditionally, the workforce age population has been thought of as constituting adults in the 18–65 year range. The age range of working age persons appears to be changing, with some evidence emerging that more adults aged over 65 continue to work, given cost of living issues and better access to medical care.

Carnevale and Smith (2013) discuss labour force composition for the age range 18–65 by ethnic racial groups based on Bureau of Labor Statistics projections from 2010 to 2050. The projections indicate that the share of White, non-Latinx persons in the workforce (aged 18-65) will decline from 66 per cent to 45 per cent between 2010 and 2050. By contrast, while the Latinx persons were 15 per cent of the workforce in 2010, they are projected to become 30 per cent of the workforce in 2050. Clearly, this doubling in the Latinx workforce eligibility will have implications for the U.S. economy and whether it can expect to have a sufficient number of workers who have attained skills through higher education and can contribute to the knowledge economy; in particular, to STEM-related occupations and fields. The changing demands of the knowledge economy on workforce skill sets are already evident and have both short term and long term implications. Importantly, regardless of time span, the new skill set demands of the knowledge economy are expanding down into occupational fields formerly conceived of as physical labour and low-level blue collar and service-counter work. New qualifications demand "technical skills", high-level communication abilities, and meaningful cross-cultural and multilingual capabilities. The situation is exacerbated because STEM-related jobs (e.g. health care worker operation of diagnostic medical equipment), even those formerly requiring moderate training now involve advanced college degrees. Increasingly specialized knowledge is becoming part and parcel of the new economy, even in sectors such as plumbing, electrical repairs, and carpentry.

Another important trend to note is that the economic recovery that followed the 2007 Great Recession transformed of the U.S. economy (Carnevale et al. 2018). Among the patterns that have emerged by 2018, and coinciding with the implementation of fiscal policies of the Trump administration, there is a strong and increased need for workers in the lowest rungs of the economy associated with temporary low-skilled labour. In other words, the demand for specialized knowledge coexists with a continuing need for unskilled and semi-skilled workers, many of whom are foreign-born. Such patterns are complex and vary from place to place; they deserve more careful analysis. The evolving demand for low-skilled workers does not mean that Latinx immigrants will uniformly benefit from what may be temporary increased employment rates shown by 2018 census figures corresponding to the lower rungs of the economy.

Regarding the recent past and the changing skill sets required by the economy, a Brookings Institution study (Muro et al., 2017) analyzed worker skill trends over the period 2002–2016, a period that witnessed the Great Recession. The investigators constructed a numerical index measure of the degree to which workers' occupations, as defined by the U.S. Bureau of Labor Statistics, required low, medium, or high advanced use and reliance on digital technologies. The results showed a major increase in the digital content of all jobs during that time span, regardless of the level of schooling required by jobs. Interestingly, but not surprisingly, by 2016, jobs requiring a secondary or below level of schooling education showed a prominent increased reliance and concentration on lower and medium level digital skills, while jobs requiring some college, a bachelor's degree, or an advanced degree – jobs which paid more and with greater job security and opportunity of advancements– showed greater concentration of required high or medium digital literacy skills.

The social mobility implications of these job skill trends tied to educational attainment across Latinx immigrant generations are clear and a reason for concern, given that so many first generation immigrants have low levels of formal education–and that Latinx second-generation immigrants forming the current Millennial generation are less likely to receive a higher education degree, compared to non-Latinx white persons. As Muro et al. (op. cit.) state:

> The spread of digital tools is underscoring the importance of digital competencies in helping less-educated workers secure basic opportunity even as it throws into relief sharp disparities among particular groups' digital preparedness. ... Moreover, the spread of digital technology into most industries is altering the circumstances within which less educated or otherwise marginalized workers strive to access solid livelihoods. ... [I]t is worth looking at changes like what have been called "good jobs" or "middle skill" jobs – jobs that have the potential to help workers without a four-year college degree earn enough to support themselves and begin to move toward the middle class. Such jobs – here defined as full-time jobs that do not require a bachelor's degree, yet pay higher than the national average wage – represent a critical first link to opportunity for tens of millions of the nation's working-age adults and struggling families. Because they are at once obtainable and stable, these positions in some 89 accessible full-time occupations provide a critical initial link to economic advancement for the two-thirds of Americans who lack a college degree.

Thus, automation and the needs of the knowledge economy are steadily accelerating the demands for workers who have attained digital information processing skills at all levels of education – despite disparities in the economic returns for lower level technical skills discussed below. With regard to knowledge economy needs in both the short and long term, Herold (2017), examining trends in workforce skill needs, notes that by the time today's Millennial 6th graders hit their prime working years in 2030s, automation and artificial intelligence may have eliminated one-half of all present jobs in the economy based on the skills sets required by current jobs, and the existing skill levels of workers now holding those jobs. Jobs of the future will become automated. More concretely, as signaled by the Muro et al. report (op. cit.) what is emerging is that jobs at all levels will require workers to develop increased proficiencies in information processing and communications literacies that rely on acquired expertise and training in using computer, microprocessor, and internet tools.

Nevertheless, these increased skill sets and proficiencies labelled as "applied tech skills" by the Career Advisory Board (Unger 2017) are not all equally appraised. They turn out to be more valued, and better compensated by firms and institutions when they involve generalizable skills across different work assignments, and not just isolated skills tied to workers operating automated machinery and performing specific information processing tasks. In a small scale survey of business leaders and hiring managers (N = 500), the Career Advisory Board (op. cit.) found that companies and firms are experiencing a shortage of needed employees with integrated technical skills that are of value to " … the benefit of an organization, not necessarily the ability to deploy specific technologies themselves. Employers are seeking individuals with these abilities more and more, but not enough are graduating with the proper skill set".

Furthermore, the Career Advisory Board (op. cit.) reports that, as a consequence, a job skills stratification system is emerging: employers are not necessarily raising the wages of workers with less than a college education who are becoming more digitally enabled. The Career Advisory Board goes on to identify what they term as "Skilled Non-College Occupations" (SNCOs) that in contrast are emerging as a much smaller, critical subset of jobs not requiring a four-year college education for job entry, but that do offer enhanced salary compensation to individuals with strong talents in computer information processing skills. Not surprisingly, businesses and institutions appear to be reluctant to compensate these workers more than is necessary – including some who are over-qualified educationally, but who are willing to take on jobs to survive. (Think of first-generation Latinx immigrants who have some degree of higher education in their natal countries but who mostly accept lower salaried blue collar or labourer jobs in the U.S, in order to support their families.) The Career Advisory Board (op. cit.) states:

Summing up, SNCOs in the U.S. represent a much smaller mass of employment compared to existing definitions of middle-skills jobs. More specifically, SNCOs (a) represent only one in five jobs that do not require a 4-year college degree for entry; (b) encompass a wide variety of occupations and industries, even though the jobs are highly concentrated in a relatively small number of occupations and industries; (c) usually pay above-average wages; (d) show a quite low correlation between wages and skills; and (e) include a significant proportion of workers who are potentially underemployed in terms of educational attainment.

Showing a cognizance of the implications of long term U.S. Demographic trends, with clear relevance to Latinx immigrants, the Career Advisory Board (op. cit.) also goes on to state that their analyses raise critical questions:

> These questions refer to the demographics of workers in SNCOs, the dynamics of SNCOs over time, and the variation in the dynamics and composition of SNCOs across subnational geographic areas. What is the composition of SNCOs in terms of age, sex, race, and ethnicity, and how has it changed over time? Have SNCOs expanded or contracted over the last decades, especially since the Great Recession? Are SNCOs expected to expand or contract in official employment projections? In terms of employment, which SNCOs have expanded or contracted, and which ones are projected to grow or decline? Do the relative size and composition of SNCOs vary significantly across states and metropolitan areas? Answers to these important questions, based on the method proposed in this paper, should offer a more accurate understanding of the nature and dynamics of SNCOs in the U.S.

Implications for Latinx educational attainment

If taken at face-value, as expressed by leading technology firms, the longer range requirements of the employment skills sets required by the knowledge economy labour force have startling implications when considering how they might affect Latinx immigrant population labour force participation and education. A 2017 report by the Dell Technologies (2017), which was prepared through the Institute for the Future (IFTF) and a panel of 20 tech, business and academic experts from around the world, estimates that 85 percent of the jobs that will exist in 2030 haven't been invented yet. The report states:

> The challenges we face as a society and the employment opportunities kids will have as adults aren't going to be nicely divided into biology, physics, chemistry, calculus or algebra . . . Solving tomorrow's big problems requires thinking across disciplines. We need kids who are ready for those kinds of careers (Dell Technologies, 2017, 15).

How Latinx immigrant background persons will fare in acquiring the emerging skill sets required by the knowledge economy deserves careful study and a proactive approach on the part of government. Of special significance is concern over Latinx educational attainment. One of our best starting points linking workforce participation development to educational attainment is the programme of research by Carnevale and colleagues at the Center for Education and Work at Georgetown University (Carnevale and Fasules 2017; Carnevale et al. 2018). While there is clear evidence that Latinx high school completion and college attainment has improved notably in the past decade, there is still a wide gap in Latinx students' attendance of highly selective institutions and completion of college degrees most responsive to their acquisition of the advanced skill sets meeting the knowledge economy needs, compared to white-non-Latinx persons. In 2016, 83 per cent of Latinx persons had completed a high school education in contrast to 90 per cent of white non-Latinx persons of post-high school age (Carnevale op. cit., 2017). And while in 2014 19 per cent of Latinx persons of college age (18–24 years of age) were enrolled in college, a rate close to their 21 per cent representation in this age-range, Latinx students were noticeably less likely to enter selective admissions institutions compared to White non-Latinx students. Twenty-four percent of Latinx students entered open-admission institutions compared to 12 percent entering selective admissions four-year institutions (Carnevale op. cit., 2017). As we mention below these differences in college enrollment and subsequent college completion are associated with challenges in acquiring cognitive and job skill sets that affect employment type and income level.

Based on NCES 2014 data, nearly one-half (48 percent) of Latinx students were enrolled in two-year community colleges, compared to 30 percent of White non-Latinx students, 32 percent of Asian background students, and 36 percent of Black students (Pew Research Center 2016). Some 80 percent of Latinx students entering community college to obtain an associate's degree aspire to receive a bachelor's degree, and some 40 percent, a graduate degree eventually. Although their aspirations are high, Latinx students in community colleges face daunting barriers in obtaining an associate's degree or transferring to four-year colleges (Carnevale op. cit., 2017). Roughly 63 percent are required to take remedial courses before being allowed to enroll in credit bearing courses, compared to 23 percent of White non-Latinx students and 11 percent of Black students (Vandal 2016).

On the other hand, longitudinal data show that bachelor's degree completion rates are low but increasing among Latinx students. NCES BPS longitudinal survey results indicate that, in 2009, after six years, only 30 percent of Latinx community college students had completed a sought after Associate's degree compared to 42 percent of White non-Latinx students (Carnevale op. cit., 2017). And with regard to bachelor's degree completion rates after 6-years enrollment in four-year institutions, the same longitudinal survey showed Latinx students lagged with a rate of 40 percent completion (as did Black students) compared to 68 percent for White non-Latinx students.

More recent NCES BPS longitudinal survey data show that just over 53 percent of Latinx students entering four-year institutions in 2009 completed baccalaureate degrees six years later in 2015 – a jump of 33 percent but still a noticeably lower rate than the one for White non-Latinx students who showed a degree completion rate of just over 63 percent (NCES 2018). In other words, data on increased baccalaureate attainment rates among Latinx students who reach four-year higher education institutions are promising with regard to the acquisition of skills in demand by the new economy. It is also true, however, that–according to CPS/PUMS data–as of 2014 only 15 percent of Latinx background students in the age range 25–29 had attained a bachelor's degree. That is in contrast to 41 percent of White non-Latinx students, 63 percent of Asian background students, and 22 percent of Black students (Pew 2016).

The Great Recession of 2008 and draconian anti-immigration policies had sensible effects on the proportion of Latinix people entering institutions of higher learning. With fewer people from Latin America entering the U.S. has paralleled a rise in the proportion of first generation immigrant Latinx persons who are 25 or older and who have attended some college. Despite such trends, lower college attainment rates among Latinx persons of working age leads them to job placements within the lowest rungs in the increasingly automated labour and service-based sectors of the economy. Such forms of employment tend to be temporary and provide minimal worker benefits.

Improved higher education access and advanced technical training should be imperative if Latinx youth are to gain mobility in the twenty-first century labour market. The trend is clear regarding necessary skills for Latinx persons to improve their position in American society. Such matters deserve further investigation. This is a daunting challenge, given the difficulty of designing and carrying out research projects resulting in accurate population estimates, given the volatility of our economy and the effects of xenophobia against Latinx and other immigrants.

Compounding such problems are increased costs of living and the limited availability of affordable housing both of which are driving Latinx immigrants away from historically welcoming urban centres in the U.S. and towards often more hostile–but also more affordable–rural and urban regions in the South and smaller Midwestern urban and rural areas. The stability of settlement in the new communities shows uneven patterns, as suggested by the findings of other papers in this Special Issue. We need more studies such as those in the present collection to make clearer how the families and children of immigrants in new areas of destination are developing intergenerational roots in terms of permanent job opportunities upward mobility, wealth accumulation, home ownership, access to education and health care, and access to retirement funds. The question remains as to how the economies and labour markets in these communities will change as a result of the introduction of automation and increased reliance on worker technical and information processing skills sets. As a whole such skills are increasing among all sectors of the American population, including Latinx people but only among the few able to attain higher levels of education.

Latinx immigrant wealth Inequality

The claim that current Latinx employment statistics portend well in terms of future improvement in social mobility is highly dubuious, given that Latinx people are concentrated at the lowest levels of the labour market in jobs unlikely to be permanent and more likely to pay little and have few benefits. Such jobs cannot be envisioned as stepping stones facilitating access to more remunerative professional jobs where wealth accumulation and upward mobility are possible. This is consistent with the profile of Latinx populations in the United States. Historically, the labour market reception of first and second generation Latinx immigrants to the U.S. has followed a pattern wherein a majority of low skilled workers and their offspring remain tethered to the lowest paying occupations and the latter advancing in educational attainment at lower rates than other immigrant populations (Portes and Rumbaut 2014).

The resulting wealth divide confronted by Latinx immigrants is an enduring demographic and sociopolitical reality that cannot be reduced by current trends in reduced Latinx unemployment. While these gains in employment are essential for survival of immigrant persons and families, and for Latinx U.S. residents as a whole, they are not enough at their pace, by any means, to significantly reduce the wealth gap between whites, and Latinx persons, or the wealth gap with respect to Blacks between now and the year 2060.

This enduring and increasing wealth gap is illustrated by data analyzed by Nieves and Asante-Muhammed (2018) from the Census Bureau Household Wealth Trends in the United States, 1962–2016. They examine trends in median household wealth from 1983 to 2016 across ethnic/racial groups, and extrapolate how household wealth would change from 2016 to 2060 should the same trends endure. Nieves and Asante-Muhammed (op. cit.) operationalize "wealth" as the fungible assets of families, and they operationalize middle class wealth as ranging from $70,200, to $210,600 in 2016 dollars. The data examined indicate that White non-Latinx persons in 2016 constituted 61.4 per cent of the population, but will be less than 45 per cent of the U.S. population by 2060. Over this same time period, Latinx persons are projected to increase from just under 17 per cent of the population to nearly 30 per cent of the population by 2060. Shockingly, the median household wealth gap between non-Latinx White persons and Latinx persons would be projected to grow rather than decline, if trends from 1983 to 2016 remained constant into the future.

The median household wealth of White non-Latinx households in 2016 was $140,500. (within the middle class range) while the equivalent figure for Latinx households was $6,300.–a gap of over $134,000 and not anywhere near the middle class range. Using 2016 dollars as an index, in 2049 when White non-Latinx persons become less than 50 per cent of the population and Latinx persons become about 26 per cent of the population, the median household wealth of White non-Latinx would be nearly $187,000., while that of Latinx households would be nearly $9,700 – a gap of over $177,000 and still nowhere near the middle class range. Moving onwards to 2060, the dwindling White non-Latinx people, constituting a little over 40 per cent of the population, would have a median household wealth somewhat over $200,000 in 2016 dollars, while Latinx persons would be nearing 30 per cent of the U.S. population with a median household wealth still under $15,000 in 2016 dollars and still far distant from the middle class range.

Conclusion: A Search for Solutions that include but Go beyond educational attainment

While it is clear that increased higher educational attainment among Latinx immigrants and their children is a necessary factor adding to chances for prosperity and social mobility and the well-being of the economy, education alone is not likely sufficient by any means to ensure employment stability and social mobility. In recent years there has arisen a more fundamental concern that human rights shared among racial/ethnic, economic, and intergenerational groups, including immigrant groups, needs affirmation as a starting point for equitable long-term population development initiatives and broader allied movements ensuring national stability and prosperity.

An important example centred on the development of U.S. immigrant populations, and of particular relevance to Latinx immigrants is described by Manuel Pastor in is his 2018 book entitled *State of Resist-ance: What California's Dizzying Descent and Remarkable Resurgence Mean for America's Future*. Pastor analyzed in painstaking detail how demographic and economic change in California; between 1969–2018, fueled primarily by Latinx and Asian immigrant settlement; was associated with political and social transformation supporting human rights and intergenerational population development. During that period, even as the state economy grew, California backed away from nativist-centred state policies–such as mandated English-only K-12 education (Proposition 187)–and implemented innovative college admissions strategies to mitigate anti-affirmative action policies (Proposition 209) affecting educational opportunities of Latinx peoples and other peoples of colour underrepresented in higher education. In the wake of these progressive reforms, the increased rate of higher education attainment among Latinx second generation immigrants in California created a critical mass of upwardly mobile professionals with awareness of the importance of civic engagement. While Latinx persons in California still lag in higher education completion rates and proportional representation in the most selective universities and graduate programmes, they have reached parity in post-high school college attendance – an important step towards their fuller participation in the California economy and civic institutions.

Pastor notes that over the 1969–80 period there was a sizeable increase in Latinx immigrant background persons successfully running for political office in California. One result was that Latinx political power grew significantly in the state legislature, especially in key roles tied to promoting and passing laws serving the needs of immigrant and low-income communities. On other fronts, the rise of Silicon Valley and other industries in California during this period propelled the state economy into becoming the 5th wealthiest in the world while at the same time attracting highly educated, technically skilled workers from other parts of the U.S. and from other (principally Asian) countries. Collectively, these new residents of California maintained liberal and progressive views on demographic population development and human rights. The resulting intermixture of persons with these shared progressive values led to support for multi-coalition legislation across a range of issues tied to equity policies, health care, and environmental/ecological maintenance policies.

Pastor argues that the California 1969–2018 experience is the harbinger for the future of other states in the coming decades aligning with the concern in this paper for the well-being and upward mobility of Latinx immigrants and their children into mid-century and beyond. He argues that California has reached a tipping point with regard to planning for the future that has led to a widespread political recognition and public will that equity and social justice concerns, including immigrant rights and well-being are central to maintaining and growing the prosperity of the state. He points out that California, nonetheless, is far from resolving its economic and social disparities as evidenced by its prohibitive cost of living, shortages in affordable housing, rising homeless rates, and intense pockets of poverty in communities – all of which coincide with major settlements of Latinx immigrant families.

Another problem is that the major technology industries are still not employing persons from Latinx immigrant backgrounds or of other ethnic/racial origins underrepresented in higher education in significant numbers in higher paying positions, in large part due to the limited size of the available pool of persons with requisite skill sets. Nonetheless Pastor argues that the die has been cast in that the growing number of younger voters from immigrant Latinx and Asian backgrounds will prevail in their prioritization of human rights and population development as primary state priorities.

If the California experience over the past 50 years calling priority attention to development of immigrant rights and well-being were to generalize to other states, which states might next follow suit? Texas will present an interesting test case. It resembles California's high density of youthful Latinx immigrant residents, an aging White non-Latinx population, and collectively, a trend towards greater liberal and progressive political views. Texas recently was identified as a new home base for Apple Computer in Austin and already is attracting Silicon Valley type industries into its major urban centres – these industries bringing with them new skilled immigrants from other countries. Another trend showing the potential for Texas to develop its Latinx population is the recent growth in the percent of Mexican immigrants who are age 25-years and older who already have earned college degrees – despite the decline in Mexican immigration overall. Eighteen percent of Mexican immigrants to Texas aged 25 years or older in 2017 had already earned college degrees in comparison to 7 percent in 2000 (Soto and Selee 2019).

Yet another auspicious sign is the rise of public policy organizations like the Latino Donor Collaborative (Schink and Hayes-Bautista, June 2017) and the Democracy and the Next American Economy: Where Prosperity Meets Justice Project (Ramos 2019) that are focused on detailed analyses of the economic wealth gap in the U.S. across demographic groups and that include the growing contributions of Latinx immigrant persons to the U.S. economy and workforce, and the gains to be obtained by increasing this populations completion of higher education (see also Cisneros 2009).

The path towards prosperity for Millennial Latinx immigrants and their Generation Z children is entangled with the capacity of the U.S. economy, polity, education systems, and social institutions to adapt to demographic, social, and economic changes occurring globally. Global ecological transformations such as climate change and other effects of the Anthropocene are adding stressors to all populations, including immigrants. For that reason, the time has come for government to take proactive measures. The prosperity and stability of the U.S. as a whole will depend as never before on how well the Latinx immigrant population can be integrated into the long term fabric of the U.S. economy and polity.

Disclosure statement

No potential conflict of interest was reported by the author.

References

Carnevale, A. P., and M. L. Fasules. 2017. *Latino Education and Economic Progress. Running Vaster but Still Behind*. Washington, DC: Center on Education and the Workforce, Georgetown University.

Carnevale, A. P., and N. Smith. 2013. "America's Future Workforce." In *All-In Nation: An America That Works for All, a Collaboration Between the Center for American Progress and Policylink*, edited by V. Cárdenas, and S. Treuhaft, 31–47. Washington, DC: Center on Education and the Workforce, Georgetown University. https://cew.georgetown. edu/americas-future-workforce/.

Carnevale, A. P., M. Van Der Werf, M. C. Quinn, J. Strohl, and D. Repnikov. 2018. *Our Separate & Unequal Colleges. How Public Colleges Reinforce White Racial Privilege and Marginalize B;ack and Latino Students*. Washington, DC: Center on Education and the Workforce, Georgetown University.

Cisneros, H., ed. 2009. *Latinos and the Nation's Future*. Houston: Arte Público Press.

Dell Technologies. 2017. The Next Era of Human Machine Partnerships. Emerging Technologies' Impact on Society & Work in 2030. Accessed 9 July 2019. http:// www.iftf.org/fileadmin/user_upload/downloads/th/SR1940_ IFTFforDellTechnologies_Human-Machine_070717_readerhigh-res.pdf.

Dimock, M. 2019. *Defining Generations: Where Millennials end and Generation Z Begins*. Washington, DC: Pew Research Center. http://www.pewresearch.org/fact-tank/ 2019/01/17/where-millennials-end-and-generation-z-begins.

Frey, W. H. 2018a. *Diversity Explosion. How new Racial Demographics are Remaking America*. Washington, DC: The Brookings Institution.

Frey, W. H. 2018b. "The US will become 'minority white' in 2045, Census projects." *Youthful minorities are the engine of future growth*. Brookings Institute. Accessed 9 July 2019. Retrieved from https://www.brookings.edu/blog/the-avenue/2018/03/ 14/the-us-will-become-minority-white-in-2045-census-projects/.

Herold, B. September 25, 2018. Jobs at All Levels Now Require Digital Literacy. Here's Proof. *Education Week*.

Leal, D. L., and S. Trejo, eds. 2011. *Latinos and the Economy. Integration and Impact in Schools, Labor Markets, and the Economy. Integration and Impact in Schools, Labor Markets, and Beyond*. New York: Springer.

Murdock, S., M. Cline, M. Zey, D. Perez, and P. Wilner Jeanty. 2015. *Population Change in the United States. Socioeconomic Challenges and Opportunities in the Twenty-First Century*. New York: Springer.

Muro, M., S. Liu, J. Whiton, and S. Kulkarni. November 2017. *Digitalization and the American Workforce*. Brookings Institute. Accessed 9 July 2019. https://www. brookings.edu/wp-content/uploads/2017/11/mpp_2017nov15_digitalization_full_ report.pdf.

NCES. 2018. Digest of Education Statistics. NCES 2018-70. Washington DC.

Nittle, N. K. 2018. States with Higher Minority Population Thought Co. https://www. thoughtco.com/states-with-majority-minority-populations-2834515.

Pastor, M. 2018. *State of Resist-Ance. What California's Dizziying Descent and Remarkable Resurgence Mean for America's Future*. New York: The New Press.

Pew Research Center. 2015. *Modern Immigration Wave Brings 59 Million to U.S., Driving Population Growth and Change Through 2065: Views of Immigration's Impact on U.S. Society Mixed*. Washington, DC: September.

Pew Research Center. 2016. *5 Facts About Latinos and Education*. Washington, DC: July.

Portes, A., and R. G. Rumbaut. 2014. *Immigrant America: A Portrait*. 4th ed. Berkeley: University of California Press.

Ramos, H. A. 2019. *Democracy and the Next American Economy*. Houston: Arte Público Press.

Sáenz, R., and K. M. Johnson. Fall 2016. White Deaths Exceed Births in One-Third of U. S. States. Carsey Research. National Issues Brief #110. Durham, NH: University of New Hampshire.

Schink, W., and D. Hayes-Bautista. 2017. Latino Gross Domestic Product (GDP) Report. Quantifying the Impact of American Hispanic Economic Growth. http:// latinodonorcollaborative.org/latino-gdp-report.

Soto, A., and A. Selee. 2019. *A Profile of Highly Skilled Mexican Immigrants in Texas and the United States*. Washington, DC: Migration Policy Institute.

Taylor, P. 2015. *The Next America. Boomers, Millennials, and the Looming Generational Showdown*. New York: Public Affairs.

Unger, A. March 6, 2017. "Career Advisory Board Reveals Growing Lack of Tech Preparedness for the American Workforce." *Research Uncovers Growing Gap in Both Applied and Hard Technology Skills*. Accessed 9 July 2019. https://www.careeradvisoryboard.org/content/dam/dvu/www_careeradvisoryboard_org/CAB-tech-skills-release_FINAL.pdf.

U.S. Census Bureau. 2018. *Projected Race and Hispanic Origin: Main Projections Series for the United States, 2017–2060*. Washington: Population Division.

Vandal, Bruce. 2016. Remedial Education's Role in Perpetuating Achievement Gaps; "Complete College America" (blog). http://completecollege.org/remedial-educations-role-in-perpetuating-achievement-gaps/.

The model minority stereotype and the national identity question: the challenges facing Asian immigrants and their children

Min Zhou and Carl L. Bankston III

ABSTRACT
A central issue in contemporary debates over immigration concerns how immigrants from diverse origins become integrated into their host nation. The children of Asian immigrants in the United States often give the impression of fitting neatly into American society and therefore into the American nation as a model minority. We argue, however, that such perception is a misleading overgeneralization and can bring about simplistic interpretations. The apparently successful integration of Asian Americans is not due to intrinsic cultural characteristics, but to the positive modes of incorporation juxtaposing unique patterns of selective acculturation. Moreover, the model minority image renders the continued distinctiveness and diversity of the Asian American population invisible and often has unanticipated consequences for individual group members. The seemingly positive outcomes result in new stereotypes, which serve as mechanisms of social exclusion for even the highly integrated immigrant groups and create new complications for understanding the national identity question.

Introduction

Numerous social forces shape negative attitudes toward immigration in receiving countries in the past and at present times, including the perceptions that immigrants would depress wages, take jobs away from native-born workers, and "eat" up social welfare; worries about the importation of global inequality and crime; and concerns about the threat to national sovereignty in a world with increasingly porous borders. Across all of the social forces, though, runs the problem of a cultural threat to national identity in a society experiencing rapid demographic change (Card, Dustmann, and Preston 2005; Hainmueller and Hopkins 2014). Some influential scholars and pundits, such as Brimelow (1995) and Huntington (2004), hold the idea that American national identity is primarily Anglo-European. They are concerned that the immigration of large numbers of immigrants of Asia and Latin American origins would pose a serious problem for national identity because these immigrants are not easily absorbed into the Anglo-European culture. In fact, the popular appeal of such worries became evident in the 2016 presidential election when Donald Trump made opposition to immigration from Mexico and Muslim countries a signature issue and drew on the emotional appeal to national identity to galvanize voter support.[1]

Since most of the overt opposition to immigration has concentrated on immigrants from Mexico and Central America and Muslim immigrants, one might imagine that national identity concerns of the era of hard borders and deportation do not affect Asian immigrants and their children because of their seemingly successful integration. Indeed, some evidence suggests that Asian Americans are well-integrated socioeconomically. The 2010 census data show that Asian Americans have the highest median household income ($66,000) of all racial groups, even surpassing native-born White Americans ($54,000); that they have the highest levels of education with 49 per cent of them (aged 25 and over) having a bachelor's degree or more, compared to 31 per cent of White Americans, 18 per cent of African Americans, and 13 per cent of Hispanic Americans; and that about half of the employed Asian Americans are in managerial and professional occupations (Pew Research Center 2013). Asian immigrants also are resettled away from ethnic enclaves and in non-traditional destinations across the United States (Frey 2014).

Since the 1960s, an emerging positive stereotype has recast Asian Americans from the uncivilized "yellow peril" to the successful "model minority" (Brand 1987; Petersen 1966; U.S. News and World Report Staff 1966). The more contemporary, pan-ethnic view of exceedingly high-achieving "whiz kids" applies to both the children of East and South Asian immigrants who are mostly well-educated and professionally trained and those of Southeast Asian refugees who are of lower socioeconomic backgrounds (Brand 1987). This model minority stereotype – family oriented, self-reliant, hardworking, resilient, and problem-free – has a powerful influence on Asian American life, especially the U.S.-born and U.S.-raised second generation (Kiang et al. 2017; Lee 1994; Ngo and Lee 2007; Wu 2014). Zhou (2004) considered whether Asians in the United States were disappearing into a slightly expanded version of an American ethnoracial identity several years ago in an article that posed the question: "Are Asian Americans becoming White?"

(Zhou 2004). In the same year, Bonilla-Silva (2004, 932) argued that most Asian Americans had reached the status of "honorary whites" in an American racial hierarchy. Similarly, in their review article on what they term the "racialized assimilation" of Asians in America, Lee and Kye (2016, 254) commented that from one perspective, "[r]ather than being relegated as racialized minorities, Asian Americans appear to be approaching 'near white' status … "

Moreover, consistent with the idea that Asians in the United States are folding neatly into the larger national identity, is the fact that Asian Americans have among the highest rates of interracial marriage in the United States (Lee and Kye 2016). Analyzing patterns of intermarriage, Hidalgo and Bankston (2010) have argued that the relatively large numbers of mixed race children with Asian ancestry necessarily means that if the boundaries between white and Asian identities have not disappeared, these have at least become increasingly blurred.

Whether and how are Asians in the United States affected by the national identity question? The answers that we offer to this question are more nuanced than a simple equation of socioeconomic outcomes with identity would suggest. In the following sections, we argue, first, that the relative success and apparent invisibility of Asian Americans is a product of changing migration contexts and hyper-selectivity. We argue, further, that this relative success does not make ethnoracial national identity irrelevant for Asian immigrants and their offspring, but that it places them in an ambiguous position in relation to national identity that may work in their favour or against them and creates special challenges of ethnoracial distinctness and social exclusion.

Recent trends in Asian immigration

Changing contexts of exit

In the contemporary world, people move faster and on a larger scale than ever before. Asian migration has changed greatly since 1970. Of the Asia-born migrants living outside Asia in 2015, 40 per cent were in North America (UNDESA 2016). Although there are some countries still plagued by poverty, war and ethnic conflict, the region has become much more developed. Even war-torn countries in Southeast Asia, especially Vietnam, experienced profound economic transformation. Globalization and development give an impetus for emigration not only among the poor and low-skilled who are displaced or outcompeted in domestic labour markets, but also among the wealthy and highly skilled who have already attained and secured middle- or upper-middle class statuses. Meanwhile, the large exodus of refugees from Asia has subsided. The United Nations estimated that there were about 3.5 million refugees in the Asia and Pacific region with the majority originating from only two countries – Afghanistan and Myanmar – fleeing from ethnic conflict and violence between 1990 and 2010 (UNHCR 2017). The United States has received only a small number (10 per cent) of these Asian refugees since 2000 (UNHCR 2017).

Asian immigrants in the United States are diverse in both national origins and socioeconomic characteristics. The largest six national origin groups (with populations over one million, such as Chinese, Indians, Filipinos, Koreans, Vietnamese, and Japanese) and many small groups (such as Cambodians, Thais, and Bangladeshis) are mostly positively selected, meaning that the average level of schooling (in years) of the immigrant group is higher than that of the general population in the home country (Feliciano 2005). Some groups, such as Chinese, Koreans, Indians, and Filipinos, are even hyper-selected, meaning that the percentage of college graduates of the immigrant groups is higher than that of the general population not only in the home country but also in the host country (Lee and Zhou 2015).

The largest number of immigrants from Asia coming to the United States arrived from relatively high human capital countries with substantial middle classes. For example, China sent more immigrants than any other countries in Asia. During the years 2015–2017, 17 per cent of immigrants from all of East Asia, South Asia, and the Middle East came from China (U.S. Department of Homeland Security 2018). The second largest number of immigrants from these three regions came from India, making up 14 per cent of the total; and third largest from the Philippines, constituting 12 per cent. Thus, even following the Department of Homeland Security's practice of including the Middle East in the Asia category, immigrants from these three relatively high human capital countries accounted for 43 per cent of Asian immigrants. As a result of the recent history of immigration, Chinese, Indians, and Filipinos make up the largest portions of the Asian population within the United States, both native-born and foreign-born. In 2017, according to *American Community Survey* statistics, Chinese constituted the largest category of Asians (24 per cent), followed by Asian Indians (21 per cent), and Filipinos (16 per cent) (U.S. Census Bureau, 2019).

Changing state policies as context of reception

State policies in immigration and refugee resettlement in the United States affect how immigrants are received and resettled, what kinds of receiving environments surround the immigrants, and what kinds of communities they form. Since the passage of the Hart-Celler Act of 1965, US immigration policy has oriented to a humanitarian goal of reuniting immigrant families and an economic goal of bringing in skilled labour needed by the increasingly globalized US economy. In the past three decades, H-1B visas, nonimmigrant visas for highly educated foreign workers in specialty occupations with predictable pathways to permanent residency and citizenship, have been disproportionately issued to Indians and Chinese who have advanced degrees in science and engineering, as well as to Filipino physicians and nurses. In 2011, 55 per cent of the H-1B visas went to Indians, 8 per cent to Chinese, and 3 per cent to British. In 2016, 70 and 12 per cent went to Indians and Chinese, respectively (U.S. Department of State Visa Office 2011, 2017).

Refugee resettlement has been another source of Asian immigration. From 1980 onward, U.S. refugee policy aimed to disperse refugees, leading to the growth of new destinations for newcomers from Asia, mostly from war-torn Vietnam, Cambodia, and Laos. In *Growing Up American*, we described how the U.S. government initially tried to spread Vietnamese refugees around the country (Zhou and Bankston 1998). However, the locations of non-governmental organizations, housing availability, and the desires of immigrants to live among co-ethnics led to the formation of interconnected Vietnamese communities across the country. The presence of active voluntary agencies in Minnesota during this same period led to the emergence of a large Hmong community in the Minneapolis-St. Paul region (Fennelly and Palasz 2003).

State policies have played an important role in shaping the dispersion of contemporary immigrants, giving rise to suburbs dominated by the influx of non-white immigrants, including "ethnoburbs" – affluent suburban ethnic communities (Li 2009) – as well as concentrations of disadvantaged immigrant populations in new destinations. Studies have found that restrictive immigration policies force circular labour migrants and undocumented migrants to permanently resettled in the United States (Durand, Massey, and Capoferro 2005; Hernández-León 2008; Hernández-León and Zúñiga 2000; Massey and Capoferro 2008; Massey, Durand, and Malone 2003). However, the outward spread of immigrants has occurred across nearly all immigrant groups of different national or ethnic origins.

Changing context of reception: the U.S. economy and public attitude

Since the 1980s, the U.S. economy has shifted from labour-intensive industries to capital- or knowledge-intensive financial, information and communications technology (ICT), and service industries (Alba and Nee 2003). Manufacturing industries have moved offshore in disproportionately large numbers to the Global South (the so-called developing world), and those that remain must compete with low-wage labour around the world (Best 2011; Portes and Walton 1981).

The growth in both ends of the American economy means that immigrant workers in the labour force are increasingly bifurcated into either the low-paid, low skilled positions on one end or high-skilled, high-paid positions on the other, with some into entrepreneurial positions created by the immigrants themselves. Responding to the change in economic structure, most contemporary immigrants fall into one of three occupational categories. First, there are low-skilled or semi-skilled, labour-intensive jobs taken up by labour migrants, including those engaged in agricultural work and labour-intensive industries, such as construction work, meat-packing, poultry and seafood processing, and textiles (Durand, Massey, and Capoferro 2005; Griffith 2006; Hernández-León 2008; Massey and Capoferro 2008). Second, there are highly skilled professional or service jobs taken up by highly educated migrants and those with relevant training and credentials, such as physicians and nurses, engineers and technicians, scientists and academics. Third, there are entrepreneurial immigrants, occupied in businesses such as small groceries, restaurants, and lodging establishments (Zhou and Bankston 2016).

Low-skilled labour migrants disproportionately come from south of the U.S. border. Geographic proximity and long-standing social networks tend to channel Mexican immigrants – the largest contemporary immigrant group in the U.S. – across the border into occupations at the bottom of the U.S. labour market. Distance, the rise of Asian nations, and selective migration tend to channel many Asian immigrants, especially those from China, India, and the Philippines, into the professional sectors of the U.S. labour market. Asians who fit into neither category rely neither on the established demand and social networks of supply of the labour migrants, nor on the credentials and qualifications of the professional migrants. Instead, their primary resource consists of family and kin relations that enable them to create employment opportunities in ethnic economies.

For the children of immigrants, this segmentation means that they grow up in highly stratified social settings, ranging from schools, neighbourhoods, and peer groups. Their outcomes depend not just on their own advantages and disadvantages, but also on the connections to their co-ethnic or other immigrant group members and to the larger American society that shape the uses they make of their advantages and disadvantages. For example, the children of Asian Indian physicians, often with abundant family resources, frequently enjoy high-performing schools in suburban middle-class communities. They are able to maximize the advantages of these schools with the additional support and encouragement of social resource-rich families and ethnic communities. In contrast, the children of Hmong refugees who were displaced and resettled in the totally unfamiliar cultural environment and extreme cold climate of Minnesota faced tremendous hardships in all aspects of life (Hein 2006). Since their families have come from a largely non-literate background in Laos, young Hmong Americans face greater challenges than many immigrants and also have fewer social resources from their families and ethnic community to overcome those challenges. Between these two extremes, the fates of the children of immigrant entrepreneurs often depend on the social and cultural resources those in their parents' generation can generate by their own efforts, just as immigrant businesses often depend on the mutual assistance and collaboration of group members (Bankston 2000; Zhou and Bankston 1998).

When the size of the newcomers into an American community is small and the local economy is good, public reception may be generally positive and welcoming. But as the immigrant population becomes visible in a locale, exacerbated by economic distress, anxiety and hostile attitudes may ensue. Hostility toward immigrants emerges from a perceived threat as well as ethno-racial prejudice. In a study of public reception of the Hmong in Wisconsin, Ruefle and associates found that the Hmong were initially welcomed but later concerns grew about their resettlement, not so much the fear that they would take jobs away from local residents but rather due to cultural differences and a generally negative attitude toward a culturally strange out-group (Ruefle, Ross, and Mandell 1992).

Although discomfort with immigration may exist in any part of American society, it has been greatest in places where natives are experiencing econ-omic difficulties and come into contact with immigrants in the bottom part of the nation's bifurcating economy. Hernández-León and Zúñiga (2006), for example, have detailed the intergroup strains created by the arrival of Mexican labourers in Appalachia. We can take this as the opposite side of the favourable "model minority" stereotype described above that has met immigrants in professional groups. At the same time, an ethos of multicultur-alism has become widespread in many professional and educational circles and many businesses have become dependent on immigrant labour (Zhou and Bankston 2016). Thus, the children of immigrants today grow up in a polarized setting, in which societal views of immigrants are deeply divided.

The polarization of attitudes toward immigrants has been part of a more general sociopolitical polarization. In the 2016 U.S. Presidential election, immi-gration became a major issue, and this issue played a large part in the rise of the ultimately successful candidate, a political outsider who initially drew pol-itical attention by broadcasting concerns about Muslim immigration and about undocumented immigration from Mexico. President Trump's two signa-ture campaign issues, re-industrialization through economic protectionism and much more restrictive immigration policies, both appealed to segments of the population who felt that they had suffered from openness to foreign connections, the economic re-structuring that had encouraged immigration, and the presence of people of new and unfamiliar national origins (Herndon 2019a).

Public attitudes toward immigrants are both more favourable more hostile than they have been in the past, depending on the part of the general U.S. public that immigrants come into contact with and on the specific social location that each immigrant group occupies in society. Hyper-selectivity of some Asian-origin groups and favourable contexts of reception for immi-grants from Asia by state policies, labour market, and the general public have neutralized the negative impacts of immigrant disadvantage through the concentration of human capital in the family and social capital, or patterned social relations, in the ethnic community (Bankston 2014; Lee and Zhou 2015; Portes and Rumbaut 2014; Zhou and Bankston 1998).

Changing context of reception: geographic distribution and variety of ethnic communities

The residential settings surrounding the children of immigrants in today's new immigrant destinations are characteristic of both diversity and structured inequality. Children of low-skilled immigrants tend to concentrate and grow up in central cities, plagued by poverty, drugs, crime, and poor schools, alongside other urban problems (Zhou 1997). Their counterparts face similar disadvantages in dispersed suburbs, where their social environments are likely to consist of native and immigrant families of low SES and similar problems associated with extreme poverty (Hein 2006). Others scattered about in ethnically diverse and decentralized clusters of various socioeconomic levels, but retain ethnic communities by focusing their social lives on an ethnically based centre, such as a temple, church, or institutions in an older symbolic urban village (Bankston 2000). Still others find themselves in affluent ethnoburbs, where ethnic identity and economic advantage are not opposed, but closely associated (Zhou, Tseng, and Kim 2008).

Generally associated with middle-class whites, suburbs are where immigrants are expected to move as a measure of residential assimilation. However, in recent decades, some suburban communities have become initial places of immigrant/refugee resettlement or have drawn secondary migration of immigrants of relatively low socioeconomic backgrounds (Zhou and Bankston 1998). For example, the pull of suburban employment lay behind the development of a Lao suburban village in southwestern Louisiana (Bankston 2000). The availability of housing and employment drives the suburbanization of many other immigrant groups as well, not just the Southeast Asian refugee groups, notably Latino immigrant groups (Donato et al. 2010; Hernández-León and Zúñiga 2000; Massey and Capoferro 2008).

New migrant destinations are often in the urban fringe or suburbs, which are stratified by race and class. However, the rise of ethnoburbs as a common residential pattern indicates that ethnic residential segregation is no longer as disadvantageous as it was in the past (Jiménez 2017; Logan and Zhang 2013; Wen, Lauderdale, and Kandula 2009). Having generally high levels of education and income, ethnoburban families may concentrate advantage, rather than disadvantage. Because of immigrant selectivity, every Asian nationality except Japanese is more segregated from whites than expected, and such residential segregation persists over time; but unlike the case of Hispanics and African Americans, Asians tend to live in neighbourhoods that are generally similar to, or even better, than those of whites, leading to a unique Asian pattern of "separate but equal" (Logan and Zhang 2013). In California, where the automobile has created vast stretches of suburbs, suburbanization has been a prominent feature of the lives of all immigrant groups. In Silicon Valley, for example, there was a rising concentration of Asian immigrants with the development of high-tech industries (Jiménez 2017; Saxenian 2006). In Orange County, Koreans established many small ethnic clusters in suburbs such as Anaheim, Buena Park, Fullerton, and Irvine (Vo and Danico 2004). Visible Chinese residential clusters emerged in almost all suburbs around the Los Angeles metropolitan region (Li 2009; Zhou, Tseng, and Kim 2008). Before 1980, immigrants were barely visible in many of today's typical ethnoburbs in California.

The fact that many Asians do not live in ethnically identifiable locations can be consistent with the image of Asians as assimilating, or disappearing, into the larger American society. However, as Lee and Kye (2016, 260) observe, "the fundamental mechanisms of spatial assimilation are not coupled with residential outcomes in a clear linear fashion", and "the spatial assimilation model may underestimate the extent to which Asian Americans, as a non-white minority group, continue to face discrimination and social distance in the locational attainment process". Ethnic communities resulting from immigration can mean that even when group members are not concentrated in a single location, network connections can maintain distinctiveness (Bankston 2014). In her study of Asian Indians in the Dallas-Fort Worth area, Brettell (2005) finds a variety of interlocking Asian Indian ethnic communities organized around primarily religious institutions. Although they are residentially dispersed, Hindu temples and voluntary associations become centres for different Asian Indian groups. Dhingra (2012) finds yet another variation on the immigrant ethnic community, the predominantly Gujarati population that dominates the U.S. motel industry. Geographically spread around the nation because of the nature of their work, the motel owners, their co-ethnic employees, and their families do constitute genuine communities because they maintain communication and cooperation, even though they are clearly physically dispersed.

Asian diversity

Asians are often referred to as a single group by the academic community and the public. Yet, they consist of multiple national origins, and within each national origin group, there is significant internal diversity, such as Chinese and Indian. Statistics from the 2001–2017 *American Community Survey* show that among the different Asian-origin groups, only Japanese, Indians, and Filipinos had lower poverty rates than non-Hispanic whites (8.5, 6.1, and 8.1 per cent, respectively, compared to 9.9 per cent among non-Hispanic whites).

Chinese and Koreans, despite relatively high median household incomes and educational levels, showed higher rates of poverty (13.9 and 14.1 per cent, respectively) than the non-Hispanic white population.

One of the biggest distinctions is between Asian nationalities who have consistently arrived and grown in numbers as legal immigrants and those who initially arrived as refugees. While the Vietnamese, the largest of the Southeast Asian refugee groups, were able to achieve relative economic success, in part through the use of tight-knit family and ethnic social networks (Bankston 2014; Zhou and Bankston 1998), other Southeast Asian refugees and their children have continued to face greater challenges. The Vietnamese, despite being the most successfully integrated group among Southeast Asian refugee groups, still had a higher poverty rate (14.8 per cent) than other major Asian national origin groups, as well as a higher poverty rate than non-Hispanic whites. Other Southeast Asian refugee groups, the Hmong (28 per cent) and Cambodians (21 per cent), showed much higher poverty rates.

The issue of diversity within and among groups also involves the interracial marriage issue. Although rates of outgroup marriage are generally high for Asians as a whole, these rates are far higher for some groups, such as Filipinos, than others (Hidalgo and Bankston 2010; Lee and Kye 2016). Moreover, there is a sharp gender distinction in out-marriage, since the majority of these involve Asian women and white men (Lee and Kye 2016). As marriage between members of different Asian groups has risen in recent years, there has arguably been a blurring of distinctions among people of different Asian national origins, rather than between Asians and the majority population (Lee and Kye 2016). Thus, marriage patterns indicate a diversity of modes of incorporation, rather than a single trajectory of assimilation.

The issue of gender raises another source of diversity hidden by broad stereotypes, connected to the mobility trajectories of the children of immigrants. Examining the role of gendered expectations on educational achievement, we found that Vietnamese ideas about gender control actually promoted among women the kind of educational performance associated with the model minority stereotype, while simultaneously reinforcing restrictive gender roles (Zhou and Bankston 2001). Park and associates (2015) found that among children of both Latino and Asian immigrants, women achieved greater educational advancement than men, with Asians benefitting from the selective migration characteristics we have identified here, while women from immigrant backgrounds also paid heavy child-bearing penalties in occupational mobility. The socioeconomic paths of immigrant women and their female children, moreover, vary according not only to the group position in the US society, but also to the gender roles of source countries (Blau 2015).

One of the most commonly overlooked aspects of Asian diversity, an aspect that has special relevance for the question of how Asians fit into the national identity concerns in an era of deportation, is that the Asian American population includes a substantial number of unauthorized immigrants. A report by the Pew Research Center has noted that:

> Asian unauthorized immigrants made up about 13 percent of the 11.1 million unauthorized immigrants who live in the U.S. Unauthorized immigrants from four nations in Asia were among the top 15 origin groups for unauthorized immigrants – India (500,000), China (325,000), the Philippines (180,000) and Korea (160,000). (López, Ruiz, and Patten 2017)

Thus, although Mexican and Central American immigrants occupy the centre of popular attention in the issue of unauthorized immigration, well over a million people from Asia and their American-born family members stand to be affected by any crackdown on undocumented immigrants.

In a time in which the idea of national identity has become a key factor in shaping popular attitudes toward immigrants, the perception that Asians are "becoming white" depends on overlooking not only the continuing social, cultural, and residential distinctiveness of many Asians, but also the fact of diversity within and between groups. Part of this distinction involves the continuing socioeconomic marginality of many Asians, a marginality that is often hidden by broad economic and educational statistics. Underlying the obscuring of this diversity is a persistent stereotyping of Asians relative to sociocultural perspectives on national identity.

The model minority stereotype and the national identity question

The role of education

Education plays a central part in popular views of Asians as an immigrant-origin minority group and makes Asians in the United States a reference group for how many Americans think of immigrants fitting in to national identity. On a nation-wide level, the children of Asian immigrants tend to outperform Hispanics, non-Hispanic blacks and non-Hispanic whites on national achievement tests, in grades, and in levels of educational attainment. Although wide variations among the Asian sub-groups exist, higher academic performance has become a distinctly Asian pattern (Jiménez 2017). Asian American students, on average, have scored higher than all other groups, including non-Hispanic whites, on the mathematics portion of the SAT test and in overall scores on the ACT test, and the gap between Asians and all other groups has been steadily rising. Asian scores of the reading portion of the SAT have been going up, and have reached the level of non-Hispanic whites (Caldas and Bankston 2015).

Moreover, the standardized test scores actually under-measure Asian school performance. The mean grade-point averages of Asian students have long been higher than those of all racial and ethnic categories (Caldas and Bankston 2015). In a study undertaken to determine whether a referendum to eliminate affirmative action in Washington State would have an adverse effect on the college enrolment of minorities, Charles Hirschman found that standardized test scores actually understated the high school performance of most Asian groups, since in grade-point averages Asians " … exceeded their potential as assessed by test scores" (Hirschman with Pharris-Ciurej 2016, 114).

As a consequence of their socioeconomic locations, meanwhile, Hispanics, who constitute a major part of contemporary immigration to the United States, not only show lower levels of school performance than Asians or non-Hispanic whites on test scores and grades, they also continue to have high, if declining, high school dropout rates (Bankston 2014). Influences on white school decisions, then, include concerns about poor educational quality in schools dominated by Hispanics and concerns about excessive competition in schools dominated by Asians (Jiménez 2017). Thus, selective patterns of immigration result in contrasting stereotypes for the two major immigrant categories, Hispanics and Asians, each with a specific distinctiveness relevant to national identity. The extraordinary educational achievement of the children of Asian immigrants has created a model minority threat, which has led to a "new white flight" (Hwang 2005; Jiménez and Horowitz 2013). Whites do not flee from poor schools, but from good schools that are seen too demanding or too Asianized. For Asian American students, such white flight can result in greater ethnic isolation and an ethnic stereotyping that constitutes an additional source of school pressure.

The educational achievement of Asians, defined as a broad, undifferentiated category, has long placed them in a particularly problematic position in debates over affirmative action. When affirmative action policies at the University of Michigan came before the courts in the early twenty-first century, opponents of affirmative action argued that such policies discriminated against high-achieving Asians. However, the *Chronicle of Higher Education* (Schmidt 2003, p. A24) reported that pro-affirmative action Asians argued that this broad generalization further disadvantaged some Asian groups. "Taking umbrage with the stereotype of Asians as an academically over-achieving 'model minority'", a legal brief filed by the Asian Pacific American Legal Center "argues that Americans from Asia and the Pacific Islands still face serious discrimination and should be beneficiaries of affirmative action in some cases". More recently, the stereotype has placed Asians at the centre of controversy over affirmative action at Harvard University, with those on both sides of the issue using a generalized image of Asians to support their positions (Hackman 2018).

Ambiguous consequences of the stereotype and the national identity problem

How do the stereotypes of Asians affect how they fit into a country reacting to demographic change through immigration and intensifying concern with national identity? The answer to this question involves a complicated and nuanced mix of positive, negative, and unintended consequences. Portes and associates developed a typology of consonant, dissonant, and selective acculturation (Portes and Rumbaut 2001, 2014; Portes and Zhou 1993). Dissonant acculturation refers to immigrant children's loss of parental language and cultural ways, which often lead to intergenerational conflict and role reversal. Consonant acculturation indicates that children and parents learn and adapt to host society's culture at about the same pace. Selective acculturation is a process where immigrant children learn host language and cultural ways selectively without abandoning ethnic culture or detaching themselves from the ethnic community (Portes and Rumbaut 2001, 2014). Each type of acculturation is consequential with significant implications for segmented assimilation. In particular, selective acculturation is generally associated with desirable outcomes for children's outcomes of education while dissonant acculturation leads to negative outcomes (Portes and Rumbaut 2014). Waters and associates (2010) use survey data from the Immigrant Second Generation in Metropolitan New York to test the association between acculturation and socioeconomic consequences. Interestingly, they find that neither any type of acculturation nor the degree of ethnic embeddedness account for mobility patterns among children of immigrants. They thus raise questions about the mechanisms considered important by segmented assimilation theorists. However, one limitation of Waters and associates' study is that it operationalizes acculturation types largely in terms of parental languages and their impacts on socioeconomic outcomes, but that it does not address the question of how varied socioeconomic outcomes may or may not be connected to continued ethnic distinctiveness. Although it may not be the intention of these scholars, this can contribute to the impression that those who achieve upward structural mobility are absorbed into a mainstream national identity.

High rates of educational success can come at a cost. In a classic theoretical study, Merton (1936) explored the ways in which purposive social action can have unintended, or unanticipated, consequences. The racialization and stereotyping of Asian Americans based on general trends of successful selective acculturation by members of some of the larger Asian groups can be taken as an instance of unanticipated consequences. The same process of selective acculturation to specific segments of American society that has produced generally high rates of success among young people in many Asian national origin groups also have negative side effects. One such side effects is to give rise to new stereotypes that mask variations across groups and individuals. The children of Asian immigrants in the professional and technical occupations have the most predictable mobility trajectory through education and the greatest security for the future. For example, Asian Indian immigrants have the highest socioeconomic scores among all Asians. U.S.-born Asian Indians on average retain the same level as their foreign-born coethnics. Chinese immigrants and their children also show high socioeconomic scores across generations.

However, averages do not tell individual stories. The children of the professionals and entrepreneurs almost certainly grow up in better neighbourhoods and attend better and safer schools than the children of low-skilled and semi-skilled labourers. Many children of foreign-born Indian and Chinese professionals start out from much more privileged positions and face fewer obstacles to school and the labour market than the children of working-class coethnics but may still have difficulties finding advantageous places in society. But what about those children whose immigrant parents lack initial social class advantages, either because the parents did not have the human capital or because parental human capital did not respond to the current demands of the American labour market? Here is where the ethnic community can play an important role. More specifically, this is where the second path, via selective acculturation, is effective for successful adaptation of the second generation predicted by the segmented assimilation theory (Portes and Rumbaut 2014; Portes and Zhou 1993). For hyper-selected immigrant groups, strong group-based human capital can facilitate the reproduction of social capital and production of ethnic resources via ethnic entrepreneurship and the preexisting ethnic community (Lee and Zhou 2015; Portes and Rumbaut 2014). For example, the ethnic system of supplementary education available in Chinatown and Koreatown in Los Angeles create additional educational resources that help not only the children of middle-class families but also those coethnics of working-class backgrounds (Zhou 2009).

Asian American youth often have a strong sense of familial obligation to succeed in school and, at the same time, parents exhibit a sense of immigrant optimism in expecting their children to do so. However, when combined with the expectations and pressure around the model minority stereotype, highly integrated Asian Americans appear unable to leverage their reported higher levels of social support in an effective way. Rather, the model minority stereotype can create unrealistic standards of success and hinder Asian-American youth from benefitting fully from their social support networks (Cherng and Liu 2017).

Consistent with the literature on stereotype threat, some experimental work has shown that the model minority stereotype can cause people to "choke" and perform poorly on a test because of the burden of actually meeting the expectations (Cheryan and Bodenhausen 2000). Lee (2012) coined the term "stereotype promise", which refers to the promise of being viewed through the lens of a positive stereotype. The students who are viewed favourably by their teachers would likely perform in such a way that confirms the positive stereotype and show positive academic outcomes as a result. Stereotype promise focuses more broadly on the way in which positive stereotypes can boost performance both in schools and in real world settings such as workplaces.

Lee and Zhou (2015) further elaborate how "stereotype promise" can become a double-edged sword, however. First, expectations of success can create uncomfortable pressure to achieve and to live up to the image, which further reinforces potentially unrealistic and unreasonable expectations. Second, teacher favouritism and other positive societal perceptions can also become source of bullying and negative attitudes toward Asian Americans as perpetrated by African-American and Latin-American peers (Liang, Grossman, and Deguchi 2007; Qin, Way, and Rana 2008). Third, the subjective experience of being stereotyped can feel restrictive, wrong, and damaging to social relationships (Lee 1994; Wang, Siy, and Cheryan 2011). Fourth, in the labour market later on, the positive stereotype can lead a "bamboo" ceiling to deter Asian Americans from attaining leadership positions (Zhou and Lee 2017).

The model minority stereotype also goes hand-in-hand with the forever foreigner stereotype. A recent research shows that nearly 100 per cent of Asian American youth who were surveyed reported having some prior experience with the dual stereotypes (Thompson and Kiang 2010). Empirically findings are mixed whether the putative benefits of the stereotype outweigh its damaging effects (Kiang et al. 2017; Wong and Halgin 2006). More significantly, if Asian Americans could be cast as models of success, then the whole idea of inequality could be upended and other racial minorities could be dismissed as complaining and disruptive (Kiang et al. 2016). Thus, the unanticipated consequences of Asian success actually steer even the socioeconomically integrated Asian Americans into the disadvantaged rungs of the racial hierarchy, which ironically prompts them to form pan-ethnicity for self-empowerment that heightens their ethnoracial distinctiveness (Zhou 2004).

Conclusion

The ambiguous position of Asians in the contemporary United States does not lend itself to easy characterizations of them as uniformly oppressed and disadvantaged or as fully incorporated into a widely accepted image of national identity. The perception of the children of Asian immigrants as high achievers has some basis in statistics. However, this perception is an overgeneralization that overlooks the wide variations among individuals and across national origin groups of varying socioeconomic backgrounds and the importance of cultural practices and ethnic formations. Both the general pattern of achievement and the group variations are results of selective acculturation to different segments of American society through ethnic relations and practices that are shaped by contemporary contexts of exit and reception. The overgeneralization, moreover, has unanticipated consequences. Even though native-born whites often develop friendly relations with individual immigrants, in many cases they still hold broad stereotypical and prejudiced ideas and feel threatened (Jiménez and Horowitz 2013).

Contemporary immigrants from Asia are tremendously diverse in origins and socioeconomic backgrounds. Yet, they are often received in host communities as a homogeneous group with two extremes, either as the poor, uncivilized, and burdensome strangers or as the wealthy, high-achieving, and problem-free newcomers (Hsu 2015). These stereotypes not only hinder a full understanding of the diversity in adaptation across Asian origin groups, they also create burdens for the relatively advantaged, as well as the relatively disadvantaged. Selective acculturation and conditional acceptance of Asian Americans into American society may be understood as a valid qualification of segmented assimilation.

The ambiguity of being Asian and American leaves a range of questions for future investigation. How is the diversity of Asians in America related to views of their distinctiveness in relation to national identity? To what extent do those who assimilate into the more advantaged segments of the society in some sense "become white" in their own eyes? Under what conditions do the more advantaged see their own opportunities threatened by policies and programmes, such as affirmative action, intended to benefit less advantaged groups?

The diversity of Asian Americans also means that researchers should give more attention to how subgroups and individuals may experience different modes of incorporation into American society. To suggest that some form of racial assimilation may affect Asians as a general category may be true at a broad level of aggregation, but the diversity means that some are approaching "becoming white" or the status of "honorary whites", while the ethnic boundary lines continue to be sharp and distinct for others. On this point, the public perceptions and self-perceptions of people of varied Asian ancestry backgrounds require more attention. What are the different ways in which those of inter-ethnic Asian backgrounds, white-Asian, and black-Asian backgrounds, for example, are seen by others and themselves?

One of the most serious gaps in the literature concerns the situation of the hundreds of thousands of undocumented Asians in an era of deportation. The stereotype of Asians as fitting neatly into American society, as well as the problem of studying people who are, in the Tagalog slang term "TNT" (*tago ng tago* or "hiding and hiding") tends to result in invisibility for this substantial portion of the population.

The issue of how contemporary concerns about national identity may affect the self-identification of members of Asian-origin groups, finally, requires investigation. To what extent do Asians in the United States respond to ethnonational pressures by attempting to quietly blend in and become versions of "honorary whites"? Does this differ by generation or by groups, with immigrant generations welcoming model minority invisibility for their children and their descendants reacting against this or with members of the more advantaged groups seeking that invisibility while the less advantaged assert distinctiveness? Or might categorical advantage work in the opposite direction?

Note

1. See, for example, the *New York Times* report on the political impact in nationwide local elections of the president's portrayal of immigrant minority group members as cultural threats to national identity (Herndon 2019a, 2019b).

Disclosure statement

No potential conflict of interest was reported by the authors.

References

Alba, Richard, and Victor Nee. 2003. *Remaking the American Mainstream: Assimilation and Contemporary Immigration*. Cambridge, MA: Harvard University Press.

Bankston III, Carl L. 2000. "Sangha of the South: Laotian Buddhism and Social Adaptation in Southwestern Louisiana." In *Contemporary Asian America*, 1st ed., edited by Min Zhou, and James V. Gatewood, 357–371. Albany: New York University Press.

Bankston III, Carl L. 2014. *Immigrant Networks and Social Capital*. Cambridge: Polity Press.

Best, Michael H. 2011. *The New Competition: Institutions of Industrial Restructuring*. UK: Polity.

Blau, Francine. 2015. "Immigrants and Gender Roles: Assimilation vs. Culture." *Journal of Migration* 4: 1–21.

Bonilla-Silva, E. 2004. "From Bi-Racial to Tri-Racial: Towards a New System of Racial Stratification in the USA." *Ethnic &. Racial Studies* 27 (6): 931–950.

Brand, D. 1987. "The New Whiz Kids." *Time Magazine* 130 (August, 31): 42–51.

Brettell, Caroline B. 2005. "Voluntary Organizations, Social Capital, and the Social Incorporation of Asian Indian Immigrants in the Dallas-Fort Worth Metroplex." *Anthropological Quarterly* 78: 853–883.

Brimelow, Peter. 1995. *Alien Nation: Common Sense about America's Immigration Disaster*. New York: Random House.

Caldas, Stephen J., and Carl L. Bankston III. 2015. *Still Failing: The Continuing Paradox of School Desegregation*. New York: Rowman & Littlefield Publishers.

Card, David, Christian Dustmann, and Ian Preston. 2005. "Understanding Attitudes to Immigration: The Migration and Minority Module of the First European Social Survey." Discussion Paper Series CDP No 03/05. London: Centre for Research and Analysis of Migration, Department of Economics, University College London.

Cherng, Hua-Yu Sebastian, and Jia Lin Liu. 2017. "Academic Social Support and Student Expectations: The Case of Second-Generation Asian Americans." *Asian American Journal of Psychology* 8: 16–30.

Cheryan, Sapna, and Galen V. Bodenhausen. 2000. "When Positive Stereotypes Threaten Intellectual Performance: The Psychological Hazards of 'Model Minority' Status." *Psychological Science* 11: 399–402.

Dhingra, Pawan. 2012. *Life Behind the Lobby: Indian American Motel Owners and the American Dream*. Palo Alto, CA: Stanford University Press.

Donato, Katherine M., Nicole Trujillo-Pagan, Carl L. Bankston III, and Audrey Singer. 2010. "Immigration, Reconstruction and Settlement: Hurricane Katrina and the Emergence of Immigrant Communities." In *The Sociology of Katrina, 2nd Edition*, edited by David L. Brunsma, David Overfelt, and J. Steven Picou, 265–290. New York: Rowman & Littlefield.

Durand, Jorge, Douglas S. Massey, and Chiara Capoferro. 2005. "The New Geography of Mexican Immigration." In *New Destinations: Mexican Immigration in the United States*, edited by Victor Zuñiga, and Rubén Hernández-Léon, 1–22. New York: Russell Sage Foundation.

Feliciano, Cynthia. 2005. "Educational Selectivity in U.S. Immigration: How Do Immigrants Compare to Those Left Behind?" *Demography* 42 (1): 131–152.

Fennelly, Katherine, and Nicole Palasz. 2003. "English Language Proficiency of Immigrants and Refugees in the Twin Cities Metropolitan Area." *International Migration* 41 (5): 93–125.

Frey, William H. 2014. *Diversity Explosion: How Racial Demographics are Remaking America*. Washington, DC: Brookings Institution.

Griffith, David. 2006. *American Guestworkers: Jamaicans and Mexicans in the U.S. Labor Market*. University Park, PA: Penn State University Press.

Hackman, Michelle. 2018 (Nov. 2). "GOP Tries New Tack Toward Asians." *Wall Street Journal*, A6.

Hainmueller, Jens, and Daniel J. Hopkins. 2014. "Public Attitudes Toward Immigration." *Annual Review of Political Science* 17: 225–249.

Hein, Jeremy. 2006. *Ethnic Origins: The Adaptation of Cambodian and Hmong Refugees in Four American Cities*. New York: Russell Sage Foundation.

Hernández-León, Rubén. 2008. *Metropolitan Migrants: The Migration of Urban Mexicans to the United States*. Berkeley, CA: University of California Press.

Hernández-León, Rubén, and Victor Zúñiga. 2000. "Making Carpet by the Mile: The Emergence of a Mexican Immigrant Community in an Industrial Region of the U.S.Historic South." *Social Science Quarterly* 81: 49–66.

Hernández-León, Rubén, and Victor Zúñiga. 2006. "Appalachia Meets Aztlán: Mexican Immigration and Intergroup Relations in Dalton, Georgia." In *New Destinations: Mexican Immigration in the United States*, edited by Victor Zúñiga, and Rubén Hernández-León, 244–275. New York: Russell Sage Foundation.

Herndon, Astead W. 2019a. How Trump's Brand of Grievance Politics Roiled a Pennsylvania Campaign." *The New York Times*, March 15. Accessed on May 1, 2019. https://www.nytimes.com/2019/03/15/us/politics/trump-white-voters-politics.html.

Herndon, Astead W. 2019b. "'Witch Hunts' and 'Fake News': Trump Grievances Go Local." *The New York Times* March 17, A19.

Hidalgo, Danielle Antoinette, and Carl L. Bankston III. 2010. "Blurring Racial and Ethnic Boundaries in Asian American Families: Asian American Family Patterns, 1980-2005." *Journal of Family Issues* 3: 280–300.

Hirschman, Charles, with Nikolas. Pharris-Ciurej. 2016. "The University of Washington - Beyond High School Project: Data and Description." In *From High School to College: Gender, Immigrant Generation, and Race-Ethnicity*, edited by Charles Hirschman, 60–115. New York: Russell Sage Foundation.

Hsu, Madeline Y. 2015. *The Good Immigrants: How the Yellow Peril Became the Model Minority*. Princeton: Princeton University Press.

Huntington, Samuel. 2004. *Who Are We? The Challenges to America's National Identity*. New York: Simon & Schuster.

Hwang, Suein. 2005. "The New White Flight." *Wall Street Journal*, November 19. Accessed on June 20, 2015. http://www.wsj.com/articles/SB113236377590902105, .

Jiménez, Tomás R. 2017. *The Other Side of Assimilation How Immigrants Are Changing American Life*. Berkeley, CA: University of California Press.

Jiménez, Tomás R., and Adam L. Horowitz. 2013. "When White is Just Alright: How Immigrants Redefine Achievement and Reconfigure the Ethnoracial Hierarchy." *American Sociological Review* 78 (5): 849–871.

Kiang, Lisa, Virginia W. Huynh, Charissa S. L. Cheah, and Yijie Wang. 2017. "Introduction: Moving Beyond the Model Minority." *Asian American Journal of Psychology* 8 (1): 1–6.

Kiang, Lisa, Vivian Tseng, and Tiffany Yip. 2016. "Placing Asian American Child Development Within Historical Context." *Child Development* 87 (4): 995–1013.

Lee, Stacey J. 1994. "Behind the Model-Minority Stereotype: Voices of High and Low-Achieving Asian American Students." *Anthropology & Education Quarterly* 25 (4): 413–429.

Lee, Jennifer. 2012. "Asian American Exceptionalism and 'Stereotype Promise'." A white paper posted on *The Society Pages*: https://thesocietypages.org/papers/asian-american-exceptionalism-and-stereotype-promise/.

Lee, Jennifer C., and Samuel Kye. 2016. "Racialized Assimilation of Asian Americans." *Annual Review of Sociology* 42: 253–273.

Lee, Jennifer, and Min Zhou. 2015. *The Asian American Achievement Paradox*. New York: Russell Sage Foundation.

Li, Wei. 2009. *Ethnoburb: The New Ethnic Community in North America*. Honolulu: University of Hawaii Press.

Liang, Belle, Jennifer M. Grossman, and Makiko Deguchi. 2007. "Chinese American Middle School Youths' Experiences of Discrimination and Stereotyping." *Qualitative Research in Psychology* 4: 187–205.

Logan, John R., and Weiwei Zhang. 2013. "Separate but Equal: Asian Nationalities in the U.S." US2010 Project Report, Brown University. http://www.s4.brown.edu/us2010/Data/Report/report06112013.pdf.

López, Gustavo, Neil G. Ruiz, and Eileen Patten. 2017. "Key Facts about Asian Americans, a Diverse and Growing Population, September 8. https://www.pewresearch.org/fact-tank/2017/09/08/key-facts-about-asian-americans/.

Massey, Douglas S., and Chiara Capoferro. 2008. "The Geographic Diversification of American Immigration." In *New Faces in New Places: The Changing Geography of American Immigration*, edited by Douglas S. Massey, 25–50. New York: Russell Sage Foundation.

Massey, Douglas S., Jorge Durand, and Nolan J. Malone. 2003. *Beyond Smoke and Mirrors: Mexican Immigration in an Era of Economic Integration*. New York: Russell Sage Foundation.

Merton, Robert. 1936. "The Unanticipated Consequences of Purposive Social Action." *American Sociological Review* 1: 894–904.

Ngo, Bic, and Stacey J. Lee. 2007. "Complicating the Image of Model Minority Success: A Review of Southeast Asian American Education." *Review of Educational Research* 77: 415–453.

Park, Julie, Stephanie J. Nawyn, and Megan J. Benetsky. 2015. "Feminized Intergenerational Mobility Without Assimilation? Post-1965 U.S. Immigrants and the Gender Revolution." *Demography* 52: 1601–1626.

Petersen, William. 1966. "Success Story, Japanese-American Style." *New York Times*, January 9.

Pew Research Center. 2013. *The Rise of Asian Americans*. Updated ed. Washington, DC: Pew Research Center.

Portes, Alejandro, and Ruben G. Rumbaut. 2001. *Legacies: The Story of the Immigrant Second Generation*. Berkeley, CA: University of California Press.

Portes, Alejandro, and Ruben G. Rumbaut. 2014. *Immigrant America: A Portrait*. 4th ed. Berkeley, CA: University of California Press.

Portes, Alejandro, and John Walton. 1981. *Labor, Class, and the International System*. New York: Academic Press.

Portes, Alejandro, and Min Zhou. 1993. "The New Second Generation: Segmented Assimilation and Its Variants." *The Annals of the American Academy of Political and Social Science* 530: 74–96.

Qin, Desirée Baolian, Niobe Way, and Meenal Rana. 2008. "The 'Model Minority' and Their Discontent: Examining Peer Discrimination and Harassment of Chinese American Immigrant Youth." *New Directions for Child and Adolescent Development* 212: 27–42.

Ruefle, William, William H. Ross, and Diane Mandell. 1992. "Attitudes Towards Southeastern Asia Immigrants in a Wisconsin Community." *International Migration Review* 26 (3): 877–898.

Saxenian, AnnaLee. 2006. *The New Argonauts: Regional Advantage in a Global Economy*. Cambridge, MA: Harvard University Press.

Schmidt, Peter. 2003. "For Asians Affirmative Action Cuts Both Ways." *Chronicle of Higher Education* 49 (39): A24–26.

Thompson, Taylor L., and Lisa Kiang. 2010. "The Model Minority Stereotype: Adolescent Experiences and Links with Adjustment." *Asian American Journal of Psychology* 1: 119–128.

U.S. Bureau of the Census. 2019. *American Community Surveys*. Accessed March 26, 2019. https://factfinder.census.gov/faces/tableservices/jsf/pages/productview.xhtml?pid=ACS_17_5YR_B02011&prodType=table .

U.S. Department of Homeland Security. 2018. *Yearbook of Immigration Statistics* 2017. Accessed March 26, 2019. https://www.dhs.gov/immigration-statistics/yearbook/2017.

U.S. Department of State Visa Office. 2011. *Report of the Visa Office 2011*. Washington, DC: GPO. Accessed May 1, 2019. https://travel.state.gov/content/travel/en/legal/visa-law0/visa-statistics/annual-reports/report-of-the-visa-office-2011.html.

U.S. Department of State Visa Office. 2017. *Report of the Visa Office 2017*. Washington, DC: GPO. https://travel.state.gov/content/travel/en/legal/visa-law0/visa-statistics/annual-reports/report-of-the-visa-office-2017.html, accessed May 1, 2019.

U.S. News and World Report Staff. 1966. "Success of One Minority Group in the U.S."

UNDESA (United Nations Department of Economic and Social Affairs, Population Division). 2016. *International Migration Report 2015: Highlights* (ST/ESA/SER.A/375).

UNHCR (United Nations High Commissioner for Refugees). 2017. "Asia and the Pacific." Accessed on March 25, 2017. http://www.unhcr.org/en-us/asia-and-the-pacific.html.

Vo, Linda Trinh, and Mary Yu Danico. 2004. "The Formation of Post-Suburban Communities: Koreatown and Little Saigon, Orange County." *International Journal of Sociology and Social Policy* 24: 15–45.

Wang, J., J. O. Siy, and S. Cheryan. 2011. "Racial Discrimination and Mental Health among Asian American Youth." In *Asian American and Pacific Islander Children and Mental Health*, edited by Frederick T. Leong, Linda Juang, and Desirée Baolian Qin, 219–242. Santa Barbara, CA: ABC-CLIO.

Waters, Mary, Van C. Tran, Philip Kasinitz, and John H. Mollenkopf. 2010. "Segmented Assimilation Revisited: Types of Acculturation and Socioeconomic Mobility in Young Adulthood." *Ethnic and Racial Studies* 33: 1168–1193.

Wen, Ming, Diane S. Lauderdale, and Namratha R. Kandula. 2009. "Ethnic Neighborhoods in Multi-Ethnic America, 1990-2000: Resurgent Ethnicity in the Ethnoburbs?" *Social Forces* 88: 425–460.

Wong, Frieda, and Richard Halgin. 2006. "The 'Model Minority': Bane or Blessing for Asian Americans?" *Journal of Multicultural Counseling and Development* 34: 38–49.

Wu, Ellen D. 2014. *The Color of Success: Asian Americans and the Origins of the Model Minority*. Princeton, NJ: Princeton University Press.

Zhou, Min. 1997. "Growing Up American: The Challenge Confronting Immigrant Children and Children of Immigrants." *Annual Review of Sociology* 23: 63–95.

Zhou, Min. 2004. "Are Asian Americans Becoming White?" *Contexts* 3 (1): 29–37.

Zhou, Min. 2009. "How Neighborhoods Matter for Immigrant Children: The Formation of Educational Resources in Chinatown, Koreatown, and Pico Union, Los Angeles." *Journal of Ethnic and Migration Studies* 35 (7): 1153–1179.

Zhou, Min, and Carl L. Bankston III. 1998. *Growing Up American: How Vietnamese Children Adapt to Life in the United States*. New York: Russell Sage Foundation.

Zhou, Min, and Carl L. Bankston III. 2001. "Family Pressure and the Educational Experience of the Daughters of Vietnamese Refugees." *International Migration* 39: 133–151.

Zhou, Min, and Carl L. Bankston III. 2016. *The Rise of the New Second Generation*. Cambridge, UK: Polity.

Zhou, Min, and Jennifer Lee. 2017. "Hyper-Selectivity and the Remaking of Culture: Understanding the Asian American Achievement Paradox." *Asian American Journal of Psychology* 8 (1): 7–15.

Zhou, Min, Yen-fen Tseng, and Rebecca Y. Kim. 2008. "Rethinking Residential Assimilation Through the Case of Chinese Ethnoburbs in the San Gabriel Valley, California." *Amerasia Journal* 34 (3): 55–83.

Index

Note: Page numbers in *italics* indicate figures; pages in **bold** refer to tables.